THE ROYAL WARRANTS

ELIZABETH R.

OUR WILL AND PLEASURE is that Letters Patent be made and passed under the Seal appointed by the Treaty of Union to be kept and made use of in place of the Great Seal of Scotland in words and to the effect following:

ELIZABETH THE SECOND by the Grace of God of the United Kingdom of Great Britain and Northern Ireland and of Our other Realms and Territories QUEEN, Head of the Commonwealth, Defender of the Faith, to

Our Right Trusty and Well-beloved Counsellor, William, Baron Hughes of Hawkhill, Commander of Our Most Excellent Order of the British Empire;

Our Trusty and Well-beloved:

Peter Maxwell (commonly called the Honourable Lord Maxwell), one of the Senators of Our College of Justice in Scotland;

Donald Buchanan Robertson, Esquire, one of Our Counsel learned in Law in Scotland;

William Brown, Esquire, Commander of Our Most Excellent Order of the British Empire;

James Reid Clark, Esquire, Commander of Our Most Excellent Order of the British Empire;

Ethel May Houston;

Laurence Colvin Hunter, Esquire;

Donald Macgregor, Esquire;

Joan Macintosh;

Geoffrey Mackintosh Shaw, Esquire;

Alexander Stewart Weatherhead, Esquire;

GREETING!

WHEREAS We have deemed it expedient that a Commission should forthwith issue to inquire into the law and practice relating to the provision of legal services in Scotland and to consider whether any, and if so what, changes are desirable in the public interest in the structure, organisation, training and regulation of, and entry into, the legal profession, including the arrangements for determining its remuneration, whether from private sources or public funds, and in the rules which prevent persons who are neither advocates nor solicitors from undertaking conveyancing and other legal business on behalf of other persons and to report:

NOW KNOW YE that We, reposing great trust and confidence in your knowledge and ability, have authorised and appointed, and do by these Presents authorise and appoint you the said Baron Hughes (Chairman); Peter Maxwell; Donald Buchanan Robertson; William Brown; James Reid Clark; Ethel May Houston; Laurence Colvin Hunter; Donald Macgregor; Joan Macintosh; Geoffrey Mackintosh Shaw; and Alexander Stewart Weatherhead, to be Our Commissioners for the purposes of the said inquiry;

AND for the better effecting the purposes of this Our Commission, We do by these Presents give and grant unto you, or any six or more of you, full power to call before you such persons as you shall judge likely to afford you any information upon the subject of this Our Commission; to call for information in writing; and also to call for, have access to and examine all such books, documents, registers and records as may afford you the fullest information on the subject, and to inquire of and concerning the premises by all other lawful ways and means whatsoever;

AND We do by these Presents authorise and empower you, or any of you, to visit and inspect personally such places as you may deem it expedient so to inspect for the more effectual carrying out of the purposes aforesaid;

AND We do by these Presents will and ordain that this Our Commission shall continue in full force and virtue, and that you, Our said Commissioners, or any six or more of you, may from time to time proceed in the execution thereof, and of every matter and thing therein contained, although the same be not continued from time to time by adjournment;

AND We do further ordain that you, or any six or more of you, have liberty to report your proceedings under this Our Commission from time to time if you shall judge it expedient so to do;

AND Our further will and pleasure is that you do, with as little delay as possible, report to Us under your hands and seals, or under the hands and seals of any six or more of you, your opinion upon the matters herein submitted for your consideration;

AND We Will and Command the said Letters Patent to be extended in the most ample form and to pass the Seal aforesaid *per saltum* without passing any other Seal or Register. For doing whereof these Presents shall be a sufficient Warrant to the Keeper of the Registers of Scotland for writing the said Commission in the Chancery Office in Edinburgh and to the Keeper of the said Seal for causing the same to be appended thereto.

GIVEN at Our Court at St James, the twenty-fifth day of October 1976, in the twenty-fifth year of Our Reign.

BY HER MAJESTY'S COMMAND

BRUCE MILLAN

Note: Councillor Geoffrey M. Shaw died on 28th April 1978.
Mrs Joan MacIntosh was appointed a Commander of the Order of The British Empire in June 1978.

Royal Commission on Legal Services in Scotland

Chairman: The Rt Hon Lord Hughes CBE

Volume One

REPORT

Presented to Parliament by Command of Her Majesty
May 1980

EDINBURGH
HER MAJESTY'S STATIONERY OFFICE

Cmnd 7846 £8.50

A

THE REPORT OF THE ROYAL COMMISSION ON LEGAL SERVICES IN SCOTLAND

VOLUME ONE: REPORT

VOLUME TWO (Parts A and B): APPENDICES

The estimated total expenditure of the Royal Commission is £500,300. Of this sum £50,700 represents the estimated cost of printing and publishing this report.

ISBN 0 10 178460 0

ELIZABETH R.

ELIZABETH THE SECOND, by the Grace of God of the United Kingdom of Great Britain and Northern Ireland and of Our other Realms and Territories QUEEN, Head of the Commonwealth, Defender of the Faith, to Our Trusty and Well-beloved George Sharp, Knight Bachelor, Officer of Our Most Excellent Order of the British Empire, Justice of the Peace;

GREETING!

WHEREAS WE did by Warrant under Our Royal Sign Manual bearing date twenty-fifth day of October, 1976, appoint Commissioners to inquire into the law and practice relating to the provision of legal services in Scotland and to consider whether any, and if so what, changes are desirable in the public interest in the structure, organisation, training and regulation of, and entry into, the legal profession, including the arrangements for determining its remuneration, whether from private sources or public funds, and in the rules which prevent persons who are neither advocates nor solicitors from undertaking conveyancing and other legal business on behalf of other persons and to report:

NOW KNOW YE that WE appoint you the said George Sharp to be a Member of the said Commission for the purposes of the said inquiry.

Given at Our Court on H.M. Yacht Britannia this eighth day of August 1978, in the twenty-seventh year of Our Reign.

BY HER MAJESTY'S COMMAND

KIRKHILL

Warrant appointing Sir George Sharp O.B.E., J.P. to be a member of the Royal Commission on Legal Services in Scotland.

ROYAL COMMISSION ON LEGAL SERVICES IN SCOTLAND

REPORT

To the Queen's Most Excellent Majesty

MAY IT PLEASE YOUR MAJESTY

We, the undersigned Commissioners, having been appointed by Royal Warrant

'To inquire into the law and practice relating to the provision of legal services in Scotland and to consider whether any, and if so what, changes are desirable in the public interest in the structure, organisation, training and regulation of, and entry into, the legal profession, including the arrangements for determining its remuneration, whether from private sources or public funds, and in the rules which prevent persons who are neither advocates nor solicitors from undertaking conveyancing and other legal business on behalf of other persons'

HUMBLY SUBMIT TO YOUR MAJESTY THE FOLLOWING REPORT.

CONTENTS

VOLUME ONE

LS—A*

Part V

THE PROVIDERS OF LEGAL SERVICES

Part VI

THE MACHINERY OF GOVERNMENT

Part VII

RECOMMENDATIONS

Part VIII

NOTES OF DISSENT

INDEX

VOLUME TWO

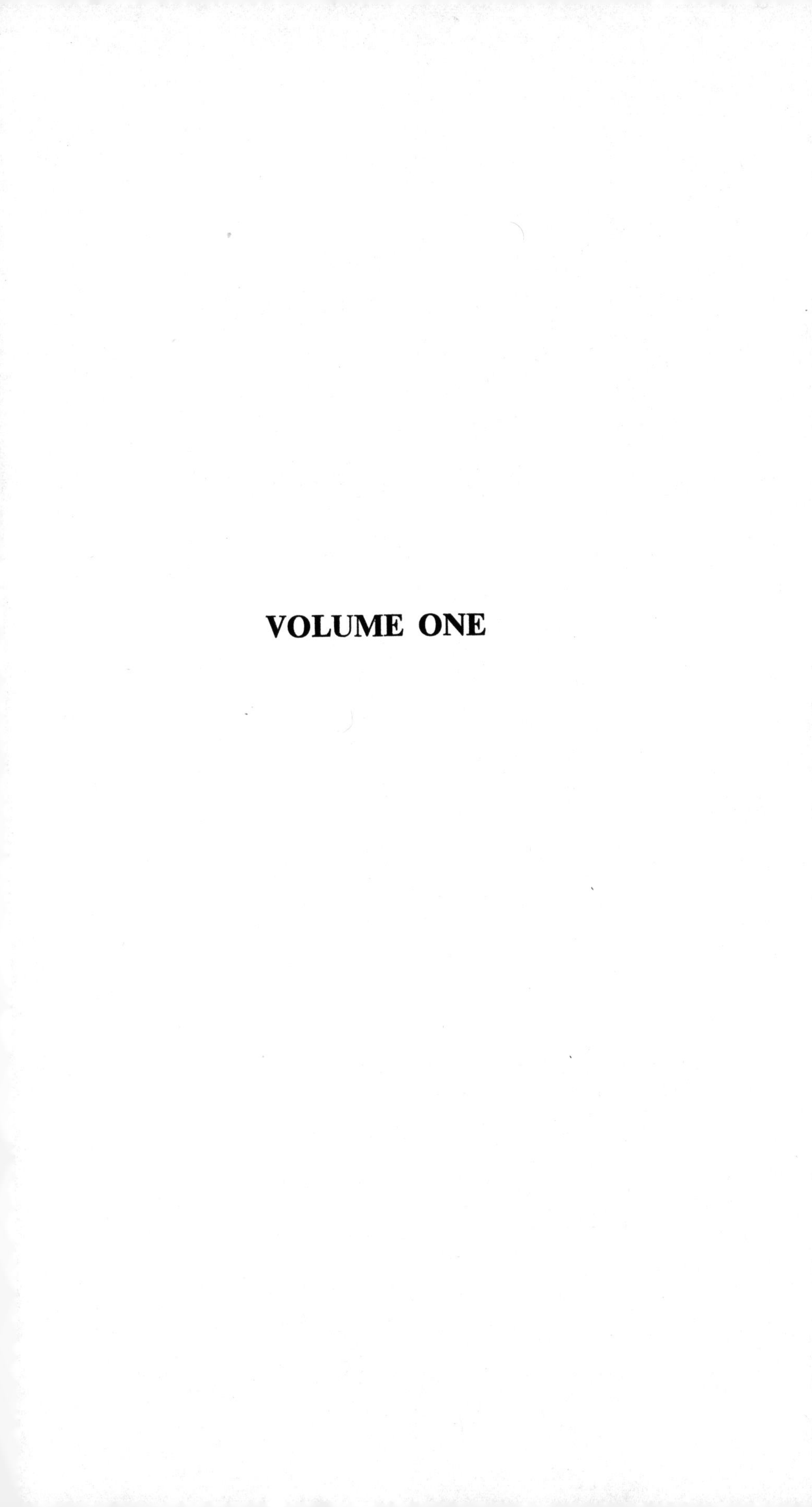

VOLUME ONE

GLOSSARY

This glossary is provided primarily for the benefit of lay persons who may not be familiar with some of the legal terms or offices mentioned in our Report. We have endeavoured to describe the terms and offices in question in simple lay language rather than provide legal definitions: as will be readily appreciated, the two rarely coincide.

Action:	Legal proceedings to establish a claim or obtain a remedy.
Administration of an estate:	Settling the affairs of a deceased person and distributing his possessions in accordance with the law and any will left by him.
Advocates:	Members of the Faculty of Advocates—professional pleaders in the courts, particularly the Court of Session and High Court. Advocates also act as consultants to solicitors seeking a legal opinion. Also known as 'counsel'. The English equivalent are barristers.
Affidavit:	A written statement made by a person who declares it on oath to be true before a Notary Public, Justice of the Peace or Commissioner of Oaths. Affidavits are acceptable as evidence in the court in some actions, particularly undefended divorce.
Aliment:	Payments to support or maintain a relative enforceable by law.
Arbitration:	The submission by parties of a matter in dispute between them to the decision of a third party.
Auditor of Court:	The person who undertakes a judicial examination (or 'taxation') of a lawyer's account to decide what should be allowed, disallowed or adjusted.
Bar, the:	The collective name sometimes given to advocates who practise in the courts because they plead 'at the Bar of the Court'. Used more narrowly e.g., 'the local Bar'—the term denotes those lawyers who appear regularly in a particular court.
Commissary Office:	A department of the sheriff clerk's office which deals with petitions for the appointment of executors and applications for confirmation of executors in testate and intestate cases.
Conciliation:	The action by a third party in disputes which assists the parties in conflict to adopt a solution voluntarily.
Confirmation:	A document granted by the court giving the executors of a deceased person's estate title to, and authority to ingather and distribute, the estate.

Consistorial actions: Actions between husband and wife which involve their status as such (mainly divorce or judicial separation).

Conveyancing: The transfer of rights of property of all kinds by written document; in particular and in general usage, the steps involved in examining the title deeds and preparing the transfer documents of heritable property (e.g., houses).

Counsel: Advocates.

Country solicitor: A solicitor whose place of business is outwith Edinburgh and who is not therefore entitled to practise before the supreme courts sitting only in Edinburgh.

Court of Session: The highest civil court in Scotland—one of the supreme courts, the other being the High Court of Justiciary. There is, in certain circumstances, a right of appeal to the House of Lords. This Court sits only in Edinburgh.

Crown Agent: The senior civil servant assisting the Lord Advocate in the prosecution of crime in Scotland.

Dean: The elected leader of the Faculty of Advocates. The heads of university faculties, including the law faculties, are also styled Deans, as are the elected leaders of a group of lawyers in an area (local faculties).

Decree: The judgment of a civil court determining the case at issue.

Defender: The party sued in a civil action. The opposite of pursuer.

Diet: The date on which a court will convene to consider a criminal matter.

Diligence: The legal procedure which a successful pursuer may have to adopt to recover from the defender what the court has awarded him.

District Court: The lowest criminal court in Scotland.

Domicile: The place which the law recognises as a person's permanent home irrespective of where he may for the time being be resident.

Edinburgh Correspondent: A solicitor or firm of solicitors in Edinburgh, described as such when instructed by a solicitor outwith Edinburgh since only solicitors whose place of business is in Edinburgh can practise in the supreme courts.

Estate: The collective assets and liabilities of a person.

Executor:	A person appointed to settle the affairs and distribute the property of a deceased person.
Faculty of Advocates:	An independent corporation consisting of persons admitted to practise as advocates before the Court of Session. In essence it is the professional body regulating admission and discipline of advocates.
Fusion:	The term used to describe the situation where there is no distinction between the two branches of the legal profession, solicitors and advocates.
High Court: (High Court of Justiciary)	The supreme criminal court in Scotland. As a court of first instance hearing serious prosecutions it goes on circuit throughout the country. As a court of appeal it sits only in Edinburgh. There is no appeal to the House of Lords.
Inner House:	One of the two branches of the Court of Session: the Inner House is divided into the First and Second Divisions presided over by the Lord President and the Lord Justice Clerk respectively. The main business of each Division is to review the decisions of single judges in the Court of Session or inferior courts which have been appealed to it.
Indictment:	The statement of a serious crime served on the accused to be tried by solemn procedure i.e., before a jury. (In lesser cases a 'complaint' is served on the accused.)
Law Society:	The Law Society of Scotland is the professional body for solicitors in Scotland. For convenience we refer to it throughout our Report as simply the Law Society.
Lawyer:	This term is used in our Report to refer to a legally qualified person who may be either a solicitor or an advocate.
Lay Observer:	The person appointed by the Secretary of State for Scotland to investigate allegations made by members of the public concerning the Law Society's treatment of complaints against solicitors or their staff. (There is a separate Lay Observer in England and Wales.)
Legal Advice and Assistance:	A scheme by which the State provides financial support to enable a person to receive advice and assistance, but not normally representation in court, by a solicitor. A contribution towards the cost may be required according to the person's means. Those whose means exceed an upper limit are not eligible.
Legal Aid:	A scheme by which the State provides financial support to enable a person to be represented by a lawyer in court in

civil actions; a contribution is required according to the person's means. Those whose means exceed an upper limit are not eligible.

Lord Advocate: The principal Law Officer of the Crown in Scotland who is responsible for all prosecution in criminal courts in Scotland. He is also the government's chief adviser on Scottish legal questions.

Lords of Appeal in Ordinary: The judges appointed to hear appeals in the House of Lords. In addition, the Lord Chancellor and peers who have held high judicial office also sit to hear appeals.

Lord Justice Clerk: The title given to the judge appointed to be the second most senior judge in the High Court of Justiciary and Court of Session. In the Court of Session the Lord Justice Clerk normally presides over the Second Division of the Inner House.

Lord Justice General: The title given to the senior judge in the High Court of Justiciary (he is always the same person as the Lord President).

Lords Ordinary: The judges of the Court of Session are known as Senators of the College of Justice or Lords of Council and Session or sometimes simply as Lords of Session; the junior ones are known as Lords Ordinary and sit in the Outer House of the Court of Session. There they sit singly taking cases being heard in the Court of Session for the first time.

Lord President (of the Court of Session): The title given to the judge appointed to be the senior Court of Session judge. The Lord President normally presides over the First Division of the Inner House. (See also Lord Justice General.)

Memorial: A statement prepared by a solicitor setting out the facts and the points of law on which he wishes counsel to give an opinion.

Notary Public: A person authorised to authenticate various legal documents. Affidavit evidence in divorce cases can be sworn before a notary. The office of notary is open only to solicitors.

Outer House: The second branch of the Court of Session (the other being the Inner House): single judges sit in judgment on cases of first instance.

Para-legals: Trained non-professional staff in lawyers' offices or advice agencies who give advice on, or carry out, routine legal matters.

Party litigant: A person who presents his own case in a civil court or at a tribunal, without the help of a lawyer.

Precognition: A statement taken from a party or a potential witness to discover the evidence which he is likely to give if a case goes to court.

Precognosce: To take a precognition.

Probative written offer: An offer in writing signed by the offerer (or his agent) which is presumed to be genuine without further evidence because of the way in which it is signed.

Process: The whole of the papers relating to a civil action lodged in court.

Procurator Fiscal: A person who prosecutes crime on behalf of the Crown in the sheriff and district courts. In addition, some duties similar to those of coroners in England in respect of such matters as fatal accident inquiries are carried out.

Proof: The stage of procedure in civil actions in which evidence is led on the facts of the case.

Pursuer: A person raising a civil action in court. Opposite of defender.

Queen's Counsel (QC): A senior advocate, so appointed by the Queen as a mark of distinction. This is called 'taking Silk' from the silk gowns which they wear. Also known as 'senior counsel'.

Right of audience: Entitlement to represent clients in court.

Scottish Law Commission: A permanent, statutory, law review body whose members are appointed by the Lord Advocate.

Senators of the College of Justice: Judges in the Court of Session. In the High Court the same judges are called Lords Commissioners of Justiciary.

Sheriff: A judge in the local (sheriff) court who must have been qualified as an advocate or a solicitor for at least 10 years.

Sheriff Clerk: A salaried officer of the sheriff court who assists the sheriff and with his staff is responsible for the administration of the courts.

Sheriff Court: The local court which tries criminal cases which are too serious for the district court but not serious enough for the High Court. The sheriff court is also a civil court with a wide jurisdiction.

Sheriff Officer: An officer of the sheriff court, appointed by the Sheriff Principal, who may for a fee take instructions from a pursuer or his solicitor to enforce a decree by obtaining payment or performance from the defender. Sheriff Officers serve summonses personally on defenders as required. They are not employed by the court but work independently for fees laid down by the courts.

Sheriff Principal: A judge with responsibility for all the sheriff courts in his sheriffdom. He may take criminal trials but not civil cases at first instance as there is a right of appeal to him from the decision of the sheriff in civil matters.

Solemn procedure: Criminal cases tried under this procedure are tried by a judge sitting with a jury.

Solicitors: Members of one of the branches of the legal profession in Scotland. They are obliged to be members of the Law Society of Scotland. Solicitors who undertake legal business on the instructions of clients require to obtain annually from the Law Society a practising certificate. Solicitors are the link between clients and advocates.

Solicitor General: The junior Law Officer of the Crown in Scotland: depute to the Lord Advocate.

Speculative action: An action undertaken by an advocate or solicitor for which the normal fee appropriate to the action will only be paid if the party represented is successful.

Summary cause: The procedure in the sheriff court for settling small actions, including debts up to a value of £500. (Cases involving larger amounts are dealt with by the Ordinary Cause procedure.)

Summary procedure: Criminal cases tried on summary procedure are tried by a judge alone sitting without a jury.

Summons: The statement by the pursuer of his claim summoning the defender to appear in court to give answer, initiating procedures in certain types of action in the Court of Session or sheriff court.

Taxation: The judicial examination of a lawyer's account for the purpose of deciding what should be allowed, disallowed or adjusted.

PART I

INTRODUCTION

CHAPTER 1

INTRODUCTION TO THE ISSUES

Terms of reference

1.1 Our terms of reference were:
'To inquire into the law and practice relating to the provision of legal services in Scotland and to consider whether any, and if so what, changes are desirable in the public interest in the structure, organisation, training and regulation of, and entry into, the legal profession, including the arrangements for determining its remuneration, whether from private sources or public funds, and in the rules which prevent persons who are neither advocates nor solicitors from undertaking conveyancing and other legal business on behalf of other persons'.

1.2 This is a wide-ranging remit; and it has required us to review legal services in Scotland in a broad, though not exhaustive, way. To have attempted the latter would have called for a much longer inquiry than seemed to us appropriate; and it would perhaps have required a range of experience even wider than that which our relatively small membership embodied.

1.3 As far as we could trace, no general review of legal services in Scotland of the kind contained in our terms of reference had earlier been undertaken by any Committee or Commission. The inquiries into legal issues which have taken place over the last few decades have invariably concentrated on particular issues such as the law of succession in Scotland (the Mackintosh Committee); legal aid in criminal proceedings (the Guthrie Committee); the registration of title to land in Scotland (the Reid Committee); civil juries (the Strachan Committee); conveyancing (the Halliday and Henry Committees); the sheriff court (the Grant Committee). Our appointment was, therefore, of special significance for the legal profession in Scotland since our terms of reference meant that its role in society was for the first time being subjected to public scrutiny in a comprehensive way.

1.4 When any organisation or service is subjected to such an examination by a Commission at the instigation of central government, there is frequently an earlier history of public discontent and controversy about the organisation or service concerned. We think it fair, however, to say at the outset of our Report that we found no evidence of strong disenchantment with the legal profession, or legal services, in Scotland during the year or two prior to our appointment. Indeed we feel that in large measure the legal profession has served Scotland well over the years. Nevertheless, there did emerge evidence that in changing times the old order of legal services must change to meet them, and that this were best done in a considered rather than haphazard fashion.

The Royal Commission on Legal Services

1.5 It is noteworthy that the terms of reference given to us were similar to the terms of reference given to the Commission appointed to review legal services in England and Wales (and later Northern Ireland). However, because of the close relationship in Scotland between the system of courts of law and the organisation of the profession, we were informed that in so far as the structure of the court system had a bearing on our terms of reference, it would be open to us to examine that system.

1.6 Since the two Commissions had similar remits, we were bound to cover much the same ground in the course of our inquiries. We kept in touch with each other as our work progressed; but the English Commission started their activities some months ahead of us and finished ahead of us also. Their Report was published in October 1979.[1]

1.7 It is perhaps not surprising that the two Commissions did not always arrive at similar conclusions. The legal system in Scotland historically developed in a somewhat different way from the systems in the rest of the United Kingdom.[2] This was the reason why it was necessary to appoint a separate Commission to review legal services and the legal profession in Scotland. Both where we have reached the same conclusions as the Benson Commission and where we have differed on topics of common interest, it has been as a result of independent consideration of the issues and of the separate evidence which we received, mainly from Scottish interests. Our object has been to arrive at recommendations which we believe are right for Scotland.

1.8 As might be expected of a Commission having wide terms of reference and comprising eleven members with varied backgrounds and experience, we have taken different views on many issues and on points of detail and emphasis. We have, however, tried wherever possible to avoid expressing these in the text of the Report, although not all of us would personally agree with each and every expression of view in the Report. Except where stated otherwise, however, we are in broad agreement on our conclusions and recommendations.

OUR PROCEDURES

Number of meetings

1.9 The royal warrant appointing us was dated 25 October 1976 and on the same day we held our first meeting.

1.10 In all, we have met as a Commission on 51 occasions; and our meetings since August 1978 generally followed a pattern of two successive days. On 7 of these occasions, the Commission met in residential sessions usually lasting three days. In addition, the Commission met on 52 further occasions to take oral evidence, mostly in private. Much detailed consideration of a number of major issues was undertaken by committees who in aggregate held 109 meetings.

Procedure adopted

1.11 There had been little significant public debate about legal services in Scotland immediately prior to our appointment. We thought, therefore, that a bald public announcement that we were now in business to examine legal services and the legal profession in Scotland, and would welcome evidence, might not yield adequate comment on existing services or constructive proposals for improvements. To help elicit useful written evidence, we first identified the

---

[1] The Royal Commission on Legal Services: *Final Report* (*Cmnd. 7648*): Chairman, Sir Henry Benson: HMSO, 1979. For convenience throughout our Report we refer to the Benson Commission.

[2] A useful description of the origins and sources of Scots law is contained in a booklet:—Scottish Office: *The Legal System in Scotland:* HMSO, 1975.

main issues on which we would welcome views, and decided to proceed by way of questionnaires. We were influenced in this direction by an earlier decision of the Benson Commission to proceed in this way. We issued three questionnaires; separate fairly detailed questionnaires were specifically directed to the Faculty of Advocates and the Law Society of Scotland. The third questionnaire, a much more general one, was designed to assist a variety of bodies and selected individuals to submit comments in a form which would be most helpful to us. Copies of the three questionnaires are at Appendix 2.

Initial publicity

1.12 In addition to inviting written evidence through the questionnaires, our Chairman held a press conference on the occasion of our second meeting. The publicity that we derived through the news media evoked only a sparse response from members of the public. In the few weeks following the press conference we received no more than 28 letters from individuals up and down the country. Some complaints were made against the cost of conveyancing; some were about delay in winding up estates; and some were about the cost of divorce actions.

Response to questionnaires

1.13 Our general questionnaire went to a large number of public and private organisations which we thought would be interested in our remit and able to make some contribution to our work. We also sent the general questionnaire to Scottish Members of Parliament as well as to the main political parties; and we invited comments from Lords of Appeal in Ordinary, Senators of the College of Justice, Sheriffs Principal and the Sheriffs' Association.

1.14 The Lords of Appeal in Ordinary who had submitted evidence to the Benson Commission agreed that we should see the comments that they had made since many topics (such as fusion of the two main branches of the profession) were of common interest north and south of the border. Wherever they thought they could make a helpful contribution about the separate Scottish legal system, they did so.

1.15 The Lord President of the Court of Session and the Lord Justice Clerk, after discussion with our Chairman, concluded that the Senators of the College of Justice collectively could best assist the Commission by commenting at our request on any particular issue or proposal for reform. The Sheriffs' Association submitted written evidence to us and we subsequently had oral discussions with some of their representatives and with individual Sheriffs Principal. We also had some helpful discussions with the Lord President of the Court of Session on a number of issues.

1.16 Most of the bodies we consulted commented on one or other aspect of legal services; but few organisations submitted detailed evidence and considered proposals for reform. Those who did included the Scottish Association of Citizens Advice Bureaux, the Scottish Consumer Council and the Scottish Legal Action Group.

1.17 Finally, so far as major submissions of evidence are concerned, we received detailed answers to our questionnaires from the Law Society of Scotland and from the Faculty of Advocates. As well as these main written submissions both the Law Society and the Faculty provided substantial further information and comments in response to supplementary points which we raised with them.

1.18 Reflecting on the differences in the evidence received by the two Royal Commissions, it seems relevant to us that many organisations whose remit or interest covers Scotland as well as England and Wales, have their headquarters in the south. The Scottish end of a national organisation, or even the independent Scottish equivalent of an English organisation, rarely, if ever, can mount the same administrative or research capability. As a result many organisations made their submissions to the Benson Commission and not to us. An example of our loss in this regard was the extensive submission made by the Equal Opportunities Commission to the Benson Commission entitled 'Women in the Legal Services'. The Equal Opportunities Commission told us that as their resources were already overstretched, they were unable to undertake the additional research that would have been needed to enable them to provide us with similar evidence relating to Scotland.

1.19 A list of all the bodies and individuals who made written submissions to us is shown at Appendix 3.

Oral evidence

1.20 In common with other Royal Commissions, we found it necessary to take oral evidence from some of those who had submitted written evidence to us in order to amplify written submissions or to seek comments on different views expressed by other parties.

1.21 We decided that our initial oral evidence sessions with the Law Society of Scotland, the Faculty of Advocates, the Scottish Legal Action Group, the Scottish Association of Citizens Advice Bureaux, the Glasgow Bar Association and the Scottish Council for Civil Liberties should be held in public; but that any subsequent sessions with these bodies, as with all others giving oral evidence, would be in private.

1.22 Our several public oral evidence sessions were advertised in the press beforehand. They failed, however, to attract the interest of the public.

1.23 As well as formal oral evidence hearings, we had confidential discussions with a number of individuals on various matters. The individuals concerned felt obliged to give their evidence in confidence, either because it was likely to be at variance with evidence submitted by the organisation to which they belonged or the organisation itself had been unable to reach a consensus on the matters in question. It seemed to us sensible to take evidence from any expert source whether on a confidential basis or not; and some of those who expressly requested that their evidence be treated as 'in confidence' were of assistance to us. We have not included the names of such individuals in the list set out in Appendix 3 of the bodies and individuals who gave oral evidence.

Research

1.24 Most of the legal research undertaken in Scotland has been primarily concerned with areas of substantive law and not with the delivery of legal services. Perhaps the most important recent research project which had a direct bearing on our terms of reference was that undertaken in 1970 by Campbell and

Wilson.[1] This research project had been commissioned by the Law Society of Scotland and was concerned with the attitudes of the public to the legal profession in Scotland. The findings, which have not been updated, showed a high degree of client satisfaction.

1.25 Some parts of our remit involved our acquiring information which could only be obtained by commissioning fresh research. Reports on these research projects are published in Volume Two; we make reference to them as appropriate in this Volume.

Visits within the UK

1.26 In order to gain some first hand appreciation of the problems confronting both the public and the legal profession, we engaged in a series of visits and discussions in various parts of Scotland; and some of us visited county courts, law centres and other organisations in England. During visits to Inverness, the Western Isles and Orkney and Shetland, the Commissioners involved took the opportunity to have discussions with representatives of the local authorities and the legal profession. Invitations were also extended through the local press to the public to meet the members of the Commission and a few people responded. Individually and in groups we also visited legal firms, Citizens Advice Bureaux, courts, tribunals and other bodies and people throughout Scotland involved in the delivery of legal services.

Examination of services in other countries

1.27 In the course of our work we made contact with two overseas bodies conducting reviews broadly similar to our own; the Law Reform Commission in New South Wales, Australia and the Professional Organisations Committee in Ontario, Canada. We have benefited from some of their work.

1.28 We also had the advantage of meeting and exchanging views with a number of distinguished lawyers from Canada, Australia and New Zealand who had come to Edinburgh for the Fifth Commonwealth Law Conference over the period 24–29 July 1977. Similarly, we took advantage of the presence in Edinburgh in 1977 of a number of young lawyers from several European countries to discuss with them various matters relative to education, training and practice on the continent.

1.29 We had not initially intended to make visits abroad to see how legal services operated in other countries. Later, however, as evidence from abroad showed interesting parallels with our own work, a majority of us considered that there would be merit in visiting a small number of countries abroad. We visited Eire since in terms of population and geography it had many features in common with Scotland. Many aspects of legal practice and organisation, however, both at central and local level were different from those in Scotland; and this itself was illuminating. Some of us later undertook a visit to various centres in Canada and the USA in September 1978. We were particularly interested to see for ourselves how the delivery of legal aid was undertaken by legal services commissions, a number of which had been established in Canada in recent years. Again, in parts of Canada and in the USA there are established

---

[1] C. Campbell and R. J. Wilson: *Public Attitudes to the Legal Profession in Scotland:* The Law Society of Scotland, 1970.

systems of public defenders whereby some persons accused of criminal offences who are eligible for legal aid can choose to be defended by salaried public employees rather than by members of private law firms paid from public funds, as is the practice in Scotland. We were also aware that the system of educating lawyers was somewhat different from that applying in Scotland, and we paid visits to the law faculties of certain North American universities.

1.30 Following a helpful discussion with officials of the Council of Europe, we decided to see for ourselves how lawyers were trained in Norway and Sweden, and also to study the provision of legal aid in Sweden. We made brief visits for this purpose. Some of us, individually, have also taken advantage of private visits abroad to undertake discussions with particular legal interests.

1.31 Throughout our work we have received willing co-operation from many people and we wish to place on record our gratitude to all who have spared the time to give us the benefit of their knowledge and expertise. The preparation of evidence to submit to us clearly took much careful thought; we are indebted to all concerned. It has also been of interest to us that the stimulus of our enquiry has of itself been sufficient to encourage changes in some matters to be made before we had completed our work.

Our Secretariat

1.32 We conclude this part of our introductory Chapter on a very necessary but very pleasant note. During the long time the Commission has been working we have had the most generous and devoted service from all members of our staff. They have not been a large body, and we have been conscious throughout our work that the burden we have placed on them has been a very heavy one. Indeed we have been astonished that so few people should have been able to tackle such an enormous amount of work with such efficiency and expedition. To our Secretary, Mr George Fair, our Legal Secretary, Mr Kenneth Barclay and our Assistant Secretary, Mr Peter Russell we give our sincere thanks. The same measure of gratitude we owe to all the other members of the staff for work so well done.[1]

THE MAIN ISSUES AND OUR APPROACH

1.33 We turn now from the mechanics of our working to indicate in general terms how we approached our remit.

Our main concern

1.34 It has been a primary objective of our work to point the way to what we think will be improvements in the provision of legal services for the people of Scotland.

1.35 In coming to the questions where and how far changes are needed in the provision of legal services, we see such services as the medium through which people with legal problems or legal business of different kinds obtain access to the legal system. Thus our primary concern is with people as users or potential users of the legal system; and we have, therefore, put great importance on the

[1] Appendix 1 lists the names of the Commissioners and the Secretariat.

access of people to the law and the provision or *delivery* of legal services to the public.

1.36 This is not to say that we have ignored the needs and preferences of those who supply these services, especially the lawyers themselves. As will become evident, we have paid a good deal of attention to this aspect, since a satisfactory system of legal services must depend on its ability to maintain a viable and adequate profession. We have also borne in mind that the profession provides services not only to individuals but also to commercial and industrial enterprises, from which a significant proportion of its income derives; and we have taken into account the probable effects of proposals for change on the balance of activity within the profession. Accordingly, while we have focussed our main attention on improving the level and standards of legal services for the general public, we have always sought to see this as part of a wider picture; and indeed at a number of points we directly make reference to changes which relate to the commercial aspects of legal services, especially in regard to the European dimension which is steadily increasing in importance. It has to be said, however, that we received little evidence from business interests, which may suggest that there is no great dissatisfaction in that quarter about the availability and the quality of the legal services which are now available.

Access to legal services

1.37 Having established that our main emphasis should be on the delivery of legal services to individual citizens (or groups of them with a common interest) we proceeded on the basis that no one should be prevented from asserting or protecting his legal rights because of lack of means. This gives rise to an important paradox which is central to our work. The State's level of assistance to citizens diminished sharply over the two decades to April 1979 as measured by the amounts spent in constant money terms on the legal aid and the legal advice and assistance schemes. Yet, at the same time, the private individual's potential need for access to legal services had been increasing. Governments in the whole of the period since the second world war have been enacting legislation which confers rights and imposes duties on citizens. Examples can readily be seen in the mass of law relative to housing, road traffic, employment, social welfare, consumer protection, and so on. In creating this plethora of rights and obligations the government has a moral responsibility to ensure that, where necessary, people can exercise these rights and are aware of their obligations. We know that the government and government agencies have done a certain amount to bring new law, new rights and new obligations to public notice, but the evidence presented to us suggested that nevertheless there was a wide gap between the needs of large sections of the public for legal services and their ability to satisfy these needs. It seemed that many people were unaware that a problem causing them great concern had a legal remedy: or, if they were aware, they were often reluctant or inhibited in seeking legal advice. It was to explore this question further that we decided to undertake research into the problems of unmet need for legal services; and the results, which are reported in later Chapters, add to those derived from research conducted by the Scottish Consumer Council and to the evidence on unmet need brought to our attention by various bodies and individuals.

Legal advisers

1.38 It does not, of course, follow that all problems which have a legal source and remedy need to be dealt with by lawyers, at least at first instance. We had evidence from a number of organisations which showed that a considerable advisory service is now provided by largely voluntary agencies for the citizens of Scotland. The value of such lay advisory services is, in our view, substantial. In the first place, they may play a useful role in determining whether a problem faced by an individual is truly one requiring legal advice or resolution. Some problems will not be recognised by the individual as legal issues: others may be thought to require legal analysis but in practice turn out to be open to remedy in other ways; while a third category may include some legal and some non-legal elements. The help of voluntary services—often with professional back-up—in resolving such difficulties is considerable; and its effectiveness is underlined by the consideration that lawyers' professional services may be expensive—or at any rate are thought to be so by large sections of the population. Accordingly, it is proper in our opinion that recourse to lawyers should be limited to the occasions when the advice and skill of the professional are really necessary. If, as we believe to be the case, lay or voluntary legal advisers can meet the initial needs of many members of society, they perform a most useful function. By its nature, however, the organisation of this sort of largely voluntary service tends to be piecemeal and less than comprehensive in its coverage of the population. We accepted that these services provided an increasingly significant element in the legal services we were instructed to examine. It was, therefore, an important part of our task to examine the main deficiencies in this area and to consider how best such services could be developed and strengthened.

The role of the State

1.39 Inevitably, evidence of unmet legal needs and uneven provision of legal services even over the relatively small (but scattered) population of Scotland calls into question the role of the State. At present the State already spends over £9m annually in Scotland for legal aid, legal advice and assistance and criminal legal aid. This expenditure is administered by the legal profession itself and the money is disbursed to the profession. In addition the voluntary lay advice agencies receive support from public funds: the largest such group, the Citizens Advice Bureaux, spend some £0·3m annually. In these circumstances it seems essential to us that the utmost care is taken to ensure that this public money is being spent to the best advantage. This meant, in effect, that we needed to look at possible alternative systems in order to determine which was the best buy having regard to both quality and cost. One such alternative is evidently that the State itself should take a more prominent role in the development and delivery of legal services. In its extreme form, this might mean a nationalised legal service, in much the same way that health services have been nationalised. The evidence presented to us contained very little argument in favour of nationalisation; but there were many instances where recommendations from those giving evidence would have involved greater public intervention in one way or another. Our approach has been pragmatic rather than resting on principle. We have examined the various issues and problems, each in its own right, and we have noted where and in what ways additional State involvement might, or might not, be beneficial. Gradually, this allowed us to build up a picture of a workable and efficient pattern of State participation; and from this we have drawn conclusions about the best overall form of organisation for this purpose.

1.40 Our own work, and the absence of relevant research studies, indicated a need for some kind of body to keep continuous watch in order to ensure that the State is getting the best possible value for the substantial sums of money it spends. Such a body would need to monitor legal service provision as it develops to meet existing and emerging needs in a changing society. We were struck by the static nature of legal services as at present provided and the slow response to changing public needs. We were also aware of fears that a possible risk to the independence of the legal profession might be threatened by over-supervision, and we were concerned to ensure that this should be prevented. It also seemed to us desirable to look at the way central government legal functions were organised to ensure that someone had a proper overview of the delivery of legal services. To ensure that this overview was well informed we also had to consider the advice available to government, and whether it was adequate.

Information about legal services

1.41 The issue of State involvement, in greater or lesser degree, raises in its turn the important matter of choice by the individual needing legal help. We believe that individuals should as far as possible have a free choice of lawyer; indeed we were concerned to improve the present provision of services to ensure that opportunities for real choice should exist for a wider section of the population, and that there should be adequate information on which individuals might base a rational choice. This implies that the private profession and other agencies should ensure that adequate information is provided to their actual and potential clientele. On this score there was some evidence of deficiency, although there were signs that the Law Society of Scotland were becoming more conscious of the needs of the public, for instance in their recent publication of a directory of legal services listing firms and giving an indication of the kinds of business they are prepared to take. Again, some marginal easing of restrictions on advertising was being introduced. Our general feeling, however, was that access to information about the types of legal service available and also their costs could be improved in the public interest.

1.42 Increasing use of advertising, as a means to these ends, introduces other considerations. Particularly in a professional field, the avoidance of misleading advertising is essential; and the advertising of specialist services raises questions about how competence and experience in specialist areas are to be assessed. As it happens, we take the view that in a small country like Scotland the development of specialisation is likely to be relatively restricted by the size of the market; but there are, and may be increasingly in the future, moves towards a greater degree of specialist practice. It is important both that proper safeguards should be provided and that unnecessary obstacles to its development should be eliminated; and we have accordingly given due attention to this matter.

Educating lawyers

1.43 The development of specialist skills, of course, is but one aspect of a much wider problem which was central to our remit; namely, the process by which lawyers are educated and trained for their professional duties. The adequacy of legal services will in great measure be determined by the effectiveness of education and training. A criticism that was expressed to us from various quarters was that the education and training of members of the legal profession were still largely related to the needs of the more affluent section of society and of corporate clients. For example, conveyancing for companies and private individuals, taxation and trusts and executries, are traditionally staple ingredients of both the university course and subsequent apprenticeship for aspiring lawyers. On the other hand, it was put to us in evidence that many legal firms lack expertise and interest in the newer areas of social, welfare and employment law which affect mainly the less affluent members of society.

1.44 Prior to our appointment, a Joint Committee of representatives of the Law Society of Scotland, the Faculty of Advocates, and the universities with law students, had formulated proposals for a postgraduate Diploma in Legal Practice. This new Diploma is to be introduced in the universities concerned in session 1980–81, and we believe it goes some way to remedy deficiencies in the present system of education and training. While this seems to be a step in the right direction, we do not think it is a full answer to some of the criticisms which have been made; we have, therefore, sought to take as comprehensive a view as possible of the whole education and training process.

Educating the public

1.45 A related matter is the general education of the public in the law and the use of legal services. The social and economic changes which have brought new developments in the relationship between lawyers and the public have not, on the whole, been matched by changes in education. The contribution which might be made on this score, both through an introduction at school to the role of law and legal services and by means of better communication to adults of legal changes and remedies, thus became a necessary part of our work.

Lawyers' remuneration

1.46 It was an explicit duty in our terms of reference that we should examine the remuneration of the profession and the arrangements whereby that remuneration was determined. This issue has many facets. An important section of the profession derives a significant amount of its income from public funds, through legal aid and legal advice and assistance. Of the remainder, coming from private sources, some will accrue through the provision of services to commercial and industrial organisations, and some again through the supply of services to private individuals. For the most part, these private transactions are subject to normal market pressures, but there are certain activities where only a qualified lawyer can undertake the work; and this means that an element of monopoly intrudes into the determination of remuneration.

1.47 While we could commence on the premise that members of the legal profession were entitled to reasonable remuneration for the work they do and are responsible for, the different considerations applying to the various components of professional income inevitably introduce a degree of complexity into the analysis. Clearly, the criteria for reasonable reward may be rather different as we move from a transaction involving a large international business, through say the monopolistic area of conveyancing of heritable property, to the defence of a person charged with a criminal offence and relying on legal aid to finance his defence. Still further adding to the difficulty is the fact that different practitioners have quite different mixes of business with the result that the proportions of income from different types of transactions may vary considerably. Thus it is quite possible for a solicitor's overall income to be reasonable in any sense we wish to define it, yet for the constituent elements to be unevenly remunerated relative to the work, skill and responsibility involved. It followed from this that we saw it as a necessary part of our task not only to examine the general level of remuneration in the profession but also, in particular, the method of determining charges both for monopolistic types of business and for functions paid for by public funds. Given the lack of information on remuneration, we had to decide early on to launch a sizeable survey of incomes in the profession conducted by the Law Society and by Coopers and Lybrand, chartered accountants, on our behalf. We believe that the information obtained provided a useful basis for a more rational approach to the whole question of remuneration.

1.48 There was, however, one important area in which we were unable to make the progress we had hoped. Especially because of the different principles under which certain portions of the lawyer's remuneration are determined, it seemed important to us to be able to obtain some information on the relative profitability of different categories of work. Unhappily, the bulk of the legal firms approached declared they were unable to assist in providing the information the Commission was seeking.

1.49 So far as salaried solicitors in the public sector are concerned, we feel that generally speaking it should continue to be possible to relate their remuneration to that enjoyed by other professionals and administrators carrying broadly the same load of work and level of responsibility.

Monopolies

1.50 The role of monopoly in certain types of legal business has already been commented upon in relation to remuneration. There are types of monopolistic practice which can be defended as being, on balance, in the public interest rather than against it. We worked from the widely accepted principle that a monopoly is undesirable unless it can be convincingly shown that the public interest is best served by its preservation. We, therefore, felt it important that the case for a monopoly or its retention, particularly in the area of conveyancing, should be carefully examined to ensure that it served the public interest.

Legal procedures

1.51 Generally speaking, court jurisdiction and procedures were outwith our terms of reference though, as noted earlier, we were told it was open to us to look at the courts in so far as they had a bearing on our task. There were two areas of court jurisdiction in which there was ample evidence indicating disquiet with present arrangements, namely divorce and small claims, both of which affected significant sections of the population, and both of which had a close bearing on our general remit on the provision of legal services. In these circumstances we thought it proper to include these within our scope.

1.52 Of related interest is our general feeling that private individuals should have greater scope than at present to undertake themselves the transaction of certain kinds of business which most people are currently obliged to put in the hands of solicitors. We do not believe that many people would in fact wish to undertake much legal business without professional advice; but we considered that it was wrong for individuals to be prevented from conducting their own affairs simply by reason of unnecessary procedural complications. Examples of legal business now simplified for the layman's benefit in England to a far greater extent than in Scotland can be seen in the procedure governing small claims; in the raising of an action for an undefended divorce; and in the obtaining of authority to wind up the affairs of deceased persons. We considered whether there was a need for change in this regard in Scotland.

Professional standards

1.53 There is one final problem which the evidence presented to us suggested should occupy our attention; the matter of complaints. No matter how good the general level of legal services provided—and in Scotland we think that the general level is high—there will inevitably be cases of incompetence or negligence.

1.54 Evidence to us indicates that the existing machinery for dealing with complaints leaves a number of complainers dissatisfied with the way that the Law Society have dealt with the complaints. The first Lay Observer was indeed appointed in 1976 to enable dissatisfied complainers to have an independent check on the way that the Law Society investigated their complaints.

1.55 It is human nature to suspect that an objective assessment of a lawyer's alleged incompetence or misconduct is more likely to be secured if the assessment is not carried out entirely or mainly by other lawyers; and we have, therefore, spent some time in formulating what we regard as necessary improvements in machinery both for examining and monitoring performance.

General

1.56 We close this brief commentary on some of the issues that we deal with at greater length in the following Chapters of our Report by predicting that the demand for lawyers' services will expand over the years ahead. Indeed our own recommendations for improved access to general advisory and legal services should themselves stimulate extra demand. Among other factors which could generate extra legal business are increasing house ownership and the increasing impact of membership of the European Economic Community. New areas of business are opening which require lawyers' services if lawyers are equipped and willing to deal with them.

1.57 We are confident that the legal profession in Scotland will expand to meet increased demand; and that implementation of the various recommendations that we make would assist the profession to provide an even better standard of service than it does at present.

TRIBUTE TO THE LATE COUNCILLOR SHAW

1.58 Before concluding this introductory Chapter we should like to place on record our deep regret at the death of our colleague Councillor Geoffrey Shaw on 28 April 1978. When he died, Geoffrey Shaw was Convener of Strathclyde Regional Council, the largest local authority in Scotland. In his early career he 'as an ordained minister of the Church of Scotland. He never, however, held a arish charge—he preferred instead to devote his early working life to youth nd community work; and it was only in his later years that local government bsorbed most of his talents and energy. Geoffrey Shaw's unusual blend of xperience and compassion would have enabled him to have made a major ontribution to the work of the Commission; and we, among many others, felt great sense of loss at his untimely death.

PART II

THE NEED FOR LEGAL SERVICES

CHAPTER 2

THE NEED FOR LEGAL SERVICES

Legal services

2.1 It is tempting to say that 'legal services are services provided by lawyers', but we reject this for two reasons. Firstly, not all work done by lawyers falls into the category of a legal service. A family solicitor, for example, may give a client advice on purely personal matters not all of which have a legal connotation. Scottish solicitors have traditionally seen themselves not exclusively as lawyers but as general 'men of business'. Secondly, not all legal services are provided by lawyers. There are many sources of legal services outwith the legal profession. Other professional people, whether they be architects, accountants or social workers, give advice to their clients on the legal aspects of their services. Much of the work of organisations such as Citizens Advice Bureaux, consumer advice centres, trade unions and motoring organisations, consists of giving information and advice about the law. Such provision is as much a legal service as the same information and advice given by a lawyer. Increasingly, Citizens Advice Bureaux and agencies like them take an active role in negotiations between, say, a consumer and a trader or a landlord and a tenant in dispute. Even though the advice centre is not strictly the citizen's agent the negotiation is no less a legal service than when it is done by a solicitor. The fact that solicitors, as specialists in the provision of legal advice and representation are, and ought to be, the ultimate source of legal services, does not in itself mean that non-solicitors may not provide legal services of adequate quality in certain circumstances. The courts also provide legal services whether directly, as the information and assistance given by a sheriff clerk to a personal applicant for confirmation as an executor, or indirectly, as the forum in which disputes are resolved in accordance with the law. We also regard as a form of legal service the dissemination of information through notices, leaflets, advertisements and booklets which give the citizen information about his legal rights and responsibilities and how he may exercise or carry them out.

2.2 Accordingly, when we speak of legal services we mean advice, information or assistance involving a knowledge of rights and obligations conferred by law and of legal procedures, whether provided by a lawyer or otherwise. These services may include action taken on behalf of a client, or facilities used by a client (whether the client is an individual, a group or an organisation). We believe that acceptance of this broad concept of legal services is essential if we are to meet the changing need for such services described below.

Factors affecting the total need for legal services

2.3 The need for legal services is not, even if we could measure it precisely, a fixed quantity; it will vary in response to a number of social pressures and tensions. We believe that the total need for legal services is growing considerably and affects sections of the community who previously regarded legal services as something outwith their experience. Before attempting to define 'need' it may be helpful to note briefly some factors which affect the total demand for legal services.

2.4 *Formalisation of relationships:* The extent to which people are content to rely on trust and status in their public and private dealings seems, whether we like it or not, to be decreasing in favour of the provision of statutory rights and formal relationships. Commercial and professional standards are now commonly made explicit in statute or published codes of practice; and machinery is established to allow complaints to be heard and challenges to be made when these standards are not met. One of the most striking developments in recent years has been the growth of statutory protection for consumers and obligations on traders and suppliers. The remoteness of management and sources of supply has made the old personal relations of seller and buyer largely impractical. The growing importance of multi-national companies and national monopolies has depersonalised relationships, resulting in a formalisation which finds its natural expression in legal procedures. Persons wishing to make complaints, and those complained against, are nowadays more likely to seek information and advice and may also require representation at hearings before courts or tribunals.

2.5 *Increase in real income:* More people now make major purchases. Home ownership has increased and is still growing; and there is also an increasing expenditure on expensive consumer durables such as cars, washing machines and freezers or services such as holiday facilities. An appeal to a legal solution in the event of difficulty is far more likely in the case of a dispute arising about a large purchase than a small one. Also, the increase in the number of major purchases made has been accompanied by an expansion of hire purchase and other credit schemes bringing further possibilities for dispute. We should also note that the influence of the consumer organisations has given rise to a much higher general level of expectation for consumers which, supported by the growth of legal protection for consumers, has resulted in a more confident assertion of rights by individuals against organisations.

2.6 *Legislation:* Accompanying these developments is the increase in the volume and the complexity of the legislation which affects us all as individuals and groups in most areas of our lives. When more and more rights and responsibilities are conferred by detailed statutes it is natural that we increasingly look to statute law for vindication of our rights and penalisation of any failure to discharge our responsibilities; and more of us require some specialist advice and information as to how we are affected. In recent years many developments in housing, welfare and employment law, have profoundly affected the daily lives of many citizens. These developments are often politically sensitive, and the law can change rapidly and confusingly. In such fields as welfare and employment law, the complexities of the primary and subordinate legislation are beyond the capacity of many people. We received much evidence about the need for clearer information on the effects of new legislation, which often takes the somewhat confusing form of amendments to existing legislation. We take up this theme further in Chapter 6.

Unmet Need

2.7 Ideally, the use made of legal services would express the total need for legal services. However, not all need results in use of legal services and in some cases the service provided may, by its inadequate quality or supply, fail to meet the whole need. The total need for legal services with which we must be concerned is the sum of actual use plus unmet needs. In broad terms the meaning of need for legal services and the nature of unmet need are clear enough. Certain causes of unmet need are clearly recognisable—shortages of lawyers in particular geographical localities and areas of the law, for example. There is, however, more to legal need than simply people having a legal problem and not being able to secure the services of an adviser. It is impossible to estimate how many legal problems there are, other than perhaps for research purposes in a small group under study. Many problems which could be resolved by legal means do not necessarily have to be. There are other non-legal solutions. So it is not much use defining problems as legal according to a researcher's idea of what the solution should be, or even according to how a wealthy person using a 'man of business' as his agent would solve them.[1] A fuller discussion of the problems in defining legal need is contained in Appendix 4.

2.8 While we received evidence that there is insufficient provision of legal services for dealing with the problems of the poorest groups in our society—problems in areas such as welfare law and tenants' rights—it is by no means clear that an expansion of traditional legal services is the best way to meet this need. As we shall see, the reasons for this unmet need are not only the absence of solicitors from particular areas but also the inhibitions of some people about consulting solicitors. Moreover, the mere existence of a potential legal solution to a problem is not in itself evidence of a need for legal services; non-legal solutions may be more convenient or suitable.

2.9 Where a citizen finds a non-legal solution which satisfies him, we would not be justified in claiming that he is deprived of legal services. That would depend on his awareness of his legal rights. In assessing the need for legal services we must therefore think in terms of two stages—firstly enabling the client to identify and, if he judges it appropriate, to choose a legal solution; and, secondly, enabling the client to pursue a chosen legal solution.

2.10 Accordingly, when we speak of a need for legal services in our Report we are speaking of a need for services—facilities, advice, assistance, information or action—to enable a citizen with a problem to assert or protect his rights in law by identifying and, if he so chooses, pursuing a legal solution, that is a solution which involves a knowledge of rights and obligations or of legal procedures. When we speak of 'unmet need' we are concerned about instances where a citizen is unaware that he has a legal right, or where he would prefer to assert or defend a right but fails to do so for want of legal services of adequate quality or supply.

---

[1] See for example:
Zander, *Legal Services for the Community* (Temple Smith; London 1978), p. 280;
Bankowski and Mungham, *Usages of Law* (Routledge and Kegan Paul; London 1976), Chapter 1.

CHAPTER 3

THE SUPPLY OF LEGAL SERVICES I: LAWYERS

3.1 In this Chapter we review briefly the way in which need is met at present by members of the legal profession, and in Chapter 4 we shall consider the place of 'other agencies' such as Citizens Advice Bureaux in the supply of legal services. At the point of contact with the client, legal services are largely supplied by the legal profession and these other agencies. We are not unmindful, however, of the vital contribution made by others such as the judiciary, officials of the courts and those who enforce the decisions of the courts, namely the messengers-at-arms and sheriff officers. We think that the contribution made by these others is best described in the context of the specific areas where the client might be expected to become aware of their role. We should also make clear that in this and the following Chapter we are concerned with the pattern of supply of legal services as it is at present. We shall not be concerned at this stage to develop to any extent our views on how the supply of legal services might be improved; this we shall do in the following Parts of the Report.

The legal profession

3.2 The legal profession in Scotland is divided into two branches: solicitors and advocates (also referred to as counsel). In this, it resembles the profession in the rest of the United Kingdom where there are solicitors and barristers. In many other jurisdictions no such distinction is made. Each branch of the profession has certain exclusive functions and privileges and some functions and privileges are exercised concurrently. A person can move from one branch to the other, but nobody can simultaneously be a member of both. The two branches of the profession have separate histories, and each has its own conditions of entry, regulations and governing body. In the following sections of this Chapter we deal in turn with the work done by solicitors and advocates in meeting clients' needs. We deal with the structure of the profession in Chapter 15.

SOLICITORS

3.3 In October 1979 the total number of practising solicitors was 4,577. Of this total, 2,749 were engaged in private practice as principals, 118 were consultants and the balance of 1,710 were in salaried employment, mostly in the public sector. Of principals in private practice, 321 practised on their own in single principal businesses, and the other 2,428 were in partnership with other solicitors.

Solicitors in public service, industry and commerce

3.4 Employed solicitors are found in 6 main areas of activity which can broadly be described as (1) local government, (2) central government, which contains a number of specialised fields such as the procurator fiscal service,

(3) public bodies, (4) commerce and industry, (5) universities and (6) private practice as assistants to the principals. The 877 solicitors in salaried employment in October 1979, excluding assistants in private practice, were employed as shown in Table 3.1:

TABLE 3.1: Areas of activity of qualified solicitors not in private practice*

Area of Activity	Number		(%)
Local government		431	(49)
Central government:			
procurators fiscal and Crown Office;	213	302	(34)
other government service	89		
Commerce and industry		71	(8)
Miscellaneous public bodies		68	(8)
Universities		5	(1)
		877	(100)

*Source: The Law Society and Crown Office.

3.5 Within these different spheres of employment, solicitors undertake a variety of tasks. In local government, solicitors, as well as being involved in administration, carry out conveyancing, court work and other legal work; they may also act as assessors to district courts or as clerks to the various licensing boards. Solicitors in central government, in the Office of the Solicitor to the Secretary of State for Scotland, perform similarly diverse tasks for their client departments and give legal advice on the wide range of functions which those departments carry out in Scotland, including the preparation and carrying through of primary and subordinate legislation. Central government solicitors also work for bodies such as the Scottish Land Court, the Scottish Law Commission and the Highlands and Islands Development Board; a few are based in the Lord Advocate's Department in London where their main functions are to assist the Scottish Law Officers and to draft government legislation affecting Scotland. Central government solicitors in the procurator fiscal service, whose official head is the Crown Agent, are engaged in the prosecution of crime. We say more about the procurator fiscal service in Chapter 17. The Solicitor of Inland Revenue (Scotland) is another central government employee who acts as adviser to the Board of Inland Revenue on Scots law and on the legal aspects of taxation questions arising in Scotland. Solicitors are also employed by public bodies, notably by the new town development corporations, for whom they carry out conveyancing work, litigation and arbitration, etc.. Various public utilities and the National Health Service also employ their own legal staff, while other solicitors are employed in universities and colleges. In addition, solicitors are directly employed by commerce, particularly by banks and insurance companies, and by industry where they advise companies on such matters as company law, taxation, consumer protection and fair trading.

3.6 The needs of those organisations which employ lawyers directly are diverse. We received little direct evidence to suggest that those who employed salaried lawyers were unable to meet their need for legal services; or that they were generally dissatisfied with the quality of the services they received. Accordingly, we have not dealt with employed lawyers in Parts III and IV of our Report although we do so in Part V. In general we decided to concentrate on the provision of legal services to individual clients by the private profession.

Solicitors in private practice

3.7 The work of the solicitor in private practice may be divided into court and non-court or chamber practice. Court work involves representing clients in civil and criminal proceedings. Solicitors may also appear in quasi-judicial proceedings such as planning inquiries and tribunals. A solicitor in chamber practice may be approached to give information and advice on almost any subject but in this variety certain major areas of practice may be identified. Conveyancing work, trust and executry work (drawing up wills and administering trusts and estates) and company business (which can include formation of companies, incorporation of businesses, acquisitions and mergers, etc.) accounted for almost two-thirds of the gross fee income earned by solicitors, according to a survey of solicitors' remuneration which we conducted.[1] The gross fee income received by the firms in the survey with detailed information on the various categories of work was as follows:

TABLE 3.2: Proportions of average gross fee income from different categories of work*

Category of Work	Average gross fee income (%)
Domestic conveyancing	33
Executry and trust business	19
Court work	13
Company and commercial work (including commercial conveyancing)	13
Insurance, building society and factorial commissions	6
Commission on sale of heritable property	5
Income tax	3
Miscellaneous work	8
	100

*Source: Appendix 7, Part I, paragraph 604. The Table is based upon information supplied by 74 firms. Whilst the figures may not be truly representative of firms as a whole, they give a measure of the relative importance of the categories of work listed. In broad terms the figures were similar to those given by the 357 firms with estimated figures.

These figures indicate the importance of the major areas of business to solicitors in private practice. On the other hand the variety of legal practice is illustrated by a passage from the Law Society's evidence to us:

> 'A solicitor in general practice is likely to find himself consulted on a wide variety of matters which come to him, not in neatly identified separate packages, but in a flood of simultaneous disparate problems. He may be called upon to advise the client on his right to reject an unsatisfactory product he has purchased in a shop, and about his divorce action; he may be consulted by his client about his investments and his road traffic summons; about his rights in respect of his children's education and the problem of bequeathing organs for use after death; about an application for a special marriage licence and his income tax return—in short, the solicitor as a general man of business, is consulted by his clients about every conceivable aspect of their affairs, not all of which have a very close, or any legal connotation. Hence the motto of the Law Society of Scotland—"Humani Nihil Alienum".'

[1] See Chapter 19 and Appendix 7.

3.8 It is clear, however, from the foregoing description and Table 3.2 that there is some substance in the claims that were made to us in evidence that the traditional suppliers of legal services concentrated on the areas of law which relate to the rights of private property (and to a much lesser extent crime), but did not provide as full a service in the areas of what we shall, for convenience, call 'social law'—that is in such rapidly growing areas as welfare law, employment law and housing law. Criminal work apart, legal aid does not yet appear to have changed the nature of solicitors' business significantly. Except for cases which go to court, solicitors' work in social law matters must be contained within the category of miscellaneous work in Table 3.2 providing altogether no more than 8 per cent of gross fee income. The Ormrod Committee, reporting on legal education in England and Wales in 1971 identified and analysed this problem of differential provision which, the Report suggests, derives from the structure of professional remuneration and the attitudes of the public:

> 'Without further developments (for example, a neighbourhood lawyer service), welfare law and many other aspects of administrative law, such as housing, will remain outside the ordinary lawyer's sphere. The extension of private practice into these new areas, though very desirable, is likely to be slow. Without a scheme for remuneration there is little inducement for the private practitioner to work in these fields or to study the law relating to them. At the same time, a new clientele will have to be created of people who are conscious of what lawyers could do to help them with these problems, and willing to seek their assistance.'[1]

3.9 Does the unmet need for lawyers' services in these areas of law described in the Ormrod Report exist in the Scottish context? We discuss the evidence of our research on this issue in Chapter 5, but we may note two pointers here. In the first place, there is the evidence cited above that for solicitors in private practice work in these areas produces only a very small fraction of their total fee income. Secondly, we can compare the number of enquiries made to Citizens Advice Bureaux about problems in these areas with the number of applications made under the legal advice and assistance scheme. This is admittedly a very crude comparison but the disparity does suggest that use made of solicitors' services to assert or protect certain statutory rights may well lag considerably behind need. In the year to March 1979, one-third of the 236,000 enquiries made to Citizens Advice Bureaux were in the following fields:[2]

Housing, Property and Land	36,692 enquiries
Social Security	23,113 enquiries
Employment	20,653 enquiries

In the same period less than one-tenth of the 65,000 applications for legal advice and assistance were identified as relating to similar problems, and break down as follows (applications in respect of social security matters are not shown separately):[3]

Employment	2,698
Housing, Landlord and Tenant	2,463

[1] *Report of the Committee on Legal Education:* Chairman, Mr. Justice Ormrod: HMSO, 1971, p. 39.
[2] Scottish Association of Citizens Advice Bureaux, *Annual Report 1978/79*, Table 1.
[3] Scottish Home and Health Department and the Legal Aid Central Committee: this information, we understand, will be included in the *29th Annual Report on the Scottish Legal Aid Scheme 1978/79* which had not been published by the time we went to print.

The ratio of total Citizens Advice Bureaux enquiries to legal advice and assistance applications was less than 4:1. The ratio in the employment field rises to approximately 8:1, and even higher in the field of housing, property and land, though there may be a significant difference between what is covered in the two sets of statistics. The ratio with regard to social security shows, of course, an immeasurable discrepancy. Many of the Citizens Advice Bureaux cases are straightforward, non-legal requests for information. We bear in mind also that, on the one hand, legal advice and assistance were available only to perhaps one-third of the population, and that solicitors might have helped many people in these fields without charge. On the other hand there were in 1978–79 only about 48 Citizens Advice Bureaux, as against more than 900 firms of solicitors. While these figures do not amount to proof of the existence of an unmet need for solicitors' services, they suggest to us that solicitors could be more actively employed in such areas of practice, particularly where there is no readily accessible Citizens Advice Bureau or other advice agency.

3.10 It is worth noting that there seems to be no declared unwillingness on the part of solicitors to take on work in these areas of social law. The following figures are derived from the 1979 legal aid referral lists in which solicitors indicate areas of the law in which they claim experience and are prepared to take clients under the legal aid and advice and assistance schemes:

TABLE 3.3: Solicitors claiming experience in certain areas for legal aid and legal advice and assistance*

House purchase/sale	871
Matrimonial/personal matters	804
Injury/accident claims	797
Wills and estates	791
Traffic offences	709
Employment law	684
Landlord and tenant problems	682
Consumer/HP/debt cases	661
Tribunal work	604
Criminal law	604
Social security/welfare benefits	449
Agriculture/crofting law	211

*Source: *Legal Aid Referral Lists, 1979.*

ADVOCATES

3.11 Advocates in Scotland correspond to barristers elsewhere in the United Kingdom. Like barristers, advocates have a sole right of audience (that is, only they are entitled to represent clients) in the supreme courts (the High Court of Justiciary and the Court of Session). Advocates also have rights of audience in every other court in Scotland and can represent clients at various tribunals and inquiries. These rights of audience are shared with solicitors in the lower courts and with solicitors and lay representatives at inquiries and tribunals. Advocates have the same right as barristers to appear before the House of Lords, the Judicial Committee of the Privy Council and Parliamentary Committees. The work of advocates falls into two main categories:

(a) representing parties before courts of law, inquiries and tribunals; and
(b) opinion work—that is, advice in relation to matters which may or may not subsequently become the subject of litigation.

All advocates are members of the Faculty of Advocates which is the governing body of this branch of the profession.

3.12 We have found it difficult to obtain information on the relative significance of the different components of advocates' work. The records which advocates keep throw little light on this question, although our remuneration survey gives some indication of the way their work loads are divided up. The survey suggests that criminal work accounts for as little as 10 per cent of income from private practice at the Bar, while civil work that is not legally aided—into which category most opinion work probably falls—accounts for 66 per cent of income.[1] Junior counsel earn a higher proportion of their fees than Queen's Counsel (QCs) from criminal work and also from civil work that is legally aided, particularly from divorce work. The amount of work done by advocates in the Court of Session is, however, reflected in the statistics of the Court's business. These show that in 1978 the Court of Session gave final judgement in 10,306 actions, of which 8,810 (85 per cent) were consistorial (mainly divorce), 803 (8 per cent) were for debts, and 540 (5 per cent) were for damages.[2] In that year the Court also disposed of 3,027 petitions by final judgement, though 1,847 of these were of an administrative character, and many did not require the services of advocates. These statistics are of little real value in assessing the importance of different types of work to the advocate profession, however, as they say nothing about the input of advocates' time, or the volume of work done.

3.13 The Lord Advocate appoints a number of Advocates Depute, at present 10, to prosecute in the High Court. Before 1970 Advocates Depute demitted office when the Lord Advocate went out of office. Since that date, however, it has been the practice for the appointments to continue and we understand that political affiliation or persuasion plays no part in their appointment. Appointment as Advocate Depute is part-time and salaried; holders of the office are debarred from private criminal practice but may (and do) continue to practise in civil matters. The appointments attract counsel of high calibre and are seen as valuable preparation for those aspiring to become judges.

3.14 We received no evidence to suggest that there was an unmet need for representation in the supreme courts and, as a result of our enquiries, we believe that the need for advocates' services in this regard is to a large extent met at present. In the lower courts, solicitors as well as advocates may represent clients; and here too we believe the need for advocates' services is fully met. Similarly, we received no evidence to suggest that there was an unmet need for advocates' services in providing opinions on points of law. Advocates are in competition in this area with solicitors and, in matters involving the interpretation of United Kingdom legislation, with barristers. There is a substantial demand for advocates' services at public inquiries, such as planning inquiries. The demand for their services at tribunals has not been great but is probably growing. In present circumstances, however, there does not appear to be any substantial unmet need for services that only advocates can supply. We understand that one area where problems have arisen is in obtaining the services of senior counsel with long experience. We discuss this problem in Chapter 15.

3.15 In saying that there is no evidence of unmet need so far as advocates' services are concerned we are aware that the practising Bar is relatively small.

[1] See Appendix 8.
[2] Scottish Courts Administration: *Civil Judicial Statistics, 1978:* HMSO, 1980.

There has, however, been a rapid growth in recent years; the practising Bar at the end of 1979 was some 140, compared with 107 in 1972. It is a feature of the Scottish Bar that it does not display the same tendency to specialisation that is found in the English Bar. This is no doubt largely due to the relatively small amount of work available in each particular field. It may also on occasion mean that clients turn to English specialists rather than to the Scottish Bar, particularly in regard to opinion work in specialised areas of the law common to all the United Kingdom, such as taxation and patent law.

3.16 In carrying out their work advocates may have to appear in courts, tribunals, etc., throughout Scotland. Advocates also normally appear in appeals to the House of Lords in Scottish civil cases (there is no appeal to the House of Lords in criminal cases). It is also competent for them to appear before the Judicial Committee of the Privy Council, the European Court of Justice at Luxembourg, the Court of Human Rights at Strasbourg and probably other international courts. The Court of Session in Edinburgh is the focal point of advocates' court work, however, and their centre of operations is the Advocates Library in Parliament House in Edinburgh. The Library, we have been informed, contains the finest collection of law books in Scotland; and in recent years the premises have undergone some renovation and adaptation to provide improved facilities for consultation with clients. The Library is adjacent to the supreme courts in Scotland where advocates, as we noted above, have the sole right of representation of clients. The excellence of the facilities now available in the Advocates Library has meant that much of the work that advocates used to undertake in individual chambers in Edinburgh is now carried out in the Library. Our survey of the costs and remuneration of advocates demonstrated that the concentration of the Faculty of Advocates in the Advocates Library was a major factor in holding down advocates' costs.[1] Advocates do not need to maintain separate chambers or consulting rooms, though some still do. The concentration of the Faculty also has the benefit of allowing regular and easy contact between advocates who can there readily discuss problems and exchange opinions and experience.

---

[1] See Appendix 8.

CHAPTER 4

THE SUPPLY OF LEGAL SERVICES II: OTHER AGENCIES

4.1 Legal services are supplied not only by the legal profession, but also by a variety of other agencies whose workers are not in the main lawyers. Many of these agencies have emerged piecemeal to meet specific needs in particular local areas or areas of the law or social provision, like housing advice centres and consumer advice centres. Other advice centres are local, independent services set up by groups in the community as a form of self-help or voluntary service; others again, are formed to meet a particular problem—for example, a planning proposal—and die when their reason for existing disappears. Local authorities themselves have increasingly seen the need to provide advice about their own services. The largest cohesive chain of voluntary advisory services is provided by the Citizens Advice Bureaux. The Bureaux were introduced at the beginning of the second world war to help with the whole range of problems faced by civilians during the emergency. They now provide impartial, independent information and advice on many subjects. More specialist agencies include organisations such as Shelter, Age Concern and the Scottish Association for the Care and Resettlement of Offenders which offer individual advice and help, but which are primarily bodies representing the interests of particular groups, pursuing particular interests, or pressing for changes in particular areas of the law or social provision.

The work of advice agencies

4.2 The work of advice agencies has been described by Rosalind Brooke under five main headings which together constitute advice giving.[1] Firstly, the simple transmission of information; secondly, the provision of advice which may involve recommending specific courses of action; thirdly, the referral of clients to other, perhaps specialist, agencies or to professionals such as lawyers; fourthly, action on behalf of clients, perhaps by writing letters or representing them at various tribunals; and, fifthly, what is described as 'feedback' which involves the agency in analysing evidence from cases they have dealt with and reporting the results to the appropriate authorities so that remedial action can be taken or inadequacies in policies or services be publicised.

4.3 Directly or indirectly, all these functions, with the exception of the last, may involve the provision of legal services in the sense in which we use the term.[2] In practice, the service given to a client by an advice centre will involve one or more of the functions in question. The Scottish Association of Citizens Advice Bureaux, in preparing their evidence to us, made an attempt to quantify the number of enquiries with a legal content made to Bureaux. The task proved difficult precisely because the individual Bureaux had divergent views as to what problems had a legal content. It is not always possible to distil the legal content of problems: a battered wife has a legal problem if she wishes to leave her husband

---

[1] Rosalind Brooke: *Information and Advice Services* (Occasional Paper on Social Administration No. 46): Bell, 1972.

[2] See Chapter 2.

and requires court action to prevent him molesting her further. However, she also has a need for accommodation, finance and support. It is part of the importance of such generalist agencies in the provision of legal services that clients who take complex problems to them can expect information and advice on all aspects of the problem, including the legal dimension. This makes it essential that the advisers are trained to identify and evaluate legal elements in problems; and that the agency has good access to professional expertise. With this in mind, we now look at the work of the major advice agencies in Scotland. A much fuller account than we can give is in 'Let the People Know', published by the Scottish Consumer Council,[1] on which some of the following paragraphs draw heavily.

Citizens Advice Bureaux

4.4 Like Citizens Advice Bureaux in the United Kingdom as a whole, the 48 Bureaux in Scotland are autonomous with local management committees drawn from the local communities and statutory and voluntary organisations within them. Each management committee is responsible for its Bureau in such matters as negotiating its annual grant from the local authority, although in some areas Bureaux conduct these negotiations jointly. The management committee is also responsible for maintaining the standards of its Bureau to the level required by the membership conditions stipulated by the Scottish Association of Citizens Advice Bureaux. The governing structure of the Bureaux movement has recently been changed, and by the time this Report is published it is expected that the Scottish Association will be an autonomous body, with associate membership of the National Association. This arrangement will give Scottish Bureaux access to information distributed by the National Association, while full authority over Bureaux in Scotland will be vested in the Scottish Association.

4.5 Citizens Advice Bureaux do not charge for their services. Individual Bureaux rely largely on grants from local authorities, though central government contributes to central administrative costs and has also provided in recent years a development grant to help in establishing new or experimental services (see Chapter 7). Once established the continuation of these services depends on local authority support.

4.6 The aims of the Citizens Advice Bureaux service are defined as being 'to ensure that individuals do not suffer through ignorance of their rights and responsibilities or of the services available, or through an inability to express their needs effectively; to exercise a responsible influence on the development of social policies and services both locally and nationally'. Commenting on these aims in their Annual Report, the Scottish Association say: 'While the CAB service sees its role as increasingly offering advice and advocacy rather than simply giving out information, the information system retains its role as a vital and valuable tool for the work of the CAB.'[2]

4.7 The Citizens Advice Bureaux provide a wide generalist service. In 1978/79, there were 236,034 enquiries made at Bureaux in Scotland, and a breakdown of these by major categories is given in Table 4.1 overleaf:

---

[1] *Let the People Know: A Report on Local Advice Services in Scotland:* Scottish Consumer Council, 1977.
[2] Scottish Association of Citizens Advice Bureaux: Annual Report 1978/1979, page 11.

TABLE 4.1: Enquiries at Citizens Advice Bureaux in Scotland, 1978/79*

Category of enquiry	%
Consumer, trade and business	22
Housing, property and land	16
Family and personal	14
Social Security	10
Employment	9
Administration of justice	8
National and international	6
Travel, transport and holidays	4
Health	4
Taxes and duties	3
Leisure activities	2
Education	2
Communications	1
Immigration and nationality	**
	100
	(N=236,034)

*Based on *Scottish Association of Citizens Advice Bureaux Annual Report 1978/79: Table 1*

**Less than 0·5%

Note: In this Table and in subsequent Tables, and elsewhere in the Report, the expression 'N=' signifies the number of cases on which the percentage is based; percentages are shown as totalling 100% even where, because of rounding, this does not appear to be the case.

4.8 Commenting on this Table in their Annual Report for 1978/79 the Scottish Association observe that 'these broad categories can conceal significant factors at lower levels of disaggregation. Thus, for example, most consumer enquiries do not concern consumer complaints, but relate to debt problems, HP and insurance queries: family and personal problems largely comprise marriage difficulties and a major proportion of housing queries concern landlord/tenant disputes and the problem of obtaining accommodation.' The major areas of enquiry which the Table identifies are consumer problems (21·7 per cent of the 1978/79 total), housing, property and land problems (15·5 per cent), family and personal problems (14·1 per cent), social security (9·8 per cent) and employment (8·8 per cent).

4.9 In their evidence to us, the Scottish Association estimated that more than 40 per cent of the enquiries made to the Bureaux had a legal content. The definition which the Scottish Association used to arrive at this figure was 'that a legal enquiry was a problem which would require a knowledge of the substantive law or court procedures for its solution'. Since many enquiries have a legal element, and some of these require a lawyer's advice, Bureaux need access to solicitors. Many Bureaux invite local solicitors to run legal sessions on a voluntary basis within the Bureaux. These clinics are entirely voluntary, and the solicitors are not allowed by the Law Society to take any cases back to their own offices. Other Bureaux have established formal rota schemes in which all local solicitors are invited to participate on a rota basis; they may be allowed by the Society to refer back to their own office any case requiring further professional help. This means that the client only has to deal with one lawyer to get the help he needs. Such schemes have been established with the approval of the Law Society, though local faculties of solicitors have not always agreed to participate when invited. Many Bureaux still rely on referring enquirers to local legal firms who are prepared to take clients from them or to advise the Bureaux staff. Other specialist advice services provided by some Bureaux may also have a legal content where Bureaux offer a service by experts such as accountants on income tax and VAT problems, by surveyors on housing, building and property maintenance and by bankers on budgeting and debt counselling, or hold consumer advice sessions run by consumer protection officers. Advocacy is of growing importance in the role of Citizens Advice Bureaux. It is normally undertaken by trained lay workers after consultation as necessary with the legal advisers to Bureaux. The Scottish Association's Annual Report for 1978/79 states that 20 Bureaux have now provided lay advisers to represent clients at one or more of the following tribunals:

Supplementary Benefits Appeals Tribunal;
National Insurance Tribunal;
Rent Assessment Committee;
Medical Appeal Tribunal;
Industrial Tribunal; and
Criminal Injuries Compensation Board.

4.10 Citizens Advice Bureaux have been accused of being slow to recognise the need to meet new challenges, such as the need for advocacy at tribunals, though there is evidence that this is changing. Although their administrative structure in Scotland has been reconstituted, there is still insufficient forward planning and corporate development of policies. Dependence upon local funding has made such planning, in fact, virtually impossible. Bureaux live from year to year and hand to mouth. The development plan of the Scottish Association of Citizens Advice Bureaux which outlines the main gaps in the system and priorities for improved services, is a move in the right direction, but without assured funding remains a paper plan. On the whole, we consider that more central responsibility is required to secure uniformly high standards. On the other hand, the real value of Citizens Advice Bureaux rests in their community role, and the essential elements in their service are the well-trained volunteers backed by adequate central information services and paid organisers. How to provide adequate resources for such a service seems to us an essential question in determining the level of legal services in Scotland.

Neighbourhood advice and information centres

4.11 This heading covers a diverse range of agencies which come into being through local initiatives within communities, usually urban ones, many suffering from multiple deprivation. They aim to provide information and advice not so much as an end in itself, but as part of a broader move towards change in the community. Such centres generally have small catchment area populations—none more than 25,000, and many are considerably smaller. The Beechwood Information Centre in Dundee, for example, serves an area of only 460 houses. Neighbourhood centres give advice on a whole range of problems and issues but a few, in particular housing and welfare benefits, tend to dominate their work. A report on the work of the Ferguslie Park Centre in Paisley found that some 60 per cent of the users had housing problems, of which 40 per cent concerned housing repairs; and almost 30 per cent of the users had welfare benefits problems.[1] Professional legal advice is usually provided voluntarily at such centres by solicitors who support their work. The centres are financially aided from a variety of sources, including regional council funds, urban aid, and other central government funds and grants from the European Economic Community Social Fund.

Consumer advice centres

4.12 Regional and islands councils were empowered to provide consumer advice in addition to their other duties of consumer protection under section 149(6) of the Local Government (Scotland) Act 1973. With funds largely provided by the Department of Trade, most Scottish authorities have made some provision, but its nature has varied. Some authorities liaise with the Citizens Advice Bureaux in their region, providing funds and back-up facilities to allow the Bureaux to provide consumer advice. Other regional councils have provided consumer advice centres run by their consumer protection departments. In January 1980 there were 15 centres in Scotland—5 of them mobile. They offered both pre-purchase information and advice to consumers who wished to make an informed choice on the range of products available to them, and post-purchase advice to those who were dissatisfied with what they had bought. In dealing with consumer complaints, the consumer advice centres can:

1. Refer complaints to the appropriate agencies under criminal legislation;
2. Advise consumers how to deal with the matter themselves;
3. Provide a mediation or conciliation service between consumer and trader;
4. Advise the consumer on ways of obtaining redress, including referrals to a solicitor.

The centres also have a public education function, including education on consumers' rights and responsibilities. Their service is by no means confined to consumers. They are equally ready to give advice to retailers who need information about their legal responsibilities and rights. A decision to cease central government grants to consumer advice centres as from 31 March 1980 has meant that all regional and islands councils are currently reconsidering their policies towards consumer advice centres. It seems likely that some will close; but a few will continue, and at least one regional council was considering extending its services.

Housing advice centres

4.13 In February 1980 there were 6 housing advice centres in Scotland, 3 of which were run by Shelter and 3 by district councils. The principal function of the district council centres was giving advice and information to clients on all sorts of housing problem—transfer of tenancies, repairs, eviction notices, etc.. Their clients included private as well as council tenants. The centres also advised those seeking mortgages, particularly at the bottom end of the house purchase market. The Shelter centres were more concerned to help tenants to assert and protect their rights, and to increase tenants' understanding of these rights.

---

[1] Jill Snaith: *The Ferguslie Park Information and Action Centre* (Department of Social and Economic Research, University of Glasgow), page 12.

Planning advice

4.14 Planning advice, in the form of information about local authority road proposals, housing clearances and developments, is generally available from offices of the local authority concerned, in some cases operating from special premises. In some areas, a non-official source of information and advice on planning issues, which can be contacted directly or through referral from Citizens Advice Bureaux or other agencies, is provided by the Planning Aid service. This consists of volunteers from local authority planning departments, university and college planning departments and planning consultants. A recent study showed that there were planning aid groups in Glasgow, Edinburgh, Dundee and Aberdeen. Subjects raised in enquiries to these groups include rights of appeal against planning permission refusal, compulsory purchase, house extension, compensation, housing proposals and objection rights in the planning process.[1] Many of the problems raised with the planning aid groups involve legal questions, particularly in the field of administrative law and the groups consult with or refer cases to solicitors as necessary.

Local authority agencies

4.15 In their 1977 report on local advice services in Scotland, the Scottish Consumer Council gave details of information and advice agencies run by local authorities, distinct from the specialist consumer and housing advice agencies, derived from a survey of all the regional, district and islands councils.[2] The report says that, in general, 'it appears that very few Councils actually operate Advice Centres as such. What is more common is that personnel in offices ordinarily open to the public give information and/or advice on a wide range of matters connected with local government.' Where they are provided, separate agencies, such as Lothian Region's enquiry centres, are primarily information services. Where problems requiring specialist advice are raised, the normal practice is to refer the client to the appropriate specialist either within the authority or another agency. In cases where the problem has a legal dimension, the information given, and the referral, may properly be described as a legal service. Another local authority source of information in the community is, of course, the library service; the libraries offer facilities for displaying and distributing information material, though they do not have facilities for giving advice.

Legal advice centres

4.16 Legal advice centres are agencies where qualified volunteers (usually either practising solicitors or academic lawyers) give advice; the term includes legal advice clinics operating (usually in an evening or on a Saturday morning) within Citizens Advice Bureaux and other general advice centres. The range of provision covers such institutions as the Edinburgh Legal Dispensary, which was established in 1900 and now operates from premises in Edinburgh University, to legal advice centres attached to social work area offices set up in the past two or three years. In 1977 there were about 40 of these centres in Scotland, and a list of them is shown at Annex 1 to this Chapter. The range of work done by these advice centres is obviously wide and varies from place to place. However,

[1] Further information may be obtained from the booklet *Planning Aid: A Report on the Scottish Experience:* Planning Exchange, Glasgow, 1978.

[2] *Let the People Know: A Report on Local Advice Services in Scotland:* Scottish Consumer Council, 1977.

some examples can be given. The Dundee Legal Advice Centre analysed its caseload between 1 October and 31 December 1978 as shown in Table 4.2.

TABLE 4.2: Enquiries at Dundee Legal Advice Centre, October–December 1978*

Category of enquiry	%
Family	19
Housing	16
Employment	13
Criminal	10
Social Security	9
Consumer	9
Other contracts	6
Delict	5
Debt	4
Wills and succession	4
Taxation	1
Complaints	1
Miscellaneous	5
	100
	(N=356)

*Source: Dundee Legal Advice Centre.

A broadly similar pattern emerges in the Edinburgh Legal Dispensary's Statistical Report for the year to 7 March 1979 (Table 4.3).

TABLE 4.3: Enquiries at Edinburgh Legal Dispensary, 8 March 1978–7 March 1979*

Category of enquiry	%
Landlord and tenant/Housing	18
Contract/Consumer/Insurance	15
Divorce	11
Criminal	10
Road traffic (accidents and offences)	9
Matrimonial (general)	7
Personal injury	6
Debt	5
Succession	4
Aliment	3
Employment	2
Neighbours	2
Complaints against solicitors	1
Social Security	**
Miscellaneous	7
	100
	(N=231)

*Source: Edinburgh Legal Dispensary, *Statistical Report for the year 8 March 1978—7 March 1979.*

**Less than 0·5%

The ways in which legal advice centres deal with the problems which are brought to them also vary; some place most emphasis on taking action on behalf of their clients; others, like the Edinburgh Legal Dispensary, refer a very high proportion of their enquiries to private solicitors. Self-referral (that is referral of a client by a solicitor at a legal advice centre to his own firm) is not allowed in most centres except in cases of emergency or other special circumstances. Normally, under guidelines laid down by the Law Society, the client will be referred to a firm with which the solicitor at the centre is not connected.

Castlemilk Advice Centre

4.17 The Castlemilk Advice Centre, which combines a Law Centre and Citizens Advice Bureau in connected premises, deserves separate consideration as it contains the first Law Centre of its kind in Scotland. The combined Centre began work, in somewhat cramped conditions, in April 1979 after discussions lasting 6 years between the Scottish Association of Citizens Advice Bureaux, the Law Society and, latterly, Strathclyde Regional Council. All callers to the Advice Centre are seen in the first instance by Citizens Advice Bureau staff and are referred to the Law Centre if the initial enquiries reveal the existence of a legal problem which calls for professional advice and assistance. Citizens Advice Bureau staff also benefit from direct access to professional legal advice in cases where they themselves are advising clients. The Law Centre is staffed by two salaried solicitors, of whom one is Director. The funding bodies have authorised a further solicitor post when the volume of work has built up. Expenditure is met by Strathclyde Regional Council (25 per cent) and central government funds (75 per cent). The Law Centre's operations are governed by the following statement of intent:

> 'The purpose of the Neighbourhood Law Centre is to provide advice, assistance and representation to clients from the Castlemilk area in areas of law not covered or insufficiently covered by private legal practitioners in the Castlemilk area. Accordingly, apart from initial advice and assistance and except in cases of emergency the Centre's solicitors will not normally undertake (but will refer to private practitioners in accordance with the principles laid down in the guidelines on the use of referral lists) work such as conveyancing, reparation, matrimonial proceedings, testate and intestate succession and criminal matters. The Centre's activities will be directed primarily to Welfare Law, Housing, Consumer Protection, Immigration and representation at Boards and Tribunals not covered by legal aid. Although the Centre will operate both Legal Advice and Assistance and the Civil Legal Aid Scheme in appropriate cases it will not take part in the Criminal Legal Aid Scheme. Only in cases of hardship will the Centre represent in any court a client who is outwith the financial limits of the Legal Aid Scheme subject to the foregoing.'

This statement is more restrictive in its terms than the waivers granted to many similar Centres in England and Wales.

Other sources of advice

4.18 Citizens Rights Offices in Edinburgh and Aberdeen, funded by the Scottish Office and the regional councils, provide information and advice on welfare rights, housing, rent and rates rebates and employment problems, and provide free representation at supplementary benefit, national insurance, rent and industrial tribunals. The Scottish Council for Civil Liberties take up broadly similar issues, both for particular clients who come to them and more generally in the political arena. In addition Welfare Rights Officers are employed by

Strathclyde and Lothian Regional Councils. The nationalised industries have consumer consultative committees or councils appointed by central government. These deal with complaints which have not been satisfactorily resolved by the industries and give direct advice to consumers.[1] A number of specialised organisations give advice to their own members or to the people for whom they are particularly concerned. Some examples of the wide range of groups in this category are the Scottish Council for Single Parents, Gingerbread, the Disablement Income Group, Age Concern and the Automobile Association and the Royal Automobile Club.

4.19 These then are some of the components in the patchwork of advice and information agencies in Scotland which, to a greater or lesser degree, provide legal services as part of their function. The question must arise as to why there is a need for these other agencies as well as the legal profession to provide legal services. We believe that the answer has at least three aspects:

(a) the nature of the problems involved,
(b) the location and nature of the offices used, and
(c) the cost to the client of seeking advice and information from the profession or other agencies.

Of course, these three aspects are closely inter-related; and running through each is the crucial question of the client's subjective perception of the problem, the offices and the cost.

The problem

4.20 To recognise a potential legal solution to a problem, the citizen must have some knowledge of the legal rights and responsibilities involved. In many cases, people are aware only of the problem and have little awareness of its relationship to the complex and ever-increasing volume of legislation surrounding their daily lives. Further, many problems are not, at least to the person who suffers from them, clear-cut single issues. Before seeking any solution it is helpful, indeed often necessary, to discuss the problem in order to identify its various aspects and discover what is really at issue. The potential client therefore requires initial advice which will help to clarify the problem and to identify the possible solutions, including potential legal solutions. Many people are reluctant to enter a solicitor's office unless they are sure that they have a real and important legal problem; but they are less reluctant to approach more informal advice agencies. An unpublished report for the Edinburgh Citizens Advice Bureau contains the results of a survey of that Bureau's users.[2] Asked how they regarded the Bureau, many clients emphasised its capacity to give reassurance and to clarify issues about which they were uncertain. They said, for example, that 'It's a good place to go when you're not sure how to go about things' and 'It gives advice on problems you can't handle yourself'.

4.21 Even when a legal solution may be the preferred or only solution, a problem might not immediately be seen by the client as one with which a solicitor might deal. The image of solicitors as a profession concentrating mainly on commercial matters, interests in private property and the interests of those

---

[1] A full account of the work of these Committees is given in the Scottish Consumer Council Report on 'Consumer Representation in the Nationalised Industries in Scotland' which forms Annex I of the National Consumer Council Report *Consumers and the Nationalised Industries:* HMSO, 1976.
[2] Ruth Hildebrandt: *The Citizens Advice Bureau:* 1977.

charged with crimes, may lead many potential clients in the areas of social law to seek advice and information elsewhere. The Edinburgh study found that the most common attitude to the Citizens Advice Bureau among its users was as a simple and acceptable way of gaining access to legal advice. Typical comments were that 'I wanted to cover all the possibilities before going to a lawyer'; 'Lawyers are so busy—they don't do it for free'; 'You go to the CAB before you go to a lawyer and commit yourself'; 'The CAB is a prop for people who are frightened to go to lawyers' and 'The CAB have the legal jargon to help you'.

The office premises

4.22 An important difference between the offices of solicitors and other agencies is their atmosphere or image. Citizens Advice Bureaux and other agencies seek to provide shop front accommodation wherever possible and generally attempt to present an atmosphere of friendly and informal helpfulness. Citizens Advice Bureaux are often located in familiar High Street surroundings. Their blue and yellow logos are clearly visible and in many towns there are street signs pointing to the Bureau. Consumer advice centres are also generally accommodated in attractive High Street premises. Neighbourhood advice centres, based in premises such as shops, converted flats and community centres, typically have windows full of posters and leaflets inviting the attention of potential clients. By contrast, many solicitors' offices are, as we have seen on our visits, somewhat austere and identified only by a reticent name plate. They are commonly located in business areas where their austerity and business-like appearance do not necessarily give an impression of the everyday concerns of ordinary people. There are exceptions, of course, and the Law Society have been receiving, and approving, an increasing number of applications to put up large shop-front signs. It is important, if clients are to receive a favourable first impression of offices providing legal services, for these to have attractive reception areas and a helpful and informative receptionist. Citizens Advice Bureaux and other information services work hard to create a good first impression. The reception points in solicitors' offices are too often impersonal.

The cost

4.23 From the client's point of view a major advantage which the other agencies have over the profession is the relative cost of consultation. Even under the legal advice and assistance or legal aid schemes a client may have to pay some contribution to the solicitor's fees: information and advice, even direct assistance, from Citizen Advice Bureaux and similar agencies are free. Once again, this is particularly advantageous to a client seeking preliminary information and advice to help him determine the scope of his problem and the possible solutions open to him. The inarticulate or uncertain client may be unwilling initially to spend money—perhaps to him substantial amounts of money—eliciting from a solicitor the advice that he has no case in law, or that the costs of an action outweigh the likely benefits. We are aware that many solicitors out of a sense of public duty do not submit an account in such cases, and this is very much to their credit. What matters, however, is that many people think they will incur expense, and the fear of commitment to large and uncontrollable expenses keeps them away from solicitors. The results of the survey, which the Scottish Consumer Council submitted to us, highlighted this fear in the remark made by one respondent about solicitors' fees: 'You don't know how much he is going to charge before you go in; maybe you couldn't afford it'. The existence of agencies giving free initial advice appears to encourage people to make enquiries which they might not have done if they had been worried about the cost.

Availability of advice services

4.24 We have noted that solicitors' offices are absent from many rural and remote areas, and are concentrated in the central business areas of larger towns and cities. For some people, particularly on the outskirts of the cities, a neighbourhood advice centre or Citizens Advice Bureau located in a community shopping area may be more readily accessible than a solicitor's office. However, the difficulties experienced by citizens in rural and remote areas are not much improved by the sparse provision made by other agencies. The number of Citizens Advice Bureaux in Scotland, for example, is proportionately much smaller than in England and Wales. In evidence to us the Scottish Association of Citizens Advice Bureaux said:

> 'There is no large region of the United Kingdom where the total coverage of the network of CABx is as inadequate as it is in Scotland. Scotland, for example, has fewer CABx than Wales.
>
> There are several important towns such as Ayr, Greenock and Paisley without Bureaux and it is estimated that only 25 per cent of the Scottish population has ready access to a Bureau.'

The distribution of Bureaux in Scotland can be seen from the map at Annex 2 to this Chapter. The majority of other advice agencies are also concentrated in the cities and in the central belt.

4.25 Various experiments have recently begun in the provision of advice services in rural areas. Some limited use is made of mobile centres, particularly by the consumer protection departments in Lothian, and Strathclyde and the Western Isles. The Scottish Consumer Council is promoting experiments with a free-phone telephone enquiry system in the Highland Region based on Inverness Citizens Advice Bureau, and with the use of village information links to provide an advice service based on Aberdeen Citizens Advice Bureau. The Citizens Advice Bureau in Castle Douglas is also conducting a village links experiment. This provides an individual trained Citizens Advice Bureau worker living in a village as contact person for his or her neighbours. Despite these developments, the provision of advice services in rural Scotland remains seriously inadequate.

4.26 We conclude that the advice agencies we have described are a necessary and valuable complement to the profession. They attract people who may need but would otherwise not seek legal advice. They provide the basic advice which can help a client to make an informed approach to the profession. They deal with areas of the law that the profession does not adequately cover; and they act as a sieve identifying cases which require the professional attention of solicitors. The services are, however, too thin on the ground.

LIST OF VOLUNTARY LEGAL ADVICE CENTRES IN EXISTENCE AT JUNE 1977

I GLASGOW

Glasgow Citizens Advice Bureaux

Bath Street CAB, 212 Bath Street.
Dalmarnock CAB, 24 Main Street.
Drumchapel CAB, 82 Ledmore Drive.
Easterhouse CAB, 46 Township Centre.

Glasgow Legal Clinics

Milton, St. Andrews Methodist Church, Liddlesdale Square.
Maryhill, Central Methodist Halls, 304 Maryhill Road.
Pollokshaws, Methodist Church, 34 Shawholme Crescent.
Govanhill, 322 Cathcart Road.

Family Service Unit, 19 Glenacre Quadrant, Castlemilk.

East End Legal Clinic, Bellfield Street, Dennistoun.
Laurieston Information Centre & Student Unit, Block 80, Stirlingfauld Road.

Glasgow University

Blackhill Legal Advice Centre, St. Paul's Church, Langdale Street, Provanmill.
Pollokshields, Glendale Community Centre, Kenmure Street.
The University, John McIntyre Building, University Avenue.

II EDINBURGH

Edinburgh Legal Dispensary, Old College, Edinburgh University.

Advice Centres attached to Social Work Offices

Craigmillar, 182 Greendykes Road.
Gilmerton, 10–12 Newtoft Street.
Gorgie/Dalry, Springwell House, Ardmillan Terrace.
Leith, 9–11 Giles Street.
Muirhouse, 34 Muirhouse Crescent.
Pilton, 40 Ferry Road Avenue.

Edinburgh CAB

58 Dundas Street.
Slateford Longstone Parish Church, Kingsknowe Road, Longstone.

The Citizens' Rights Office, 70 Nicolson Street.

III DUNDEE

Citizens Advice Bureau, 125 Nethergate.

Dundee Legal Advice Centres, (University of Dundee)

Perth Road.
Fintry Church Hall, Fintry.

IV ABERDEEN

Citizens Advice Bureau, 38 Castle Street.

V PERTH

Citizens Advice Bureau, 10–12 New Row.

VI OTHER ADVICE CENTRES SPONSORED BY CITIZENS ADVICE BUREAUX

Bellshill CAB, 20 Motherwell Road.
Buckhaven CAB, Wellesley Road.
Clydebank CAB, 13 Kilbowie Road.
Dalkeith CAB, 8 Buccleuch Street.
Hamilton CAB, Brandon House, 27 Brandon Street.
Largs CAB, 32–36 Boyd Street.
Livingston CAB, 8 Victoria Street, Craigshill.
Penicuik CAB, 27–29 John Street.
Stirling CAB, 4 Albert Place.

VII ADVICE CENTRE SPONSORED BY SOLICITORS IN PRIVATE PRACTICE

The Shotts Advisory Centre, Shotts, Lanarkshire.

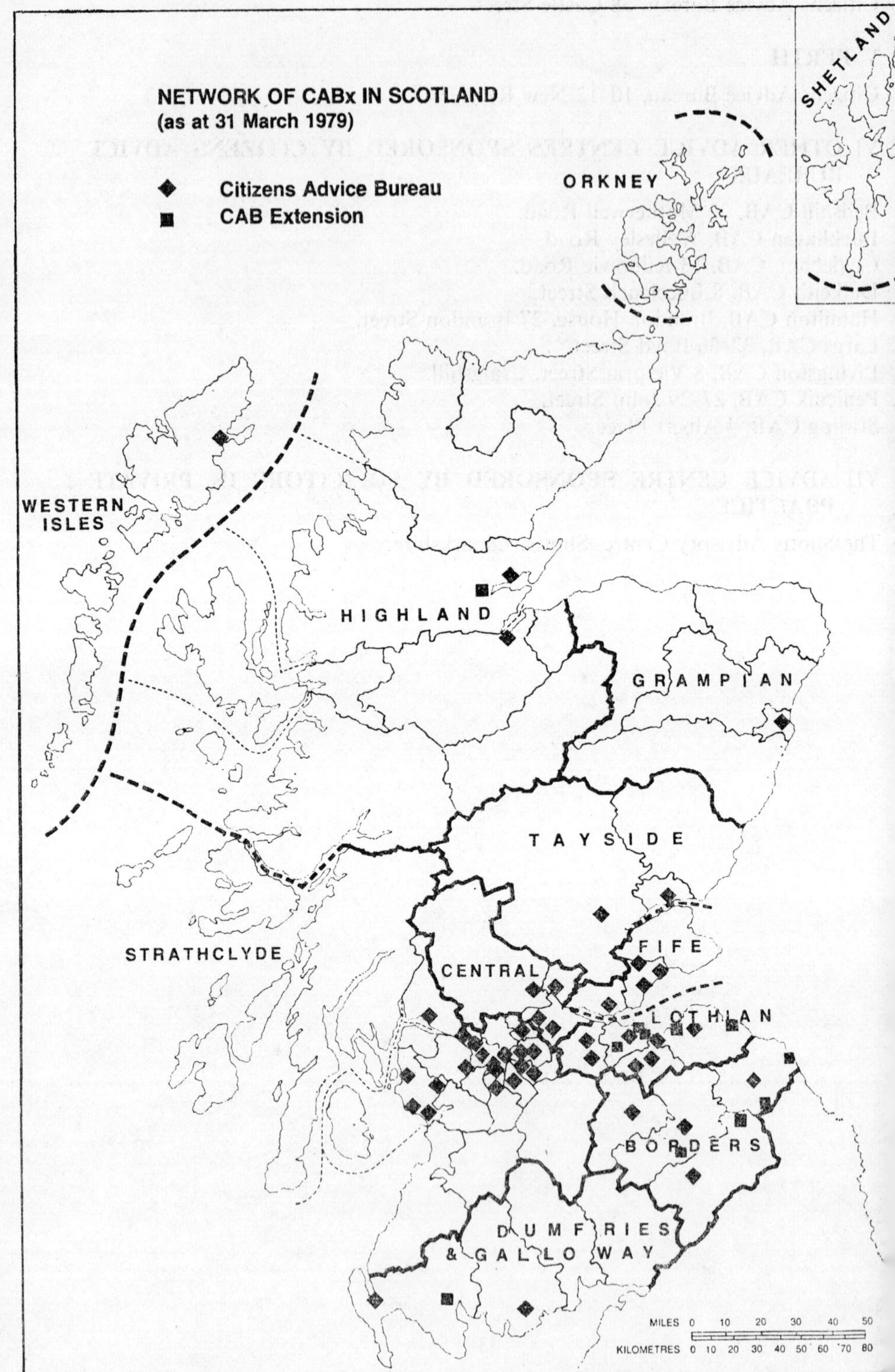
NETWORK OF CABx IN SCOTLAND
(as at 31 March 1979)
Citizens Advice Bureau
CAB Extension
SHETLAND
ORKNEY
WESTERN ISLES
HIGHLAND
GRAMPIAN
TAYSIDE
FIFE
CENTRAL
STRATHCLYDE
LOTHIAN
BORDERS
DUMFRIES & GALLOWAY
MILES 0 10 20 30 40 50
KILOMETRES 0 10 20 30 40 50 60 70 80

CHAPTER 5

USE AND NON-USE OF LEGAL SERVICES

5.1 In Chapters 3 and 4 we have described the services provided by solicitors and by a variety of advice agencies, and have given some indication of the number of people who use these services. To focus our concern about unmet need for legal services we decided that we had to look not only at users of legal services but at non-users, and to this end we undertook an investigation into how people attempted to solve problems of a relatively serious nature. A full report of this study is at Appendix 4. In this Chapter we draw on the findings of that survey, and on some other relevant material, to analyse the extent and causes of unmet need, and to identify what seemed to be the main obstacles to the use of legal services.

5.2 In designing our survey we were concerned to identify the needs for legal services which people had actually experienced, rather than to discover how people thought they would respond to hypothetical situations. This seemed essential to help us evaluate the conflicting claims made about the existence and extent of unmet need for legal services in Scotland. In particular, we wanted to identify reasons why people did not use legal services when they might have done so. Was it that they were poorly informed about their rights, or about sources of advice? Was it that they could not conveniently get to a lawyer or other adviser? Was it that they could not afford to go—or thought they could not? We, therefore, asked respondents to say what had been the most important or worrying problem they had actually experienced. Our survey went on to ask respondents whom they had consulted about their problem, since failure to take appropriate advice will in certain circumstances result in an unmet need for legal services. If, after taking advice, the person was dissatisfied with the outcome, his need for legal services may not have been fully met; and we therefore sought information on this point as well.

5.3 The problems which respondents identified as the most important or worrying they had experienced are shown in Table 5.1. The major categories of problems identified are consumer problems, accidents and injuries, and landlord/tenant disputes.

5.4 Respondents were then asked whom, if anyone, they had consulted when faced with their problem. Table 5.2 shows that more than one in five—the largest single group—sought advice from no one. Almost one in three sought advice from someone such as an employee of a shop or company, a local government official or a superior at work. More detailed analysis shows that in most such cases those consulted were directly connected with the problem. Fourteen per cent of respondents went to a solicitor in private practice, and three per cent to an advisory agency. Table 5.3 shows this in more detail according to the nature of the problem.

5.5 We then asked respondents whether they were satisfied with the way their problem was finally disposed of. Table 5.4 shows that dissatisfaction was greatest among those who had consulted friends and relatives where 2 out of 3 were dissatisfied, closely followed by those who went to a superior at work (generally about a work-related matter). Those who consulted legal or para-legal advisers were more often satisfied than those who relied entirely on themselves.

TABLE 5.1: Most important problems discussed with respondents*

	%
Involved in accident caused by other party	20
Injured at work	14
Trouble with services (such as repairs)	13
Trouble with complaint to a shop	11
Trouble with landlord over repairs	10
In trouble with police	8
Unfairly treated by employer	5
Felt cheated over a holiday	5
Problem over state benefit (such as social security allowance)	4
Difficulty recovering debt	3
Eviction or threatened eviction	2
Party to tribunal proceeding	2
Taken to court over debt	1
Problem in evicting tenant	1
Other	3
	100
	(N=853)

*Source: Appendix 4, Table 1.

TABLE 5.2: Advisers consulted by respondents*

	%
No-one	21
Employees of shops and companies	17
Solicitor in private practice	14
National/local government officials	11
Professional (e.g. doctor, bank manager)	7
Friends/relatives	7
Member organisations (e.g. trade union, motoring organisation etc.)	4
Superior at work	3
Para-legal/consumer advisory body (e.g. citizens advice bureau)	3
Member of parliament/councillor	1
Social worker	1
Other legal officer (e.g. employed solicitor, procurator fiscal)	1
Miscellaneous	10
Not stated	1
	100
	(N=853)

*Source: Appendix 4, Table 3.

TABLE 5.3: Use of own resources and use of legal resources by type of problem*

		Legal Resources	Own Resources	Other Resources	Total
Consumer	(%)	13	22	65	100(N=236)
Accident (excluding work)	(%)	21	24	55	100(N=172)
Injury at work	(%)	15	32	53	100(N=118)
Landlord/tenant	(%)	10	23	67	100(N=110)
Police	(%)	34	41	25	100(N=61)
Employment	(%)	14	47	40	100(N=43)
Debt	(%)	18	67	15	100(N=33)
Other	(%)	25	21	54	100(N=71)
All problems	(%)	17	28	54	100(N=844)

*Source: Appendix 4, Table 6.

TABLE 5.4: Satisfaction with outcome by adviser used*

		Satisfied	Not Satisfied	Total
No-one	(%)	47	53	100(N=182)
Employees of shops and companies	(%)	47	53	100(N=145)
Solicitor in private practice	(%)	53	47	100(N=117)
National/local government member or official	(%)	44	56	100(N=103)
Miscellaneous professional	(%)	70	30	100(N=69)
Informal contacts	(%)	32	68	100(N=56)
Other legal and para-legal advisers	(%)	57	43	100(N=30)
Member organisation	(%)	47	53	100(N=30)
Superior at work	(%)	38	62	100(N=29)
Other	(%)	69	31	100(N=87)
All	(%)	50	50	100(N=848)

*Source: Appendix 4, Table7.

5.6 A number of respondents said that they had thought of consulting a solicitor about their problem, but failed to do so. Most had concluded that such consultation was not necessary. About one in four, however, said that they had decided against consulting a solicitor because they thought such a course of action would have been too expensive. This is shown in Table 5.5.

TABLE 5.5: Reasons for not consulting a solicitor*

	%
Unnecessary	69
Too expensive	24
Others	7
	100 (N=58)

*Source: Appendix 4, Table 12.

5.7 The respondents who had not thought of consulting a solicitor were asked whether they now thought that it would have been helpful to do so. Eleven per cent said yes, 72 per cent no and 17 per cent were uncertain. Respondents' reasons for thinking a solicitor would not have helped are shown in Table 5.6. One in three thought it was unnecessary to see a solicitor, and almost half (44 per cent) thought that their problem was not important enough a matter to go to a lawyer, or 'not the sort of case for a lawyer'.

TABLE 5.6: Reasons for thinking solicitor would not have helped*

	%
Unnecessary	35
'Not the sort of case for lawyer'	23
Not important enough	21
Too expensive	7
Would not have affected outcome	6
Other	9
	100
	(N=460)

*Source: Appendix 4, Table 13.

5.8 There are comparable findings in the results of a survey which the Scottish Consumer Council submitted to us in evidence. Their respondents were asked what they would do in circumstances such as being excluded from rented accommodation because of arrears, being in debt to a shop, or being threatened with disconnection from gas or electricity services. A minority of respondents would have reacted aggressively and taken unilateral action—for example forcing entry to the rented accommodation, and awaiting the next move from the landlord. They would say that this was permissible because it was 'illegal' for the landlord to attempt to exclude them. The majority, however, reacted submissively: they were typified by one respondent who said '. . . you are in the wrong, it's you that are in arrears. A solicitor couldn't help you'. Similarly, when asked what they would do if they had bought a faulty electric kettle and the shop refused to replace it, respondents said that they would try to obtain satisfaction by reasoning with the shopkeeper, writing to the manager or contacting the manufacturer of the kettle. If these courses of action failed they would simply buy a new kettle. They saw this problem as 'too trivial' to involve a solicitor.

5.9 It would be wrong for us to conclude that all those who fail to take legal advice after an accident had an unmet need for legal services. On the other hand, we think it reasonable to assume that some respondents thereby failed to assert their legal rights of redress. When someone is in dispute about a faulty kettle he may well be right to say a solicitor's services are unnecessary or inappropriate. We have seen, however, that many respondents were not satisfied with the resolution of their problem. A person who deals with a faulty new kettle by buying a replacement has failed to assert his rights.

5.10 Our survey did not simply concentrate on how respondents had dealt with their most worrying problem, but asked them, if they felt they required legal assistance, whether there were any obstacles which might prevent them from going to see a solicitor. As Table 5.7 shows, two-thirds of them said that there was no such obstacle, and the reasons given by the others were to do with cost, their attitude to lawyers, and the accessibility of lawyers' offices. We examine these three obstacles in the following paragraphs.

TABLE 5.7: Potential obstacles to consulting a solicitor*

	% agreeing
Lawyers are likely to cost too much	26
People like me don't go to lawyers	6
Lawyers make me feel uncomfortable and ill-at-ease	4
Lawyers' offices aren't open at suitable times	3
Lawyers' offices are too far away to get to easily	2
Other considerations	1
No likely obstacle	64

Note: Total does not sum to 100% as more than one answer could be given by each respondent. N=1658 respondents.

*Source: Appendix 4, Table 48.

5.11 The obstacle most frequently mentioned by respondents was the likely cost of a solicitor's services. As the legal aid and the legal advice and assistance schemes exist to provide financial help to those who have only moderate means with which to pay for legal services, our respondents were asked what they knew about these schemes, and about the legal aid symbol (two figures seated at a table) which indicates an office where legal aid is available. Some 40 per cent of respondents did not know what legal aid was, over 90 per cent did not know what legal advice and assistance were, and about half did not recognise correctly the legal aid symbol.[1] Lack of knowledge was greatest among those in the lower socio-economic categories. Ironically, those who are most likely to be eligible for legal aid are least likely to know what legal aid is. This is shown in Table 5.8, and suggests that some of those who thought a lawyer's services would be too expensive did not appreciate the financial support to which they would be entitled in making use of such services.

TABLE 5.8: Knowledge of legal aid and legal aid symbol, by socio-economic status*

	Proportion (%) of respondents in each group having no or very inaccurate knowledge about:	
Socio-economic status	Legal Aid	Legal Aid Symbol
Higher professional/managerial	19	47
Lower professional/managerial	24	42
Other non-manual	31	40
Skilled manual	39	48
Semi- and unskilled manual	47	53
Other	55	64
All non-manual	28	41
All manual	43	50

*Source: Appendix 4, Table 66.

[1] See Appendix 4, Table 65.

5.12 Table 5.7 showed that some respondents felt ill-at-ease about approaching a lawyer. Our survey also attempted to assess the attitude of respondents to the legal profession. The results indicate that the most favourable attitude towards the profession is held by those in the higher socio-economic categories, such as professional and managerial workers, whereas semi-skilled and unskilled manual workers were most likely to have an unfavourable attitude.[1] The use made of solicitors follows the same pattern. Two out of every three higher professional and managerial workers had consulted a solicitor at least once in their lives, but only one in three of semi-skilled and unskilled manual workers had done so. This finding is in line with research carried out for the Law Society in 1972, as summarised in the following comment:

'You will not be surprised to know that our research identified class variations in knowledge of, and attitudes to, lawyers, as well as contact with lawyers. Lower social class groups tended to regard lawyers in *curative* terms, whereas higher social class groups saw them in *preventive* terms. Lower class people view the law and lawyers with suspicion and saw lawyers as people they might have to contact if they have problems that need resolving or are "in trouble"; higher-class persons on the other hand relate more easily to lawyers, accept the legal system and its working with approval, and use lawyers as helpers and advisers'.[2]

5.13 Attitudes to the profession are important whether or not an objective observer may think them justified. Our survey showed that people's actual experience of using a solicitor was unlikely to prejudice them against the profession. On the contrary, users' satisfaction with a solicitor's services was generally high, as Table 5.9 shows.

TABLE 5.9: Dimensions of satisfaction with solicitor*

	% in agreement
Solicitor easy to talk to	97 (N=417)
Solicitor kept client informed	90 (N=373)
Solicitor easy to get hold of	89 (N=369)
Fee as expected or lower than expected	84 (N=249)
Work completed as quickly as or more quickly than expected	81 (N=367)
Fee about right or too low for the work involved	74 (N=252)
Satisfied or very satisfied overall	83 (N=410)

*Source: Appendix 4, Table 31.

5.14 A number of respondents to our survey said that lawyers' offices were inaccessible or not open at suitable times. There are undoubtedly a number of communities where access to a solicitor is difficult. The Scottish Legal Action Group said to us in their written evidence:

'Even quite thriving small communities such as Mallaig . . . and Ullapool have no solicitors. For residents in these districts to consult a solicitor involves the time and expense of a full day's journey to Fort William . . . or Inverness with possible loss of earnings'.

[1] See Appendix 4, Table 50.
[2] C. M. Campbell: *Lawyers in their Social Setting:* W. Green & Son, 1976, pages 206–207.

A particular dimension of need in remote and rural areas is the desirability for opposing parties in contentious transactions to have independent legal advice. This means that communities with only a single legal firm, who can provide an adequate service in most cases in relation to wills, winding up estates, and taxation, are inadequately served in matters like conveyancing and divorce when conflict of interest between clients is implicit.

5.15 Almost 50 per cent of practising solicitors are to be found in Edinburgh and Glasgow, and in the major cities solicitors' offices are traditionally concentrated in the business areas.[1] In recent years some improvement in the distribution of city offices has been made, with a few firms opening branch offices in under-provided areas (some of them opening at weekends). We understand that there is sometimes difficulty in negotiating leases for suitable property in such areas, or in obtaining appropriate planning permission from the district council for the use of shop premises as legal offices, or in arranging to lease a local authority house as an office.

Conclusions

5.16 Our evidence suggests that the unmet need for legal services in Scotland is not the result of people's dissatisfaction with the services they have obtained from lawyers. Those of our respondents who had consulted a solicitor were generally satisfied with the help they received. The problem is rather a considerable unwillingness on the part of the public to consult a solicitor in the first place—61 per cent of our respondents had never done so, although the proportion is smaller among younger people.[2] It appears in particular that many people fail to take *independent* advice when faced with a comparatively worrying problem such as an accident or injury, a consumer complaint or a landlord/tenant dispute. Most judged these problems not appropriate for a solicitor. There are undoubtedly cases where the sum at issue is so small that it would be out of all proportion to incur the expense of employing a solicitor to recover it. If, as a result, people fail to assert their rights, this suggests that an alternative form of legal service may be needed. The small numbers taking legal advice as shown in Table 5.3, coupled with the level of dissatisfaction at the outcome shown in Table 5.4, suggest strongly to us that significant numbers of people make decisions as to the value of legal advice on the basis of inadequate information. In paragraph 2.10 we referred to these decisions in terms of the citizen's capacity to identify and, where appropriate, to choose a legal solution to a problem. This is the first element in a person's need for legal services, and the evidence is that important minorities find this need unfulfilled.

5.17 The second element in the need for legal services is the citizen's ability to pursue a legal solution to an identified problem. We have seen from Table 5.7 that while many people say they would have no difficulty about going to see a lawyer if they thought they had a legal problem, perhaps one in three would be reluctant or would fail to do so, whether because the adviser is remote (or seen as remote) or because of the cost (or what is thought to be the cost).

5.18 From this analysis we can identify three major causes of unmet need for legal services. The first barrier the citizen has to overcome is one of information—he must know that he has a legal right. A further aspect of this barrier is that the

[1] See Table 19.5.
[2] See Appendix 4, Tables 14 and 16.

citizen must know what sources of help are available to him, what order of costs might be involved, what financial assistance could be available, and in particular whether he is eligible for legal aid. In Chapter 6 we consider how public knowledge about the law and legal services might be improved.

5.19 A second barrier between the citizen and legal services is ease of access. Not only must legal advisers be available in a convenient place at a convenient time, they must be seen as approachable. In Chapter 7 we consider how to improve the initial accessibility and approachability of legal services.

5.20 A third barrier to use of legal services is cost. We have already seen that some people are badly informed about cost, and we deal with that as an information problem in Chapter 6. Fear of cost is also a factor in whether an adviser is seen as approachable, and we bear in mind the importance of free initial advice in considering access in Chapter 7. This alone will not remove the financial barrier. Extended legal advice and assistance can be expensive, and so can litigation where there is added uncertainty about the likely cost. In Chapter 8, therefore, we consider how to help the citizen to pay for legal services.

5.21 Our review of the evidence convinces us that these barriers are substantial ones for various groups. Information about legal aid is poorest among those in the lower socio-economic groups who are most likely to be eligible, and with the smallest contributions, if any. (Ignorance of the legal advice and assistance scheme on the other hand is almost universal.) In the same way manual workers are less well-disposed towards lawyers than non-manual ones. The financial barrier, however, is most real for those who are not eligible for legal aid. By contrast there is little evidence that experience of using a solicitor creates any barrier to future use. On the contrary, respondents who had been clients expressed a high degree of satisfaction with the service received.

The delivery of legal services

5.22 In addition to problems of access to legal services there can be problems in the delivery of the service. Where a required service is expensive we cannot rest content with ensuring that all citizens are given financial assistance to pay for it. We must go on to consider what can be done to reduce the cost of providing the service. Indeed the public interest in keeping down costs is all the greater to the extent that public funds are deployed in paying for the service. However, we have been concerned not simply with cost in a narrow sense. In evaluating the efficiency of services we have also paid close attention to quality. The efficient delivery of services of adequate quality is as important in legal services as anywhere else.

5.23 Accordingly, throughout Parts IV to VI of our Report, we shall be concerned less with ensuring that the need for legal services is met (which is the focus of Part III) than with ensuring that legal services are delivered efficiently. It is, indeed, with the efficient meeting of the need for legal services that the whole of our Report is concerned.

PART III

IMPROVING ACCESS TO LEGAL SERVICES

CHAPTER 6

INFORMING THE PUBLIC

6.1 All the evidence available to us suggests that a major obstacle to the efficient use of legal services is the relatively poor state of public information about the law and legal services in this country. There is widespread ignorance about the individual's rights and duties under the law and about the range of legal services available, and of the ways in which these services can help the individual to find solutions to his problems. There is also much misconception and ignorance about the implications of seeking a legal solution to a problem through the use of the available legal services. This is not to say there are no deficiencies in the existing provision of legal services or that these deficiencies are not in some cases considerable; but no matter how good the provision of legal services, the level of public information and education about those services must be high in order that the best use of them is made.

Our aim

6.2 In looking at all the ways in which the public are informed about the law and legal services we have kept in mind that the principal object of public information should be to ensure that every citizen knows the overall framework of his legal rights and responsibilities; knows where to seek advice on the precise nature of those rights and responsibilities; and knows where to seek advice and assistance on how to assert and protect his rights.

LEGAL EDUCATION IN SCHOOLS

6.3 Given the lack of knowledge about even very basic matters concerning the law as it affects individuals in their daily lives, we have had to consider what role the schools could play. Providing some element of legal education in the school curriculum has obvious attractions, because we do not think that people are fully fitted for adult life if they lack basic knowledge about how the law affects them and about how to use legal services. Moreover, if legal education is introduced to school pupils at an appropriate stage of compulsory schooling, it means in the long term that all adults will have had at least some insight into the importance of law and legal services. No form of adult education can hope to have as wide a coverage. At school, education about the law and the legal system can be readily located within the more general context of social education, thus emphasising that the legal system and recourse to the law are part of the normal machinery of society. This would be helpful because our evidence shows that some people regard the law as something special and 'not for the ordinary man'. Indeed, it seems to us a proper task for the schools to ensure that school leavers have a basic knowledge of how laws affect them and how the legal system is a key part of society.

6.4 On the other hand, we recognise that there are many competing demands on the school curriculum. Most official bodies or pressure groups think that their subject is so fundamental to everyday life that no member of the community can afford to be without some knowledge of it and that, therefore, the schools should teach that subject to all pupils. We also recognise that specific information about the existing law might be of only limited use in later life; even if it is remembered, some of it might well soon be out of date, and this could be more dangerous than knowing nothing about the law on a particular matter. Finally, it is necessary to ask whether the resources to meet any obligations we might wish to put on the schools could realistically be made available: it would, of course, be pointless to suggest that all pupils should study a particular subject if there are no teachers to teach it and no learning materials with which to work.

6.5 Some elements of legal education appear at present in the modern studies curriculum in the secondary school. Modern studies is an examinable subject but it is an optional course which many pupils do not take. Even those who do may omit the legal parts by choosing other options. What is taught varies from school to school and depends on pupils' interests and the resources available to teachers, among other factors. At best, however, the examination syllabus at 'O' grade provides an opportunity to study such matters as the constitutional relationship between the judiciary, the executive and Parliament; the role of the legislature and of the courts; and relationships between central and local government. This seems to us to be an admirable syllabus for the study of these particular constitutional issues, but it does not provide for a practical appreciation of the role legal services might play in the solution of an individual's problems.

6.6 We think that pupils leaving school should have acquired an understanding of the distinction between civil and criminal law, the work of the courts and the role of civil law in regulating disputes in the community. We also think that they should have an understanding in broad and simple terms of a few of the absolutely basic concepts of the law. School pupils should also learn about the more important tribunals; and they should be taught about agencies to whom they can turn for help including, of course, the legal profession. The principles governing the availability of legal aid should also be taught. We do not suggest that these are minimum requirements of any course that might be devised, but we mention them here as indications of the essentially basic and practical nature of the course we have in mind. Detailed development of courses will, of course, be a matter for the appropriate professionals. We would not wish to preclude, for example, the integration of a study of the legal system with other forms of social education, or with studies of the historical development of social welfare provision. We do not intend a general exhortation to teachers to include some elements of a study of the law and legal services in their curricula. We believe that the study of the law, the legal system and legal services should be an identifiable part of the school curriculum and we **recommend** that all pupils should be taught for one period per week in the third year of their secondary school curriculum about the issues which we have outlined. What we have in mind, in terms of the Munn Report, is an S3 social education module on legal services and the law.[1]

6.7 As we have recognised, this recommendation necessarily has implications for educational resources. Teachers will be required who have a suitable know-

[1] *The Structure of the Curriculum in the Third and Fourth Years of the Scottish Secondary School* (The Munn Report): HMSO, 1977.

ledge of the legal system and legal services. This will mean either new teachers being employed or in-service training being made available to existing teachers to enable them to teach the subjects we envisage. Colleges of education will, therefore, need to adjust their programmes to take account of this development. Appropriate teaching materials will also be required. We have seen examples of some work at present in preparation on the Scottish legal system under the auspices of the Scottish Curriculum Development Service, in co-operation with the Law Society. While the scale of such work may need to be expanded, we believe that the facilities already exist to produce the necessary materials. In addition, this is an area which should appeal to those responsible for educational television and radio broadcasting. A development of such a sort would have the added bonus that it would undoubtedly attract an audience from among adults who are at home during the day. Indeed, educational television and radio broadcasts and published materials for use in schools may well all be of value in other forms of provision for legal education—for example, evening classes or community initiatives (see below, paragraphs 6.14 and 6.16 to 6.19).

6.8 Particularly at a time when, as we have said, many different groups are pressing for space in the school curriculum for their particular subject, we do not think it is entirely fair to leave the initiative for the developments we have in mind entirely with teachers and other educationists. The responsibility will primarily be theirs, but we see value in some central body with a legal interest maintaining some over-view of the provision made. We therefore **recommend** that our proposed Department of Legal Affairs (see Chapter 20) should be associated with the Scottish Education Department in ensuring that appropriate school courses are made available. We **recommend** also that the Departments, in conjunction with the Law Society, should consider what part solicitors might play in the provision of legal education in schools.

PUBLIC INFORMATION

6.9 The school courses which we have recommended should in time give all citizens a better picture than most now have of how the law affects them, how the legal system works and where to go for assistance. This is a minimum requirement for life in a society which is increasingly ruled by detailed and complicated legislation. However, we cannot rely on school education alone to provide such basic understanding. Most of the people who will be affected by our recommendations are already adult and some basic information must, therefore, be made available to the public at large by other means. In addition, there is always a need for specific up-to-date information about how the law affects people in particular circumstances which people can get hold of when they need it.

6.10 Information can be made available to the public in a variety of ways, though not all of these are necessarily appropriate for the expanded provision which we believe to be necessary. The principal forms of public information include printed literature—books, booklets and leaflets; institutional advertising such as that carried out by the Law Society; information provided by the mass media such as 'Your Problems Answered' pages in magazines; further education in the form of evening classes and college courses; community initiatives such as the involvement of guest speakers at meetings of clubs, guilds and youth groups, or at public meetings arranged by, say, a neighbourhood law centre; and information provided by central government. We consider these various sources and make recommendations for their development in the following paragraphs.

6.11 *Printed literature.* Short of reference to the original legislation, or to highly technical legal text books, there is little in the way of printed information available to the general public about Scots law and its effect on individuals and their rights. The Law Society and the Scottish Association of Citizens Advice Bureaux, for example, publish some leaflets on particular aspects of the law at present, but the general level of provision is poor. Sometimes the only information circulating in Scotland on a legal matter refers exclusively to the law of England and, far from assisting individuals to seek the correct kind of help in dealing with their problems, these misleading sources serve only to confuse. To meet the need for specifically Scottish information leaflets and booklets the Scottish Legal Action Group have recently established the Scottish Legal Education Trust, whose purpose is to prepare and publish leaflets and booklets giving details of Scots law on a variety of matters, particularly those affecting the least advantaged sections of the population, such as the law relating to welfare benefits, rented housing and employment.

6.12 *Institutional advertising.* Although individual solicitors are not permitted to advertise (a question which we consider in paragraphs 6.20 to 6.36 below) the Law Societies both in England and Wales and in Scotland have mounted extensive institutional campaigns intended to educate the public as to the availability of services and the benefits and costs of using a solicitor. The advertising campaigns have covered such matters as house purchase, running a business, claims, disputes, accidents and making a will. Such advertising, though valuable as far as it goes in explaining how a solicitor can be of help, can never be sufficient to maintain an adequate state of public knowledge about legal services. In particular, those not experiencing the problem covered in an advertisement are likely to ignore it, and will generally not be able to refer to it in time of need.

6.13 *Editorial material.* Under this head we include articles and 'Your Problems Answered' pages in journals and magazines, and broadcast programmes such as 'What's Your Problem?' There seems to be an extensive market at present for 'advice journalism', and also for features which include both advice and investigative journalism. We see this as a reflection of a public need for information and advice. We think that such material is valuable where it serves a real interest in drawing attention to particular rights or duties, rather than merely providing entertainment at the expense of, say, some hapless trader. Indeed, we think there is scope for presenters and editors to draw general conclusions from individual case-study material and to exploit specifically educational opportunities. In United Kingdom presentations it is, of course, vitally important that attention is drawn to any differences between Scottish law and practice and that of the rest of the United Kingdom. Apart from 'advice journalism', material of a directly informative kind is less common. We have, however, noted that the Law Society and the BBC together produced a series of programmes on rights and responsibilities for Scottish radio in 1977. More recently, a television programme introduced viewers to the inside of a sheriff court and to its normal procedure. There is educational value in programmes of this nature for both schools and adult audiences. We consider that the audience for such programmes is probably growing and the broadcasting authorities may find that material produced for schools programmes whets a larger appetite.

6.14 *Further education.* Many local authorities include courses dealing with aspects of the law and legal services in their adult education programmes. These courses may be related to particular needs such as those of the motorist or householder, or take the form of more general and necessarily superficial courses on such themes as 'law and the citizen'. While we support the idea of such courses, we think that they probably have only a limited value in introducing information about rights and responsibilities, since many people who take the trouble to enrol for courses are likely to be already well informed about their needs for advice and where to go for it.

6.15 *Government information.* Several bodies suggested to us in evidence that the government should have the principal responsibility for providing the information and education which the public require as to their general legal rights and duties. We agree that government departments have a responsibility for publicising and explaining new legislation as it is introduced, but we doubt whether they are the best agency for disseminating general information. The government view of the effect of particular statutory provisions is not necessarily right: it is the courts that give authoritative interpretations of statute. For this reason, the government is understandably reluctant to give what many people would assume to be an authoritative description of their rights despite any disclaimers to the contrary. Therefore, we do not see central government departments as the right people to provide a comprehensive information service. Where government has a real responsibility is for advising the public of the factual implications of new amendments to legislation affecting public rights. In this regard we are critical of the level of provision already made by governments to advertise existing statutory provisions in the legal services field. We consider the amount spent by central government on publicity for the legal aid schemes in Scotland, for example, to be wholly inadequate. There has been a startling decline in the amount spent on publicity for legal aid, as the following figures, given to us by the Scottish Office, show:

1973–74	£138,000
1974–75	117,000
1975–76	69,000
1976–77	42,000
1977–78	14,000
1978–79	15,000
1979–80 (estimated)	600

The 1977–78 figure of £14,000 compares with the £40,000 which the Law Society proposed to spend on institutional advertising in the same period. When governments seek to reduce public expenditure, economies in publicity seem to them an attractive target; but it seems to us that the considerable expense of passing legislation is largely wasted unless adequate efforts are made to ensure that effective use is made of the result. We believe that there should be a more extensive use of television and radio broadcasts by government to explain the impact of new legislation as it is brought into effect. We **recommend** that it should be the responsibility of government to ensure that important changes in the law are widely advertised in the press and by radio and television as they are implemented. To ensure that adequate thought is given to this issue, we also **recommend** that the financial and explanatory memorandum introducing each government Bill should include a statement of the amount proposed to be spent on initial publicity for the measures the Bill contains.

Community Initiatives

6.16 At present, local Citizens Advice Bureaux, advice centres, legal clinics and consumer protection departments undertake very little in the way of wider education. We consider, however, that the community base is the best foundation for effective public education. Centralising the information services, say on the Scottish Information Office of the Scottish Office, would put the service at too great a remove from its clients. Those providing the information need to have sufficient knowledge of the information requirements of those to whom they are providing publications and other services. Local bodies are best placed to judge the information and education needs of the local area, and best placed to make good use of the facilities available to meet those needs. Moreover, information requirements vary from place to place: the information needs of a rural area will obviously be different from those of an urban area.

6.17 Community education should be more than simply providing information in response to enquiries. We mentioned in paragraph 6.10 above the role of guest speakers addressing community groups; but at present this is very haphazard. We **recommend** that community education should be recognised as an important part of the work of Citizens Advice Bureaux and Law Centres. In making this recommendation, however, we are aware of one possible source of difficulty. In England and Wales where Law Centres have taken an active part in community education this has tended in some quarters to arouse a hostile political reaction. A centre which actively publicises tenants' rights, for example, does not endear itself to the local authority against whom the tenants may act. In principle, there is nothing wrong with this so long as the advice centre is not seen to be playing a leading part in a campaign; at such a point the distinction between education and political action becomes almost impossible to sustain. We deal with the role of Law Centres generally in the following Chapter.

6.18 While the actual provision of information for local communities has to be tailored to local needs, the job of producing leaflets and other material explaining rights which apply nationally is obviously something to be done centrally. In the following Chapter we will recommend that an executive Legal Services Commission should be responsible for funding advice services. It will be in a good position to assess the need for particular kinds of information, and to know what form any leaflet, say, should take to be of most use. We therefore **recommend** that the Legal Services Commission should carry initial responsibility for securing the adequate provision of public information on legal rights and legal services in Scotland. We think that the Commission could in practice best discharge its information duty by commissioning material from appropriate specialists. The Commission should also have power to mount national advertising. We saw this being done very effectively in Montreal in Canada where the Quebec Legal Services Commission paid for short radio and television advertisements on particular legal rights and services. Such advertising is relatively expensive, of course, and would have to come out of the total funds available to the Commission we have proposed. While we do not envisage extensive advertising in the national press or on television, the Commission should be able to undertake it when it judged the cost worthwhile.

6.19 Material produced nationally should, as we have said, be made available locally. It is wasteful, and ineffective, to give people information they do not need at the time. That is why we lay so much emphasis on getting people to know where to go for help. Advice services stock leaflets. People often do better to see an adviser first and then get the proper leaflet, rather than waste time and effort by taking the wrong leaflet and failing to understand that it does not deal with their particular problems.

ADVERTISING BY SOLICITORS

6.20 It is important not only to educate people about the scope of their rights and duties and the general availability of legal services, but also to help them to find an appropriate adviser when they need one. There are a number of initiatives which the Law Society have taken to help clients get in touch with a solicitor who will be able to help them with their problem. For example, the Law Society have introduced a directory of general legal services which lists practitioners and areas of the law in which they are prepared to accept instructions. Legal firms themselves decide whether or not to have an entry in the directory. They also compile their own entries which are not approved or vetted in any way by the Law Society. This is made clear in the directory which is widely distributed by the Society to libraries, Citizens Advice Bureaux, sheriff courts, the police, consumer protection bodies, local authorities and others. The Law Society also issue, to agencies such as Citizens Advice Bureaux, legal aid referral lists which give details of solicitors' firms prepared to take legally aided cases. The lists show the areas of the law in which each firm claims experience, although the Law Society do not offer any guidance as to what depth of experience these entries imply. In addition the Law Society if approached directly will put a client in touch with a suitable practitioner in his local area.

6.21 Perhaps the most obvious way of telling potential clients where a suitable service was available would be for solicitors to advertise. This is the practice in most markets for services, but the Law Society, in common with similar bodies in many parts of the world, have long regarded advertising by solicitors as unethical and a form of professional misconduct. There are very limited exemptions from this rule, but they did not even meet the case of one solicitor, in a town serving a large rural area, who wrote to us. He had wanted to start opening his office on Saturday mornings, for the convenience of clients who in the normal course came to town only on Saturdays. The Law Society, however, had not allowed him to advertise this initiative.

6.22 The restrictions on advertising by solicitors were the subject of a report by the Monopolies and Mergers Commission published shortly before we began our work.[1] That report rehearses the reasons for the Law Society's opposition to advertising by solicitors. The principal objections are that advertising would undermine the trust on which the solicitor-client relationship is based, by suggesting that the relationship was one from which the solicitor expected to gain; and that solicitors' wider duty to society, going beyond their relationship with their clients, precluded the advertising of their services. The Monopolies

[1] The Monopolies and Mergers Commission: *Services of solicitors in Scotland; A report on the supply of services of solicitors in Scotland in relation to restrictions on advertising:* HMSO, 1976.

and Mergers Commission found these grounds to be overstated. We agree. In particular, our research shows that the public, so far from believing that solicitors do not profit from their practice, are to a degree deterred from consulting solicitors for fear of what it might cost.

6.23 Since the Monopolies and Mergers Commission report was published the Law Society have relaxed some restrictions on advertising, so that press advertisement is now allowed when a new firm is set up, or a branch office opened, or when a firm changes its address. Some limited advertising by firms in 'under-lawyered' areas has also become allowable. These changes, though welcome, are marginal ones.

Trust in the solicitor-client relationship

6.24 In evidence to us the Law Society argued, not so much that there should be no suggestion that the solicitor stood to gain from his relationship with his client, but rather that advertising would increase the risk that some solicitors might have too much regard to their own interest in the relationship. We think that this argument undervalues the sense of responsibility of the profession. The Law Society also suggested that the public would suspect the motives of those who advertised. If this argument is sound, then it seems to us better to leave the decision whether to advertise with the individual firm rather than to prevent firms from judging for themselves the value of advertising. We ourselves do not think it likely that the public would shun firms who advertised, provided certain restrictions on what could be advertised were retained.

The directory instead of advertising?

6.25 The Law Society put it to us that advertising by firms would be haphazard, ineffective and uncontrolled. They agreed that to rely on people getting the right solicitor for their purpose solely by personal recommendation was inadequate; and they contended that the directory of legal services was the right answer since it provided comprehensive information and showed all firms on the same basis.

6.26 The Law Society accept that there is a risk that potential clients could be misled into believing that the directory entries have been vetted by the Law Society, despite the printed disclaimer, or into believing that the entries represent expertise in specialisms. They think, nevertheless, that the benefits of publishing the directory outweigh the disadvantages of this acknowledged risk.

6.27 When it comes to advertising by individual firms, however, the Law Society consider that the balance of advantage tips the other way and that the risk of misleading the public, for example by some firms placing larger advertisements in bolder type, becomes unacceptable. We do not agree. We cannot see that solicitors should not be allowed at the very least to advertise at their own hand what is, to all intents and purposes, advertised on their behalf by the Law Society in the directory. We do not think that the public are so naive as to infer that the biggest or boldest advertisement is placed by the best firm.

6.28 Notwithstanding the existence of the directory, it could be argued that if we are to allow solicitors to advertise a service in, say, planning law, we ought to minimise the risk of misleading the public by ensuring that such a solicitor is competent to offer that service. We have considered whether it would be practical to achieve this by some system of certification of specialism, but we have felt obliged to reject this (Chapter 16). We think we must rely on steps taken by the Law Society to maintain and improve the general standard of competence, a question on which we make specific recommendations (Chapters 16 and 18). An effective system of monitoring competence generally should have the incidental effect, in most cases at least, of deterring a solicitor from advertising a willingness to undertake types of work which he is not competent to perform adequately. A further argument presented against advertising is that it would tend to be used most by the 'black sheep' of the profession. We do not find this argument convincing. If there are 'black sheep', the solution should lie in more effective methods being adopted by the Law Society to maintain professional standards, not in prohibiting all solicitors from giving reasonable information to the public as to the service they provide.

6.29 Accordingly, we support the advertising of the services offered by solicitors. Unless the Law Society are prepared to certify special competence in limited areas of practice, and we do not specifically recommend that they should, the services advertised should not be described as specialisms, or areas of expertise, or in any other term which implies superior quality. We should not object to the phrase 'preferred areas of practice' in advertisements, however, and indeed we think that the directory might usefully restrict each solicitor to, say, four or five preferred areas, in addition to 'a general service'. This would be better than the present practice of some solicitors who, to indicate that they offer a general service, state a willingness to accept work in each and every area of law.

Price advertising

6.30 Should solicitors be restricted to advertising only such information as their name, address, telephone, hours of business, and preferred areas of practice, or should they be allowed to advertise their fees? The nature of legal work makes fixed price advertising difficult, as every case is different. Nevertheless, it is not hard to envisage a firm taking the rough with the smooth and advertising the drafting of all wills for a fixed fee. Alternatively, even if the advertisement only quotes a fee recommended by the Law Society potential clients will have an indication of the order of costs involved. In Chapter 5 we have said that uncertainty as to cost is a major obstacle to many people using legal services. If solicitors were able not only to advertise the wide range of services they provided but also to give some idea of the order of costs, many people who have hesitated to use a solicitor in the past may feel encouraged to take their business to him.

6.31 The Law Society have told us that they fear that price competition would lead to firms cutting corners to provide a cheap service. We do not think that firms would be likely to take such risks should our proposals for encouraging competence, as suggested in Chapter 18, be implemented. In any case, although there is at present a rule requiring solicitors to quote only the Law Society's recommended fee to any potential new client making enquiries (that is, overt price competition is not allowed) we are aware that this rule is not always observed; indeed its existence is not universally known in the profession.

6.32 In Chapter 19 we recommend that while maximum fees for certain items of work should be prescribed, solicitors should be at liberty to charge less, and should not be inhibited from giving prospective clients an estimate for a piece of work. It is consistent with this approach that solicitors should be able to advertise their prices though, as we have said, they will only be able to advertise a fixed price if they can specify what that fee is to include. We want to encourage firms to offer a competent professional service at competitive prices. The Monopolies and Mergers Commission took the view that the restrictions on advertising had an adverse effect on competitiveness and efficiency, on the introduction of innovatory methods and services and on the setting up of new practices. We are convinced of the need for greater use of aids to efficiency, and we consider that to permit advertising, including price advertising, would be a useful way to further that end.

6.33 There is another reason why we want price advertising. Solicitors should be able to advertise free or cheap diagnostic interviews, to reassure prospective clients that if they wish to go no further than one interview it will cost them nothing, or no more than £5, for example. It would be quite wrong to limit price advertising to this scheme, however, since firms could readily offer a free initial interview but charge relatively high fees for subsequent work.

6.34 When the Monopolies and Mergers Commission reported on this question they recommended that a solicitor should be permitted to use whenever he thinks fit, such methods of publicity as he thinks fit, subject to certain provisos which they phrased as follows:

'(1) No advertisement, circular or other form of publicity used by a solicitor should claim for his practice superiority in any respect over any or all other solicitors' practices.

(2) Such publicity should not contain any inaccuracies or misleading statements.

(3) While advertisements, circulars and other publicity or methods of soliciting may make clear the intention of the solicitor to seek custom they should not be of a character that could reasonably be regarded as likely to bring the profession into disrepute.'

The Monopolies and Mergers Commission proposed that these principles should form the basis of practice rules regulating advertising by solicitors which would be drawn up by the Law Society following consultation between themselves and the Director General of Fair Trading.[1]

6.35 While reasonably informative and sober advertising is no more than a sensible way for solicitors to communicate with potential clients to their mutual advantage, soliciting business in an improper manner should be rigorously excluded. Such practices would in our view include the citing in advertisements of previous successful cases, say in the field of personal damages; and attempting to procure business for personal accident claims in the casualty wards of hospitals ('ambulance chasing').

6.36 We therefore **recommend** that, as proposed by the Monopolies and Mergers Commission, the Law Society should replace their present rules on advertising with practice rules drawn up after consultation with the Office of Fair Trading, breach of which should be treated as professional misconduct.

[1] Monopolies and Mergers Commission: *Services of Solicitors in Scotland*, pages 33 and 34.

These practice rules should embody the principles set out by the Monopolies and Mergers Commission and reproduced in paragraph 6.34 above.

Quality and style of legislation

6.37 One further important matter in relation to keeping the public informed as to the law as cheaply and effectively as possible is the quality and style of our primary and secondary legislation. The legal rights and duties of the individual have been vastly increased and elaborated in recent times. Unfortunately, like so much of our legislation, the statutes conferring rights and duties on the individual are more often than not expressed in terms of such great complexity and obscurity that the average layman cannot be expected to understand them. The Consumer Credit Act 1974 is a case in point. Indeed, even the trained lawyer cannot grasp such legislation without hours of work and consequent expense to someone. This is a United Kingdom problem though it is particularly acute for Scotland, since so much legislation for Scotland is in Miscellaneous Provisions Acts, or in application sections in Acts primarily designed for the English system, or by means of references to previous Acts. We are aware that this question has been the subject of concern and study for years. However, we see little sign of substantial improvement; and while we consider that it would be beyond our terms of reference to make specific proposals in this matter, we cannot believe that improvement is impossible. To make the legislation affecting Scotland simpler and more intelligible is a matter of prime importance.

RECOMMENDATIONS

			Paragraph
Legal education in schools	R6.1	All pupils should be taught for one period per week in the third year of their secondary school curriculum about the law, the legal system and legal services.	6.6
	R6.2	The Department of Legal Affairs (see R20.1) should be associated with the Scottish Education Department in ensuring that appropriate school courses are made available.	6.8
	R6.3	The Department of Legal Affairs and the Scottish Education Department, in conjunction with the Law Society, should consider what part solicitors might play in the provision of legal education in schools.	6.8
Public information	R6.4	It should be the responsibility of government to ensure that important changes in the law are widely advertised in the press and by radio and television as they are implemented.	6.15
	R6.5	The financial and explanatory memorandum introducing each government Bill should include a statement of the amount proposed to be spent on initial publicity for the measures the Bill contains.	6.15
	R6.6	Community education should be recognised as an important part of the work of Citizens Advice Bureaux and Law Centres.	6.17
	R6.7	The Legal Services Commission (see R20.3) should carry initial responsibility for securing the adequate provision of public information on legal rights and legal services in Scotland.	6.18

			Paragraph
Advertising by solicitors	R6.8	As proposed by the Monopolies and Mergers Commission, the Law Society should replace their present rules on advertising with practice rules drawn up after consultation with the Office of Fair Trading, breach of which should be treated as professional misconduct. These practice rules should embody the principles set out by the Monopolies and Mergers Commission and reproduced in paragraph 6.34.	6.36

CHAPTER 7

ACCESSIBILITY OF ADVICE

7.1 In this Chapter we are concerned with the channels for improved access to legal services. We discussed in the previous Chapter some methods by which the public might be better informed about their legal rights and responsibilities. We now turn to how the client makes contact with the appropriate service.

7.2 As has been observed often enough, it is pointless to say that all men are equal before the law if some cannot afford to use the law to protect their rights. In the same way, we believe that there is little merit in Parliament conferring rights and imposing duties on citizens (for example, by social welfare legislation) unless at the same time it provides an effective means of informing people of those rights and responsibilities. Indeed, this obligation has already been acknowledged through the introduction of legal aid, and in particular the legal advice and assistance scheme which, as explained in Chapter 8, allows a solicitor to provide advice and assistance at public expense subject to a simple means test applied by the solicitor. Central government also gives financial support to Citizens Advice Bureaux and some other advice services, presumably for the same reason. Nevertheless, in our view the obligation on the government is not being adequately discharged.

7.3 We believe that there is an important place for subsidised legal advice and assistance and we welcome the more generous conditions of eligibility introduced in April 1979. We do not consider, however, that this scheme can or should be the only vehicle for securing the substantially improved access to legal services that is necessary. In defining the need for legal services, we identified two elements: a need for initial advice to allow a citizen to identify and, if he judges it appropriate, to choose a legal solution to his problem; and a need for further advice and assistance to pursue a chosen legal solution (see Chapter 2). In Chapter 4 we have seen that an important part of the demand for legal services can be effectively and economically met by agencies providing general advice, initially through laymen, but with suitable back-up facilities (including referral to legal firms) to provide necessary further advice and assistance. These agencies can be particularly effective in helping clients to define the nature of their problems, which will often be complex and without a clearly identifiable 'legal' component; in providing a service in a convenient and familiar location; in assisting those with misgivings about the costs of legal help; and in reassuring clients who may not know their legal rights, or may have inhibitions about consulting solicitors.

7.4 It would, in our view, be an inefficient use of relatively scarce resources for solicitors to provide the kind of initial advice we have described. In 1978–79 Scottish solicitors were paid some £895,000 for over 34,000 cases under the legal advice and assistance scheme, at an average cost per case of £26.[1] In the

[1] Source: Scottish Home and Health Department and the Legal Aid Central Committee: this information is to be included in the *29th Annual Report on the Scottish Legal Aid Scheme, 1978–1979* which had not been published by the time we went to print.

same year the Citizens Advice Bureaux in Scotland dealt with some 236,000 cases at a cost of approximately £315,000; and the average cost per Bureau enquiry was therefore in the region of £1.50.[1] These figures, we hasten to add, are not directly comparable. It is likely, for example, that solicitors deal mainly with the more complex, time-consuming cases—and this is undoubtedly true where cases are taken on by a solicitor through referral from a Citizens Advice Bureau. Many Bureau enquiries, on the other hand, are simple requests for information and involve no action on behalf of the client. Nevertheless, it is clear that the Citizens Advice Bureaux provide at low cost a very useful service to a great many people. Further development of that kind of information and advice service seems to us the most cost-effective way to improve the accessibility of advice. The legal profession has, of course, a vital role to play in supporting the advice centres with specialist knowledge; but specialist service is an expensive commodity and it is wasteful to use a solicitor's skill to carry out tasks which a trained layman can perform effectively.

GENERALIST ADVICE SERVICES

7.5 We **recommend** that improved access to legal services should be promoted by the development of generalist advice centres which can in appropriate cases provide the first access point to the machinery of legal services.

7.6 We stress, however, that we do not see an improved generalist advice service as in any way eroding the need for a legal advice and assistance scheme. Ultimately in any serious legal problem there is no substitute for professional advice. In some areas the provision of services by private practitioners may well be the most efficient way of meeting need: for example, some rural or remote areas may provide sufficient work to support a single office of a legal firm, but not enough to warrant an advice centre. Moreover, many people correctly identify their problem as requiring a solicitor's services and approach a solicitor directly. In our survey of legal needs 14 per cent of respondents went directly to a solicitor in private practice with their problem.[2] The services of advice centres will be complementary to the services provided by solicitors, and experience shows that they would be likely to lead to more rather than less use of legal services.

Advice centres

7.7 The advice centres which we envisage will be based, at least initially, on existing forms of advice agency and will, therefore, develop from a variety of models. This is not a bad thing. Citizens Advice Bureaux are the most widespread and organised system of non-professional advice centres, but flexibility and variety of provision to meet differing local needs are important features of the developments we wish to see. However, there are certain basic features which we can stipulate. Firstly, the greatest need is for centres which are generalist in nature. Problems do not always fall neatly into specific categories; if they did, we could recommend a greater number of specialist advice centres. Even then, access would be a problem. Specialist agencies would of necessity be much thinner on the ground, and the smaller use made of them would make

[1] Source: *Scottish Association of Citizens Advice Bureaux Annual Report 1978/79*, and figures supplied to us by the Association.

[2] See Appendix 4, Table 3.

the provision much harder to justify. (We discuss in paragraph 7.9 how specialist advice should be made available as necessary through generalist centres.) The advisers too should normally be generalists, able to answer simple queries over a range of topics. We believe it makes for better use of resources for the client to speak first to a lay adviser before consulting, if it proves necessary, a solicitor or other specialist adviser. The client can then be helped to clarify his problem and identify its salient features, without having the implicit judgement that he has 'a legal problem' made for him by virtue of the specialist knowledge of the adviser.

Trained volunteers

7.8 A second feature of the provision we envisage is that the generalist adviser should normally be a volunteer, but not an amateur in any pejorative sense. In their development plan, the Scottish Association of Citizens Advice Bureaux argue the case for the role of the volunteer in terms which we fully endorse:

> '. . . part-time volunteers can make positive contributions to the Service which paid workers cannot make or are less likely to be able to make. The voluntary workers are a major source of the independence of Citizen Advice Bureaux because their contribution and voluntary effort increases the independence of the Bureaux. They can bring a freshness, an informality and a variety of background and experience to the Bureaux which full-time advice workers cannot match. Therefore, it should be a major objective of each Bureau to actively recruit the widest variety of members of the local community able to offer, with training, a quality service to the public. Many Bureaux have already made real progress in recruiting from new sources of voluntary help such as shift workers and mothers of young children. With the exception of the city centre Bureaux, experience has shown that Bureaux obtain most of their usage on the basis of their local reputation and that this reputation is greatly enhanced where the Bureaux workers constitute a cross-section of the local community.'

Any adviser must be adequately trained, of course, and we have been impressed by the readiness of volunteers with the Citizens Advice Bureaux and other agencies to take appropriate training. We deal with the training of lay advisers in Chapter 17.

Specialist support

7.9 The third feature of the centres we envisage is the provision of suitable support. Volunteers need a stiffening of paid organisers if they are to operate most effectively. In addition to efficient administrative services, however, they need access to a range of specialist advisers. This must include solicitors, but will also extend to contact with planning advisers, consumer experts, surveyors etc.. The various methods of providing professional legal advice through a generalist agency include:

(a) *volunteer support.* It may be possible for the centre to call on the services of solicitors who are willing to give time to the centre without charge; sometimes they may hold regular clinics at the centre, sometimes be at the end of the telephone. For the most part, however, such volunteer solicitors are not allowed by the Law Society to take cases from the centre back to their own offices;

(b) *rota schemes.* In some Citizens Advice Bureaux, local solicitors provide legal clinics on a rota basis, referring difficult or lengthy cases back to their private practice (under the legal advice and assistance scheme where appropriate). Such arrangements require the prior approval of the Law Society;

(c) *referral.* In some centres it may be appropriate simply to refer clients to a solicitor in private practice. All Citizens Advice Bureaux make some use of this method, using the Law Society referral list and their own knowledge of local solicitors;

(d) *salaried solicitors.* A centre might employ its own solicitor to advise the staff on questions they refer to him or occasionally to give initial advice direct to a client. Such an appointment might be full-time or part-time; a full-time appointment might be made to serve a number of centres.

7.10 These various options are not exclusive. Many of them can be used in combination, and the form of provision made at individual centres should vary in response to local needs and to regular assessments of the efficiency with which the chosen pattern of provision meets those needs. We believe that solicitors involved in the work of generalist advice centres should have an important part to play in the training of lay advisers. With particular reference to clients who are to appear before tribunals, for example, these solicitors should train lay representatives to appear on behalf of citizens at appropriate tribunals. They should also give advice to individuals on how to present their own case to a tribunal. Salaried solicitors should be entitled to represent citizens at tribunals, though we would expect them to do so only in exceptional instances, such as in a test case. Only rarely would we expect such solicitors to provide legal representation in a court.

Lay representation at tribunals

7.11 We recommend in Chapter 8 an extension of legal aid to enable claimants to be represented before tribunals by a solicitor—but only in limited circumstances. We believe that the best way to meet the needs of claimants before many tribunals is to encourage the development of lay representation at tribunals. Although a number of organisations such as Citizens Advice Bureaux, trade unions and claimants rights groups do excellent work in representing tribunal claimants, there is considerable variation in the help and advice available to claimants appearing before tribunals. The availability of representation also varies with the subject matter of the particular tribunal. Most claimants making an application to a tribunal both lodge the application and appear before the tribunal without the benefit of any informed and independent advice. This is unsatisfactory.

7.12 We know that a number of projects to try to build up lay representation before tribunals have been encouraged in England. From our observations such projects have helped both to extend the amount of representation and advice available before tribunals, and also to improve the quality of such representation and advice. There have, however, only been a few projects of this nature. Some projects have concentrated on the training of lay representatives while others have built up teams who could provide representation before particular tribunals. Yet another scheme was aimed at providing a 'duty representative' at National Insurance Tribunals, who could advise all claimants and appear on their behalf if necessary. The source of funding of the different projects varies and is often only guaranteed for a short period. The future of the existing tribunal representation units, given the present funding basis, appears to be very insecure. While the inquisitorial approach of a tribunal may mean that the quality of presentation of a claimant's case is less critical to the outcome of his case, there is considerable scope for developing the system of lay representation before tribunals, and we are strongly of the opinion that finance should be made available for this purpose. While we recognise that there are a variety of kinds of tribunal, we **recommend** that encouragement should be given to developing the provision of lay advice and representation before those tribunals in which lay participation is appropriate, and that adequate training should be provided for lay representatives. (We deal more fully with the training of such advisers in Chapter 17.) We also **recommend** that the responsibility for developing the system of lay advice and representation before tribunals, and for ensuring that adequate financial resources are made available, should be given to the Legal Services Commission which later in this Chapter we recommend should have overall responsibility for the funding and oversight of publicly funded advice services.

LAW CENTRES

7.13 Although the priority, as we have said, is to provide generalist advice centres using trained volunteer advisers in the first instance, with access to specialist advice if necessary thereafter, we believe that Law Centres could perform a useful function in meeting the need for legal services in some areas in Scotland. Scottish experience with regard to Law Centres is extremely limited. We have described the only such Centre, a combined Citizens Advice Bureau/Law Centre at Castlemilk, established after six years of difficult negotiation between the Law Society, Citizens Advice Bureaux and Strathclyde Regional Council, the funding agency. Even this Law Centre has not had the same scope as busy centres we visited in England, some of which offered legal services for both groups and individuals, operating under a Law Society waiver more generous than the Castlemilk statement of intent. Still less does Castlemilk resemble the legal advice centres we saw abroad. In the United States of America and in Canada we visited publicly financed Law Centres providing striking innovations in legal resources for communities with inedaquate legal services. In Sweden we saw handsome, well equipped Law Centres in city centres providing direct subsidised competition with private firms and collecting fees and legal aid on much the same basis. In one way and another all these reflected a widely felt response to the new pressures of law upon groups and individuals in society.

7.14 In the long term the aim should be to provide Law Centres which can serve the whole community, wherever there is an unmet need. They should not be seen as a service for particular groups in society, or as a second-class form of legal service. We might, however, hesitate to follow the Swedish example so far as to site Law Centres in central commercial areas of towns, since we believe that the service should be provided where the clients are. In the more immediate future the first Law Centres should be established where the unmet need is greatest, and should offer a service in areas of law for which there is no adequate provision. Indeed, any excessive emphasis on requiring Law Centres to break even financially might undermine this aim by encouraging them to concentrate, like private firms, on the most profitable areas of law. Nevertheless, we do see value in Law Centres keeping accounts to show the cost of the services they provide, and in the long term they may be able to provide a general yardstick for the cost of these services.

7.15 We **recommend** that the Legal Services Commission (which we propose later) should study and experiment with the best use of Law Centres in Scotland. In doing so they should bear in mind the following principles:

(i) Law Centres should give a free service of initial legal advice to all comers, using para-legals to supplement expensive professional advisers. Where suitable, individuals should normally be referred for help with traditional problems to the solicitor of their choice in private practice;

(ii) Law Centres should concentrate their work on whatever areas of law are not adequately catered for locally by solicitors. There should be no prohibition on their doing other work, however, as long as they do not neglect the areas of need;

(iii) Law Centres should play an active educational role in the community, ensuring that groups and individuals know the legal resources available to them;

(iv) Law Centres should be managed by local committees representing the community on the widest possible non-partisan basis. Their independence of special interests should be written into their constitution, which will need to be approved and monitored by the Legal Services Commission from which, as we later recommend, their funds should come.

7.16 The special concern of Law Centres for groups may produce problems. Group interests express themselves very often in political terms and these can colour the public image of the Law Centres. Even more undesirably the political motivation of individual Law Centre advisers can colour the image of community organisations or campaigns. Law Centres should avoid becoming bases for political campaigning without losing their pioneering spirit. We believe that groups concerned with social issues must have access to legal advice, and that Law Centres could play an essential educational role in advising community organisations about the legal facilities that exist for maintaining and enforcing their legal rights and responsibilities. We would not wish to place any inhibition on groups consulting Law Centres for independent, impartial legal advice and, when necessary, representation. On the contrary, it seems to us wrong that Law Centres should refuse help to any particular types of clients (such as landlords) except insofar as a real conflict of interest between individuals using the Centre may arise. A Law Centre should help to conciliate and resolve local differences, not harden them on partisan lines.

7.17 Particularly in deprived areas there should be one open-door type of legal service to which anyone can resort for an initial opinion without the discouragement of means-testing. We see little advantage in saddling Law Centres with the administrative complexities of applying for legal aid for the initial enquiry. However, if an enquiry develops into further extended action it seems fair to the client, to the Law Centre and to the competitive private profession that payment should be made through legal aid or through fees. Clients with individual problems requiring legal advice could then either be dealt with on the spot or referred to private firms in the knowledge that the cost would be the same either way. In this way fair competition could be ensured. We **recommend** that a code of practice regarding the circumstances in which clients should be required to pay for Law Centre services should be drawn up by the Legal Services Commission after consultation with the Law Society and lay users.

ADMINISTRATION

Scale and cost of advice services

7.18 The Scottish Association of Citizens Advice Bureaux submitted to us details of their development plan for 1979–84; and the Scottish Legal Action Group in their evidence to us argued the case for a national network of 'citizens aid centres'. Both groups arrived at the same conclusion, that the equivalent of some 100 centres would be needed to provide a reasonably adequate advice service throughout Scotland. This very round figure need not mean the provision of 100 individual offices because, as the Scottish Association of Citizens Advice Bureaux pointed out in evidence to us, some areas might be better served by two or more part-time Bureaux in different locations rather than one full-time Bureau at a single location. Experiment will be needed to determine what kind of service works best in particular areas. The library service and various advice agencies use mobile caravans, for example. On the other hand mobile services have had mixed success. One of the few imaginative enterprises by a private firm providing a mobile legal service in Dundee failed recently for lack of support. Another possibility is the use of a free telephone enquiry service. An experiment in the provision of such a service based on the Inverness Citizens Advice Bureau is taking place in Wester Ross, under the aegis of the Scottish Consumer Council and the Highland Regional Council, to determine whether it will prove cost-effective and make good use of staff resources.

7.19 Accepting that the figure of 100 generalist advice centres is only the roughest of estimates, we find the arguments of the Scottish Legal Action Group and the Scottish Association of Citizens Advice Bureaux persuasive. How should these be developed and what would such provision cost?

7.20 Firstly we had to consider whether advice services could be expected to earn money on their own account. We were unanimous that the generalist advice centres should provide a service free of charge. This is crucial if the public are to be assured of a hearing without the suggestion of further commitment of the individual's resources. Consequent upon our recommendations that Law Centres should charge fees and operate the legal aid scheme where they act for a client beyond the initial interview, however, we considered whether salaried solicitors employed by Citizens Advice Bureaux should receive payment, for instance when representing a client. Since the essence of a Citizens Advice Bureau is that it should be free, we are unwilling to recommend that a Citizens Advice Bureau solicitor should act under legal aid or charge fees. Normally he should only give initial advice—or advise the lay advisers. Clients with cases that are likely to be extended should be referred to private practitioners or to Law Centres. However, there may be special cases which for some reason other lawyers are unable or unwilling to handle, and we **recommend** that in such cases Citizens Advice Bureaux management committees should be able to authorise their solicitor to proceed under legal aid, if applicable, or to charge fees.

7.21 The cost of such a nationwide service as we are recommending is obviously difficult to estimate as the precise form of local provision cannot be prescribed in advance. Very roughly, however, we estimate that £2·5 million might allow the provision of 100 centres each with one full-time (equivalent) solicitor (and/or other specialist) and one full-time (equivalent) para-legal generalist worker/centre manager, the rest of the staff being volunteers. Bearing in mind that there are already 48 Citizens Advice Bureaux in Scotland on which to base development, as well as other types of information centre, we believe that the Legal Services Commission could make a fair if not lavish start with funds of the order of £2·5 million. The running cost of Law Centres will be somewhat offset by our proposal that they should receive payment in appropriate cases from clients or the legal aid fund.

7.22 We think that there should be national co-ordination of the development of advice centres, starting with the provision already made by existing advice agencies. Not all such agencies will wish to seek public funding and there will always be an independent role for groups who specialise in particular areas, such as Shelter or Age Concern. (Even then individual advice centres run under the auspices of such a group might be the best basis for a generalist advice service in a particular area.) A central authority, the form of which we discuss below, should make grants to whatever advice centres it judges to be the most effective way of meeting need in a particular area. There are considerable advantages to be gained from a measure of national co-ordination: the information and training schemes provided for individual Citizens Advice Bureaux by the National and Scottish Associations are good examples of such benefits; and national planning will facilitate the application of common standards throughout Scotland. Moreover, it is also likely to be the best way to develop new ways of providing advice services following experiment and research. However, any central authority's judgements on local requirements would need to be based on information from local sources, which we discuss below.

Management and finance

7.23 In considering who ought to be responsible for funding advice services, we looked at four possibilities:

(a) A central government department;

(b) Local government (with exchequer funding through the rate support grant);

(c) The Law Society (with exchequer grant);

(d) A Legal Services Commision (with exchequer grant).

7.24 *Central government department*. In this model, the department would have responsibility for giving grants to a wide variety of bodies, on the basis of information received from local committees established for the purpose. Such an arrangement would provide direct public accountability for the funds spent on such a service. We think, however, that this would expose the service to direct political pressures in an undesirable way; and we want to avoid creating any possibility of this happening.

7.25 *Local government.* Although it would not meet our preference for a nationally co-ordinated provision, there would be certain advantages in giving the responsibility for local services to local authorities. The service would be responsive to local priorities and could have access quickly and easily to all departments of the authority. This could lead, through internal mechanisms, to better feedback and to a consequent improvement in local authority practices and policies. Those taking the decisions would be accountable directly to elected representatives. On the other hand, we have borne in mind that many problems brought to the advice centres would arise from the action of the local authority in one capacity or another; and it seems to us that there would be little public confidence in an advice service run by the same authority. Those clients who failed to get satisfaction would feel that the advice service had been taking the side of the authority, even if it had in fact acted vigorously on behalf of the client. In addition, we are aware of the vulnerability of these services to changes in the political complexion of councils: a number of Law Centres in England, and some Citizens Advice Bureaux, have had their financial support terminated or reduced by local authorities or have lost the use of their premises. We do not think it right that the citizen's access to advice should be put at risk in this way. Although we have said that it is desirable that the form of provision should vary from area to area in response to local needs, there is a danger, if local authorities have control of the service, that the quality of provision might vary widely in different areas. It would be difficult for local authorities to arrange for national planning of the service. We conclude that local authorities should not be responsible for advice services. Nevertheless, representatives of local authorities should participate in the management of advice services.

7.26 *The Law Society.* The Law Society recommended to us that Part II of the Legal Advice and Assistance Act 1972 should be implemented in order to allow the Law Society to employ salaried lawyers. These lawyers would be empowered to provide services for clients under the legal aid and the legal advice and assistance schemes and, in advice centres, give legal advice to the centre, give clients oral advice and refer clients to private practitioners. It would be for the Law Society to decide which of these tasks were performed. We would doubt whether the Law Society would wish to develop an adequate network of advice centres to meet the need as we see it; and even if centres were provided, we believe that there is a danger that the service would be too restrictive. We say this, firstly, because the specifically legal expertise of the Law Society would militate against the development of a generalist service; and, secondly, because it would be open to the Law Society to restrict the activities of its directly employed solicitors. It would in our view put the Law Society in an invidious position in so far as their responsibilities towards their members and their duties towards the public interest could come into conflict. Support for private practice or the implementation of Part II of the 1972 Act might, in certain circumstances and particular localities, be an appropriate solution. The experience of the Castlemilk Law Centre convinces us, however, that the Law Society would find it difficult to be responsible for the energetic development of the service we wish to see.

7.27 *Legal Services Commission.* In their evidence to us, a number of bodies recommended that some national authority should be appointed to plan and co-ordinate the provision of legal services, using information gathered at a local level by subordinate committees or by contact with local government and representatives of voluntary movements. We agree that a central authority could best exercise strategic responsibility for the funding, oversight and development of publicly-funded advice services (including the legal element) throughout Scotland. As we said in paragraph 7.24, this authority should not be a government department, and we call it a Legal Services Commission. Such a body will be well placed to conduct experiments with different forms of provision and to act on the results. A single body would be an important advance on the present involvement of different central and local government departments in the provision of advice services, which makes for a disjointed and uncoordinated approach. It should also be responsible for disseminating information to the public on the law and legal services, as recommended in the previous Chapter.

7.28 A central authority responsible for advice services could either run the services itself or simply provide funds to local agencies. The first option was advocated by the Scottish Legal Action Group. We believe that this option would inevitably create a substantial bureaucracy, and that it is based too heavily on specifically legal advice provided by legal specialists. We prefer a service relying primarily on the use of lay volunteers at the point of delivery; we think local control of the service essential; and we do not wish to create a large bureaucracy. We therefore **recommend** that the Legal Services Commission which we propose in Chapter 20 should, with funds allotted to it by central government, give grants to advice centres and Law Centres, conduct research, experiment with ways to provide services and set standards for advice services. We also **recommend** that the Legal Services Commission should not run advice services directly itself, but each centre should be run by an independent local management committee much as Citizens Advice Bureaux are at present.

Area advice services committees

7.29 If a Legal Services Commission is to carry out effectively the responsibilities we have proposed for it, it will need to have information and advice about local needs and resources. We **recommend**, accordingly, that area advice services committees should be established. It would be for these committees to identify local needs. Where further expenditure is needed, for example to set up a new advice centre or Law Centre, or to recruit extra salaried staff, the local committee would need to make a bid for funds to the Legal Services Commission, which would in its turn allocate funds to projects in accordance with its national priorities. Local initiatives requiring funds should be channelled first through the local area advice services committees, though organisations should be able to appeal direct to the central authority if their local application were rejected. National projects, such as Scottish Association of Citizens Advice Bureaux development plans, should go initially to the Legal Services Commission which should consult with the area committees about local implications. We hope the Commission would give established centres assurance of funding for, say, five years ahead in order to encourage forward planning.

7.30 Area advice services committees should be locally appointed or elected, to represent local information providers, users, local law faculties, local authorities and other elements varying with the needs and interests of different areas. It should be for the Legal Services Commission (in consultation with regional councils) to set up these committees, to formulate standard constitutions and to establish direct relations with them; but the Commission should not have powers of appointment.

Remote areas

7.31 The provision of adequate legal services is particularly difficult in remote areas. We were impressed by the concern about this shown in evidence to us from bodies such as the Highlands and Islands Development Board, the Crofters Commission and the Western Isles Islands Council. In such areas the proposed area advice services committees will enable measures to be devised which take full account of local circumstances. The kinds of experiments mentioned in paragraph 7.18 will be of particular value in remote areas, and these areas should also benefit especially from the recommendation we make in the next paragraph.

Assistance to legal firms

7.32 There is a further way in which the Legal Services Commission should be able to use its funds to secure improved access to legal services. In their evidence to us, the Law Society argued that rather than establish advice centres or Law Centres, the most effective way of meeting need would be to provide incentives to private practitioners to enter areas of unmet need, for example by local authorities making premises available at preferential rates. We **recommend** that the Commission should have power to provide financial assistance to firms of solicitors to establish offices in under-provided areas of the country. It should be open to the Commission to decide whether a grant, a loan or other form of incentive would be most appropriate in the particular circumstances. This recommendation follows from evidence we received about the difficulties of establishing lawyers' offices in peripheral areas, where the first year is almost always loss-making and where even the second year is likely only to break even. However, we do not recommend that the Commission should undertake to subsidise private firms on the basis of either a continuing deficit subsidy or a guaranteed 'target income'. In cases where a private firm would be unable to support itself in the medium term we suggest that other devices, such as the use of peripatetic lawyers, might provide better solutions. We also believe that the recommendations on advertising of prices and services which we made in Chapter 6 will help new practice units establish themselves more quickly than at present. We further **recommend** that district councils should be ready to give planning permission for solicitors' offices in shopping centres and residential areas, and to let residential property to solicitors for use as offices where this will make legal services more readily accessible.

7.33 We would note here our preference for encouraging existing firms to set up branch offices in new areas rather than creating new single-handed practices. A branch of a larger firm makes available greater resources to the community it serves than does a single-handed practice.

Conclusions

7.34 The role we have in mind for our proposed Legal Services Commission in relation to the national advice system is primarily strategic: it should become responsible for grants to Citizens Advice Bureaux and to such local advisory bodies as it thinks meet a real need. Although the priority for development is a generalist service, the Commission should be able to give grants to specialist groups if the local committee thinks that this is the most effective way, perhaps only in the short term, of meeting an established need. The Commission should, of course, draw up priorities and it will exert considerable influence on practice at the local level by the way in which it allocates funds. It should also fund research into better methods of delivery of legal services, and establish new forms of centre where it thinks them appropriate. It should ensure that the need is met for published guidance, advice or information, both for the public and for the advisers in the advice centres.

RECOMMENDATIONS

			Paragraph
Generalist advice services	R7.1	Improved access to legal services should be promoted by the development of generalist advice centres.	7.5
Lay help at tribunals	R7.2	Encouragement should be given to developing the provision of lay advice and representation before those tribunals in which lay participation is appropriate, and adequate training should be provided for lay representatives.	7.12
	R7.3	Responsibility for developing the system of lay advice and representation before tribunals, and for ensuring that adequate financial resources are made available, should be given to the Legal Services Commission.	7.12
Law Centres	R7.4	The Legal Services Commission should study and experiment with the best use of Law Centres in Scotland, bearing in mind the principles stated in paragraph 7.15.	7.15
	R7.5	A code of practice regarding the circumstances in which clients should be required to pay for Law Centre services should be drawn up by the Legal Services Commission after consultation with the Law Society and lay users.	7.17
Administration	R7.6	In special cases Citizens Advice Bureaux management committees should be able to authorise their solicitor to proceed under legal aid, if applicable, or to charge fees.	7.20
	R7.7	The Legal Services Commission should, with funds allotted to it by central government, give grants to advice centres and Law Centres, conduct research, experiment with ways to provide services and set standards for advice services.	7.28

			Paragrap
	R7.8	Each centre should be run by an independent local management committee.	7.28
	R7.9	Area advice services committees should be established.	7.29
Assistance to legal firms	R7.10	The Legal Services Commission should have power to provide financial assistance to firms of solicitors to establish offices in under-provided areas of the country.	7.32
	R7.11	District councils should be ready to give planning permission for solicitors' offices in shopping centres and residential areas, and to let residential property to solicitors for use as offices where this will make legal services more readily accessible.	7.32

CHAPTER 8

PAYING FOR LEGAL SERVICES

8.1 The generalist advice service which we have recommended will meet many people's need for legal services. However, there will still be many others who will require the specialist services of the legal profession and in this Chapter we consider some of the ways in which the cost of meeting this need can be met. We are not concerned here with the question of whether lawyers' fees for particular items of work are too high or too low, or with the arrangements whereby lawyers' fees are set and assessed. We deal with such questions in Chapter 19. Our concern here is with the sources of finance, both private and public, to pay for legal services. Legal aid is an arrangement under which private practitioners are paid from public funds. In fact, the generic term 'legal aid' covers three separate schemes: criminal legal aid, civil legal aid, and legal advice and assistance. The criminal legal aid scheme provides for payment of public funds to meet professional fees and outlays incurred in the defence of persons charged with crime; the civil legal aid scheme provides for such payments to meet all or part of the professional fees or outlays of persons involved in civil litigation; and the legal advice and assistance scheme provides for payment of all or part of the professional fees and outlays of persons getting legal advice on any question of Scots law and assistance by the solicitor in taking action to follow up that advice other than court action. We deal in this Chapter with these schemes and with a number of other ways of providing for legal services either privately or from public funds.

LEGAL AID BACKGROUND

History

8.2 Civil legal aid in more or less its present form was introduced in Scotland in 1950. Prior to that date, however, the Scottish legal profession had long accepted the representation of the poor without fee as a professional duty. An Act of 1424 made provision for the court to appoint an 'advocate' in civil cases for 'onie pure creature, for faulte of cunning, or expenses, that cannot, nor may not follow his cause'. In 1535, two advocates for the poor were appointed and received a stipend from the Treasury; but the system was probably rudimentary until the seventeenth century when there developed the practice of appointing members of the Society of Writers to the Signet as agents for the poor in the Court of Session. An Act of Sederunt of 10 August 1784, which probably for the first time formalised the procedure for admission to the poor's roll, required the Faculty of Advocates to appoint six advocates and the Writers to the Signet and the other agents practising in the Court of Session each to nominate four of their members to act for the poor in civil cases in the Court of Session. The applicant was required to produce a certificate of indigence from the minister and two elders of his parish and a report on the merits of the case by lawyers appointed for this purpose. This was, accordingly, the beginning of a system where the means of an applicant and the merits of his case are first examined before legal aid may be granted. From at least the 16th century, the legal profession accepted as a public duty the defence of poor persons on criminal charges. The statutory basis is uncertain, but two Acts of the Scottish Parliament in 1587 are thought to have regulated the provision of this service. Formal provision for the appointment of poor's agents in civil and criminal cases in the sheriff courts was made by the Act of Sederunt of 12 November 1825. Local schemes for providing representation for the poor were modified from time to time in the years after 1825, but the 'Poor's Roll' remained substantially in the same form until 1950. At an earlier stage, however, there had been recognition that radical reform was necessary, and a committee under the chairmanship of Sheriff Morton was appointed in 1936 to review the facilities available to poor persons as parties before the civil courts and as accused persons before the criminal courts.[1] Before action could be taken on the Morton Report, the second world war intervened. In 1945, the Cameron Committee[2] reviewed the need for legal aid in Scotland following a report on this subject which had been made by the Rushcliffe Committee relative to England and Wales.[3] After considerable debate there emerged the Legal Aid (Scotland) Act 1949, which envisaged a system whereby persons of limited means could receive civil and criminal legal aid and advice. However, because of economic considerations at the time, civil legal aid alone was introduced in 1950. It was not until 1964 that criminal legal aid was introduced following a further review, this time by the Guthrie Committee.[4] In 1972, legal advice and assistance (providing for limited advice and assistance short of representation in court) were added to the system.[5]

Administration of legal aid

8.3 From the outset, the administration of legal aid has been in the hands of the Law Society, who administer the various schemes through a committee structure which divides responsibility for various aspects of the schemes as shown in Diagram 8.1.

8.4 In their evidence to us, the Society said that their Council through their own committees exercised the following functions:

(i) to determine matters of policy in relation to future development of the schemes;

(ii) to provide premises, furniture and equipment and employ staff for legal aid purposes;

(iii) to appoint solicitor members to the central, supreme court and local legal aid committees;

(iv) to deal with complaints against solicitors in respect of their services under the legal aid schemes.

The Council also have power to give directions to the central committee. The central legal aid committee consists of not more than 9 solicitors appointed by

[1] *Report of the Poor Persons' Representation (Scotland) Committee (Cmd. 5435)*: The Morton Report: HMSO, 1937.
[2] *Report of the Committee on Legal Aid and Legal Advice in Scotland (Cmd. 6925)*: The Cameron Report: HMSO, 1946.
[3] *Report of the Committee on Legal Aid and Legal Advice in England and Wales (Cmd. 6641)*: The Rushcliffe Report: HMSO, 1945.
[4] *Legal Aid in Criminal Proceedings (Cmnd. 1015)*: The Guthrie Report: HMSO, 1960.
[5] A fuller historical account is in C. N. Stoddart: *The Law and Practice of Legal Aid in Scotland*: W. Green and Son Ltd., 1979.

DIAGRAM 8.1: ADMINISTRATION OF LEGAL AID*

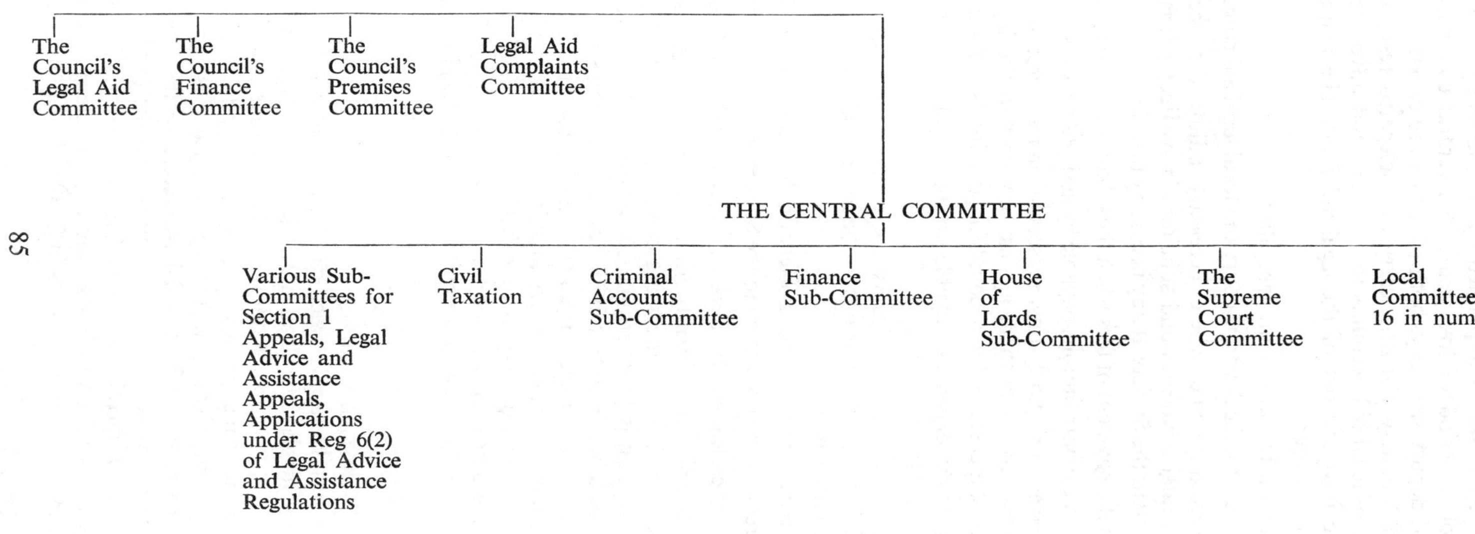

*Source: The Law Society.

the Law Society, not more than 5 advocates appointed by the Faculty of Advocates, and 2 lay members appointed by the Secretary of State. Members are appointed for a period of five years. The central committee has a full-time secretary and deputy secretary, both of whom are experienced solicitors, and a staff of approximately 120 who carry out delegated responsibilities involving the payment of legal aid accounts to solicitors and advocates and the control of sums paid into and out of the legal aid fund. The major functions of the central committee are:

(i) to administer the scheme generally;

(ii) to supervise the supreme court and local legal aid committees;

(iii) to scrutinise and where necessary adjust the accounts payable to individual advocates and solicitors in particular legal aid cases and to represent the Society at any necessary taxations;

(iv) to make payment of fees when these have been adjusted or taxed;

(v) to collect contributions payable by assisted persons;

(vi) to receive principal sums preserved or recovered on behalf of assisted persons; to apply them against any cost to the legal aid fund of the particular case; and to account for such funds to the assisted person;

(vii) to recover expenses payable to the legal aid fund by unsuccessful opponents;

(viii) to determine appeals against decisions of the supreme court committee in civil cases and decisions of the local legal aid committees in civil and in criminal cases;

(ix) to report annually to the Society on the administration of the schemes;

(x) to prepare for submission to the Society, estimates for legal aid;

(xi) to grant certificates for appeals in civil cases to the House of Lords.

These functions are predominantly administrative. The supreme court committee and the sixteen local committees are composed entirely of practising lawyers; their major function is to determine, as regards each application for civil legal aid, whether certain statutory criteria for the granting of legal aid are fulfilled, though they also are involved in sanctioning the use of expert witnesses and the exercise of certain other supervisory functions. Most of the local committees are serviced by solicitors on a part-time basis; but in addition to the 120 staff employed at the central committee and the local committee in Edinburgh, 60 are employed at the supreme court committee and at the local committee in Glasgow.

Legal aid in civil cases

8.5 To apply for civil legal aid, a potential client must approach a solicitor who is willing to take legally aided clients. Normally, solicitors who participate in the schemes display the legal aid logo (a blue sign showing in white two figures seated at a desk) in a window or near the door of their offices. Otherwise, the potential client can approach the Law Society who will inform him of solicitors in his area participating in the legal aid schemes; or he may approach a Citizens Advice Bureau which will have access to the 'legal aid referral lists' produced by the Law Society; or he may consult the Law Society's directory of general services provided by solicitors. The solicitor will first determine whether the case is of a kind for which legal aid is available. Legal aid is available for actions in all cases in the civil courts in Scotland with minor exceptions, principally actions of defamation or verbal injury, election petitions and the recovery of certain small debts.

8.6 The solicitor will then forward the client's application for legal aid to the appropriate committee. The application will contain details of the client's case and of his financial position. For cases in the Court of Session (or the Restrictive Practices Court) the application will be made to the supreme court committee. For cases in the sheriff courts, the Scottish Land Court, the Lands Tribunal for Scotland or the Employment Appeal Tribunal, the application will be made to the local legal aid committee. The committee considers the client's case as stated by the solicitor to determine whether the client has 'probabilis causa'—that is, a reasonable prospect of success; and also to determine whether, in all the circumstances, it is reasonable that the applicant should be granted legal aid. It is only if these two statutory criteria are fulfilled that legal aid may be granted.

8.7 Additionally, the applicant must satisfy certain financial criteria. In the first place legal aid is not available to people who have alternative facilities to meet the costs of litigation—for example, when a trade union will pay for the case as one of the benefits of membership. Secondly, the applicant's income must be assessed according to certain statutory formulae in order to determine his 'disposable' income (his net income after deduction of all the allowances permitted by the regulations). The assessment is made by the Supplementary Benefits Commission, whose determination is not open to appeal. Applicants whose disposable income exceeds a given limit are ineligible for legal aid. Thirdly, the applicant's disposable capital must also be similarly assessed. Once again, he may be refused legal aid if his disposable capital exceeds a given limit. If the applicant falls within the eligibility limits he may be awarded legal aid free or, depending on his disposable income and capital, he may be liable to pay a contribution to the cost of his action. In this case the Supplementary Benefits Commission will assess what is called his 'maximum' contribution. The supreme court committee or the local legal aid committee will then assess the likely cost of the proceedings and will fix the applicant's 'actual' contribution. The actual contribution required will never exceed the maximum contribution; but in instances where the committee considers that the probable cost of proceedings will be less than the maximum contribution, the actual contribution will be set at that lower figure. Payment of the actual contribution to the legal aid fund is usually made by monthly instalments over a period of one year. If, on the conclusion of the proceedings, the actual contribution proves to be insufficient to cover the cost to the legal aid fund, the applicant may be asked to pay all or part of the difference between his actual contribution and the maximum contribution originally assessed by the Supplementary Benefits Commission.

Legal aid in criminal cases

8.8 In criminal cases, legal aid is granted by the court—normally the court before which the accused makes his first appearance. There is no appeal from the court's decision. The procedure for processing legal aid applications in criminal cases, and the criteria applied in awarding legal aid, are somewhat different from those applied in civil cases. There is no requirement for 'probabilis causa' to be established: such a requirement would run contrary to the principle that an accused is considered innocent until he has been proved guilty. There is also no time for the complex investigation into the financial means of the applicant which is used in civil cases. The financial test which applies to all cases is that the court should be satisfied, after consideration of the financial circumstances of the accused, that the likely expenses of the case cannot be met without undue hardship to the accused or his dependants. In most cases, this requires a spot decision by the sheriff or justice of the peace or magistrate before whom the accused appears. In summary cases (those tried without a jury), the additional test of whether it is in the interests of justice that legal aid should be available has to be applied. Legal aid will, therefore, frequently not be available for minor cases heard before the sheriff and district courts. In certain other cases, the applicant may not be entitled to legal aid by virtue of his having rights or facilities for obtaining representation in other ways; for example, in a road traffic offence case the applicant may be a member of a motoring organisation which would offer him representation for the case. Where the person concerned is a member of a body which might reasonably be expected to give him financial help towards the cost of his defence, the court is required to obtain from the applicant, before he can be granted legal aid, an undertaking to pay the legal aid fund any sum received on account of the expenses of his defence.

Legal advice and assistance

8.9 The legal advice and assistance scheme covers the giving of advice on any question of Scots law, and assistance by the solicitor with the exception of representation before courts or tribunals.[1] In such cases, the solicitor himself applies a relatively simple means test; and, if the client qualifies, the solicitor may advise him and start work on his behalf immediately. The only restriction is that if the necessary work involves an expenditure of more than £25 the solicitor must seek the approval of the local legal aid committee to exceed that sum. The committee will give such authority, up to a further limit fixed by it, if it considers that it is reasonable that the advice and assistance should be given, and that the estimated cost of giving such advice or assistance is fair and reasonable. In accordance with the general philosophy of legal aid, where any sum of money (other than alimentary payments, one half of redundancy payments and certain other benefits) or any other property is recovered or preserved as a result of advice and assistance, the cost to the legal aid fund in giving the advice and assistance is the first charge on the sum recovered. However, the solicitor can apply to the central committee for authority not to enforce payment of his account in this way if he feels that to do so would cause grave hardship or distress to the client, or that it could be effected only with unreasonable difficulty because of the nature of the property.

The duty solicitor scheme

8.10 As well as administering the criminal legal aid scheme, the Law Society administer the duty solicitor schemes whereby the services of a solicitor are available to all accused held in custody on their first appearance in court. Thereafter, the accused person who pleads not guilty and is granted legal aid may continue to use the services of that solicitor; or he may choose another, though only a minority do so. Each local legal aid committee has the responsibility of preparing a 'duty plan' for every sheriff court and district court within

[1] The Legal Aid Act 1979 provides for assistance by way of representation under this scheme, but no orders have yet been made to make such assistance available in Scotland.

its jurisdiction. The plan, which provides the services of solicitors undertaking criminal legal aid work in the courts concerned on a rota basis, is approved by the legal aid central committee, after taking into account any views of the appropriate Sheriffs Principal (in the case of sheriff court plans) or justices committees (in the case of district court plans).

8.11 When the duty solicitor is informed that a person has been taken into custody charged with murder, attempted murder or culpable homicide and that he wishes the duty solicitor's services, he is required to visit that person in custody and to advise him and act for him until he is brought to a sheriff court for his judicial examination. In all cases where the accused is in custody and is dealt with under solemn procedure (those tried with a jury), the duty solicitor is required to visit the accused before his judicial examination and represent him at that examination. In summary cases, the duty solicitor is required to interview any accused person in custody who wishes his services and to represent that accused up to the first diet at which he is called on to plead. If a plea of guilty is tendered, the duty solicitor will continue to act for the accused until the case is terminated. Typically, this will involve the presentation of a plea in mitigation.

8.12 We should note that the foregoing account is a simplified one. The law governing legal aid has been described as 'a morass of fragmentary information, difficult to assimilate and frustrating to construe'.[1] The Scottish Legal Action Group's evidence to us stated that:

> 'Virtually each year since Legal Aid was introduced in 1949 there has been an annual accretion of new law. The section of the lawyer's bible, the Parliament House Book for 1977, which deals with the three forms of Legal Aid, legal aid in civil cases, in criminal cases and legal advice and assistance, runs to 253 closely-printed pages, comprising 52 Acts of Parliament, Acts of Sederunt, Orders, Schemes and Regulations. It is little wonder that even lawyers often confess to being baffled by the intricacy of the law...'

During the course of our work we learned that the Scottish Home and Health Department had established a working party to review the legal aid legislation. This working party has not yet reported.

THE NEED FOR LEGAL AID

8.13 Is it right that the State should provide assistance to those who need it to secure legal services? In the following paragraphs we consider from first principles the forms which such State aid should take, and whether there should be any limits to the circumstances in which it should be provided.

8.14 There is no compelling reason why State support should take only the form of payment to private practitioners. Wholly new approaches to State-financed legal services were suggested to us. We received evidence proposing that the existing pattern of legal services should be radically revised with the introduction of a 'national legal agency'; in effect, a legal parallel to the national health service. The Scottish Legal Action Group proposed to us that State finance for legal services should depend on whether a service was 'essential, desirable or likely to produce gain for the individual'. In their scheme, essential services—for example, legal representation in defence against a criminal charge

[1] C. N. Stoddart, op. cit., page 16.

which carried the penalty of loss of liberty and in civil actions relating to the preservation of jobs and homes—would be freely available to all; desirable services—such as legal representation against a criminal charge which carried the penalty of a fine but not imprisonment, and the making of wills, obtaining of divorces and adoptions—would be available subject to a flat rate contribution, except for people receiving supplementary benefit or family income supplement who would be exempt from the contribution; and services likely to produce gain —such as conveyancing—would be paid for by the individual.

A national legal service

8.15 The analogy with the national health service seems at first sight attractive: if the State is to fund the provision of legal services there are obvious arguments for the foundation of a fully-developed State service. There are, however, a number of fundamental objections to such a service. The first stems from a distinction between medicine and law: whereas all medical clients are individuals, a significant part of the legal clientele comprises companies and other associations. We can see no case for providing free legal services to businesses, or for requiring businesses to hire only State lawyers. Secondly, much personal legal business falls outside our concern with the assertion and defence of rights (see paragraph 8.17): conveyancing and the administration of estates are examples. In our view, clients in such matters have no call on State subsidies. Thirdly, the assertion and defence of rights necessarily involves parties with conflicting interests. It is a basic principle that such parties should be separately represented: a single national agency cannot ultimately guarantee independent representation to opposing parties. Fourthly, the law develops through adversary pleading in the courts; and we would not want this process to be replaced by internal debate within an agency as to the correct construction of the law. We cannot, therefore, support a monopolistic national agency or indiscriminate State subsidies. This does not, however, rule out the provision of some legal services by State salaried lawyers: indeed this possibility is catered for in existing legal aid legislation.

The scope of legal aid

8.16 The Scottish Legal Action Group proposal contains a number of points. For example, it does away with the principle of contribution on the basis of means. We know that many people find means testing abhorrent; but we believe that it is only fair that those who are able should make some contribution to the cost of the legal services they use. Some form of assessment of means will thus continue to be essential. The Scottish Legal Action Group said to us:

> 'Many people must find this means testing by a body whose main function is the relief of the poorest [the Supplementary Benefits Commission] very degrading and it may well lead to their not availing themselves of civil legal aid.'

There is, of course, no way of saying how many people have been dissuaded from applying for civil legal aid because of the form of the means test used; but from our evidence, we have no reason to believe that the numbers are significant. Nevertheless, we hope that our proposals will eliminate any sense of 'degradation'. In the case of criminal legal aid, the Scottish Legal Action Group consider the means test at present employed (an immediate assessment by the court) erratic and unreliable, producing wide variations in practice between different sheriffs, justices of the peace and stipendiary magistrates. Here too our proposals should improve matters. Our approach, as will be seen later, has been to adopt the principle of a scheme with contributions based on an assessment of means, while eliminating the most serious defects of the existing arrangements.

8.17 The Scottish Legal Action Group proposal also involves what might be called 'needs testing': a categorisation of kinds of case some of which would attract free legal aid; some of which would attract legal aid subject to a flat rate contribution; and some of which would attract no legal aid at all. In the way in which this was presented to us we were not convinced that the proposal was sound; and we thought it could lead to injustice. As regards civil matters we do not think it desirable for us, the legislature, or anyone else, to attempt to define in general terms for others what types of cases are 'important' to them. Unless the category for which unlimited or generous legal aid is to be available were drawn so widely as to make this proposal meaningless, we think it inevitable that the proposal would result in legal aid being granted in cases of relative triviality and being withheld in cases where hardship cries out for it to be available. Nevertheless, we believe that there should be a limit, in principle, to the scope of legal aid. In civil matters, as we have already said, we believe it is right that the State should help a citizen to take legal action to assert or protect his rights; but we do not think it justifiable that public funds should be expended to assist individuals in arranging their affairs for the benefit of themselves or for others. Conveyancing is perhaps the most obvious example. We do not see why public funds should be expended on assisting a person in the legal aspects of purchasing a house any more than on the cost of furniture removal. Conveyancing is, however, only an example. Other examples of cases where legal advice may well be sought, but not be concerned with assertion or defence of a right, are the making of wills or setting up of trusts, and advice as to whether a person should enter into a proposed contract. However, once a contract is entered into, advice or representation in relation to a dispute as to the parties' rights under it would be a matter concerning assertion or defence of a right. Our proposal to limit legal aid to this principle will in practice only be relevant to what is presently covered by legal advice and assistance. Defence in criminal proceedings and pursuit or defence in civil proceedings always or almost always falls within the principle of assertion or defence of a right. We **recommend**, therefore, that legal aid for advice and assistance and for representation in civil matters should only be available to help citizens to assert or protect their rights, and not to assist them in arranging their affairs for the benefit of themselves or others. In criminal cases, we believe that legal aid should be available to provide all accused persons with advice on how to plead and, if appropriate, help in the preparation of a plea in mitigation. Beyond this, in criminal cases, we think that to a very limited extent the availability of legal aid should depend on the importance of the case. We do not think it necessary or desirable that public funds should always be made available for the defence of persons charged with offences where the outcome of a conviction could not be a serious matter, either as regards penalty or as regards damage to reputation (see paragraph 8.52).

Tribunals

8.18 Those who appear before tribunals do so to assert or protect rights and should, therefore, qualify for legal aid in terms of the principle we have enunciated. In support of this view, it can also be argued that where legal representation is allowed and one side can afford to use it, it is wrong to refuse legal aid to the other party. However, there is a difference between most tribunals and courts. Our courts traditionally rely on the adversarial procedure which generally demands a degree of skill and knowledge of the law on the part of the pleader. Tribunals of the kind we have in mind, such as the Industrial Tribunal, are accustomed to proceed by a more inquisitorial approach, which makes the quality of presentation less crucial to the outcome. We think that this form of procedure is well suited for tribunals of this type and should be encouraged. We had this in mind in recommending in Chapter 7 that lay representation at such tribunals should be developed by generalist advice agencies. We certainly would not prohibit the employment of lawyers for this purpose. No doubt there are cases where difficult questions of law arise in which the assistance of lawyers appearing for the parties is valuable to the tribunal in question, but we think that the use of lawyers ought not to be encouraged in the general run of these cases since they tend to introduce adversarial formality to which the proceedings are not well suited.

8.19 The Scottish Committee of the Council on Tribunals recommended to us that legal aid should only be available at tribunals in the absence of suitable lay representation. We endorse that approach, though we consider that a solicitor should be entitled to claim from the legal aid fund for undertaking representation if the tribunal certify that a substantial point of law was at issue. So that it might be widely known whether there is 'suitable lay representation' locally available, each tribunal should publish a list of agencies providing what is, in the view of the particular tribunal, suitable representation. However, though it is important to provide representation where needed, tribunal proceedings are intended to enable citizens to appear without a legal representative to conduct their case; and we do not wish to encourage representation where the person himself could, after receiving advice as to what was involved, adequately present his own case. Legal aid should, therefore, be made available for representation at tribunals only if the client would otherwise be unable to follow the proceedings, and then only where there is no lay representation locally available which is recognised by the tribunal as suitable.

8.20 Tribunal hearings can involve substantial points of law. In addition, therefore, where the chairman of the tribunal, on an application made before the hearing, considers that a substantial point of law is likely to arise it should be competent for the tribunal to grant legal aid. If a substantial point of law arises during the course of a hearing, the tribunal should be able to authorise legal aid and to adjourn the hearing to allow legal representation to be obtained. In many such cases, the individual may already be represented by a full-time trade union official or by a lay representative, and although persons with such alternative means of representation should not be granted legal aid in straightforward cases, in cases where a substantial question of law is likely to arise they should be treated as regards legal aid in the same way as others using the tribunal system. We do not expect that such cases will arise frequently, and experienced chairmen and clerks of tribunals will readily recognise the cases where substantial questions of law are likely to arise. In practice, this extension of legal aid to tribunals will best be made tribunal by tribunal. The Legal Aid Act 1979 makes provision for legal aid to be extended to tribunals by regulation. It is clear that such regulations will need to be preceded by an examination of tribunals individually to see which require (or allow) legal representation and before which the exclusion of legal aid might cause inequity. An examination should be undertaken to identify those tribunals at which a substantial point of law is most likely to arise. All such tribunals should include a legally qualified member.

8.21 To sum up as regards tribunals, we **recommend** that legal aid should be available for representation at a tribunal, but only if the client would otherwise be unable to follow the proceedings and if there is no lay representation available locally which is recognised by the tribunal as suitable. We **recommend** in addition that a tribunal should have power to grant legal aid where it considers that the matter before it gives rise, or is likely to give rise, to a substantial point of law. We further **recommend** that all tribunals at which a substantial point of law is likely to arise should include a legally qualified member.

Matters presently excluded from legal aid

8.22 Legal aid is not currently available either to pursue or to defend an action of defamation. While we would wish to prevent frivolous or vexatious litigation being pursued at public expense, we think that the present total exclusion of defamation is wrong. It is particularly unjust in preventing persons from defending such actions. However, it would be wrong to grant legal aid in such actions to defenders and not pursuers. We think that frivolous and vexatious cases can, and will, be excluded from legal aid by a proper and careful use of the reasonableness test. Accordingly, we **recommend** that legal aid should be available to pursue or defend an action of defamation.

8.23 There are a few summary actions for which legal aid is not available, notably summary causes where the debt is admitted. In most of these cases there is no need for legal representation; what the debtor may need is help in managing his resources. We think that our proposals in Chapter 12 are the best way to meet this need, and it would not be appropriate to extend the availability of legal aid to cover such cases.

Eligibility

8.24 Who then should be eligible for legal aid to assert or protect his rights? In November 1976, just after we began our work, the eligibility limits in civil legal aid were as follows: legal aid was available only to people whose disposable income did not exceed £2,085 per year and whose disposable capital was £1,400 or less.[1] Contributions were required from disposable income in excess of £665 per year and from disposable capital in excess of £300. We received considerable criticism of these limits which were said to result in only the very rich or the very poor being able to litigate. The capital limits were particularly attacked. The Law Society and the Scottish Association of Citizens Advice Bureaux, for example, drew our attention to the position of widows and pensioners with small savings who were in effect penalised for their thrift because their savings, against which they could claim only small allowances notwithstanding their very low income, made them ineligible for legal aid. The Crofters Commission pointed out that crofters who had only one cow would be excluded from legal

---

[1] Although the capital limit is not an absolute bar, it is extremely rare for anyone whose capital exceeds the limit to be awarded legal aid.

aid by this capital limit. The limits were, however, radically increased in April 1979 and at the time of writing (February 1980) legal aid is available to those whose disposable income does not exceed £4,075 per year, and whose disposable capital (from which is excluded in particular the value of the applicant's home) is no more than £2,500. Legal aid is free to those whose disposable income does not exceed £1,700 per year and whose disposable capital is £1,200 or less.

8.25 Although we welcome the increases in the financial eligibility limits, the upper limit operates in a grossly unfair way. The citizen who just squeezes in below the limit is awarded legal aid and knows his maximum liability. If his own solicitor's fees cost more than that, the legal aid fund will pay; and if he loses his case, the court will be required to restrict the award of expenses against him to such an amount as it considers reasonable in all the circumstances. This means in practice that the legally aided party is rarely left with any liability for the expenses of his successful opponent beyond what he can fairly readily afford. No such restriction on liability for expenses is made in the case of a non-legally aided party; so that the disadvantage suffered by those whose disposable income just exceeds the upper legal aid limit is out of all proportion. If the non-legally aided party is successful he has a theoretical claim for expense against the legally aided party; but this is often of little or no value in view of the requirement that the courts must restrict that claim to what the legally aided party can reasonably afford. The successful non-legally aided party has no resort against the legal aid fund except in the very restricted circumstances provided for in section 13 of the Legal Aid (Scotland) Act 1967, which gives the court a discretion to award him some or all of his expenses against the legal aid fund. Even this power is limited as regards proceedings at first instance to cases where the non-legally aided party is the defender, a limitation for which we can see no justification; and in such cases the non-legally aided party has to demonstrate 'severe financial hardship'. The cost of civil litigation can rarely be predicted in advance. A person falling within, perhaps only just within, the eligibility limits knows in advance the maximum that the litigation will cost him, win or lose, except only that the court has an element of discretion to restrict his liability for expenses if he loses to what he can reasonably afford. His opponent who may be only marginally better off, but who is above the eligibility limit, cannot know what the litigation will cost him; but he does know that as likely as not, even if he is successful, he will recover no part of his expenses.

8.26 To remedy this glaring inequity, we **recommend** a scheme which has no upper eligibility limit of disposable income. However, we also think that public funds should only be provided to pay for litigation in so far as a person cannot afford to pay for it himself without gross financial hardship to himself or his family. To achieve this object we **recommend** that the scheme should have a scale of contributions which rises sharply with income, so that in effect the contribution of those with a substantial income will often be greater than the actual costs of litigation. We suggest a possible scale of contributions in Table 8.2 below. We also **recommend** that the contribution levels should be reviewed annually.

8.27 We have considered whether a scheme with no upper income limit to eligibility should retain an upper capital limit to eligibility. While there would be presentational advantages in excluding the very wealthy by applying some kind of capital limit, when we looked closely at the question we could see little or no practical benefit. In view of what we regard as the valid criticisms of the present low capital limit, and of our own proposals for a steeply progressive scale of contributions, we would have wished to exclude only the very largest holders of capital from the scheme. We concluded that the value of such a cut off point would be largely cosmetic since the great majority of individuals in possession of substantial capital would almost certainly, by virtue of that capital, have a large disposable income and be liable for a substantial maximum contribution under our progressive scale of contributions. Moreover, the assessment of capital can be extremely difficult to undertake accurately and quickly where, for example, life policies are involved, or unquoted shares, or works of art. On the whole, it seemed to us better to have a simpler scheme which assumes that capital holdings will be reflected in income even if this carries the risk that one or two individuals might be notionally eligible for legal aid with a maximum contribution that did not adequately reflect their true financial worth. We therefore **recommend** that no account should be taken of capital in assessing eligibility for civil legal aid, or in computing the contribution payable.

TABLE 8.2: Example of a graduated scale of legal aid contributions.

Disposable Income £	*Rate of Contribution (%)*		*Contribution at top of Band*	
	Existing	*Proposed*	*Existing* £	*Proposed* £
0 — 1700*	0	0	0	0
1700 — 2000	25	5	75	15
2000 — 2500	25	10	200	65
2500 — 3000	25	20	325	165
3000 — 3500	25	30	450	315
3500 — 4000	25	40	575	515
4075†	(25)	(50)	594	553
4000 — 5000	—	50	—	1015
5000 — 6000		60		1615
6000 — 7000		70		2315
7000 — 8000		80		3115
8000 — 9000		90		4015
9000+		100		+

Example:
Disposable Income £3200 — Proposed Contribution £225 (£165+30%×£200)

*Current free limit
†Current upper eligibility limit

8.28 The existing civil legal aid scheme excludes from its benefit all 'bodies of persons corporate or unincorporate'. It is, therefore, only available to individuals. It makes no distinction, however, between litigations in connection with the business affairs of an individual and those concerned with his personal or private affairs. We see difficulties in applying our new proposed scheme to one man businesses, because the income of the business may well bear no relation to its value. This is not significant where, as now, there is a low eligibility limit; but under our proposals it would possibly involve undue use of public funds in support of relatively affluent businesses. We accordingly **recommend** that civil legal aid should not be available to businessmen or traders for litigations relating to a business or trade even if the business or trade is owned by an individual, this exclusion to be in addition to the exclusion of bodies corporate or unincorporate. We think that this additional exclusion is justifiable on the ground that business and trade may be able to set off litigation expenses against tax, and also on the ground that it would be prudent for businesses and trades to insure against the risks of litigation expenses.

Losers' liability for expenses

8.29 The unsuccessful legally aided party should, as now, be protected from having to meet all his opponent's expenses. The approach we prefer, however, is to make the assessed contribution the maximum which the legally aided litigant should have to pay. For example, if Mr. A were granted legal aid subject to a contribution of £800, and his own expenses were £600, then the most he should have to contribute to his opponent's expenses should be £200. The present rule about the award of expenses against an unsuccessful legally aided party is unjust. We **recommend** that the expenses of the successful opponent of a legally aided party should be recovered from the unused balance of the legally aided party's contribution; and to the extent that they exceed any such balance, they should be met by the legal aid fund. Ideally, in justice, this should apply whatever the nature of the successful party. We see good practical reasons, however, for making an exception in the case of parties presently excluded from the legal aid scheme, that is to say 'bodies of persons corporate and unincorporate'. When the successful party is such a body, it should not be entitled to recover any expenses from the legal aid fund unless it can satisfy the court that inability to do so would result in severe hardship to individuals. While we have proposed that one man businesses and sole traders should be excluded from legal aid for litigation connected with their business or trade, we do not think that, where they are successful opponents of legally aided parties in such actions, they should be excluded from the right to recover expenses from the legal aid fund in so far as these expenses exceed the unexpended part of the opponent's contribution; and we so **recommend**.

Civil legal aid: an integrated scheme

8.30 Civil legal aid was introduced in 1950, and legal advice and assistance in its present form in 1973; but the two are governed by separate Acts, regulations and schemes, although both are administered by the same body, the legal aid central committee. Many civil legal aid cases develop from initial advice and assistance given under the legal advice and assistance scheme, and provision has to be made to relate the two certificates, the two assessments of contribution, and the two sets of solicitor's accounts. The present distinctions between legal aid and legal advice and assistance are confusing to the public at large, and a composite scheme would, we think, make for better public understanding. In our survey of legal needs, only 39 per cent of respondents did not know what legal aid was; but 90 per cent were ignorant of the advice and assistance scheme.[1] Integration of the schemes would require that publicity would have to be given only to one scheme and there would, we consider, be greater knowledge of the scheme and of the availability of its benefits to those who required them. A further advantage of integration would be to remove the need for two separate

[1] See Appendix 4.

means tests. At the present time two such tests are required if an applicant changes over in mid-stream when the problem in which he has been obtaining advice requires recourse to litigation.

8.31 We have said earlier that people should contribute what they can afford towards the cost of legal aid. At present, there is a fundamental inconsistency between the contributions required for legal aid and for advice and assistance. Although the upper income limit is roughly the same for each scheme, the maximum contribution from income towards advice and assistance is £49 whereas for legal aid it is £594. In practice, not many advice and assistance cases exceed £50; but that is no reason for supposing that the client could not afford more. To put the point bluntly, if the State considers that a person can afford a contribution of £600 towards legal services which take the form of litigation it seems odd, to say the least, that that same individual's maximum contribution towards legal services in the form of advice and assistance should be only £50. His ability to pay has nothing to do with the cost of the service. Integrating the two schemes would remove this anomaly. As Table 8.2 shows, we have proposed a more finely graduated scale of rising contributions than at present, which mitigates the worst effects of abolishing the cheap rate advice and assistance scale. Although there may be some technical difficulties in integrating the two schemes, we are confident that they would not prove insurmountable. We therefore **recommend** that civil legal aid and legal advice and assistance should be integrated into a single scheme, which should simply be a legal aid scheme. We think that there would be clear benefits in convenience both to clients and to the legal aid administration in doing this, although our proposals for a fresh approach to civil legal aid do not depend on it.

Assessment of contributions

8.32 The present statutory means test procedure operated by the Supplementary Benefits Commission is, in our view, unnecessarily complex and sophisticated. Evidence shows it can be a substantial cause of delay in civil litigations. Moreover, we question whether the expertise of the Supplementary Benefits Commission would make it an appropriate body to carry out means testing under the scheme we propose, where in some cases assessment will be required in the cases of persons of substantial means. The experience of the legal advice and assistance scheme, where a simpler assessment is carried out by the solicitor himself, leads us to believe that it would be more efficient and more cost-effective to have a simplified assessment of eligibility for legal aid carried out by the solicitor to whom an application is made. We therefore **recommend** that the assessment of an applicant's eligibility for civil legal aid and the setting of a maximum contribution should be done by the solicitor to whom the client applies.

8.33 Before deciding on this recommendation we sought the views of the Law Society. They impressed on us, firstly, the impossibility of a solicitor being able to assess capital at all readily; and that is one reason why we were prepared to ignore capital completely in assessing means. Secondly, they stressed that the income assessment would have to draw the right balance between simplicity and equity. The present advice and assistance means test is very simple, whereas the legal aid test takes much greater account of individual circumstances. A middle course between these present tests is what we want. The calculation to be performed by the solicitor (or one of his staff) can be reduced to the extent that ready reckoner tables are provided (as is done in Sweden).

8.34 We propose that the client should provide the solicitor with a signed declaration as to the particulars which are relevant to the assessment of contribution in accordance with a simplified ready reckoner. If the client provides false or incomplete information he should be liable to penalties similar to those prescribed for false declarations in income tax matters. On this basis, the solicitor will determine the maximum contribution. There should be a procedure by which the solicitor will adjust the maximum contribution if the client's means change during any matter of prolonged duration. When the matter is finally disposed of, the legal aid fund should pay to the solicitor the amount of fees or outlays properly incurred in so far as these exceed the maximum contribution, and also any part of the contribution collected by the legal aid fund rather than the solicitor himself (see below). In the event that the maximum contribution assessed by the solicitor is too high, either because the solicitor has not ensured that the required information is completed on the declaration or because he has calculated his assessment incorrectly, the loss will fall on the solicitor. In the event that the assessed maximum contribution is too low because the statements in the declaration are wrong (whether intentionally or not), the loss will fall on the legal aid fund, which will have a right to recover the loss from the client. The legal aid administrators will have to make at least spot checks for this purpose.

Collection of contributions

8.35 For many persons payment in advance of the whole cost, or likely cost, of the contribution may be quite impractical. The existing scheme provides for the fixing of a figure known as the actual, as opposed to the maximum, contribution which is related to the probable actual cost of the litigation; and upon the basis of this figure, an instalment rate of payment of contributions is fixed. It is plain that payment by instalments must be retained. We are not, however, entirely satisfied that it is essential to fix an actual contribution figure. If this were dispensed with, it might be that a litigant would find himself having to pay more than his own total expenses, but if he did he should recover the excess. If the retention of the actual contribution is considered necessary we think that this, as well as the maximum contribution, could be fixed by the solicitor and not, as at present, by the local legal aid committee. The amounts and frequency of the instalments would also be fixed by the solicitor in accordance with rules laid down in the ready reckoner. It would be for the solicitor to explain to the client the difference between the actual and maximum contribution and the fact that he may be called on eventually to pay the latter. We understand that this is not at present always understood by assisted persons.

8.36 Had it been practical, we would have preferred that in all cases the contributions should be paid direct to the solicitor, who would then only charge the legal aid fund for any balance. This would simplify and cheapen the operations of those administering the fund. However, we were convinced by evidence from the Law Society that this would not be practical. The expense and trouble of recovering or attempting to recover a large number of small instalment payments and of accounting for them would make the operation so uneconomic that many firms might cease to offer legal aid. In the circumstances we regretfully came to the conclusion that the central administration equipped with the machinery for carrying out the work on a large scale must continue to provide the facility of collecting clients' contributions and paying the solicitor. For this purpose, the solicitor would have to inform the central administration of the maximum and actual contributions and the instalment rate. Spot checks could be made from time to time at this stage to ensure that solicitors were fixing these figures properly on the basis of the client's declaration as to his means. We **recommend** that where contributions are to be paid by instalments to the central administration every effort should be made to introduce alternative and convenient methods of payment, such as by post office giro.

8.37 Notwithstanding the preceding paragraphs, we also **recommend** that it should always be possible for the solicitor and client by mutual agreement to make their own arrangements for payment of the contribution direct to the solicitor, and we would hope that this would become the normal practice.

Assessing the merits of proposed litigation

8.38 Once the financial decisions have been made, there remain, at present, the professional legal questions about a legal aid application: does the client have 'probabilis causa' (a reasonable prospect of success) and is it reasonable, in all the circumstances, that legal aid be granted? To ensure that hopeless cases are not pursued at public expense, decisions on probabilis causa should continue to be taken by lawyers. We also think that some test of reasonableness should be applied since it is not always reasonable to pursue even the strongest of cases—for example, where the defender is a person with little or no means from which to satisfy any award made by the court.

8.39 However, it is not necessary for these tests to be applied by a legal aid committee in every case. In England and Wales most secretaries of legal aid committees have delegated powers to grant, but not to withhold, legal aid; and only cases of doubt, particular complexity or high cost are actually considered by members of the committee. In Scotland, the Law Society are only now considering whether the authority of two committee members is necessary to authorise every case, and delegated authority for the secretary is not yet contemplated.

8.40 Giving limited delegated authority to secretaries of local committees would be an improvement, but we do not think it goes far enough. We think that approval of a grant of legal aid on probabilis causa can, and should in the majority of cases, be left to the professional judgment of the solicitor himself. We were, however, impressed by the evidence of the Law Society that to give the solicitor the duty of refusing legal aid on one of these grounds could create problems in the solicitor-client relationship. Accordingly, we **recommend** that:

(i) where the solicitor has assured himself that the 'probabilis causa' and reasonableness tests are satisfied, he should be able to grant legal aid himself;

(ii) where the solicitor is in doubt he should refer the application to a statutory independent committee to be set up by the body responsible for administering legal aid; and

(iii) where the solicitor thinks the tests are not satisfied he should have no power to refuse legal aid, but should have to refer the application to the committee, unless the client is satisfied, on the solicitor's advice, that such a referral would be hopeless.

We hope that this system would greatly reduce the amount of work requiring to by dealt with by committees. We think that local committees would no longer be needed for this purpose and that the relatively few cases requiring to be referred could be dealt with more economically by one central committee. This committee should comprise mainly solicitors, but there should be a lay voice in deciding questions of reasonableness. We will later recommend that the administration of legal aid should be the responsibility of a Legal Services Commission, but whoever is responsible there will need to be a statutory independent committee of this kind.

8.41 We appreciate that what we propose in the preceding paragraph could lead to abuse by an unscrupulous solicitor. We do not believe that this is a serious risk; but the legal aid administration would require to keep a check on the situation and would need to be able to identify any solicitor who was making a practice of granting legal aid in cases where it was not in accordance with the criteria laid down.

Legal aid certificates

8.42 There is a danger that our recommendations for simplifying the granting of legal aid could result in a deluge of paperwork descending on the central administration. Almost every litigant will want legal aid, if only for the insurance it will provide against having to meet the other side's expenses. In addition, the integration of legal advice and assistance with civil legal aid may mean that everyone seeking legal advice in connection with the assertion or defence of a right will get legal aid in the broad sense in which we now use the term at the outset, just in case the dispute goes to court—or indeed in the ultimate case to the House of Lords. This could clutter the central administration with files on cases in many of which the client's contribution will be enough to meet the expense without any payment from the legal aid fund.

8.43 There is, we think, a way out of this potential difficulty. The solicitor granting legal aid should issue a certificate to the client and should keep two file copies. If litigation is proposed at this stage, the certificate should indicate the nature of the action; if litigation is not envisaged at first but becomes necessary later, a supplement to the certificate should then be issued. Only if, on conclusion of the matter, the client's contribution will not be sufficient to meet his expenses, should one copy of the certificate be sent to the central administration, in which case it should accompany the solicitor's account. (In cases where the client wants to pay his contribution by instalments to the legal aid fund from the outset, the certificate might be used as the authority to open the client account, and be submitted by the solicitor to the central administration at that stage.)

8.44 Our recommendations thus far, if adopted, will greatly reduce the administration involved in granting legal aid. The full-time equivalent of some 66 staff will be freed for other duties at the Supplementary Benefits Commission at an estimated total saving of £450,000 at current (January, 1980) levels. Some 40 per cent of the whole-time legal aid staff of the Law Society are committed to local committee and supreme court committee duties, and annual savings of perhaps £250,000 should be possible in salary, national insurance and superannuation costs if these committees are disbanded. The combined costs of the new committee we recommended in paragraph 8.40, and its staff, and of the staff to carry out increased monitoring, should be more than offset by further savings in the cost of the present central administration which should arise from our recommendations. Other savings of perhaps £300,000 per annum will also result in salaries to part-time local secretaries and local representatives; travelling and subsistence allowance and committee attendance fees; rent, rates, insurance, heating maintenance, etc. and other administration costs. We conclude, therefore, that savings in administrative costs of the order of £1 million per annum (some ten per cent of the cost of legal aid) will be possible if our recommendations are accepted.

Recovery of expenses

8.45 We think that when a legally aided litigant is successful he should be entitled to recover direct from his opponent, or from the legal aid fund as the case may be under the recommendations which we made in paragraph 8.29, an amount of expenses equivalent to his actual contribution. We therefore **recommend** that the present rule, whereby the legal aid fund undertakes the recovery of all the expenses awarded to successful assisted persons should be changed. Under our proposed scheme we think that the legal aid fund should only have responsibility for recovering from the unsuccessful opponent an amount equivalent to any sum which it has to pay towards the successful party's expenses; the successful party's solicitor should be responsible for recovering the amount equivalent to his client's contribution. The solicitor for the successful party could, however, be required in the first place to collect the whole of the expenses. He would only be entitled to recover from the legal aid fund any expenses in excess of the amount of his client's contribution, in so far as the excess was not met by any sum recovered by him from the unsuccessful opponent. Under this procedure, arrangements would have to be made for the legal aid fund to take on the burden of collecting that part of the expenses for which it was responsible, when the solicitor could show that he had endeavoured over a period of, say, six weeks to recover those expenses himself without success. In cases where the opponent was willing to pay promptly this would avoid involving the legal aid fund at all in the recovery of expenses.

Consistorial actions

8.46 We will suggest in Chapter 10 that legal aid (for litigation) should no longer be necessary for undefended divorces. This will, incidentally, relieve the legal aid fund of some but by no means all of the burden of work on the recovery of expenses. Divorce dominates the legal aid scheme, but it dominates the central committee's casework in recovering expenses still more. Adoption of the proposition which we put forward in Chapter 10, that no award of expenses be made in undefended divorce actions, would further reduce the burden of recovering expenses which the legal aid fund has to bear.

Sums recovered

8.47 There is a rule that any sum or property recovered for an assisted person is payable to the legal aid fund in the first instance and applied to defray the cost of the litigation to public funds. The effect is that, if there is difficulty about recovering expenses from the other side, it is primarily the litigant who suffers rather than the fund. In this situation assisted persons are in just the same position as any other litigant, and we have considered whether this should continue. Certainly, it would be wrong to encourage a party to litigate when the expense would be out of proportion to the sum at issue and there was doubt about the prospects of recovering expenses from the other party. On the other hand, clients find it hard to accept that, having paid their contribution and won their case, they may be no better and perhaps actually worse off. We **recommend,** therefore, that while the legal aid fund should still look to sums recovered to defray its expenses when the recovery of expenses from the other side is difficult, the assisted person should have first claim on a part of any sum recovered. It is difficult to set a value on how much: at current prices £500 might be reasonable, or perhaps the amount of the contribution plus £500.

The statutory deduction from civil legal aid fees

8.48 When civil legal aid was introduced by the 1949 Act it was provided that solicitors participating in the scheme then introduced (Civil Legal Aid Scheme) would have their fees reduced by 15 per cent. This was intended to represent half of the solicitor's profit margin. The deduction was subsequently reduced to 10 per cent in 1960. The arguments advanced in favour of the deduction were that before the introduction of legal aid many solicitors had worked in the past on a speculative basis, and that the introduction of the fund meant that they were guaranteed payment. Other arguments advanced were that to the profession's credit they were already known to reduce fees for poorer clients; and that, since the system was to be administered entirely by the legal profession, the acceptance of the deduction was some guarantee to the public that the scheme would be operated in a disinterested manner and would dispel any impression that the profession were unduly profiting from the scheme at the expense of the State. Against the deduction, it was argued that once the system of representing the poor without charge had been changed the profession should be paid the full and proper rate for the job. If there were to be a deduction, the public might feel that they were getting a second class service at cheaper rates, while those who could afford to pay would get a first class service by paying the full fee. When the subsequent legal aid schemes dealing with legal advice and assistance and criminal legal aid were introduced no similar deduction was proposed. We are not clear how this anomaly arose.

8.49 We do not believe that there is now any justification for retaining the principle of a statutory deduction in the legal aid scheme, particularly since it does not apply to all parts of the scheme. In view of the changes which we have proposed in the way in which legal aid is to be awarded, especially the greater responsibility being placed on solicitors, we **recommend** that the deduction should now be abolished.

LEGAL AID FOR ACCUSED PERSONS

8.50 It is arguable that, given the presumption of innocence under our system of justice until proved guilty, all accused persons should be entitled to legal aid for their defence. To provide such a service would be extremely costly, however, because although some 225,000 people are proceeded against in the summary courts each year, only about 22,000 are awarded legal aid.[1] We have, therefore, tried to acheive a reasonable balance between the needs of the accused and the cost to the public purse. At the same time we want a system that requires minimal administration.

8.51 As at present, those proceeded against under solemn procedure should be entitled to legal aid without any test of the 'interests of justice'. Also, those accused held in custody before their first appearance in court should, as now, be entitled to the services of the duty solicitor for advice on how to plead and, if appropriate, for help in presenting a plea in mitigation. Indeed, it seems to us right that such limited assistance should be available to all accused persons, so that no-one fails to advance a valid defence because he does not consult a solicitor, perhaps for fear of what it would cost. We therefore **recommend** that legal aid should be provided to enable all accused persons to receive initial advice on how to plead and, where appropriate, to be given help in the preparation of a plea in mitigation. Duty solicitors should be paid as now on a sessional basis. To minimise administrative costs the service to accused persons not held in custody should be charged at a flat rate per case. Those who would be entitled to free civil legal aid should pay nothing; and the solicitor should be reimbursed from the legal aid fund. Everyone else should pay the flat rate charge.

8.52 The problem of deciding which summary cases should be legally aided, beyond what is proposed in the previous paragraph, is not a new one. It was considered in some detail by the Widgery Committee who recommended that, where one or more of the following features was present, there were grounds for thinking that representation (and therefore legal aid) was desirable.

(a) that the charge is a grave one in the sense that the accused is in real jeopardy of losing his liberty or livelihood or suffering serious damage to his reputation;

(b) that the charge raises a substantial question of law;

(c) that the accused is unable to follow the proceedings and state his own case because of his inadequate knowledge of English, mental illness or other mental or physical disability;

(d) that the nature of the defence involves the tracing and interviewing of witnesses or expert cross-examination of a witness for the prosecution;

(e) that legal representation is desirable in the interest of someone other than the accused as, for example, in the case of sexual offences against young children when it is undesirable that the accused should cross-examine the witness in person.[2]

Although these criteria have no statutory authority in Scotland, they were commended to district courts at their inception by the Scottish Home and Health Department. Despite this, and although sheriffs must bear similar considerations in mind in deciding whether it is in the 'interests of justice' that legal aid be granted, we have received valid criticism that the grant of legal aid varies between sheriffs, and between justices of the peace and magistrates, in an arbitrary way. We therefore **recommend** that the criteria for granting criminal legal aid to defend a summary prosecution should be laid down in statute.

[1] *Criminal Statistics, Scotland 1977*. (Table 9). (Cmnd. 7339): and figures supplied by the Scottish Home and Health Department and the Legal Aid Central Committee. This information, we understand, will be included in the *29th Annual Report on the Scottish Legal Aid Scheme 1978–79* which had not been published by the time we went to print.

[2] *Report of the Departmental Committee on Legal Aid in Criminal Proceedings:* The Widgery Report (Cmnd. 2934): HMSO, 1966.

8.53 We have little difficulty in accepting grounds (b), (c) and (e) as proposed by the Widgery Committee. The Law Society told us, however, that almost any case could be presented in such a way as to satisfy ground (d); so we think that a more restricted form of words would be appropriate here. Ground (a) poses the greatest problems, particularly in relation to the risk of imprisonment. For many minor statutory offences imprisonment is not a competent sentence; but common law offences all carry the theoretical possibility of a prison sentence. The difficulty is that for many offences the risk is extremely small, so that it would be very wasteful to provide legal aid in all such cases to catch the few likely to result in imprisonment. Of almost 205,000 persons convicted or found guilty in the summary courts in 1978, fewer than 5 per cent were sentenced to some form of detention. Among the 170,000 who were charged with an offence in Class VII (miscellaneous offences) the proportion was less than half as great (2 per cent). In numerous categories of offence within Class VII no sentences of detention were imposed, and in others covering large numbers of accused persons the proportion was trivial—for example 32 (0·3 per cent) out of 12,300 convicted or found guilty of being drunk and incapable, and 440 (0·6 per cent) out of 71,700 in offences relating to motor vehicles (excluding drunk in charge).[1]

8.54 If there were a clear hierarchy of crimes and offences, or even if imprisonment were not a competent sentence in the district courts, then drawing a line for legal aid purposes would be much easier. However, we believe a line can be drawn; and we **recommend** that legislation should specify the offences where there is no risk of imprisonment or where the risk is so small as not to justify a grant of criminal legal aid.

8.55 The risk of imprisonment depends not only on the offence but on the accused, and in particular on his criminal record. Were we to take account of this, the granting of legal aid would become more complex; and, of more importance, it could readily lead to established criminals getting legal aid that is denied to first-time accused persons. Accordingly, the grant of legal aid should not depend on the accused person's criminal record.

Who should grant legal aid?

8.56 If the criteria for granting criminal legal aid are statutory and predominantly objective, as we have recommended in paragraph 8.52, solicitors in our view should be able to grant criminal legal aid to their own clients. Objective criteria can be checked fairly readily, so that any abuse would be capable of being detected easily. The Law Society told us, however, that solicitors would not want this responsibility, largely because they are from time to time subjected to what they regard as unjust criticism in some quarters for allegedly abusing criminal legal aid. While the Law Society had no hesitation in rebutting these criticisms as unsubstantiated, they said that they would not want to run the risk of solicitors being the object of further hostile comment if they were to be able to grant criminal legal aid at their own hand.

8.57 We feel we must have regard to the Law Society's considered and emphatic view. However, we do not accept the Society's alternative suggestion, that local legal aid committees should be given the responsibility for granting criminal legal aid. In the first place, our recommendations relative to civil legal

[1] *Criminal Statistics Scotland 1978*, (Cmnd. 7676), Table 9.

aid would remove any need for these committees. Secondly, there is a suggestion that these committees could enquire into the merits of the defence in a way that a sheriff, justice or magistrate cannot. We do not think it proper, however, to refuse criminal legal aid because of the nature of the defence: to do so would inevitably be to usurp the powers of the court of trial and to anticipate its verdict. Thirdly, if the criteria for granting legal aid are largely objective, and prescribed by statute, there is no need for a committee to make decisions. Our conclusion, therefore, is that if criminal legal aid, for the reasons advanced by the Law Society, cannot be granted by solicitors themselves, there is no option but to leave the responsibility where it now is, with the courts. We wish to **recommend**, however, that authority to grant, but not refuse, criminal legal aid should be delegated to sheriff clerks in suitable cases, provided that the clerks receive adequate training for the purpose. It should not normally be necessary for accused persons or their agents to attend court in connection with legal aid applications. We also **recommend** that where a decision on an application for criminal legal aid has to be taken by a judge, it should be done in chambers and not in open court, as we understand is already the case in some sheriff courts.

8.58 Any person who is to be prosecuted under solemn procedure should be entitled to legal aid, without any test of the 'interests of justice', until the case is disposed of. Any person who is in custody should be entitled to full legal aid until either his case is disposed of on a plea of guilty, or he is released with or without bail. This legal aid will normally be provided in the person of the duty solicitor, but the accused should be entitled to engage the services of another solicitor whose fees and outlays will be chargeable against the legal aid fund. Any other accused person, that is a person who has not been detained in custody at all, or, having been detained in custody, has been released, will be entitled to legal aid up to and for the purposes of making a plea in mitigation (if he pleads guilty), up to and for the purposes of making an application for full legal aid for his defence. The solicitor will be able to make the necessary enquiries as to the accused's means and the applicability of the statutory criteria to the particular case and prepare a brief written application to the sheriff. The sheriff (or sheriff clerk) will normally proceed upon the basis of this application to grant legal aid. He should not, however, be entitled to refuse it without giving the applicant or his solicitor a chance to be heard.

A contributory scheme?

8.59 We have proposed a rough and ready rule on contributions for initial advice. Contributions towards the cost of full representation pose greater problems. On the one hand the present system, with no contributions, does not always produce a fair outcome. For example, if a man can afford £600 for his defence, which is likely to cost £800, why should he pay nothing rather than the first £600? Equally, criticism arises when the estimate of cost turns out to be badly wrong so that the accused who pays nothing could easily have paid the full cost as things turned out. On the other hand, the Benson Commission found that the cost of collecting the contribution in England and Wales was often out of all proportion to the sum recovered. It would also be wrong to demand contributions from those acquitted; and, in the case of those who are convicted and fined, it hardly seems sensible for separate arms of the State to be chasing the assisted person, one for the amount of his fine and the other for his legal aid contribution. Accordingly, we **recommend** that accused persons who receive criminal legal aid, and are tried and found guilty, should be liable to contribute to the cost of their defence. Applicants for legal aid to defend a criminal prosecution, whether under solemn or summary procedure, should certify that they understand that, if they are tried and found guilty, they will be liable for a contribution. Their solicitor should assess their contribution on the civil legal aid scale so that the accused person knows what his contribution will be on the basis of his present earnings.

8.60 If an accused person is tried and found guilty, the court should determine formally his legal aid contribution. Those sentenced to imprisonment may have no financial resources, in which case they should pay nothing. If the convicted person is fined, he should not pay a separate legal aid contribution, but the judge should take a notional contribution into account in fixing the fine, based on the solicitor's assessment of the contribution and modified as necessary by any change in circumstances. If it is thought desirable to keep account of the notional contribution, the judge should be able to direct how much of the fine should be paid over to the legal aid fund. Assessing a contribution in the case of convicted accused persons disposed of in other ways is more straightforward; and in such cases it should be for the legal aid fund to recover the contribution determined by the court.

8.61 We were frequently told that in criminal cases late changes of pleas from not guilty to guilty were a cause of disruption to court timetables and considerable inconvenience to witnesses who had been cited to appear. Such late changes of plea were also costly to the legal aid fund. We understand that there are proposals contained in the Criminal Justice Bill presently before Parliament which should alleviate the problems; and we do not, therefore, make any recommendation about recovering contributions from accused persons who change their pleas at a very late stage.

The duty solicitor scheme

8.62 It will be clear from what we have already said that the duty solicitor scheme is an essential feature of criminal legal aid as we would wish to see it develop. In paragraphs 8.10 and 8.11 we give a simplified account of how the scheme presently operates on the basis of duty plans prepared by the local legal aid committees for every sheriff court and district court. The duty solicitor sees only persons who have been kept in custody; and as a result of changes in the law, and in the procedures adopted, fewer persons are now being kept in custody prior to an appearance in court. An obvious consequence of this is that they do not have access to the duty solicitor although they would be entitled, if eligible, to advice under the legal advice and assistance scheme, or to make a formal application for criminal legal aid if they intended to plead not guilty. We do not think that this is what is required as many simply wish advice on the plea which they should make. Our recommendation in paragraph 8.51 will ensure that all accused persons will be entitled to advice on how to plead and, if necessary, assistance in making a plea in mitigation. This advice and assistance will be available from any solicitor participating in the legal aid schemes. For those accused persons who are detained in custody the services of a solicitor present at the court to advise and assist will still be necessary. In order that such a solicitor can properly advise and assist the accused person it is necessary that full details of the crime or offence with which the accused is charged should be available. However, we are concerned that in some courts, on some occasions, this may not be the case, and the complaint or indictment may only be made available to him a short time before he appears in court. This means in practice that the duty solicitor must often interview the accused before he knows in detail what he is accused of. In such circumstances the advice must often be to plead not guilty, since it will be crucial to know whether an accused has been charged for instance, with a careless driving offence or with murder. We have had evidence that this degree of uncertainty in fact occurs. Clearly the solution is to ensure that no accused person in custody is obliged to appear in court to answer the charges against him unless he has had full details of these in time for him to discuss them with the duty solicitor. We **recommend,** therefore, that all accused persons in custody should be entitled to see a duty solicitor and that before they do so they should have full details of any crime alleged against them. We appreciate that in practice this will mean that procurators fiscal will on occasion have to arrange speedier service of particulars of the offence with which the accused is charged.

8.63 As we indicated, the local legal aid committees prepare duty plans which ensure that a solicitor (or solicitors in busy courts) will be available to provide legal services for persons in custody. Our proposals on legal aid will eventually result in the local committees disappearing and we have considered, therefore, where the obligation of preparing a duty plan should then lie. There are four options open to us: firstly, the Legal Services Commission which we propose for administering legal aid; secondly, the local advisory committees which we proposed in Chapter 7; thirdly, the court advisory committees which we will propose in Chapter 15; and, lastly, the clerks of the sheriff and district courts. We think, on balance, that the court advisory committees would be the most appropriate body to take responsibility for the preparation of a duty plan to ensure the attendance of solicitors to provide legal services for accused persons, and we so **recommend**.

Legal advice in prison

8.64 Untried prisoners can have an anxious time awaiting news from their solicitor. Sometimes this is occasioned by the solicitor's failure to keep his client up to date with developments. Not all prisoners have a solicitor, and although prisons have copies of the Law Society's directory of general legal services, prison officers cannot be sure to identify all those persons who need to obtain the assistance of a solicitor. We **recommend** that public funds should pay for regular legal clinics in prisons to make available a solicitor to advise untried prisoners of their rights, help them to get a solicitor to act for them, and liaise as necessary with the prisoner's own solicitor. The solicitor attending the clinics would not act for prisoners himself. We do not think that such work should be carried out on a daily rota, because of the need for continuity. A small number of solicitors regularly at the prison would be most likely to win the confidence of those within it. The work might appeal to retired solicitors or to women solicitors temporarily unable to work full-time.

8.65 Such an arrangement could benefit newly-convicted prisoners too as they may need advice about the procedure for lodging an appeal. Appeals must be lodged within ten days following sentence; and some prisoners who instruct their solicitor to appeal only learn that he has done so when they receive intimation from the court, perhaps a few days after the period of appeal has expired. Here again, the fault lies with the prisoner's own solicitor; but the prison clinic solicitor ought to be able to ensure that prisoners are kept in touch about the lodging of appeals. Newly convicted prisoners are often too disorientated to comprehend what they are told about their right of appeal, and it is important to ensure that they can have ready access to authoritative advice about the procedures. The prison clinic solicitor would be well able to provide such a service as well as advise prisoners on various other legal problems which may arise during their period of imprisonment such as housing, matrimonial and debt matters. Evidence was submitted to us pointing out the inadequacies of the present access by prisoners to legal services on these matters, and we take the view that the clinics which we recommend will meet these needs.

8.66 We received evidence that there was a need for legal representation in prison disciplinary procedures. We know that the matter is under active consideration, and we do not make a recommendation about it. We are clear, however, that prison clinic solicitors should not be involved in disciplinary matters as this would necessarily involve them on one side of a dispute between staff and prisoners.

ADMINISTRATION OF LEGAL AID

8.67 Legal aid has been administered by the Law Society since its inception in 1950; and we do not doubt that this was the best arrangement that could have been made at that time. We had to consider, however, whether this arrangement was necessarily right for the future, especially bearing in mind the radically different system of operating legal aid which we have recommended.

8.68 It has been put to us that it is wrong in principle for the governing body of the legal profession to be responsible for supervising the payment of public funds to its own members. No-one has suggested that anything the Law Society has done is improper; nor have we found anything to suggest that. Rather the argument is that lawyers benefit financially from legal aid, and it is not proper that their professional organisation should be seen to be the body responsible for administering it. We think that the principle of this argument is sound.

8.69 In recommending, as we have, that solicitors rather than local legal aid committees should grant legal aid, we clearly open up a new possibility of abuse. It is a measure of our confidence in the high standard of professional integrity of Scottish solicitors that we are prepared so to recommend. Nevertheless, this recommendation makes it all the more important that those administering the scheme centrally should be seen to be independent of the profession. In addition, as we are recommending that the Supplementary Benefits Commission should cease to be responsible for the means test, we must provide an alternative monitoring authority so that any abuses, for instance by clients making false declarations of means to their solicitor, can be followed up.

8.70 The Law Society are diligent in their scrutiny of legal aid accounts submitted for payment by solicitors and advocates. The profession will testify to this. Nevertheless, we are not convinced that effective action is taken where particular solicitors' accounts regularly require extensive adjustment. Indeed, we were surprised to find that solicitors have not been required to sign the accounts they submit as being claimed in accordance with the relevant rules. The major shortcoming, however, in the present arrangement—and this may be no fault of the Law Society's—is that it does not give the managers of the legal aid fund sufficient independent authority. The legal aid fund has no voice of its own in relation to the setting of tables of fees, even though it is involved in substantial fee payments out of the fund. When a solicitor and the legal aid fund take an account to be settled by the Auditor of Court, the legal aid fund actually pays for the solicitor's attendance at the hearing whether his arguments are upheld or not. The management of legal aid from day to day is in the hands of the central committee; but while this committee is a statutory body it is a committee established and maintained by the Law Society, and the minutes of its meetings are circulated to all Council members. The committee is established under a scheme made by the Law Society and approved by the Secretary of State for Scotland, with the concurrence of the Treasury. While the power to make the scheme enabled the Society to have up to five lay members, the scheme only provides for two, both of whom are appointed by the Secretary of State.

8.71 Most of us came to the conclusion that the management of the legal aid fund is not sufficiently independent of the Law Society to assert effectively the interests of the public purse, where these interests conflict with those of the profession on a wider front than simply the scrutiny of the amount of individual accounts submitted for payment. We do not seek to blame the Law Society in any way. Their dual responsibility of simultaneously promoting the public interest and safeguarding the interests of their members is an unenviable one.

8.72 We have looked at the administration of legal aid not solely with a view to the efficient and accountable management of the scheme. It is important not only that value for money from legal aid should be monitored, but that it should be compared with alternative modes of provision, such as those which we have recommended in Chapter 7 should be developed. We draw this argument together more fully in Chapter 20.

8.73 Having reviewed the principles and practice of administration of legal aid by the Law Society, we **recommend** that legal aid should be administered by an independent authority in the form of the Legal Services Commission which we propose in Chapter 20.

8.74 In relation to legal aid the principal responsibilities of the Legal Services Commission should be:

(1) to keep the operation of the scheme under continuous critical review. This will mean, for example, pressing for amending legislation where necessary and keeping statistics to identify what the money is spent on, and where significant savings might accrue if some changes to the scheme, or to operating procedures, were introduced;

(2) possibly, to scrutinise accounts submitted for payment (but see paragraph 8.75), and to make payment;

(3) to experiment with new forms of delivering legal aid, or alternative legal services with a view to securing the most effective use of public funds;

(4) to carry out spot checks, and whatever investigations they think appropriate to identify and to deter abuse. This will mean calling for solicitors' files in a sample of cases and checking up on assisted persons' earnings. In appropriate cases it would be necessary to make formal complaints against lawyers under the complaints procedure which we discuss in Chapter 18.

(5) to establish machinery (the central committee referred to in paragraph 8.40) to rule on 'probabilis causa' and 'reasonableness' in cases referred by solicitors, and to promulgate any general guidance as may be needed on the interpretation of these tests.

This is, in effect, a blueprint for a new legal aid scheme. No doubt some of the detailed provisions currently in force will need to be retained, but the aim should be to reduce the 'fine print' to a minimum. Our proposals will enable much simplification—for example, there will be no need for 'emergency certificates'—but consolidation is overdue in any case. The work of the departmental working party on this topic to which we referred in paragraph 8.12 should enable rapid progress to be made in drawing up a new scheme.

Scrutiny of advocates' and solicitors' accounts

8.75 A particular point we have considered is whether the legal aid fund managers should employ staff to check accounts before authorising payment, or whether they should send accounts to the Department of the Auditor of Court which we recommend in Chapter 19. In that Chapter we set out the arguments on this issue, and record that we are equally divided among ourselves on which option to recommend.

OTHER METHODS OF PAYING FOR LEGAL SERVICES

8.76 In the following paragraphs we deal with schemes which are sometimes proposed as alternatives to State-financed legal aid. We have already stated our belief that such a legal aid system should be maintained, and we have recommended how the present system should be developed. We will, therefore, consider these alternative methods of providing and financing legal services as possible additions to the system we wish to see rather than as replacements for it.

A public defender

8.77 It was suggested to us in evidence that a public defender system should be considered as a means of providing legal services at public expense to those charged with criminal offences. A public defender would be a salaried State lawyer who would act for accused persons. The State would thus supply the service directly, rather than paying for the cost of private provision through legal aid. It is also claimed that a public defender system would be considerably cheaper than the existing criminal legal aid scheme. Though this claim cannot be substantiated in the absence of relevant experience, neither can it be refuted; and with annual expenditure on criminal legal aid now running at over £4 million it would be irresponsible to ignore a potential saving if this could be achieved without a reduction in the quality of the service to accused persons. On the other hand, the Law Society raised several strong objections to the concept of a public defender. They said, firstly, that it would destroy the accepted public view of the independence of the legal system; secondly, that it would interfere with the normal professional relationship of confidence between the client and the solicitor; and, thirdly, that it would be unlikely that the public would accept it. The Law Society also detailed a number of practical difficulties which they foresaw.

8.78 Those of us who visited Canada and the USA took the opportunity to look closely at several public defender systems in operation there. In some parts of North America the public defender system is long established, and in some instances is the only form of criminal legal aid. We found that the system was held in high regard by many members of both the judiciary and the private profession to whom we spoke. Those responsible for running the schemes claimed that the cost was less than that which would have been incurred if the work had been undertaken by private practitioners. However, we are aware of criticisms in some states that the public defender works too closely with the prosecutor and that the interests of administrative convenience and cheapness are sometimes put before the interests of the accused. We are also aware that some research projects are underway to examine in detail the existing schemes.

8.79 The evidence before us is finely balanced. On the one hand, there is evidence that a public defender system in other countries works well, is acceptable to the public, and is an economical way of providing legal aid. On the other hand, there are claims that the system provides second-class representation for at least some accused persons. The argument that a public defender service would interfere with a long standing principle of Scottish criminal justice, namely the right of the accused to decide on his own representative, is vitally important. One argument against the introduction is that, whether it was intended or not, the introduction of a public defender system would in fact cause the alternative availability of legal defence for accused persons on legal aid from the private profession to wither away. This is not a result we would wish, and it is a matter which should be watched carefully in any experiment. It is not, however, necessary to make the use of a public defender compulsory on any client, and we **recommend** that an accused person should be entitled to choose his own defence agent, using legal aid if he is eligible. At the same time, we see no reason why a public defender should not provide the duty solicitor service. Provided that this principle is adopted, the other arguments against a public defender can be tested by experience. If accused persons dislike the idea of the judge, prosecutor and defence agent all being employees of the State, they will choose solicitors in private practice. The same will apply if they feel that they cannot place the same trust and confidence in a public defender as in a private practitioner.

8.80 Any public defender scheme would need to provide for the separate representation of multiple accused persons in a single case who had conflicting interests. This can readily be done, for example, by providing that the public defender should act for only the first accused to approach him, or for none at all. Arrangements on these lines have been made elsewhere.

8.81 We reach the view then that a public defender is an acceptable way to provide State assistance to accused persons, provided that no-one is compelled to use his services. Such a service might be better value for money than criminal legal aid; and public defenders operate successfully in other parts of the world. There was, in fact, an office of 'public defensor' in the Edinburgh Police Court some years ago, and both the Morton and Guthrie Committees recommended the introduction of a limited public defensor service.[1] Indeed, the present law on legal aid permits salaried officials to be appointed by the Law Society to perform some or all of the functions of representation of accused persons. There is, however, no guarantee that a public defender would be acceptable to potential clients in Scotland, or that he would be better value for money than legal aid. We therefore **recommend** that there should be an experiment to assess whether or not a public defender system could with advantage be introduced in Scotland to run in parallel with the service provided by solicitors in private practice supported by legal aid.

8.82 The choice of area in which to conduct the experiment we recommend, and the length of time it should take, are matters for expert consideration; but we **recommend** that the following points be borne in mind by those constructing the experiment. Firstly, it will be extremely important to ensure that recruits to the public defender service are of high quality and sufficient in number to cope with the demands made on it. The experiment should, therefore, run for a sufficiently long period to allow service in the public defender's office to be an attractive part of a lawyer's career development. The payment of adequate salaries will also be important as there is little doubt that inadequate salaries would result in inadequate service and the ultimate failure of the experiment. Indeed, we consider that the experiment should if necessary be delayed until adequate staffing is possible. Secondly, it will be desirable for the staff involved to remain, if possible, for the duration of the experiment. A series of short-term appointments to any of the posts involved will not provide a fair or reliable test. Thirdly, a precise monitoring system will have to be established to measure both the use made of the service and its effectiveness; cost alone is not an adequate basis of assessment. Fourthly, to minimise potential impact on the private sector it might be necessary to mount an experiment of a limited size within a large area so that a reasonable proportion of defence work would remain available to solicitors in private practice. We think the experiment might best be held in an area in which the courts serve some quarter of a milllion people—some 5 per cent of the population of Scotland—which should provide a range of crime that is fairly representative of Scottish experience as a whole. Finally, we suggest that the public defender should not have a right of audience in the High Court but should be responsible for instructing advocates in the same way as do solicitors at present.

Contingency fees

8.83 An alternative to publicly funded legal services which is used in some states in the USA is the 'contingency fee'. This is an arrangement under which a lawyer acts for his client on the basis that if money is recovered the lawyer will receive an agreed proportion, while if the case is lost he will receive nothing. There are three main grounds on which such a system can be advocated:

(1) contingency fees enable pursuers who would not otherwise be able to afford it to take their claims to court;

(2) lawyers accepting cases on this basis will have a stake in winning the case and, therefore, will be more committed and more diligent in their preparation and presentation;

---

[1] The Morton Report: op. cit., page 33.
The Guthrie Report: op. cit., page 65.

(3) contingency fees might benefit lawyers by simplifying the administrative procedure by which they were paid and by increasing their earnings.

However, we do not believe that contingency fees, which are at present forbidden by professional rules, should be allowed. The temptation with such a basis of feeing would be for certain lawyers to concentrate only on strong cases and, in particular, on those cases with prospects of considerable sums being recovered. In Scotland, unlike in the USA, the loser is liable to meet his opponent's expenses, and a contingency fee arrangement would not change that. We also believe that it is a bad principle for the lawyer to have a direct financial interest in the outcome of the case. For example, under this arrangement a substantial proportion of money recovered will go to the lawyer, and as the lawyer pays all the costs of the case in return for his proportion of the money recovered he is exposed to strong temptation to settle the claim before incurring the heavy expense of preparing for trial and of trial itself although it may not be in his client's best interest to have a settlement made out of court. Moreover, as the legal aid scheme which we have recommended is available to all persons we do not consider that there is any need for contingency fee arrangements. The prohibition on contingency fees should, therefore, remain.

A contingency legal aid fund

8.84 It has also been suggested that a contingency legal aid fund could be set up which would retain the advantages of the contingency fee system but would avoid some of the major disadvantages. The scheme would involve setting up a fund, initially provided by the government, which would provide financial guarantees to pursuers who would otherwise be unable to afford to bring their cases to court. The proposal is that in the event of success the pursuer would contribute to the fund a proportion of the money he recovered with his legal costs being paid, in accordance with the usual practice, by the losing side. If the case were lost the fund would guarantee to meet the expenses of both parties. The administration costs of the scheme would be met by charging a registration fee to all applicants; and the money to pay expenses in unsuccessful cases would be built up from the contingency fee paid in successful cases out of the sum recovered. An applicant for aid from the fund would have to pass a test of 'probabilis causa'.

8.85 This scheme would avoid some of the disadvantages of the contingency fee system. The lawyer conducting the case would have no personal interest in the amount of money to be recovered but would receive his normal fee whether the case was won or lost. This, together with the need to show 'probabilis causa', would prevent vexatious litigation being encouraged by the scheme. However, the fund would provide an instrument for pursuers and not, in most cases, for defenders. Again, however, we do not believe that there will be any need for a contingency legal aid fund if our proposals for the further development of the civil legal aid scheme are accepted. We do not, therefore, recommend that a contingency legal aid fund should be established.

Speculative actions

8.86 There is in Scotland a long tradition of a lawyer acting on a 'speculative' basis. The arrangement here is that the lawyer will be paid his normal fee if the case is successful, and if the case is lost he will be paid nothing. Although they suffer from the disadvantages of offering no protection against the award of expenses and of being more readily useful to pursuers rather than defenders, speculative actions have traditionally been useful to pursuers who have a reasonable case but who have been excluded from legal aid on financial grounds. Their use in future, however, should be largely made unnecessary, given our proposals on legal aid. Nevertheless, the speculative action might remain attractive to small businesses excluded from the scope of legal aid although in our view businesses ought properly to obtain insurance to cover their needs as potential litigants. Speculative actions should, therefore, continue to be available to those who wish to use them.

A suitors' fund

8.87 A further proposal which we have considered is that there should be established a 'Suitors' Fund' which would compensate litigants who incur exceptional legal costs through no fault of their own.[1] Such a fund would reimburse a litigant for extra costs incurred as a result of:

(1) the reversal of a decision of a lower court on appeal;

(2) the illness or death of a trial judge; or

(3) the need to determine an unsettled point of law of public importance.

Litigants in receipt of legal aid would benefit from the suitors' fund only if this involved their being relieved of the need to pay part of a contribution. We do not believe that such a system should be available for cases in which the decision of a lower court is reversed on appeal. The conduct of the case is under the control of the litigant, and its complexity and the risk of an appeal can be assessed beforehand. Nor do we think that such a system should be available should a case have to be re-heard (for example, because the judge died during the course of the hearing). Insurance protection can be, and on occasion is, obtained against such risks; and cases need not invariably be re-started if a judge is unable to see it to a conclusion. We do not, therefore, recommend that a suitors' fund be established.

Legal insurance schemes

8.88 Insurance to meet legal expenses is available in a number of countries including some where legal aid is not available. In recent years some insurance companies have been offering legal costs insurance in this country to individuals as well as to companies, in addition to the more traditional insurance cover for personal injury and damage to property. Currently, the annual premium for such cover is around £15 for general and consumer (excluding motor) protection which compares very favourably with the contribution to the legal aid fund for which many people will be liable in terms of our recommendations.

8.89 Legal services for groups are perhaps more common in North America than here, although it is common for trade unions and motoring organisations to provide 'group legal services' in particular circumstances as a benefit of membership. These schemes are usually limited to assistance in connection with employment matters and motoring offences respectively. There is ample scope

[1] This proposal is published as an appendix in *CLAF: Proposals for a Contingency Legal Aid Fund:* Justice, 1978.

for other groups to make similar provision for their members. A development of this facility allows members of the group to pay a supplementary subscription (or premium) entitling them to a range of benefits, for example, a free half-hour interview with a solicitor, or reduced fees from members of a panel of solicitors. In such schemes the group effectively use their membership to negotiate special terms for the supply of services to members. The schemes vary greatly in the precise rules and benefits, and in North America they are sometimes financed by employers as a 'fringe benefit'.[1]

Group interest and public interest litigation

8.90 One way to make certain kinds of litigation more readily affordable is to provide a method whereby all those with a similar grievance can unite to bring a single court action. Classes of potential litigants, such as all those who bought motor cars with a common defect, or residents with a common complaint about faulty housing construction on their estate, could thus make common cause without relying on a 'test case' which does not always provide a satisfactory solution. This approach involves complex questions of substantive Scots law which we are not equipped to resolve. We understand, however, that the Scottish Consumer Council have established a working party, comprising both lawyers and laymen, to study the whole issue and to make recommendations. The report of this working party should provide a basis for further consideration of what could, and should, be done. This is an important issue and deserves such thorough treatment. If group actions become admissible, the question of how legal aid might be made available to such litigants will need to be considered.

8.91 One other use for legal aid in Scotland could be to provide opportunities to test adequately legal issues of public importance. This could be done on appeal or even at first instance. We have been told that many important parts of the law of Scotland have never been tested thoroughly in court because of a general unwillingness to enter into expensive litigation, possibly for little personal benefit. If Scots law is to develop on sound and tested lines, there is an argument that, in cases where an important legal point is at issue, judges should be empowered to award free legal aid to either party or to both in order to facilitate appeals. We have not been able to consider all the implications of this issue but we **recommend** that it should be considered by the Department of Legal Affairs which we propose in Chapter 20.

---

[1] A fuller discussion of such schemes is in A. A. Paterson—'Paying for Legal Services' in *Journal of the Law Society of Scotland, 1979 Volume 24, No. 6.*

RECOMMENDATIONS

			Paragraph
The scope of civil legal aid	R8.1	Legal aid for advice and assistance and for representation in civil matters should only be available to help citizens to assert or protect their rights, and not to assist them in arranging their affairs for the benefit of themselves or others.	8.17
	R8.2	Legal aid should be available for representation at a tribunal, but only if the client would otherwise be unable to follow the proceedings and if there is no lay representation available locally which is recognised by the tribunal as suitable.	8.21
	R8.3	A tribunal should have power to grant legal aid where it considers that the matter before it gives rise, or is likely to give rise, to a substantial point of law.	8.21
	R8.4	All tribunals at which a substantial point of law is likely to arise should include a legally qualified member.	8.21
	R8.5	Legal aid should be available to pursue or defend an action of defamation.	8.22
	R8.6	The civil legal aid scheme should have no upper eligibility limit of disposable income, and should have a scale of contributions which rises sharply with income and is reviewed annually.	8.26
	R8.7	No account should be taken of capital in assessing eligibility for civil legal aid, or in computing the contribution payable.	8.27
	R8.8	Civil legal aid should not be available to businessmen or traders for litigations relating to a business or trade, even if the business or trade is owned by an individual, this exclusion to be in addition to the exclusion of bodies corporate or unincorporate.	8.28

			Paragraph
Liability for expenses	R8.9	The expenses of the successful opponent of a legally-aided party should be recovered from the unused balance of the legally-aided party's contribution; to the extent that they exceed any such balance, they should be met by the legal aid fund.	8.29
	R8.10	The right of recovery from the legal aid fund should extend to individuals and one-man businesses, but not to litigants who are bodies corporate or unincorporate unless such a body can satisfy the court that inability to recover from the legal aid fund would result in severe hardship to individuals.	8.29
An integrated scheme	R8.11	Civil legal aid and legal advice and assistance should be integrated into a single scheme, which should simply be a legal aid scheme.	8.31
	R8.12	The assessment of an applicant's eligibility for civil legal aid and the setting of a maximum contribution should be done by the solicitor to whom the client applies.	8.32
Collecting contributions	R8.13	Where contributions are to be paid by instalments to the central administration every effort should be made to introduce alternative and convenient methods of payment, such as by post office giro.	8.36
	R8.14	It should always be possible for the solicitor and client by mutual agreement to make their own arrangements for payment of the contribution direct to the solicitor.	8.37
Assessing the merits of proposed litigation	R8.15	(i) Where the solicitor has assured himself that the 'probabilis causa' and reasonableness tests are satisfied, he should be able to grant legal aid himself;	8.40

			Paragraph
		(ii) Where the solicitor is in doubt he should refer the application to a statutory independent committee to be set up by the body responsible for administering legal aid;	8.40
		(iii) Where the solicitor thinks the tests are not satisfied he should have no power to refuse legal aid, but should have to refer the application to the committee, unless the client is satisfied, on the solicitor's advice, that such a referral would be hopeless.	
Recovery of expenses	R8.16	The present rule, whereby the legal aid fund undertakes the recovery of all the expenses awarded to successful assisted persons, should be changed.	8.45
Sums recovered	R8.17	While the legal aid fund should still look to sums recovered to defray its expenses when recovery of expenses from the other side is difficult, the assisted person should have first claim on a part of any sum recovered.	8.47
The statutory deduction from civil legal aid fees	R8.18	The ten per cent deduction from civil legal aid fees should be abolished.	8.49
Legal aid for accused persons	R8.19	Legal aid should be provided to enable all accused persons to receive initial advice on how to plead and, where appropriate, to be given help in the preparation of a plea in mitigation.	8.51
	R8.20	The criteria for granting criminal legal aid to defend a summary prosecution should be laid down in statute. Legislation should specify the offences where there is no risk of imprisonment or where the risk is so small as not to justify a grant of criminal legal aid.	8.52–8.54

			Paragraph
	R8.21	Authority to grant, but not refuse, criminal legal aid should be delegated to sheriff clerks in suitable cases, provided that the clerks receive adequate training for the purpose.	8.57
	R8.22	Where a decision on an application for criminal legal aid has to be taken by a judge, it should be done in chambers.	8.57
	R8.23	Accused persons who receive criminal legal aid, and are tried and found guilty, should be liable to contribute to the cost of their defence.	8.59
Duty solicitor	R8.24	All accused persons in custody should be entitled to see a duty solicitor and before they do so they should have full details of any crime alleged against them.	8.62
	R8.25	Court advisory committees (see R15.2) should prepare duty plans to ensure the attendance of solicitors to provide legal services for accused persons.	8.63
Legal advice in prison	R8.26	Public funds should pay for regular legal clinics in prisons.	8.64
Administration of legal aid	R8.27	Legal aid should be administered by an independent authority in the form of the Legal Services Commission which we propose in Chapter 20.	8.73–8.74
Choice of defence agent	R8.28	An accused person should be entitled to choose his own defence agent, using legal aid if he is eligible.	8.79
Public defender	R8.29	There should be an experiment to assess whether or not a public defender system could with advantage be introduced in Scotland to run in parallel with the service provided by solicitors in private practice supported by legal aid. The points detailed in paragraph 8.82 should be borne in mind in the design of the experiment.	8.81–8.82

			Paragraph
Public interest litigation	R8.30	The Department of Legal Affairs should consider the use of legal aid to facilitate appeals where an important legal point is at issue.	8.91

PART IV

IMPROVING THE DELIVERY OF LEGAL SERVICES

CHAPTER 9

CONVEYANCING

Introduction

9.1 In this Chapter we look in some detail at certain aspects of the services which are provided in connection with the process of buying and selling houses in Scotland. Although most of the services are provided by solicitors there are others involved, particularly the building societies and chartered surveyors, and we have considered questions of valuation and surveys of houses. In our examination of these matters we had it in mind to see where it might be possible for the process to be made simpler, cheaper and better.

EVIDENCE AND PUBLIC OPINION

Evidence received on conveyancing

9.2 Our remit specifically charged us to consider 'the rules which prevent persons who are neither advocates nor solicitors from undertaking conveyancing . . . on behalf of other persons'. The reference in our remit to the 'monopoly' of the legal profession in conveyancing can be seen as a recognition of the importance of this issue to many members of the public and to the profession. That conveyancing business is important to the profession was confirmed in our survey of solicitors' remuneration. In this survey, some 33 per cent of the gross fee income of all firms who responded was derived from domestic conveyancing, while a further 5 per cent came from commission on sale of heritable property.[1] Buying a house, as is often pointed out by the legal profession, is the largest and most important single purchase most of us ever make. In another of our surveys, conveyancing, not surprisingly perhaps, was the most often quoted single reason why people seek the services of a solicitor.[2] This same survey suggests that 32 per cent of those who have recently consulted a solicitor last went on conveyancing business. It is also of interest that a substantial proportion (37 per cent in 1979) of the complaints made each year to the Law Society against solicitors were in connection with conveyancing matters. We should make clear, however, that we received no evidence at all from commercial or public bodies to suggest that their needs for conveyancing services were not adequately met; and we have not, therefore, investigated the provision of legal services in the field of commercial conveyancing.

9.3 In the evidence we received, the main weight of criticism of legal services in relation to conveyancing related to the high cost of legal fees in the buying and selling of houses. Delay was not seen as a great problem. The evidence also pointed to the need to simplify the procedures, documents and language used in conveyancing. The principal argument advanced for making conveyancing simpler was to reduce costs; but it was also argued that if domestic conveyancing were simpler, it would be easier for clients to understand what was involved.

[1] See Table 3.2 and Appendix 7.
[2] See Appendix 4.

Indeed, some of those giving evidence specifically wanted 'do-it-yourself' conveyancing to be more readily possible than it now is. Frequently, the intention behind the evidence was to enable the client to become more involved in the transaction, to improve communications between solicitor and client, and perhaps to reduce the amount of work for which a solicitor was needed.

9.4 We also received evidence about the 'conveyancing monopoly' enjoyed by lawyers. The principal argument used in defence of the monopoly was that it safeguards the public, whereas those who attack it argued mainly that greater competition would be in the public interest and would lead to reduced costs. Before dealing with the monopoly in detail, however, there are a number of matters which we think it would be helpful to consider as a preliminary.

Public attitudes

9.5 We did not feel that the evidence we had received was necessarily a reflection of public attitudes to conveyancing. Inevitably perhaps, the evidence told us more about what clients had found unsatisfactory in the services they had received than about the services which solicitors had given satisfactorily. Accordingly, we commissioned a survey into consumer attitudes to conveyancing. Full details of this survey are given in Appendix 5. In briefest summary, however, the facet of house purchase which attracted the greatest criticism concerned the valuation surveys instructed by building societies. Frequently a number of potential buyers of a house wish to make an offer for it, but first require to be sure that a necessary mortgage will be available. Several building societies may be approached and all will commission a valuation survey on the property in question to be satisfied that mortgage facilities should be provided. These multiple valuations were widely seen by the respondents to our survey as unnecessary. A number of respondents objected that although they were paying for the valuations, the results were not made available to them. Both buyers and sellers were unhappy with the practice whereby prospective buyers bid 'blind' against each other, whereas the less common practice of the seller simply asking a fixed price was almost universally praised (even by those sellers who had actually received more than their asking price for their property). The law on conveyancing was felt to need simplifying; and in conjunction with this, the involvement of solicitors in the process was felt by a substantial number to require change. The contractually binding effect of the exchange of missives, however, was thought to be good, and was occasionally contrasted favourably with the English system of 'offers subject to contract'.

Satisfaction with the service provided

9.6 Table 9.1 shows how many clients were satisfied with the services of their solicitor. Seventy-seven per cent of solicitors' clients said that they would use the same solicitor again in buying or selling a house.

Attitudes to costs

9.7 For a large number of people, the total account of fees and outlays incurred when either buying or selling a house was higher at the end of the day than they had expected. Only 40 per cent of respondents said that they had correctly anticipated what the costs would be. Purchasers found the solicitors' professional fees even less reasonable than any other of the costs incurred, none of which, of course, was popular; and this was the case even among people who were not dissatisfied with the services provided by their solicitors. Dissatisfaction with solicitors' charges was even greater among people selling property; and this dissatisfaction was about the same as that expressed by the clients of estate agents over their charges, even though the services of estate agents were more often criticised. However, many people seemed confused about the distinction between solicitors' professional fees and the other charges connected with the 'legal aspects' of the buying and selling transactions paid by solicitors on behalf of their clients (stamp duty, for example, and charges paid for recording the disposition or conveyance). It may be that solicitors' accounts were insufficiently clear, or that people were not aware that these charges constituted items separate from the solicitors' professional fees. What is not in doubt is that the costs incurred in buying and selling properties were generally felt to be too high, and this was so largely irrespective of the opinion people had of the quality of the services they had obtained.

TABLE 9.1: Client satisfaction with solicitors' services – domestic conveyancing*

Respondents agreeing that:	Proportion (%) of clients who were	
	Buyers (N=334)	*Sellers* (N=142)
The solicitor gave enough advice	84	87
The solicitor did enough	83	82
The solicitor kept them informed enough	80	85
The solicitor was competent	92	88
They would use the same solicitor again	77	77

*Sources: Appendix 5, Tables D1–5.

Summary of evidence of areas of satisfaction and dissatisfaction

9.8 Although some of the evidence was conflicting, particularly on matters such as the 'conveyancing monopoly', clients seemed to be broadly satisfied with the quality of service they received from their solicitors. They were also satisfied with the decisiveness and finality of the exchange of missives. On the other hand, there was some dissatisfaction with the complexity of legal procedures involved in the transfer of title; with the conveyancing monopoly; with the cost, both in fees and outlays, to sellers and purchasers; and, especially among first-time buyers, with the extent to which the solicitor keeps the client informed. We have, therefore, examined certain aspects of the process of buying and selling houses in Scotland to see where it might be made simpler, cheaper and more comprehensible.

CONVEYANCING PROCEDURES

9.9 The work of the solicitor in Scotland in connection with the purchase and sale of a house is not confined to carrying out the strictly legal work of conveyancing proper—that is, the preparation of the deeds or writs required to transfer the title or legal ownership of the property from the seller to the purchaser, or to constitute or discharge a security over the property. To a much greater extent than his English counterpart, the solicitor in Scotland is also engaged in the negotiations leading up to the purchase and sale. Indeed, solicitors may now describe themselves as 'Solicitors and Estate Agents'. There are, of course, estate agents in Scotland; but in the house buying and selling business they are only in recent times, and in certain areas, providing a service on a scale which is in competition with that traditionally provided by solicitors.

9.10 In Scotland a contract for the sale of heritable property is constituted by a probative written offer and acceptance. The most common method of arranging such a contract is through missives of sale, often simply referred to as missives. Missives generally take the form of an exchange of letters, by which an offer to buy or sell is made and accepted by the parties involved or by their agents. Completion of this process constitutes a binding contract and thereafter the seller's solicitor has to produce his client's title deeds to the purchaser's solicitor who will then examine them to make sure that the seller owns and is entitled to sell the property and that his client, the purchaser, can receive a valid title. An Act of the Scottish Parliament in 1617 established the Register of Sasines, a public register of deeds relating to heritable property, now kept by the Keeper of the Registers in Edinburgh. It is a statutory requirement that to obtain a real right in land in Scotland the relevant documents must be recorded in the Register of Sasines. The recording of a deed does not, however, guarantee the title to the property, so that any interested party (for example a purchaser) or his agent must examine the various deeds making up the title to satisfy himself that there is a good title. Examining the seller's title and preparing the documents to transfer the title to the purchaser so that it can be recorded in the Register is one of the major elements in the time taken by the solicitor acting for a purchaser. To eliminate this time-consuming examination without leaving the purchaser or a lender on the security of the property open to unacceptable risk would clearly be a most worthwhile single contribution to making the process of buying a house simpler and less costly.

Registration of title

9.11 A committee under the chairmanship of Lord Reid reported in 1963[1] in favour of the introduction in Scotland of a system of registration of title whereby on the first subsequent occasion of a sale of property a once and for all examination of the relevant deeds would be carried out by officials of the Department of the Registers of Scotland. The Keeper of the Registers would thereafter issue to the new proprietor a certificate of title guaranteed by the State. This proposed procedure would obviate the need for examination of bundles of deeds each time a property changed hands and, as a result, the process of buying and selling houses should become cheaper as well as simpler. A further committee in 1969 under the chairmanship of Professor Henry[2] devised a detailed scheme for implementing the recommendations of Lord Reid's committee and a pilot scheme was instituted by the Department of the Registers of Scotland to test the proposals. In April 1979 the Land Registration (Scotland) Act, which provides for a system of registration of titles and the issue of State guaranteed land certificates, was enacted. We understand that the introduction of the scheme for registration will be phased over a period of 9 or 10 years, beginning in January 1981. Once the scheme is introduced in a particular area registration will be compulsory on the first sale of a property thereafter. Properties registered in the new Land Register will be identified on an ordnance survey map and details of matters affecting the title will be recorded on a computer system. When the

[1] *Registration of Title to Land in Scotland,* (Cmnd. 2032): HMSO, 1963.
[2] *Scheme for the Introduction and Operation of Registration of Title to Land in Scotland* (Cmnd. 4137): HMSO, 1969.

Keeper has completed registration he will issue to the purchaser a land certificate being a copy of the relevant details of the property in the title sheet of the property in the Land Register. Although houses are said to change hands every six or seven years on average, many properties—and particularly those held by local authorities or large landed estates—may be held without change of ownership for very long periods. This means that the present system will continue in use alongside the registration of title system unless and until registration is made universally compulsory.

9.12 The principal advantage of the Land Register will be that a title recorded in it will be guaranteed by the State through the Keeper, and the purchaser or his agent will only need to check the title sheet of the property in the Land Register from the entry describing the ownership of the seller (or the person from whom he has derived right by, for example, a will). The Reid committee suggested that solicitors' fees might be reduced by as much as 25 per cent with registration of title. Any such reduction would be welcomed but we have had no evidence to show what the proper reduction would be. We have, however, been made aware that the work involved on a first registration will be much greater than on subsequent registrations, both for the purchaser or his solicitor and for the staff of the Land Register. The land certificate when issued by the Keeper will impose much greater obligations on him than the recording under the present system, but we hope that the registration charges under the registration of title system will not be such as to negate any reduction in legal fees. We appreciate that the Department of Registers is required to operate generally on a self-funding basis, but we **recommend** that any extra cost incurred on first registration of properties over what might be charged for recording under the present system should be borne by the State.

Overriding interests

9.13 At the present time as part of the examination of the title, a solicitor will have the Register of Sasines searched to check that no adverse interests are recorded against the property. There may, however, be a number of overriding interests affecting the property which would not be disclosed by such a search. Such overriding interests could include, for example, leases, public rights of way and various orders affecting the property made by central and local government. Under the registration of title system, the land certificate will include the burdens and conditions in the title other than those which have clearly become obsolete, and it will be possible to take account of some matters which could not be noted under the present system. The Land Register will also record any entries (presently kept in the separate Register of Inhibitions and Adjudications) which record deeds or processes which legally restrict the owner of a property from disposing of it. At present a separate search of this Register is required. The land certificate will not, however, disclose all overriding interests and we understand this would not be practically possible. We do **recommend,** however, that as many of these interests as possible should be shown on the land certificate.

Letters of obligation

9.14 Under the existing system the period which elapses between the date of receipt of a deed in the General Register of Sasines and the date of completion of the registration process varies between seven and nine weeks. At the date of settling a property transaction there is, therefore, a period which will not be covered by a search of the Register of Sasines. During this period, a purchaser or lender is at risk as the seller could, at least theoretically, have sold the property to someone else, or could have granted securities or created burdens over it, or a third party may have registered a writ inhibiting the sale of the property, and none of these actions be disclosed by the earlier search. Such risks are normally covered by a personal undertaking given by the seller's solicitor which is known as a letter of obligation. This states that down to the date of recording of the disposition in favour of the purchaser (that is, the final record of title in the purchaser's name) there will be no writs or charges granted in respect of the property contrary to the interests of the purchaser (except in so far as these may have been granted by him). On introduction of registration of title it is estimated that the first registration may take as long as five to seven weeks to complete but in subsequent transactions the period should be very considerably shortened. In practical terms the risk period will eventually be reduced to under 24 hours and it may be, therefore, that letters of obligation will no longer be required.

9.15 The introduction of the Land Register will go a considerable way towards streamlining the conveyancing system in Scotland and towards meeting some of the criticisms which have been made of the present system. The proposed scheme is not, however, without complications but we do not feel it is appropriate for us to criticise details of the scheme, particularly as it is not yet in operation and some of the details are still being worked out. We do, however, **recommend** that there should be set up a Standing Committee appointed by, and reporting to, the Secretary of State for Scotland which should have responsibility for overseeing the new system, recommending such improvements and simplifications as seem desirable, and considering the longer term operation of the system. The Standing Committee should comprise members of the Land Register staff, of the legal profession, of other related professions and of the general public. Though the Register of Sasines and Register of Inhibitions and Adjudications will need to continue in use alongside the Land Register we believe that registration of title should be made compulsory soon after the Land Register is completely phased in to ensure that the two systems run in parallel for the minimum feasible period of time. We **recommend** that the Standing Committee should advise when this should be done and that where the registration is made compulsory for all properties and is undertaken because of this and without any change in ownership the full costs of such a registration should be borne by the State.

9.16 With the introduction of registration of title we believe there may be possibilities of further reform of the system of transferring property in Scotland. Once the State is guaranteeing the title recorded in the Land Register it may in time be possible with the development of computers to devise a more modern system of transferring property linked to a number of computer terminals throughout the country. We therefore **recommend** that the Standing Committee proposed in paragraph 9.15 above should be charged specifically with the duty of examining the feasibility of introducing a simpler system of transferring property which might be provided by the State at a much reduced cost to the public.

Log-book system

9.17 One suggestion which has been made to us in evidence, but which we do not feel should be pursued, is that conveyancing should be done on a 'log-book' system. The proposal depends on an analogy between, say, a motor car or a boat and a house when it comes to the processes involved in changing ownership. It is said that some people may pay less or no more for a house than for a car or a boat and that, although cars or boats being moveable may be more easily stolen, the change of ownership is effected by a much simpler process than that for a house. The suggestion is that there should be a registration form which would serve as a certificate of identity for the property and also as a certificate of ownership for the proprietor. This form would be forwarded to a register of titles for alteration and stamping together with a form signed by both parties when a change of ownership was being made. If a mortgage on the property were involved the lender would hold the certificate. However, such a system could not extend to all properties. Ownership of a house or flat (apartment) includes ownership rights in the land on which the building stands and consequently involves a variety of relationships with other proprietors. When objections of this kind were raised with those who proposed the system, they suggested that the simplified system should apply only to certain types of property which would not involve, for instance, the complicated relationships which exist where there is common ownership of parts of a property, for example, in a tenement block of flats or apartments. We do not accept that such a simplification should be available only in the case of certain properties; and, in any case, we believe that the Land Register will meet most of the criticisms of the present system made by those who advocate a 'log-book' system and will provide a more comprehensive means of simplifying the conveyancing process.

Simplification of deeds etc.

9.18 Reform of the title registration system is only one approach to simplifying conveyancing. The language and the nature of the documents and practices used in conveyancing were criticised by various people in evidence to us. A chartered surveyor spoke of 'archaic methods of description' and 'complex, repetitive and old fashioned language' used in dispositions. A professor of law said that 'the whole practice of conveyancing is really anachronistic and must be updated', and he drew particular attention to the lengthy, repetitive form of deeds and documents which he considered wholly unnecessary. There were several suggestions that standardised forms of documents should be brought into use. We wholly approve of this concern to simplify. Not only are simpler documents easier for laymen to understand, they also reduce the time it takes for a lawyer to understand what they contain. While we are aware that there are pitfalls in redrafting descriptions or conditions in older documents into modern language, we nevertheless **recommend** that the legislature and the profession should ensure that the documents used for conveyancing are always in as straightforward English as possible.

9.19 As well as making documents simpler there is scope for a measure of standardisation. For example, the Scottish Legal Action Group, suggesting that standardised forms of missives should be introduced, said that:

> 'Missives in fact vary so little that many firms have pro forma offers for property, where only the essentials . . . are left blank. While such forms may vary in wording and layout between firms their purpose and effect are almost identical in every case.'

The Scottish Legal Action Group suggest that recommended forms should be provided by statute but that the use of such forms should not be compulsory. We agree that such forms should not be compulsory mainly because of the risk that important matters peculiar to a particular transaction may be overlooked when a standard form is used, particularly by a layman.

9.20 Recommended standard forms or styles need not of course be statutory. Indeed, the Law Society from time to time in their monthly Journal recommend styles or forms of various types of legal documents; and many others are incorporated in legal textbooks and are provided as part of teaching materials in the law faculties at universities. We hope that this will be continued in the new Diploma in Legal Practice and also that the materials provided for Diploma students will be readily accessible to all users. We **recommend** that a specialist committee with lay representation should be appointed to review the scope for simplification and standardisation of legal documents used in conveyancing.

THE LAWYERS' MONOPOLY

9.21 We turn now to the 'lawyers' monopoly'. It is laid down in statute that only practising solicitors or advocates may carry out conveyancing on behalf of another person for a fee.[1] Advocates do not now normally engage in conveyancing work; such involvement as they have generally arises in cases concerning a dispute about title. The precise restriction or 'monopoly' is on the drawing or preparation for a fee of any writ relating to heritable (or moveable) property. The Law Society informed us that this monopoly appears to have originated in England in connection with a tax payable on the annual certificate or licence required by solicitors who carried on conveyancing business. Legislation in 1804 applying to English solicitors provided that only solicitors paying the tax should prepare deeds for reward. This monopoly appears to have been extended to Scotland by the Stamp Act of 1870 and has since been continued by a number of statutes. Prior to 1870 any person would have been entitled to practise in Scotland as a conveyancer.

9.22 Three important points should be made about the nature of the monopoly Firstly, there is nothing in the monopoly which prevents a person doing his or her own conveyancing. A person can prepare a disposition in his or her own favour, have it stamped and sign the warrant of registration to enable the deed to be registered in the Register of Sasines. Secondly, as we have already noted, the statutory provisions prohibit a person who is not a solicitor or an advocate from preparing a writ relating to heritable or moveable property (with certain specific exceptions) only where such a writ is prepared for a fee, gain or reward, or the expectation of some reward. Thirdly, the monopoly has regard only to the drawing or preparing of a writ relating to heritable or moveable property, which means, in the case of domestic conveyancing, the preparation of the disposition by the seller in favour of the purchaser, the discharge of any existing standard security and the drawing of any new standard security. There is no monopoly with regard to negotiating the sale or purchase of a property, the exchange of missives, the making of searches in the Register of Sasines or the various other steps involved in the purchase or sale of a house. Having said this, however, we should say that it appears that solicitors have a virtual monopoly in all conveyancing work after the completion of the missives. The Keeper of the Registers has told us that it is very rare indeed for a writ to be presented for

[1] *Solicitors (Scotland) Act 1933*, Section 39.

recording by anyone other than a solicitor. The difficulties and complexities of the legal procedures on which we have already commented, and the requirement for personal undertakings to be given in letters of obligation, have all helped to maintain a monopoly for solicitors in conveyancing work which is in practice more extensive than that conferred by statute.

9.23 Evidence to us on the monopoly question came mainly from the professional bodies and others who might be expected to have a certain amount of specialist knowledge in the field. The principal arguments in defence of the monopoly—and indeed in favour of an extension of it—came from the Law Society and the Scottish Law Agents Society. The Law Society said to us that the statutory provisions which comprise the conveyancing monopoly exist now, if not in their origins, to protect the public. They are designed to ensure that the client's affairs are dealt with by trained and skilled persons and that all writs relating to heritable property are properly prepared in order to maintain an accurate Sasine Register. The Law Society pointed out that members of the legal profession in Scotland are subject to strict regulations in matters such as entrance qualifications, training and discipline; they are subject to the ethics and standards of the profession; and they are bound to comply with the Scottish Solicitors' Accounts Rules which lay down rules for the depositing and safekeeping of clients' funds. Further, the Scottish Solicitors' Guarantee Fund, financed by members of the Law Society, is available to compensate members of the public who suffer loss arising out of any solicitor's dishonesty; and, in addition, solicitors are now covered by compulsory professional indemnity insurance. In addition to what they regard as extensive safeguards for the public in the existing monopoly, the Law Society proposed to us that the conveyancing monopoly should be extended to cover all steps in a conveyancing transaction, including the preparation of missives whether of sale or purchase or in respect of the letting of property.

9.24 The Scottish Law Agents Society told us that the solicitor has what they call a 'quasi monopoly' with regard to conveyancing because he is a recognised trained specialist in his subject. Like the Law Society, they believe that there is a need for a clear and unambiguous land register and they say that this demands a degree of technicality, specialism and integrity in the preparation of deeds that can only be provided by solicitors. They claim that the special rights of solicitors are essential in the interests of consumer protection; and they also urge the extension of the monopoly to include missives. They state that at present, purchasers can enter into contracts for the purchase of property through estate agents who are acting primarily for the seller. The solicitor has to look at any proposed sale or purchase of property in the context of the client's whole affairs; and he must, therefore, consider whether the client should buy or sell at all, and, if so, on what financial basis and under what conditions.

9.25 The principal evidence submitted to us which argued against the monopoly came from the Glasgow Law Services Study Group, the Scottish Legal Action Group and the Labour Party (Scottish Council). The Law Services Study Group said that the professional monopoly in conveyancing was unjustifiable provided that other persons undertaking such work had attained a sufficient level of competence in this field. They recommended that a code of conduct should be established which would impose specific duties on all persons buying or selling property on behalf of clients. Their view was that while examination of title requires a specialist knowledge of property law and procedure and should be carried out only by persons who have obtained adequate competence in these areas, such persons need not necessarily have acquired qualification in other branches of law and thus need not necessarily be lawyers. This Group were not in favour of extending the monopoly to include missives. They stated that the main requirements on the part of an agent completing a missive were: (a) a basic understanding of the law of contract and of property law; (b) experience of the property market; and (c) ethical integrity. They argued that such requiiements were not exclusively the preserve of people possessing a formal legal qualification.

9.26 The Scottish Legal Action Group suggested that there should be no real need to maintain the existing monopoly in the drafting of writs for gain, but their argument appears to be based on the introduction of a system of Registration of Title. They wish to admit to the monopoly 'suitably trained lay persons subject to the supervision of the Scottish Legal Services Authority' (their recommended supervisory body for legal services). The Scottish Legal Action Group were not in favour of missives being brought into the solicitors' monopoly; but in view of the fact that missives conclusively determine the terms of a contract they suggested to us that any agents who may deal with missives should only be permitted to do so when they have obtained permission from the Scottish Legal Services Authority who would be required to examine the competence of such agents and ensure that they had sufficient professional indemnity insurance for the amount of such work as they undertake.

9.27 The Labour Party (Scottish Council) stated that:

> 'It is clear from experience with other agencies that conveyancing services can be provided more cheaply, and that these services are professionally competent and backed by sufficient guarantees in the event of mistakes being made. The solicitor's monopoly on conveyancing is *not* therefore in the public interest.'

The Council go on to recommend that the field of conveyancing should be opened up to other groups who meet certain prescribed standards.

9.28 Finally, the Scottish Labour Party advocated that there should be a national legal agency within which there would be a housing agency staffed by solicitors who would act in the buying and selling and conveyancing of private houses. Private practitioners would continue to act within the field but 'unqualified third parties would not be entitled to so act'. The Scottish Labour Party were of the view that by creating a free market with the importation of cut price conveyancing and unqualified third parties acting as conveyancers the law would be brought into disrepute and the resulting level of service would not be in the public interest. Their argument was, therefore, not against the solicitors' monopoly, but only against solicitors in private practice having the sole right to undertake conveyancing for a fee.

9.29 The arguments in favour of the monopoly are that it protects clients' monies; that it provides a sure and dependable land register; and that the best service to both buyers and sellers is provided by properly qualified lawyers. The arguments against the monopoly are that conveyancing does not require a full legal training (although adequate training would be required as a safeguard for the public interest); and that the monopoly tends to lead to higher fees and, therefore, to higher costs to the public.

Our assessment of the monopoly

9.30 We have approached this question from the standpoint that any monopoly to be justified must be shown to be clearly in the public interest. Indeed, the Law Society stated this general principle in evidence to us. The public interest is not, of course, restricted to the interests of individual clients, and the argument about the value of a dependable register of titles rightly recognises that. We assess the strength of public interest in the monopoly in terms of the arguments for and against its retention.

9.31 It has been suggested to us that the monopoly should not only be retained but should actually be extended so that the missives stage of the purchase and sale of heritable property would be brought within the monopoly. If this argument were sound we should have received evidence that the present arrangement was in practice seriously detrimental to those who used agents other than solicitors to conclude missives on their behalf. Although, in our survey,[1] clients expressed greater satisfaction with the services of solicitors than with those of estate agents, the dissatisfaction with estate agents does **not** amount to a case for depriving them of the right to conclude missives. Many clients no doubt share the views of the Law Society and the Law Agents Society that they should consult a solicitor about the whole business of buying and selling houses, but that is no reason for compelling everyone to do so. We conclude, therefore, that it would be wrong to extend the present monopoly so as to bring within it the missives, and we so **recommend**.

9.32 It has been stated to us in evidence by the Law Society and by the Scottish Law Agents Society that the monopoly is necessary to ensure a dependable register of titles in Scotland. There are two elements to this proposition: firstly, that the skill of solicitors ensures a reliable register; and, secondly, that no other person could acquire this level of skill without qualifying as a solicitor. The 1979 report by the Keeper of the Registers records that 29,934 writs were withdrawn (11·4 per cent of the intake) either at the agent's request (4,533) or because of errors. These figures do not include some 7,500 writs returned for amendment before entering the register. While not all the errors represent fault on the part of solicitors, the fact is that most do; and we find these figures a cause for disquiet. They suggest to us that the dependability of the Sasine Register is at least partly the result of diligent scrutiny by the Keeper's staff, and cannot be wholly ascribed to the high standard of professional competence displayed by solicitors.

9.33 It might, nevertheless, be argued that persons other than solicitors would commit an unacceptably larger number of errors. We agree with the evidence submitted to us that high standards of competence should be required of anyone who wishes to undertake conveyancing for gain. We do not accept, however, that a person needs to be a solicitor to become a competent conveyancer. Largely because of the present monopoly, of course, few persons other than solicitors are currently sufficiently competent, though some non-legal staff in solicitors' firms may be (and formal instruction for them is envisaged in Chapter 17). Many of the steps in a conveyancing transaction are undeniably of a routine nature, and need not be carried out by a solicitor. The routine nature of the work will further increase with the introduction of registration of title when

[1] Appendix 5, Tables D1–D5.

the strict conveyancing involved will be a much simplified operation, and even less likely than at present to require the full skills of a solicitor. The review of the scope for simplification and standardisation of documents which we have recommended is another factor which would add strength to the case for the involvement of trained non-legal staff in conveyancing work.

9.34 We therefore conclude that the need to safeguard the dependability of the title register does not justify retention of the solicitors' monopoly.

9.35 Another argument in favour of the retention of the monopoly is that one effect of it is the safeguarding of clients' monies. The Solicitors' Accounts Rules and the existence of the guarantee fund, are important safeguards for clients. For most citizens the loss of the price of their house would be ruinous. Nevertheless, similar protection could be required of other agents, and indeed legislation has recently been introduced which will require estate agents to provide guarantees for clients' monies.[1] While, therefore, such guarantees are necessary, they cannot be said to justify a monopoly in favour of solicitors.

9.36 The critics of the monopoly also assert that it leads to prices (professional fees) that are higher than the work of conveyancing justifies and that the monopoly is, therefore, against the public interest. We describe in Chapter 19 our efforts to establish the degree of profitability of conveyancing work and we need only state here our disappointment that we were unable to get firm information from the profession.

9.37 Such information as we have been able to obtain suggests that conveyancing may be for many firms a very profitable part of their business. We see no compelling reason, however, why the buyers and sellers of houses should have to pay legal fees which in effect are subsidising other kinds of legal business. A somewhat different argument that has been advanced to us by the Law Society in oral evidence is that any high profits in conveyancing are made on the more costly houses and that these compensate for the low or nil profit made at the lower end of the market where the purchase of tenement flats, for example, often involves complicated or time-consuming conveyancing. We deal with the question of cross-subsidisation in Chapter 19.

9.38 The crux of the matter, however, is whether the public interest would be better served if the conveyancing monopoly were to be broken. The factors that we have examined in the immediately preceding paragraphs do not in our view justify retention of the monopoly. Before finally concluding in this sense, however, we felt it necessary to consider whether the breaking of the monopoly might lead to some legal firms, particularly in rural and relatively remote areas, losing some conveyancing work and thereby being forced out of business. We doubt very much whether this would happen; but even if it did, we would not regard this as a compelling argument for retaining the monopoly. If it were in the public interest that a legal firm should be maintained in a particular area, this could better be secured through a State subsidy rather than by high charges for particular clients; and this is a matter which our proposed Legal Services Commission (Chapter 20) would consider in its use of Exchequer funds to promote the provision of legal advice services in areas at present, or likely to be, inadequately served.

[1] *Estate Agents Act 1979*. The regulations which will make the detailed provisions have not yet been brought into operation although we understand that it is hoped that this will be done later this year (1980).

9.39 Our conclusion is, therefore, that the case for the legal profession retaining the present monopoly has not been established.

Extending the monopoly beyond the legal profession

9.40 We reached the point, therefore, when we had to consider whether we would want some non-solicitors to undertake conveyancing for reward, while still preserving essential safeguards for the public. Let us make it clear in this connection that we were concerned only with people's homes—residential domestic property. We had no body of evidence against the monopoly relative to commercial conveyancing and we make no recommendation for breaking it in this area of work. So far as domestic conveyancing is concerned, we were clear that if non-solicitors were to be allowed to do this work they would have to satisfy set standards of competence and meet prescribed safeguards for clients' money.

A new profession?

9.41 We considered whether to recommend the establishment of a new profession of conveyancers to share the monopoly with solicitors. Admission to the profession would be conditional on the applicant satisfying prescribed standards of competence or obtaining a prescribed qualification. Members of the profession would, like solicitors, be required to practise independently of any other commercial undertaking. A new profession would, like any other profession, evolve rules about ethics and the handling of complaints as well as meeting requirements for insurance and for safeguarding clients' monies. In a country as small as Scotland, however, it seemed to us that evolution of such a new profession would take many years; and that in any event the end we had in view—the provision of conveyancing at competitive prices—could be more quickly and effectively achieved by other means. We decided, therefore, against recommending the creation of professional non-solicitor conveyancers who could set up in practice on their own account.

9.42 This led us to consider, as an alternative, extending the present conveyancing monopoly to other established organisations or professions which were already involved in domestic property transactions. Again, they would need to meet certain criteria. Our first criterion is that those wishing to undertake conveyancing should provide adequate safety for clients' funds. Many professional bodies have the power to require their members to comply with rules of this kind. Estate agents, as we noted, are now being obliged by statute to keep proper accounts for clients' money, and to obtain insurance cover.

9.43 Our second criterion is one of competence. This involves education, training, prescribed qualifications and continuing training. Many professional bodies already provide these and we think that they could provide a specific conveyancing qualification for their members who studied for and passed appropriate examinations in conveyancing; and to enable this to become practicable we consider that our proposed Department of Legal Affairs (Chapter 20) should discuss with professional bodies who wish to provide this qualification and with the universities and with the Scottish Business Education Council, the provision of courses in conveyancing at a number of centres for persons who wish to acquire an appropriate conveyancing qualification. There would be no reason, of course, why legal firms themselves should not employ such non-solicitor conveyancers. The more limited qualification of the non-solicitor conveyancers compared with that of solicitors should mean that they would be less well remunerated; and the conveyancing service could be provided by firms at less cost to themselves and to their clients than at present.

9.44 Our third criterion would be that the members of the professional bodies who offered conveyancing services would be required by the rules of the body to have adequate indemnity insurance, to conform to rules of conduct, and to adhere to proper procedures for dealing with complaints which would be similar to those under which the legal profession has to operate, or will have to operate if our recommendations in Chapter 18 are accepted.

9.45 We accordingly **recommend** that domestic conveyancing should no longer be restricted exclusively to the legal profession; and that members of other professional bodies, who satisfy prescribed standards of safety for clients' monies, who have the education, training, and competence to provide a conveyancing service, and who have adequate indemnity insurance and conform to proper rules of conduct and procedures for dealing with complaints, should be entitled to undertake such work for a fee. We think that the widening of the monopoly which we recommend will bring to the field of domestic conveyancing greater competition than is evident at the present time and this should be reflected in keener charges for conveyancing work. The proposals which we make in Chapter 6 will have a like result.

Valuations and surveys

9.46 As we noted earlier in this Chapter, our survey showed public satisfaction with the conclusive nature of the exchange of missives, but dissatisfaction with the need for multiple valuation surveys which it entails. The one entails the other because missives cannot always be based on a 'subject to survey' condition, particularly when there is a seller's market such as has recently obtained in Scotland. The system in England and Wales where purchases are 'subject to contract' enables a purchaser to have a valuation or survey undertaken before the final exchange of contracts. We have, therefore, thought it necessary to examine this aspect of the process of buying domestic property.

9.47 There are two elements to what is generally referred to as the 'multiple survey problem'. Firstly, though no purchaser is obliged to obtain for himself a survey report on a house he wants to buy, some people think it prudent to do so. However, they must instruct this survey to let them decide whether they want definitely to submit an offer for the house, and before they know if their offer will be accepted. Where several persons make an offer the unsuccessful ones will have lost the cost of the survey. It is not unknown for people to make offers for three or four houses before being successful. For each house, however, several surveyors may have prepared reports on the property on behalf of different prospective purchasers.

9.48 The second element of the problem arises whenever the would-be purchaser is relying on a building society loan. Building societies are bound to have properties valued before lending on them, although this does not require a full structural survey. If a client wants a loan on a house the society will instruct a valuation of the property, on the basis of which they will offer a loan to the

to provide to all potential purchasers a standard form of report on the property by a surveyor. This report would be designed to meet the building societies' valuation requirements and could indeed be designed to provide further information for the buyer, although falling short of a complete structural survey. Unfortunately, there are strong reasons for not adopting this seemingly attractive solution. The building societies would find difficulty in accepting a value established by the seller's agent as a basis on which to lend to a purchaser. The surveyor would run into the same liability difficulties as with the proposal to make valuation reports available to borrowers. Moreover, the requirement for the seller to furnish a report might make his house impossible to sell. The idea of a 'seller's survey' is thus beset with difficulty.

9.59 The principle of 'caveat emptor' (let the buyer beware) governs the purchase of houses at present. This principle is, however, not a sacred one, and is at odds with the general trend towards consumer protection. Much consumer legislation in particular has, in recent years and in other areas, modified it extensively, and sellers of many goods are liable to the buyer should a variety of deficiencies emerge after sale. In principle, there is no reason why the buyers of houses should not receive similar protection although most house sale contracts are between individual citizens for neither of whom is the transaction part of a business. We therefore **recommend** that the expert committee we have proposed should also examine fully whether the difficulties in requiring sellers to provide a survey report can be overcome.

9.60 Short of requiring the seller to provide a survey report, it might be possible to require the seller to furnish prospective buyers with certain prescribed information before entering into any contract to sell. Not only would this ensure that buyers were better informed, it would mean one person (the seller or his agent) doing the work once, instead of several buyers or their agents doing it separately. Such information might include some or all of the following:

—the desirability of taking professional advice both as regards the condition of the property and as regards entering into a final contract to purchase;
—information on the binding effect of missives;
—what a building society valuation covers or does not cover;
—whether there are any known major defects in the condition of the house;
—the disclosure of any information the seller may have concerning planning proposals which might affect the house;
—information which the seller may have about any local authority orders restricting the use of the property;
—any unusual or onerous conditions in the title which might have similar effects;
—whether any financial obligations exist over the house (for example, in the form of securities or mortgages).

In the event of a purchaser entering into a contract through missives, the contract would either be voidable up until the time of entry or occupation of the house or the purchaser would have grounds for a claim for damages against the seller for a certain period if:

(i) Any of the requisite information had not been given and was material; or

(ii) Any of the information given was incorrect to a material extent.

9.61 This proposal does not hinge on exactly what information would be included in the statutory requirement. We have not gone into this in detail, not least because we appreciate that some of the information we have suggested could give rise to difficulties of definition and that the suggested effect involves consideration of the law of contract. There is also a question of whether a purchaser who has had the benefit of professional advice from a solicitor should get the benefit of this type of provision. We **recommend** that the expert committee which we have suggested should also be charged with responsibility for examining the feasibility of proposals along these lines.

9.62 We **recommend** that the same committee should also consider whether a person who instructs a survey but does not buy the house should pay the surveyor for his time only, and not for the responsibility element since the surveyor will owe him no continuing liability for his advice.

Conditional contracts

9.63 Another suggested solution to the problem which was put to us in evidence was the introduction of an implied suspensive condition in the contract between seller and purchaser. This would be a condition implied by law in all such contracts which would allow the buyer to withdraw within a specific period if a survey subsequently carried out revealed unacceptable deficiencies in the property. We do not support this proposal and, indeed, most of the evidence we received was overwhelmingly opposed to it. There are a considerable number of drawbacks. Firstly, there is the length of time which might elapse between a first conditional contract and the eventual completion of a binding contract; the finality of the existing Scottish system of missives was much appreciated in the responses to our survey of public attitudes to conveyancing. Many purchasers are also sellers. Secondly, there would be no guarantee that a potential buyer would not still have to commission a number of surveys before finding a satisfactory property. Thirdly, we think the difficulties which would arise in fixing an appropriate time limit and defining the grounds on which a purchaser might claim that the condition of the property was unsatisfactory would, while not necessarily being insuperable, result in the creation of disputes which might require recourse to civil litigation. Fourthly, we felt that there has to be very strong evidence in support of such a condition to make it mandatory in all cases and thus interfere with or restrict the general freedom to contract. Finally, we consider that this system would put unnecessary hardship on a seller if the conditional contract were not completed—for example, the probable loss of other potential offers during the period of the conditional contract and the resultant need for the seller to re-advertise.

Solicitors' fees

9.64 We have seen that many people think that they have to pay solicitors too much for conveyancing. We are concerned that solicitors should charge only what is fair and reasonable for the work done, that the work should be necessary and that it should be undertaken by appropriately qualified persons. Proposals which we hope will contribute to these objectives are made in Chapter 19. In the case of conveyancing, however, the public interest and concern are such that we think a fuller examination of the problem and our approach to it are justified. In particular, we make reference to the complex structure of the charges for property transactions, and to aspects of the role in these charges of the scale fee which seem to us objectionable.

Stamp duty and VAT

9.65 Before looking at the structure of costs in total, we wish to draw attention to the significance of stamp duty, which is widely seen as unreasonable. It is now difficult to buy any new house in Scotland without incurring a liability to pay stamp duty. Clients are obliged, moreover, to pay value added tax (currently at 15 per cent) on solicitors' fees and on other of the charges relating to the purchase or sale of property. Taxes are thus a significant element in the costs associated with conveyancing. This tax burden at the point of purchase contrasts with the tax allowance on loan interest repayments once the house has been bought. While broader considerations of fiscal and social policy must weigh heavily in any review of the tax framework, there is no doubt that the present structure adds substantially to the costs associated with housing transactions.

Typical costs

9.66 In addition to the costs associated with conveyancing on which we have commented there are others such as advertising, commission to a selling agent, search dues and registration dues. The amount of these charges depends in practice largely on the price at which the property is being purchased or sold and it is not possible, therefore, to be specific about them. As we describe in Chapter 19 (19.44–19.47) and Appendix 11, we carried out a limited survey into the costs of domestic conveyancing. We were concerned at the high overall cost of domestic purchases and sales—transactions which are regular facts of life for a large proportion of the population, often due to changes of job or changes in family circumstances. As Table 9.2 shows, the average costs for sales were £536 at the average price of £17,200 and for purchases £484 at the average price of £16,800. A simultaneous sale and purchase of an average property would result in a person having to meet a bill of over £1,000 which is a substantial sum in relation to average household income. As the Table makes clear, however, this bill is composed of a number of elements, some of which are outside the solicitor's control.

9.67 It follows that even if savings in cost can be made on any one of these items, this may have comparatively little effect on the total amount paid. To achieve a significant reduction in the costs of buying and selling domestic property, therefore, we have thought it necessary to tackle the problem over as wide a range as possible. It may be useful to summarise at this point our various proposals put forward with a view to alleviating this burden of cost:

(i) We recommend in Chapter 19 how the fees for work undertaken by solicitors should be calculated. This should lead to fees being charged on a basis which is more closely related to the costs of the particular transaction. In particular, it should remove one source of increased costs which derives from the scale fees applied in conveyancing. Under the existing system, solicitors' charges increase broadly in line with rising house prices. But in addition to this kind of inflation-proofing, solicitors have also benefited from periodic upward revision of the whole scale by the Law Society. This seems to us very difficult to justify and we are

TABLE 9.2: Average costs of purchases and sales*

	Average Costs	
	Sales £17,200	Purchases £16,800
	£	£
Commission where solicitor sold the property	156	—
Solicitor's fee (including fee for missives and mortgage work)	217	245
VAT on commission and fee	55	37
Advertising costs	40	—
Survey fees	2	12
Stamp duty	—	137**
Search dues	13	2
Recording dues	4	26**
Other outlays	49	25
	£536	£484

*Source: Based on Appendix 11, Table 6. (The figures for advertising costs, survey fees, stamp duty, recording dues, search dues and other outlays in this table are the average figures for those cases in which a detailed breakdown was provided by the solicitor; as such they are not calculated from the same base as 'total outlays' in Table 6 of Appendix 11 and this accounts for the slight inconsistency in totals between the two tables.)

**These are not the amounts which would be payable on a transaction where the price was £16,800 but are the average of all the purchase transactions in the survey.

concerned that this two-fold source of increases in conveyancing charges should be eliminated.

(ii) We recommend in Chapter 6 that solicitors should be allowed to advertise fees in order to introduce some competition into the conveyancing market, with a view to decreasing costs.

(iii) We recommend in this Chapter (a) that conveyancing should cease to be the exclusive preserve of solicitors; and (b) that there should be an investigation of possible simplification of conveyancing documents.

(iv) Although it is outwith our remit, we also think that the burden of stamp duty and VAT is substantial and we hope that some consideration will be given to reducing their effect: the effects of house price inflation in particular have greatly increased the incidence of stamp duty and raised the costs of buying quite modestly priced property.

(v) Our recommendations regarding valuations will also remove a source of discontent and possibly reduce costs.

(vi) While we have not been able to deal directly with every problem brought to our notice the expert committee we have suggested will no doubt find solutions which will further improve the situation.

These measures, taken together, should contribute to a desirable reduction in the costs of housing transactions; and we see no reason why progress on most of them should not be made quickly.

9.68 In the longer term, we think still more substantial savings in costs may be possible. Our concern in the short run has been to try to ensure that the charges for work necessarily undertaken should be fair and reasonable to solicitor and client. Over a longer time period, we see possibilities that the necessary work in conveyancing may be reduced and simplified, and that costs may be further reduced in consequence. We have noted that a system of registration of title is to be introduced in Scotland. Although we have no evidence to show the effect of this on solicitors' fees, it has been suggested that a reduction of the order of 25 per cent should result. Given this innovation and the associated State guarantee of titles, together with the scope opened for simplification and computerisation of title registration and transfer, we think it feasible that a further more radical change in the system can be brought about, enabling the sale and purchase of domestic property to be transacted at much lower costs. This we would see as a goal which is well worth striving for, and we would wish to commend it strongly, as reflected in our recommendation at paragraph 9.16 above.

INFORMATION FOR CLIENTS

9.69 We have dealt in general terms with information for the public in Chapter 6. Specifically in relation to conveyancing, we know that many clients do not understand what the solicitor actually does for them; they come up against obscure language and it is clear from correspondence which we have had from private individuals with grievances about the handling of their house sales or purchases that the solicitors involved, although probably blameless in other respects, could very often be criticised for failing to explain their actions, or apparent inaction, to their clients. Finally, we have also mentioned the considerable ignorance regarding the costs involved in conveyancing; many respondents in our survey were unable to distinguish, for example, between the solicitor's fee and necessary outlays. We have no doubt that while the public do not expect to be told all the intricacies of the procedures involved they do want to understand the broad outlines of the service for which they are paying. Similar trends can be seen in public attitudes to other professions, such as teaching and medicine. Solicitors must aim, therefore, to involve the client adequately in the decision-making process, and ensure that he knows enough to play an effective part.

9.70 Some general points are important in deciding what information should be made available to the client:

(a) Only information which will significantly improve the knowledge and understanding of the recipient should be included;

(b) A decision to give information must balance the risk of giving so much detail as to discourage the client from trying to understand and become involved; and

(c) Plain language should always be used; it will, however, be helpful to add a note of any technical term in common use.

Many solicitors already do this orally. We think this approach should be supplemented by printed information which the client can consult at his leisure. The two main objectives of any information leaflets produced should be:

(1) To enable people to have greater understanding of the conveyancing process and more effective control over decisions taken in these transactions; and

(2) To enable people to have a better understanding of the costs involved in a conveyancing transaction.

To attain the first objective would ensure that clients are able to do more than simply aquiesce in any course of action which might be suggested by the solicitor. Fulfilment of the second objective will make people readier to accept reasonable accounts for work done by solicitors and, when necessary, to make a judgement as to whether or not they should dispute the account.

9.71 The Law Society have produced a leaflet entitled 'Buying or Selling a House?' which meets the aims we have described. Solicitors should make much more effective use of it. Similar printed information will be just as important for any other persons who undertake conveyancing in the future. We should stress finally that we intend such leaflets to be complementary to sound advice by the conveyancer, and not in any sense a substitute for it.

OTHER MATTERS

Instalment purchase

9.72 In considering what information should be given to potential purchasers we became aware that there was one special kind of transaction into which people often entered in ignorance of the very real risks they faced without legal or other disinterested advice. We made enquiries about this kind of arrangement which is normally known as rental purchase or instalment purchase. The properties involved in such purchase arrangements are usually the poorer tenement properties, very often in twilight areas ripe for re-development. The fact that building societies or local authorities will often not lend on such properties may lead an intending buyer into entering a contract under which, following payment of an initial deposit, fixed monthly instalments and periodical payments of interest on the outstanding amount of the price become due. Title to the property is not transferred until full payment is made.

9.73 In some cases the system seems to work well enough; but it is clear that it is open to abuse and that purchasers who do not understand the legal requirements for the sale and purchase of heritable property may, in certain circumstances, find themselves at great disadvantage. The contract often includes unreasonable conditions. For example:

(i) One missed instalment may result in ejection, the loss of all that has been paid and even a court action for the unpaid balance;

(ii) The seller instead of the purchaser may claim compensation if the property is acquired compulsorily by the local authority; or

(iii) The purchaser may be required to take out life assurance through the agency of the seller and be penalised for failure to comply.

9.74 It has been suggested that property companies use such arrangements as a device to circumvent the provisions of the Rent Acts; whether or not this is so, there is evidence that many purchasers do not understand their obligation to maintain the tenement property and still regard the seller as their landlord. Problems can also arise where there is a chain of instalment purchase agreements for a single property; and in some cases of which we have heard payment is made in full but proper title may not be completed.[1]

[1] Further information is given in an article entitled: 'House Purchase by Instalments'; *SCOLAG No. 9*, pages 48 to 50.

9.75 The difficulties involved in instalment purchase cannot be solved by a simple recommendation in our Report. Purchasers should be afforded better protection in instalment sales. We know that the Office of Fair Trading is aware of these problems; it should perhaps be given powers to pursue the matter further. We are not clear, however, whether the passing of the Unfair Contract Terms Act 1977 has made any impact on the problem. We therefore **recommend** that a detailed study should be made of the problems of instalment purchase contracts with a view to effecting changes in the substantive law which will offer the purchaser in an instalment sale better protection than the law at present affords.

Oppressive conditions in missives

9.76 It was represented to us that members of the public, sometimes without proper advice, enter into missives for the purchase of property which contain conditions that are described as oppressive. This is not so much a matter of legal services, but as missives are contracts which may be entered into without proper advice we **recommend** that the question of oppressive conditions in missives be referred for study to the Office of Fair Trading.

Crofters

9.77 As we noted earlier, we do not think it sufficient for government to give people rights unless they also inform them of the rights and give them the means to take advantage of them. During discussions which we had with the Crofters Commission we were given an example of a failure to meet the latter. The Crofting Reform (Scotland) Act 1976 provided for crofters acquiring title to their croft houses and land; but because of the inadequacy of legal services, and particularly because of a difficulty in getting plans of the property prepared, the take up of the rights and the transfer of titles have not been as quick as was expected. The Crofters Commission thought that matters could be improved if they could provide a legal service and if the Department of Agriculture and Fisheries for Scotland could provide the surveying services. We understand that additional costs would have to be incurred if this were the case, but we are of the view that the proposals are worthy of consideration.

RECOMMENDATIONS

			Paragraph
Registration of Title	R9.1	Any extra cost incurred on first registration in the Land Register of properties over what might be charged for recording under the present system should be borne by the State.	9.12
	R9.2	The land certificate should disclose as many as possible of the overriding interests affecting a property.	9.13
	R9.3	There should be set up a Standing Committee appointed by, and reporting to, the Secretary of State for Scotland which should have responsibility for overseeing the new Land Register, recommending such improvements and simplification as seem desirable, and considering the longer term operation of the system. The membership should comprise representatives of the Land Register staff, the legal profession and any other related profession, and the general public.	9.15
	R9.4	The Standing Committee should advise when registration of title should become universally compulsory. When this happens without any change of ownership the full costs of such a registration should be borne by the State.	9.15
Simplification of procedures and documents	R9.5	The Standing Committee should examine the feasibility of introducing a simpler system of transferring property which might be provided by the State at a much reduced cost to the public.	9.16
	R9.6	The legislature and the profession should ensure that the documents used for conveyancing are written so far as possible in simple language.	9.18

			Paragraph
	R9.7	A specialist committee with lay representation should be appointed to review the scope for simplification and standardisation of legal documents used in conveyancing.	9.20
The conveyancing monopoly	R9.8	The present monopoly should not be extended to bring within it the missives stage of the purchase and sale of heritable property.	9.31
	R9.9	Domestic conveyancing should no longer be restricted exclusively to the legal profession; members of other professional bodies who satisfy prescribed standards as detailed in paragraph 9.45 should be entitled to undertake conveyancing work for a fee.	9.45
Building society valuations	R9.10	Building societies should adopt standard specifications for valuations, appoint a common panel of valuers and instruct all valuations through a common agency.	9.53
	R9.11	An expert committee should consider the difficulties involved in making building society valuation reports available to potential borrowers.	9.57
	R9.12	The same expert committee should examine whether the difficulties in requiring sellers to provide a survey report can be overcome.	9.59
	R9.13	The same expert committee should consider whether sellers should be obliged by statute to provide certain information to purchasers.	9.61
	R9.14	The same expert committee should consider whether a person who instructs a survey but does not buy the house should pay the surveyor for his time only.	9.62

			Paragraph
Instalment purchase	R9.15	A detailed study should be made of instalment purchase contracts with a view to effecting changes in the substantive law which will offer the purchaser in an instalment sale better protection than the law at present affords.	9.75
Oppressive conditions in missives	R9.16	The question of oppressive conditions in missives should be referred to the Office of Fair Trading.	9.76

CHAPTER 10

DIVORCE

10.1 As we mentioned in the introductory Chapter to our Report, divorce was one of the specific areas of court business and jurisdiction which we felt it necessary to consider in detail. There were several reasons. Firstly, Scotland like the rest of the United Kingdom has experienced a steadily increasing resort to divorce by couples to end formally what they regard as irretrievably broken marriages. Divorce can only be secured by court action; and this involves legal services. Although the law regarding divorce has changed substantially under the Divorce (Scotland) Act 1976 there has been little corresponding change in legal procedures except for the admission of affidavits for undefended divorces. We wished to see if the machinery needed adaptation to meet the new demands. Secondly, legal costs for divorce in undefended actions—and these constitute the great majority—are considerably higher in Scotland than in England and Wales. We shall discuss the reasons for this later; but there is no doubt that this factor was responsible for much of the evidence which we received arguing for change in the legal processes governing divorce in Scotland. Thirdly, we were concerned to secure better arrangements than exist at present to safeguard the welfare of children of divorcing parents. The courts have a statutory responsibility for taking into account, before granting a divorce, whether or not the arrangements for the care of the children are satisfactory; and we were concerned to see whether existing legal procedures were adequate in this regard. Fourthly, we thought that we should consider whether defended divorce actions should continue to be held in open court; and, lastly, we wanted to see whether the recommendations which the Finer Committee had made relative to family courts could be usefully developed in Scotland.[1]

Divorces and their cost

10.2 In Scotland the Court of Session has sole jurisdiction in actions for divorce. In 1978 the Outer House of the Court of Session disposed of 11,921 actions, of which 8,794 (74 per cent) were consistorial actions (that is, actions relating to marriage, divorce or separation).[2] Of the total of 8,794 consistorial actions, 8,330 were undefended divorces. A divorce may, of course, be undefended as regards whether there should be a divorce, but defended on matters such as custody of children and financial arrangements. The statistics do not appear to draw this distinction. In the rest of this Chapter when we speak of an undefended divorce we mean one that is not being defended on any matter.

10.3 While actions for divorce constitute the largest number of actions in the Court of Session they do not represent a proportionate part of the workload of Scotland's supreme civil court. Actions for divorce normally present comparatively little legal complexity. Nevertheless, the sheer weight of numbers is

---

[1] *Report of the Committee on One-Parent Families* (*Cmnd. 5629*): HMSO, 1974.
[2] *Civil Judicial Statistics, 1978*, (*Cmnd. 7762*), Table 3: HMSO, 1980.

formidable, and so is the cost. Actions for dissolution of marriage in the Court of Session cost the legal aid fund some £2·9 million in the year ending 31 March 1979. That was more than three-quarters of the total paid from the legal aid fund in respect of civil actions (£3·6 million).[1] Such a substantial commitment of public funds and court time required investigation.

The Finer Report

10.4 As is clear from our introductory comments in paragraph 10.1, we have looked at divorce in a context wider than that simply of cost. We appreciate that divorce is generally a traumatic experience for one or both of the parties involved, and a hapless situation for any children concerned. We felt obliged, therefore, to consider what changes we might recommend which would reduce the trauma of divorce for all immediately affected, bearing in mind particularly that rather more than half of the consistorial actions in the Court of Session involve children.[2]

10.5 We took into account the Report of the Finer Committee who advocated a system of family courts for England and Wales; and we noted that the Committee had also said that the consideration of principle which led them to that view applied equally to Scotland, although the application in detail would require to be looked at in the context of Scots law. The family courts envisaged in the Finer Report were founded on six major criteria:

'(1) The family court must be an impartial judicial institution, regulating the rights of citizens and settling their disputes according to law;

(2) The family court will be a unified institution in a system of family law which applies a uniform set of legal rules, derived from a single moral standard and applicable to all citizens;

(3) The family court will organise its work in such a way as to provide the best possible facilities for conciliation between parties in matrimonial disputes;

(4) The family court will have professionally trained staff to assist both the court and the parties appearing before it in all matters requiring social work services and advice;

(5) The family court will work in close relationship with the social security authorities in the assessment both of need and of liability in cases involving financial provision;

(6) The family court will organise its procedure, sittings and administrative services and arrangements with a view to gaining the confidence and maximising the convenience of the citizens who appear before it'.[3]

10.6 We had no doubt that divorce courts modelled on these criteria could lead to a significant improvement in the provision for the settlement and conduct of matrimonial disputes. The interests of all the parties affected, particularly children, would be given better consideration than at present seems possible.

---

[1] Scottish Home and Health Department and the Legal Aid Central Committee: this information, we understand, will be included in the 29th Annual Report on the Scottish Legal Aid Scheme 1978/79 which had not been published by the time we went to print.
[2] Scottish Courts Administration told us that in 1978 4,946 cases out of a total of 8,782 involved children.
[3] *The Finer Report*, paragraph 4.283.

However, the present government, like its predecessor, has stated that it is currently unable to enter into any commitment on the recommendations of the Finer Committee.[1] We therefore concluded that we should seek to make recommendations which might be practicable in a period of public expenditure constraint such as is now being experienced; which endeavour to give effect to the principles quoted in the preceding paragraph; and which would not prejudice further developments on the lines of the Finer Committee's recommendations.

10.7 We appreciate that in addition to dissolution of marriage on divorce, there are procedures relating to nullity of marriage and for the presumption of the death of a spouse. We are, however, here concerned primarily with divorce; and in the following paragraphs we deal in some detail with the criticisms that we ourselves would make of existing divorce procedures in Scotland. We also suggest how, in our view, these procedures might be simplified and improved, and also be made less costly.

DIVORCE JURISDICTION

10.8 We received a substantial body of evidence that sheriff courts should be enabled to hear divorce actions. In summary, the arguments were as follows:

—Sheriff courts have jurisdiction in most consistorial actions (for example, adoption, separation, aliment) and have proved their competence.

—Sheriff court procedures would be cheaper for the individual parties and be more convenient.

—Sheriff court procedures would be cheaper for the public purse in regard to legal aid.

—Sheriff court procedures would facilitate the investigation and follow-up of custody arrangements.

10.9 We also received some evidence to the effect that divorce should no longer be a matter of court proceedings at all, but that parties should be able to obtain a divorce from registrars of births, deaths and marriages. The argument is that marriage can be, and to an increasing extent is, contracted through a civil ceremony conducted by the registrar; and there is, therefore, no obvious reason why this same official should not be empowered to terminate the contract of marriage so long as prescribed conditions for termination are fulfilled. Indeed, there are some who take the extreme view that the institution of marriage is now no more than one of the arrangements which society regards as appropriate for licensing; and that the termination of the marriage, if this is the wish of both of the parties concerned, should be secured simply by completion of an appropriate form at any post office. We do not discount these as possibilities in the longer term; but we are unable to consider them seriously at this stage. While marriage may start as a simple licensing operation, it evolves through the years into a very complex relationship in which the interests of people of several generations are involved. At best, we can see 'easy divorce' in the foreseeable future as being appropriate only to undefended divorces where no

[1] *House of Commons Official Report, 16th July 1979:* Written Answer Col. 405.

children are involved; and even then there may be difficulty in ensuring that proper financial arrangements are made. No doubt the grounds for divorce, and the way it can be procured, will continue to be subjects for debate whether or not the recommendations which we make for change are implemented.

Legal status

10.10 We now return to the arguments for and against giving sheriff courts jurisdiction in divorce actions. It is argued that as divorce has such a special importance, petitions for divorce ought to fall exclusively within the jurisdiction of the supreme civil court. The special importance of divorce is said to arise because it affects the legal status of individuals and has effects on rights to property. It seems to us that there is now increasing legal as well as lay scepticism about this argument; and we ourselves do not consider that the Court of Session could justifiably retain sole jurisdiction in divorce simply for the reason that divorce affects the legal status of persons. So does adoption, but that comes within the ambit of the sheriff court.

Economies of scale

10.11 We also attach little significance to the argument that the Court of Session achieves economies of scale by undertaking all divorce work. Whatever merit this argument has in regard to court costs is outweighed, in our view, by the high cost to litigants of present procedures. We are aware that following the introduction of affidavit procedures, the Court of Session now processes undefended divorce actions more quickly and efficiently than before. There is no reason to think that sheriff courts could not do equally well. We also recognise that the time an action takes in court is only a part of the time that it is in the hands of the legal profession. So while we accept that the Court of Session now despatches its undefended divorce business much more quickly and at greater convenience to the parties than was the case prior to our appointment, we do not consider that this constitutes sufficient argument on which we could justifiably recommend that the Court of Session should retain sole jurisdiction in divorce actions.

Convenience of the parties

10.12 We have already alluded to the important change that took place subsequent to our appointment in the procedure relative to undefended divorces in the Court of Session, namely, the admission of affidavit evidence by pursuers and witnesses. Prior to April 1978, it was necessary in divorce actions, undefended as well as defended, for the parties and witnesses to appear personally in court. For many people this meant a costly journey to Edinburgh, and possibly an overnight stay. Since April 1978, however, it has been possible for the evidence in undefended divorce actions to be presented by means of affidavit evidence—that is, written statements which are sworn to on oath by the person concerned before a notary public or justice of the peace. These affidavits together with the other papers in the case are now dealt with by the judge in private and there is, therefore, no longer any necessity for a formal court hearing. Only in defended divorce actions do parties and their witnesses still need to travel to Edinburgh and appear in person at the Court of Session. There is no doubt that this development has made less strong the argument earlier advanced that sheriff court divorces would be more convenient for parties and witnesses living outwith Edinburgh. The argument remains fully valid of course in relation to defended divorces; and here we must say that we cannot see any justification for requiring parties and their witnesses to go to the expense of having to travel to Edinburgh to obtain a divorce. It is not simply that costs are needlessly high because of having to attend before the Court of Session. There are other factors.

Number of lawyers involved

10.13 Litigants in divorce actions, as in all other Court of Session business, require the services of an advocate to present their case to the court. Moreover, litigants instructing solicitors outwith Edinburgh will require the services not only of their local solicitor but also of one who works in Edinburgh—an 'Edinburgh correspondent'. (We refer to this requirement generally in Chapter 15.) These three lawyers are not, of course, doing the same work; and the client pays only once for any particular item of business. Nevertheless, because one solicitor has to prepare instructions and papers which have to be read and put into effect by another solicitor who has to go to yet a third lawyer, this time an advocate, the system seems to us wasteful of resources. The client inevitably must pay more, since he has to pay one solicitor to prepare the instructions and the other to read them and put them into effect; but even if this were not so, the present arrangement is not efficient. Cases are bound to take longer than they need, if only because papers have to be transmitted from client to 'country' solicitor, 'country' solicitor to Edinburgh correspondent, and Edinburgh correspondent to advocate. An examination of accounts suggests that a very large part of the heavy cost of executing procedures is incurred in the initial enquiries and preparation of precognitions and affidavits which are normally undertaken by the local solicitor. The transfer of jurisdiction to the sheriff court would not of itself and without simplifying procedure reduce the cost. However, we believe that the need to employ Edinburgh solicitors and advocates must mean a significant addition to the expense of the procedure. While we appreciate that there are differences in the two types of consistorial action, we have noted that the average cost to the legal aid fund of actions in the sheriff court for judicial separation in the year to 31 March 1979 was some £185, as against an average cost per case of Court of Session divorces of £315.[1] These figures at least suggest that divorce cases could be performed more cheaply in the sheriff court.

Extended role for sheriff court

10.14 We earlier said that we do not want to prejudice in any way the eventual implementation of the Finer Committee's proposals relative to family courts; and to this end it would make sense to develop the sheriff court as the forum capable of resolving all family legal matters. Sheriff courts undertake a variety of other business of course; but it would be an improvement on present arrangements if they had jurisdiction over all consistorial business. It certainly seems to us anomalous that sheriff courts now have jurisdiction in actions of separation and aliment which may sometimes present difficulties, while all divorce actions

---

[1] Scottish Home and Health Department and the Legal Aid Central Committee.

no matter how straightforward are reserved to the Court of Session. Developing the sheriff court as a family court is not simply a matter of giving it jurisdiction in all consistorial matters; it extends to ensuring that the sheriff court is seen as an integral part of the resources available locally for dealing with family problems. In particular, the court must establish effective working relationships with social work departments and other agencies concerned with family support. This is something which the Court of Session cannot hope to achieve as readily because it is not a local court.

Load on the sheriff courts

10.15 It has been suggested to us that in practical terms the sheriff courts would not be able to cope with the extra work which a jurisdiction in divorce would entail. This argument would have some force if the personal attendance of parties and witnesses in all divorce actions were necessary. Dispensing with this need, however, in undefended actions reduces considerably the pressure on court facilities and we would expect such procedures to be adopted in sheriff courts. In individual sheriff courts which are already suffering pressure on their accommodation, any extra work created by divorce jurisdiction might cause some difficulty, but we are satisfied that in general the sheriff courts would be able to cope. We would not regard the problems of one or two courts as an adequate argument for retaining the present centralised procedures.

Effect on junior advocates

10.16 We were aware that a consequence of the transfer of divorce work away from the Court of Session would be a loss of work for junior advocates. Our survey of advocates' remuneration for 1976–77 showed that over half the fee income of the most junior advocates (those of three years' standing or less) came from civil legal aid work, and the larger part of this must have been derived from actions for divorce. This survey, however, was conducted before the introduction of the affidavit evidence; and we have been told that junior advocates are already suffering a reduction in the divorce work available to them because solicitors are now more readily able to secure the services of experienced advocates since court appearance is no longer necessary. We believe that the Bar would be able to adjust to the loss of divorce work which would happen if the Court of Session lost its current exclusive jurisdiction; and while there might be transitional difficulties, we do not think that they need to be so serious as to represent a major counter-argument to the transfer of jurisdiction in divorce to the sheriff courts. It would be wrong in any case to retain divorce work in Edinburgh for the benefit of the junior Bar and at the cost of the divorcing public.

Jurisdiction to sheriff courts

10.17 Having assessed the jurisdiction issue against various criteria—cost, convenience, creation of family courts etc.—we are in no doubt that the arguments point conclusively to granting the sheriff courts jurisdiction in divorce matters, and we so **recommend.**

Concurrent jurisdiction

10.18 The question remains whether the sheriff courts should have an exclusive jurisdiction in divorce matters, or whether they should have a concurrent jurisdiction with the Court of Session. In favour of a concurrent jurisdiction it can be argued that there is already concurrent jurisdiction between the Court of Session and the sheriff courts relative to most other civil business; and that if similar arrangements applied in divorce, cases would 'find their own level'. This implies that complex cases would tend to be taken in the Court of Session whereas the more straightforward cases would go to the sheriff court. We are not, however, persuaded that the present concurrent jurisdiction in most civil matters is wholly desirable, and indeed we recommend in Chapter 14 that this should be reviewed. We do not, therefore, recommend concurrent jurisdiction in respect of divorce actions. There are, in our view, a number of strong arguments against concurrent jurisdiction. In the first place, it does not ensure that any case will necessarily find the appropriate level of court. Where there is concurrent jurisdiction the selection of the court rests with the pursuer, which probably in practice means with his or her solicitor. No reason requires to be given for the selection, and we do not think it is necessarily made on an objective assessment as to which court is most appropriate. Moreover, it gives an option to the pursuer which is denied to the defender. This seems to us wrong in principle. It would enable a pursuer to select the Court of Session with a view to threatening expense or inconvenience to the defender, thereby inducing him or her not to defend. Further, we later recommend more effective machinery for dealing with questions relating to children; and if the Court of Session were to have a concurrent jurisdiction a procedure would have to be maintained by which that court had access to that machinery. This would not be impossible to devise, but it would introduce unnecessary complexity. The giving of exclusive jurisdicition to one level of court would not be inconsistent with modern statutory trends. For example, recent consumer legislation confers exclusive jurisdiction on the sheriff courts in certain consumer matters up to a high financial limit; conversely, recent patent legislation has conferred exclusive jurisdiction on the Court of Session. We therefore **recommend** that the sheriff court should have exclusive jurisdiction as a court of first instance in divorce matters.

Sheriff to have power to remit

10.19 We think it sensible, however, to provide an opportunity for matters of particular complexity to be resolved by the Court of Session. Just as a sheriff on cause shown by the parties, or of his own accord, can at present remit separation and aliment cases to the Outer House of the Court of Session, we **recommend** that he should have power to remit divorce actions in the same way.

Designation of particular divorce courts

10.20 We earlier noted that individual sheriff courts might be faced with practical difficulties in assuming a jurisdiction in divorce. If this were so, it would be justification for only a restricted number of sheriff courts to deal with divorce business. Accordingly, we **recommend** that Sheriffs Principal, when they think it appropriate, should designate particular courts within their sheriffdom to deal with divorce cases. In designating courts for this purpose, however, Sheriffs Principal should bear in mind not merely questions of administrative efficiency but also the convenience of the parties and others involved. We believe it is important that, as far as possible, separate accommodation should be available for consistorial cases, but bearing in mind our recommendation relative to privacy in paragraph 10.40, this accommodation does not require to be pretentious.

Right of pursuer to select court

10.21 At present, as all divorce actions must be raised in the Court of Session, parties are not in any doubt as to which court has jurisdiction. Now that we have recommended that jurisdiction be transferred to the sheriff courts, however, we have to consider in which sheriff court the action for divorce should be lodged. In the majority of civil actions in the sheriff courts the choice of court is based on the residence or place of business of the party being sued. There are various rules covering other situations, including actions of separation, which are, of course, in many respects similar to actions of divorce. In separation actions the pursuer can choose to raise the action in the sheriff court of the area in which he or she resides, or in the sheriff court of the area in which the other party resides. The present rules for determining jurisdiction in divorce as between different parts of the United Kingdom are based on similar principles, namely the place of residence of either party. We think that similar principles should also be applied in determining jurisdiction in divorce as between sheriff courts. We **recommend,** therefore, that the pursuer should be able to choose between raising the action in his or her local court or in the defender's local court if this were different. If for some reason it is desired to have the action dealt with in a sheriff court other than one in the area of residence of either the pursuer or defender, the pursuer should be entitled to apply accordingly to the sheriff at his or her local sheriff court. The sheriff should have sole discretion whether or not to accede to the request. Moreover, we **recommend** that a sheriff of his own accord should have power to remit any divorce action to any other sheriff court where, for instance, he has grounds for believing that this would be in the best interests of any children affected by the action.

DIVORCE ACTIONS: THE CENTRAL ISSUES

Divorce based on separation

10.22 We wish to comment briefly on certain aspects of separation on which a substantial number of divorces are based. We are concerned to ensure that the financial arrangements following divorce are equitable, particularly in cases where children are involved. We have noted the opportunity for what amounts to 'blackmail' in the present arrangements. A person seeking a divorce on the basis of a period of separation of less than five years requires the consent of the other spouse and this consent may in some cases be granted on conditions, particularly financial conditions, which are unfair. Typically, the situation we have in mind is where a wife with children seeks a divorce with her husband's consent after a separation lasting two years. The husband might be indifferent to the wife's desire for divorce, and may be willing to consent only if the wife is prepared to accept lesser financial provision for herself than her circumstances would normally occasion. The wife, to get the divorce she wants, may accept this condition knowing that there is 'social security' to which she can turn if the need arises. We are concerned at the potentially harmful effect such an arrangement could have on the future welfare of the children concerned.

10.23 In our view, it will be impossible to eliminate the 'blackmail' so long as 'consent' is an essential element in one of the grounds of divorce. On the other hand, we do not think it reasonable simply to abolish the 'two years with consent' ground. This would mean that where a marriage has obviously broken down and neither party particularly wishes it to continue, nevertheless the parties would either have to prove one of the 'fault' grounds—adultery, intolerable conduct or desertion, or else wait for five years. We are aware of views sincerely held that divorce should be available, without consent, after only one year's separation. We are inclined to doubt whether such a relatively short period would protect the interests of the party who did not wish a divorce. However, we venture to suggest that the present two categories of separation (which constitute evidence of irretrievable breakdown of marriage justifying divorce) should be replaced by a single category not requiring consent. We therefore **recommend** that Parliament should consider the proposition that there should be only one category of divorce based on separation; that this category should not require consent; and that the period of separation which would establish evidence of irretrievable breakdown of marriage should not be longer than two years. If this proposition were accepted there would be no point in retaining the 'desertion' ground. We would not, however, suggest abolishing the adultery and intolerable conduct grounds, since we think that these should still be available even though there has not been two years' separation.

Custody of children

10.24 Under section 8 of the Matrimonial Proceedings (Children) Act 1958, the Court of Session at present has a duty to consider the arrangements proposed for the welfare of any children affected by an action for divorce before granting a decree. Unlike England and Wales where the county courts dealing with divorce have court welfare officers who can at the court's request make enquiries into custody and access arrangements, the Court of Session in Scotland has no court welfare service. Instead, in cases where the judge dealing with a divorce action considers he needs more evidence to be satisfied as to the welfare of children involved, he has to call for a report from the appropriate social work department or ask for a special report to be made by a solicitor or an advocate. We believe that these arrangements are less than adequate to enable the Court of Session to perform the duty imposed on it by section 8. The court is not provided with any funds for the purpose of making any such enquiries. This is a disturbing example of central government imposing a duty on the court without providing adequate resources to discharge the duty. The situation in this matter has been worsened by the introduction of the affidavit procedure, since the court is deprived of the opportunity of questioning the pursuer and witnesses. Accordingly, we have considered whether the courts should have any duty to deal with custody and access issues which are ancillary to actions of divorce, or whether the safeguarding of children's welfare in this as in other situations should rest entirely with the other agencies statutorily concerned, namely social work departments and children's panels. Although we recognise the limitation of courts of law in dealing with the sensitive area of child welfare we believe that the courts could not be seen to be doing their public duty if they disregarded what most people would consider the main issue arising from divorce—that is, the children's welfare. The problem, as we see it, is how to harness responsible expertise to advise the courts; but we are in no doubt that the courts should still have a duty to ensure that the welfare of children affected is safeguarded as best it can be in the particular circumstances before a decree of divorce is granted.

How should the courts safeguard children's welfare?

10.25 As we consider that the courts should have a statutory duty to ensure that the welfare of children is safeguarded, we have had to consider how best this duty can be discharged. In the majority of cases involving children the custody arrangements agreed and proposed by the parties will probably be the best that can be made. Only in a limited number of cases will protracted scrutiny of the arrangements for custody, and perhaps the intervention of the court in suggesting other arrangements, be necessary. Consequently, we do not think it would be an unreasonable or improper burden on the public purse to provide that a special report on the custody arrangements for children of the marriage should be required in all divorce actions involving children. The importance we attach to the welfare of children involved in divorce cases dictates that this degree of care is taken of their interests and we so **recommend.**

How is the court to get such reports?

10.26 Ideally, the person preparing this report should be qualified to assess domestic situations, and be skilled in conciliation since we believe he should have power to invite the parties to reconsider any arrangements which appear unsatisfactory before submitting a report to the court. We have considered four ways of providing such reports to the court:

(i) creating a new department of the court with appropriate staff;

(ii) creating a new court official with few, if any, support staff;

(iii) seconding social workers to the court service; and

(iv) using the reporters to children's panels.

10.27 It was brought to our notice that the county courts in England and Wales dealing with divorce have special administrative and judicial staff to examine both the custody arrangements and the arrangements for financial provision following divorce. This led to some of us visiting the county court in Newcastle upon Tyne and we were given much helpful information about the English procedures. There are obvious attractions in recommending that special court staff and services of the kind available in the English county courts relative to divorce should be established in Scotland also. However, we do not believe that such a recommendation would be realistic in present economic conditions. In any event, we were concerned to make the best use of resources available in Scotland. Some sheriff courts would be unlikely to have enough divorce business to merit the provision of a special staff; and the creation of a new range of officials might appear to be extravagant.

10.28 Nevertheless, we were much impressed by the assistance which the registrars in the English county courts are able to provide to the judges in divorce actions. The registrar in England is a judicial officer of a kind which we do not have in the Scottish legal system: he can deal with a limited number of actions such as small claims; and his reports, particularly in undefended divorce cases where the parties do not appear, are clearly of great assistance to the judge. Again, however, we concluded that the practice in England, attractive though it seemed, was not for the foreseeable future a practicable proposition in Scotland. Apart from the fact that registrars in England rely on supporting court staff for whom we see no immediate justification in Scotland, we doubted whether there was any need to introduce into our sheriff courts a judicial officer who would in effect be an assistant sheriff.

10.29 The third option, perhaps more cost effective and readily practicable, which we considered, was to rely solely on social work departments for the provision of reports on children involved in divorce actions. In the busier sheriff courts, we contemplated that a social worker might perhaps be seconded to the court for a period of, say, up to two years of full-time service; in other courts one seconded social worker might serve a group of courts from a main court base; while in yet other areas, reports might best be provided *ad hoc* by the social work department. We thought that perhaps some 20–25 extra social workers throughout Scotland would be needed to provide the service which we think the courts should have.

10.30 The fourth possibility which we considered was to make use of the expertise and the administrative and specialist services available in Scotland through the reporters to the children's panels. These services involve, of course, a close working relationship with social work departments. We looked into the method of operation of the children's panels in the Lothian and Strathclyde regions; and we were impressed with the scope and detail of the case files prepared in connection with children referred to the panels, and also by the understanding approach taken by the reporters and the panels to the children who become their responsibility. One disadvantage which was expressed to us is that the panels are widely regarded by the public as a form of court for dealing with juvenile criminals. This, therefore, at first sight hardly seemed a propitious or appropriate forum in which to examine the custody and access arrangements proposed for the innocent child victims of divorce. However, we finally considered that no other organisation offered quite the same scope for the sensitive assessment of children's needs which we thought was required. The fact that crime gets more publicity than other aspects of the work of children's panels is not surprising. We believe, however, that such an attitude is damaging to a valuable Scottish social innovation; and we would hope that by using panel expertise in another non-criminal sphere the balance of public opinion could be modified. Nevertheless, we did not disregard present attitudes and took this into account, as will be seen.

10.31 In deciding, on balance, that there would be great advantages in making use of the reporters and children's panels to assist the courts to discharge the duty Parliament placed on them in 1958 to safeguard the welfare of children affected by divorce, we had in mind that the expertise of reporters and their staff and of the voluntary members of children's panels lies in assessing domestic situations and the quality of child care and supervision provided by parents.

The reporters have well established links with social work departments, schools etc., and would, we think, be in the best position to single out cases where proposed custody and access arrangements gave cause for disquiet. We also had in mind that children's panels were not intended to be organisations solely concerned with deliquent children and that to give them a new but limited involvement in civil work relative to divorce would be in accordance with their original conception. We would expect reporters to be alert to the need for treating custody cases referred to them by the courts with consideration for the feelings of parents and children who are going through domestic stress. We **recommend,** therefore, that in every divorce action (defended as well as undefended) where children under the age of 16 are involved, the case should be referred by the court to the appropriate reporter to the children's panel for special reports on custody arrangements.

The procedure we envisage

10.32 When a case is referred to the reporter he, through the regular contacts which his department have established, will consider whether the proposed custody and access arrangements are the best that can be made for the children concerned. Normally, this should require one interview with either or both parents. We believe it is important that in appropriate cases—say children of 6 years and above—the reporter or his staff should seek the views of the children themselves. In most cases what has been proposed by the divorcing parents relative to custody, access and financial provision will be acceptable; and the reporter should within a relatively short period of time be in a position to provide the court with the information which it requires. In a minority of cases the reporter may have reason to be uncertain whether the welfare of the children concerned is being adequately safeguarded. In such cases the reporter himself should invite the parents to discuss the doubtful issue with him; and if he remained in doubt or were dissatisfied he would then refer the matter to the children's panel. We would expect that children's panel sittings for this type of divorce enquiry would be at separate times from hearings dealing with children in trouble. The opinion reached either by the reporter or by the children's panel would be conveyed to the court and it would be for the judge or the sheriff to make his decision. The sheriff would, of course, be free to accept or reject the advice tendered to him by the reporter or the children's panel, and he would also be free to ask for any further information or reconsideration that he deemed necessary. We have considered whether the reporter should be given a power to cite parents to appear before him for the above purposes. Obviously the pursuer will generally be willing to appear because if he or she failed to do so the divorce being sought might be withheld. Normally we would hope that the other parent, having been invited, would also willingly appear; failure to do so might imply a lack of interest and this would be a factor which the sheriff would doubtless take into account. On balance, we do not think that a power to cite ought to be granted to the reporters; but this is a matter which could be reviewed in the light of experience.

Review of financial arrangements

10.33 We would add that while reporters and children's panels would be primarily involved in the provision of information to the court about custody and access arrangements we are in no doubt that the trained staff of the reporter's department might also in many instances be able to spot cases of the kind we have referred to in paragraph 10.22 where a wife is accepting lesser financial provision than she might be able to obtain from the husband whom she is divorcing. Although the interest of the children should be the central concern of the reporters it is arguable that adequate financial provision for the mother is related to the children's welfare. We think that the reporter in some cases might usefully advise the pursuer as to what would be an appropriate financial provision having regard to the means of the parties and the interests of the children. In the event of there being a dispute as to the amount of any financial provision the reporter would be in a position to provide the sheriff with some advice as regards the financial arrangements so far as they affect the children.

Review of custody orders

10.34 We have considered to what extent custody and access orders should be subject to review. At the present time, they are only reviewed if the matter is raised by one or other of the parties. We do not think that this is adequate. On the other hand, we think it would be wrong that divorced parents should be, as it were, under constant supervision as regards the care of their children. We **recommend** that in any case where a court has made an order for custody or access, the reporter should be under a duty to review the working of the order after a period of, say, six months, and to report to the court if he considers that any change is required. The court on receiving such a report should have power to make a further order, even if no such order were sought by either of the parties. Before making such further order the court should have power to remit the question to the children's panel for further advice if this were thought necessary. We have had evidence to the effect that children to whom custody and access orders relate are sometimes justifiably unhappy with the effect of those orders and are quite capable of expressing a sensible and responsible view as to what should be done. At present such children have no remedy. We **recommend** that any child over the age of 10 to whom a custody or access order relates should be entitled as a matter of right to contact the reporter directly and seek a review. In such cases the reporter would have a duty to review and report to the court if he considered a change were required.

10.35 A similar question of review arises in relation to orders made by the court in respect of children of divorced parents where neither parent can be relied on as a custodian, at least without supervision, so that such children are placed under the supervision of, or are committted to the care of, a local authority. At present once such an order is made, that is normally the last the court hears of it. We **recommend** that any local authority subject to such an order should be required after, say, one year after the making of the order to report to the court as to whether or not the order should remain in force. Moreover, the local authority should be under a clear obligation to report to the court at any time whether the terms of any particular order should be changed.

Cost of our proposals

10.36 We have not found it possible to estimate the extra cost that would be involved for the children's hearing system if our proposed use of reporters and children's panels were accepted. Our own view is that the extra burden that would be placed on the reporters would not be insupportable although some extra staff would probably need to be engaged in areas where there are considerable numbers of divorces. It would be unfair to expect the local authorities responsible for the children's hearing system to shoulder such extra costs since the service is required by the courts which are a central government responsibility. We **recommend,** therefore, that the Department of Legal Affairs which we propose in Chapter 20, in discussion with the local authorities concerned, should make *ad hoc* grants to cover the extra costs which our proposals would involve.

Privacy for divorce actions

10.37 We sought views from a number of individuals experienced in divorce matters as to whether divorce actions should continue to be held in public, or whether the time had come when they ought to be conducted in private. This issue arises now only in respect of defended actions since, as earlier noted, undefended actions no longer require the presence of the pursuer and witnesses in the Court of Session. As undefended divorce petitions are dealt with by judges in chambers this of course means that the great bulk of divorce actions are already being considered in private. In 1978 of 8,152 divorce actions in which the court gave final judgement 7,869 or 96·5 per cent were undefended.[1] We are proposing that when there is no matter in dispute between the parties, the sheriffs should normally deal with the case on the basis of papers only, and the question of privacy will similarly not arise.

10.38 In favour of hearing defended divorces in open court it can be argued that the courts should be open to the public in order that justice can be seen to be done; and that if an exception is made in the case of divorce, pressure will arise for other kinds of action similarly to be held in private. The administration of justice in open court has also been stated to be a protection for the judge because an aggrieved litigant, if cases were held in private, could subsequently assert unfairness on the part of the judge. The proponents of open court hearings also argue that the interests of children involved are better safeguarded by the exercise of powers to restrict press reporting than by restricting the attendance of the public.

10.39 The majority of those who gave evidence to us on this matter, however, were against divorce actions being heard in open court. By their nature, defended actions inevitably involve a 'washing of dirty linen' in public; and the process invariably hardens attitudes further and generates even greater bitterness between the parties. The breakdown of the marriage is usually a painful experience for at least one party; and it can be in nobody's interests that this final step in dissolving the marriage should be taken in the full glare of publicity. The proponents of privacy in divorce also argue, no doubt with justification, that many members of the public who sit in the public benches during divorce proceedings do so not to see justice being done, but to savour any evidence of scandalous behaviour on the part of one or other of the spouses. Those who argue for privacy also contend that the public interest can adequately be safeguarded by allowing the press to be present, but subject always to restrictions on reporting whenever children are involved.

10.40 We ourselves are in favour of divorce actions being heard in private.

[1] These figures exclude 630 actions disposed of under the pre-1976 divorce law. See *Civil Judicial Statistics, 1978*.

We think that both the public interest and the position of judges can be adequately safeguarded by allowing the press to be present. We doubt whether the special nature of divorce could readily be founded on by others seeking similar treatment for other categories of action; but, in any event, any claims for the extension of private hearings to other forms of action would have to be made on their own merits. We have, therefore, no hesitation in **recommending** that defended divorce actions in the sheriff court should be heard in private, subject to the right of the press to attend and report the minimum that is considered essential in the public interest. We do not consider that the press can always be relied on to be sufficiently sensitive to the position of children of divorcing parents; examples of sheer insensitivity to the harm that can be done to children by newspaper reporting are by no means rare. There already exists provision in the criminal law to protect from press publicity children who appear as accused persons or as witnesses in criminal cases; and we consider that similar restrictions should by legislation be applied in the case of children involved in divorce proceedings. Our wish for privacy in these proceedings appears with particular force where children are involved. Accordingly, we **recommend** extending privacy of proceedings with restrictions on press reporting to all cases concerning custody of children, whether they are divorce actions or not.

Law reports

10.41 Finally, it is an important part of the development of the law, and of the continuing education of lawyers, that practitioners should be able to study the law as it develops in court. It would be a retrograde step if defended divorce actions held in private could not be reported in the law journals. We therefore **recommend** that such reporting should continue. The reports, however, should not refer to parties by name, but should adopt the 'A v B' technique.

Special court facilities for divorce business?

10.42 In Chapter 14 we recommend that parties in civil business should be separated from those involved in criminal business in the sheriff courts. We think this argument applies with particular force to the segregation of consistorial business from criminal trials. If sheriff courts have in the future, as we recommend, an exclusive jurisdiction in divorce actions the number of defended actions in which the parties will be required to attend individual courts will be relatively small. There should, therefore, be no difficulty in making appropriate arrangements.

The need for representation in undefended cases

10.43 In Scotland prior to April 1978, as we have observed, pursuers in undefended actions had to appear personally in the Court of Session along with their witnesses who testified to the evidence on which the divorce was sought. This procedure meant that the pursuers had to be legally represented in court.

10.44 The introduction in April 1978 of affidavit procedures and the consequent removal of the need for pursuers and witnesses to attend court has not, however, resulted in the cessation of civil legal aid for undefended divorces in Scotland as happened in England and Wales in April 1977. The reasons are, we understand, that the procedures in Scotland are such that it is difficult for any pursuer to petition for divorce without legal assistance. Affidavits, which set out the grounds on which the divorce is sought, have to be sworn before a notary public or a justice of the peace; and the form of the affidavits and the other paper work involved are so daunting that lay pursuers require considerable legal advice and assistance. The fact that legal representation in court is no longer required has not reduced the cost of the general run of undefended divorces in Scotland. According to information supplied by the Legal Aid Central Committee the average cost of undefended divorces over the last four years has been:

1976–77	£240
1977–78	£310
1978–79*	£310
1979–80†	£344

The costs in 1979–80 reflect an increase in solicitors' fees as well as the higher cost of outlays.

* based on figures up to 22 February 1979 only.
† based on a sample of accounts.

Evidence and corroboration

10.45 Where a civil action is not defended the law of Scotland normally allows the pursuer to succeed simply on the basis of written assertions. This, however, is not the case in divorce. In divorce, even if there is no defence, sworn evidence of the facts is required. It is for this reason that when the court altered procedure to avoid the need for attendance of parties at court it had to introduce instead affidavits sworn before notaries. This procedure involves expense. We think that in cases where there is no dispute, sworn evidence of this kind should be unnecessary, and we **recommend** that the court should be able to proceed upon a written form completed by the pursuer with a signed declaration that what is stated is the truth. No doubt some sanction against false declarations will be required. There is a further complication that, as in most, but not all, other matters where proof is required, evidence in divorce actions needs to be corroborated by at least one witness in addition to the pursuer. For this reason the present procedure requires not only one but at least two affidavits. We think that the requirement is unnecessary and **recommend** that it should be abolished in divorce proceedings. If these recommendations are implemented it will be possible to move to a simplified system which in suitable cases could be carried out by the pursuer, perhaps with some assistance from a Citizens Advice Bureau or from the sheriff clerks. These recommendations only apply in so far as there is no dispute. We have not considered and make no recommendations regarding requirements of proof in respect of contested matters.

Simple forms for undefended actions

10.46 Petitioners in England and Wales, with some assistance from solicitors or court staff, are able themselves to furnish on forms specially designed for the purpose, all the information which the court requires. From our own investigations we believe that the paper work in England and Wales could be even simpler than it now is; and the aim should be to produce in Scotland likewise forms that most laymen could complete with only limited need for legal advice and assistance. There is no reason why forms that are readily comprehensible to laymen should not be devised within the framework of the law. The forms would have to be accompanied by an explanatory leaflet; and it would be desirable that sheriff clerks should be trained to assist intending litigants to complete the forms. We therefore **recommend** that simple forms should be introduced which would enable a litigant to apply personally for a divorce if he or she so wishes.

Cessation of legal aid for divorce

10.47 If our recommendations for sheriff courts having divorce jurisdiction, for changes in the law of evidence and corroboration, and for the introduction of simpler paper work are all implemented, we see no reason why legal aid in its present form should continue to be available for undefended divorce actions. To remove any doubt on this matter, we would make clear that any party contemplating divorce could, under our integrated legal aid scheme proposed in Chapter 8, seek initial advice from a solicitor. If, after this initial legal advice, a party raises an action for divorce and there are no contested matters the subsequent steps to procure the divorce should not involve any further charge on the legal aid fund. We therefore **recommend** that initial legal advice and assistance only (as at present in England and Wales) should be available under our proposed new legal aid scheme when there is no matter under dispute as soon as the new procedures which we propose are introduced.

Entitlement to expenses

10.48 The law as to entitlement to expenses of a person in an undefended divorce action is at present undergoing some change in view of certain recent decisions of the Court of Session. However, there are now and are likely to remain many cases in which a husband defender is found liable for expenses, even though he does not defend. There is indeed an anomaly at present in that, rather than refrain altogether from defending the action, it may be cheaper for a husband to defend the action, apply for legal aid for his defence, and then seek modification of his liability for expenses. We think that there would be much to be said for changing the law so that in an undefended action of divorce no expenses would be awarded against the defender. We have not considered the full implications of this, but we **recommend** that it should be studied.

Net cost effect of our proposals

10.49 We have recommended some changes which will add to present costs—for example, the involvement of reporters and children's panels in providing reports for the courts on custody issues. We have also recommended extra duties for sheriff clerks and their staff in the processing of divorce papers and in assisting parties who wish to complete the appropriate forms without legal assistance. These extra costs, which we cannot quantify, should not in any event be substantial. There will, on the other hand, be savings which the State would secure under the head of legal aid if the basis on which such aid is available is altered as we have proposed in paragraph 10.47. We expect that many pursuers would still need to seek initial legal assistance under our recommended new integrated legal aid scheme; but there would be bound to be substantial savings on the civil legal aid bill which amounted to some £3·6 million in the year ending 31 March 1979.

Occupancy rights in the matrimonial home

10.50 There is one other matter which was drawn to our attention and which we should mention before leaving the subject of divorce. This is the difficulty judges at present face through lack of powers to make orders relative to occupancy rights in the matrimonial home when granting decrees of divorce. The typical situation which gives rise to the difficulty is where a mother with children seeks divorce and also custody of the children. In many cases the mother will be in a rented public authority house, the tenancy of which is in the father's name. The public authorities it seems are reluctant to grant a change of tenancy to the mother until the divorce is granted; and a hiatus can then ensue when the mother and children may be at risk. We were glad to learn that this problem had already been under examination by the Scottish Law Commission; and we express the hope that their work on this matter will speedily be concluded and that their recommendations will be implemented with the least possible delay.

RECOMMENDATIONS

			Paragraph
Jurisdiction to sheriff courts	R10.1	Sheriff courts should be granted jurisdiction in actions for divorce.	10.17
	R10.2	In divorce actions the sheriff court should have exclusive jurisdiction as a court of first instance.	10.18
Power to remit cases to Court of Session	R10.3	A sheriff on cause shown by the parties, or of his own accord, should have power to remit divorce actions to the Outer House of the Court of Session.	10.19
Designation of particular divorce courts	R10.4	Sheriffs Principal, when they think it appropriate, should designate particular courts within their sheriffdom to deal with divorce cases.	10.20
Right of pursuer to select court	R10.5	The pursuer in a divorce action should be able to choose between raising the action in his or her local sheriff court or in the defender's local sheriff court if this were different.	10.21
Sheriff's right to remit action to another sheriff court	R10.6	A sheriff of his own accord should have power to remit any divorce action to any other sheriff court where, for instance, he has grounds for believing that this would be in the the best interests of any children affected by the action.	10.21
One category of divorce based on separation	R10.7	Parliament should consider whether there should be only one category of divorce based on separation; whether this category of divorce should not require consent; and whether the period of separation which would establish evidence of irretrievable breakdown should not be longer than two years.	10.23
Special reports on custody of children	R10.8	Special reports on custody arrangements should be obtained in all divorce actions involving children.	10.25

			Paragraph
	R10.9	In every divorce action (defended as well as undefended) where children under the age of 16 are involved the case should be referred by the court to the appropriate reporter to the children's panel for special reports on custody arrangements.	10.31
Review of custody or access orders	R10.10	In any case where a court has made an order for custody or access, the reporter to the children's panel should be under a duty to review the working of the order after a period of, say, 6 months and to report to the court if he considers that any change is required.	10.34
	R10.11	Any child over the age of 10 to whom a custody or access order relates should be entitled as a matter of right to contact the reporter directly and seek a review. In such cases the reporter would have a duty to review and report to the court if he considered a change were required.	10.34
Review of supervision or committal orders	R10.12	Any local authority subject to an order which has placed children of divorced parents under its supervision or care should be required after, say, one year after the making of the order to report to the court as to whether or not the order should remain in force.	10.35
Grants to authorities for services of reporters	R10.13	The Department of Legal Affairs in discussion with the local authorities concerned should make *ad hoc* grants to cover the extra costs incurred by the courts' use of reporters' services.	10.36
Privacy for divorce actions	R10.14	Defended divorce actions in the sheriff court should be heard in private, subject to the right of the press to attend and report the minimum that is considered essential in the public interest.	10.40

			Paragraph
Restrictions on press reporting in custody of children cases	R10.15	Privacy of proceedings with restrictions on press reporting should apply in all cases concerning custody of children, whether they are divorce actions or not.	10.40
Law reports	R10.16	Divorce actions held in private should still be subject to reports in law journals but using the 'A v B' technique to preserve privacy.	10.41
Evidence and corroboration	R10.17	In undefended divorce actions the court in place of affidavit evidence should be able to proceed on written forms completed by pursuers with a signed declaration that what is stated is the truth, and without need for corroborative evidence.	10.45
Need for simple forms in divorce actions	R10.18	Simple forms should be introduced which would enable a litigant to apply personally for a divorce, if he or she so wishes.	10.46
Cessation of full legal aid for undefended divorce actions	R10.19	Only initial legal advice and assistance under the proposed integrated legal aid scheme should be available to parties seeking divorce where there are no matters in dispute.	10.47
Entitlement to expenses	R10.20	Consideration should be given to the proposition that no expenses should be awarded against the defender in undefended divorce actions.	10.48

CHAPTER 11

SMALL CLAIMS

11.1 Some of the evidence we received showed dissatisfaction with the complexity and difficulty of court procedures. We deal with the general problem of civil procedures in Chapter 14. However, as earlier noted, the two areas where the greatest concern was expressed were divorce (which we discussed in the previous Chapter) and small claims. Despite the existence of a special procedure for small claims in Scotland—the summary cause in the sheriff court—there was a substantial body of evidence to the effect that the needs of claimants in cases involving small sums are at present inadequately met. The existing summary cause procedures were described as too expensive and too complex. It was further represented to us by many bodies and individuals, that disputes arising from simple every day transactions ought to be dealt with under simple court procedures. The evidence presented to us stressed the deterrents that prevent potential individual consumer litigants from using the summary cause procedure to settle a small claim. The procedure is such that a lawyer's services are virtually essential for certain steps in it, and if a solicitor is employed the outlay can soon exceed the sum claimed. Although the successful pursuer is entitled to recover at least some of his expenses, this is a possibility that even the most confident litigant cannot take for granted. From the evidence we received, and from the further studies we undertook, we believe that there is a need in Scotland for an informal and speedy procedure for settling small claims, facilitating self-representation by the parties to the dispute.

11.2 Although the evidence shows substantial agreement on the need for a new system of dealing with small claims, views differed as to whether the system should be court-based or not. Some of the evidence recommended a system of informal tribunals or arbitration for small claims, whereas other evidence recommended improvements or simplifications in court procedures. The various schemes proposed differed considerably. We therefore had to consider the nature of the problems with which any such system would have to deal, and in doing so we studied how some other countries had attempted to meet the need for a small claims procedure.

The nature of small claims

11.3 Most of those who gave evidence to us saw small claims as relating to consumer protection and involving the enforcement of the consumer's rights and the redress of his grievances, often about disputes regarding the adequacy of goods or services supplied. This is not, however, what actually constitutes the majority of the smaller claims that come before the sheriff courts. Most of these relate to the recovery of debts, and the summary cause is, in practice, to a very large extent a debt collection procedure. In most such cases, the person sued has simply failed to make payment. We decided to define a small claim in terms that will encompass undisputed as well as disputed claims. The specific feature of a small claim, in our view, is that the sum involved (whether as a debt, a sum claimed as damages, or the value of goods involved in a dispute) is sufficiently small to represent the value of a common rather than an exceptional loss or domestic transaction.

Systems in other countries

11.4 Procedures for dealing with small claims have been introduced in many countries. Some prefer using the courts while others have adopted quasi-judicial arbitration procedures. We studied systems in England and Wales, in Toronto and Vancouver in Canada, in Los Angeles and New York in the USA, and in Sweden; and we also studied published accounts of procedures elsewhere.

11.5 There is much literature on this subject and it is unnecessary for us to summarise the great variety of procedures we have seen and from which we have drawn various general principles. A few examples will suffice. In England and Wales, we studied the county court procedure wherby cases involving sums of less than £200 can be referred to arbitration at the request of either party. If the amount involved is greater than £200, both parties need to agree to arbitration. The registrar (a judicial officer in the county court) normally acts as the arbiter, taking an inquisitorial role, asking questions and probing for information as the need arises rather than merely listening to the parties putting their case. The litigants may meet the registrar at a pre-trial review, where the case may be settled informally or where the papers necessary for evidence will be explained. England also has two experimental 'small claims courts' in London and Manchester which, despite their name, are not part of the English courts system. Essentially, they are experimental arbitration procedures that enable litigants to obtain judgement quickly and cheaply. These two small claims courts have no statutory jurisdiction, and both parties must agree to be bound by the courts' decisions. The adjudicators in London are mostly lawyers, while in Manchester they include a number of experts such as architects and engineers. In both the London and Manchester courts, the procedure is informal and the arbiter takes an inquisitorial role.[1]

11.6 In Norway, all small claims first come before a local conciliation board which attempts to arrive at a settlement between the parties. These boards have an entirely lay membership. In Sweden, on the other hand, a simplified procedure for small claims has been introduced in ordinary civil courts. Fees for legal representation cannot be recovered and the courts have legally qualified clerks to help litigants prepare their cases. The existence of a Public Complaints Board in Sweden to deal (free of charge) with consumer disputes means that relatively few cases actually reach the courts.

11.7 Most states of the USA have some system of small claims court, the majority of which prohibit legal representation and use informal and private hearings. The small claims court in New York has attracted considerable interest with six small claims offices throughout the city open in the evenings to provide the service of arbiters. Nearly 90 per cent of small claims in New York are heard by arbiters. In the Canadian province of Ontario the small claims courts comprise a specific branch of the court system. Their procedure is comparable with our own summary cause, but it includes unusual features.

[1] Provision for small claims is fully discussed in: National and Welsh Consumer Councils: *Simple Justice:* 1979.

Debt problems may be taken to an official known as a referee. His function is to provide a mediation and conciliation service between debtors and creditors, seeking to establish the most suitable and acceptable means of settling a debt, preferably without further legal action being taken. The referee may also be approached by debtors or creditors before action is initiated in the small claims court, and settlement of the debt can be arranged, perhaps by instalments, without any legal action being taken. We consider the role of the referee in debt enforcement and debt counselling further in Chapter 12.

The European Economic Community

11.8 Small claims procedures in member states of the European Economic Community have recently been under consideration and the Economic and Social Committee has produced a report on consumer protection which considers small claims in this context. The basic principles which the report recommends for any small claims procedure seem to us to express very well the best practices we have seen:

'—the procedure should be simple and free of unnecessary formalities; the complainant must be able to bring his case before the judge himself, the complaint being stated by filling in a simple form. Help should be provided in filling in the form, by the court officials, for instance, or a consumer advice centre;

—there should be no obligation to be represented in the proceedings. A ban on the use of lawyers does not, however, seem desirable, in the consumer's interests as well. The financial risk could be limited (precisely because the amount at stake is not great) by not consistently ordering the losing party to pay the other's costs. The consumer should also have the opportunity of being represented by a representative consumer organisation;

—it should be possible for the case to be dealt with orally;

—the judge should have great freedom regarding the way in which the proceedings are conducted. This freedom should embrace inter alia: the ways in which evidence may be furnished, the interrogation of the parties or witnesses, outlining the proceedings to the parties;

—the costs of the actual proceedings should be very low;

—high costs for expert investigation should be avoided. The judge must weigh the claim against the probable cost of expert opinions and take account of the nature of the product and the financial means of the complainant. The judge should inform the consumer about the costs and offer the possibility of an expert opinion free of charge if the consumer's financial position or other circumstances so warrant.'[1]

Our recommendations were developed independently of the principles adumbrated in that report, but it is clear that we are thinking on much the same lines and that there is, indeed, considerable international consensus on this issue.

---

[1] European Economic and Social Committee: *Study of the Section for Protection of the Environment, Public Health and Consumer Affairs on the Use of Judicial and Quasi-Judicial Means of Consumer Protection in the European Community and their Harmonisation:* Brussels, 1979. Pages 40–41.

Conciliation and negotiation

11.9 Small claims do not, of course, begin as court actions; there are other ways of resolving disputes such as negotiation and conciliation. Citizens Advice Bureaux workers, local authority consumer protection officers and solicitors may all attempt to negotiate settlements between consumers and traders either by negotiating directly or by making use of special procedures under commercial codes of practice. There may be an implied threat of legal action but the purpose of all these advisers will normally be to achieve a mutually satisfactory solution without more formal procedures. The principal benefits of conciliation and negotiation are informality and, at best, speed and cheapness, and they may often result in a compromise solution. On the other hand, conciliation cannot settle authoritatively any point of law at issue or reach a decision where the parties remain in disagreement. We believe that advisers ought always to attempt negotiation before raising a court action; and the court procedures we favour would provide for potential litigants to be told what local conciliation services, if any, are available.

Procedures existing in Scotland

11.10 The very brief summary we have given of some of the provision made for small claims in other countries is intended to suggest the variety of ways in which other countries meet what they see as a real need—a simple, cheap, quick, conclusive small claims procedure. We have said that in Scotland the procedure for raising small claims actions is the summary cause in the sheriff court. In Dundee, however, an experimental small claims procedure has been available since 1 January 1979.

Summary cause

11.11 The present summary cause procedure in the sheriff court was introduced in 1976 in the light of the recommendations of the Grant Committee.[1] The main purpose of its introduction was to provide a procedure that was both efficient and cheap. The summary cause does not normally involve written pleadings and the lengthy procedure of adjustment that goes with the ordinary cause; there is no recording of evidence at the hearing itself. In most actions for the payment of money, the procedures can easily be carried through without the parties being required to appear in court—a considerable advantage in preventing loss of wages and travelling expenses. Appearance is required only when the action is defended, or when there is some dispute about the method of payment. Broadly speaking, the actions which may be brought by the summary cause procedure include most consumer claims, actions by corporate bodies for the recovery of debts, claims for the recovery of heritable property (for example repossession by commercial landlords or local authorities following non-payment of rent) and claims for damages where the sum involved does not exceed £500. The rules setting out the procedure and forms are complex and extend to some fifty pages. A somewhat simplified account is given in the 'Guide to the New Summary Cause in the Sheriff Court', copies of which are available in courts and at Citizens Advice Bureaux.

---

[1] *Report of the Committee on the Sheriff Court (Cmnd. 3248)*: HMSO, 1967.

11.12 The person raising the action (the pursuer) must obtain from the sheriff clerk's office one of ten different forms of summons. With the completed form the pursuer goes to the sheriff clerk's office again where payment of the appropriate fee is made ranging from £1·50 to £7·50 depending on the amount of the sum being claimed. The sheriff clerk signs the summons and marks on it the date when the case may be called in court. Next the copy summons must be served on the defender, normally by recorded delivery post; and this can only be done by a solicitor or sheriff officer. The certificate showing that the summons has been served must be returned to court before a stated date.

11.13 Where the case is one for the payment of money, the defender must indicate whether he will attend court or not. If no form is returned to the court, the case will be decided in favour of the pursuer by default. If an offer of payment by instalments is made and the pursuer agrees to accept it, there is no need for an appearance by either party. Otherwise, the pursuer must attend or be represented in court. Subject to the court's approval, either party may be represented by a person who is not a lawyer, but there are various limitations on the court's discretion in this regard. Expenses may be granted against the loser: these expenses may include the summons fee; the cost of serving the summons and of conducting the case (including any solicitor's fee); reasonable outlays which could include travelling expenses and any loss of wages or earnings; and the expenses of necessary witnesses.

11.14 An analysis of the records of the Edinburgh Sheriff Court for November 1976 revealed that of 1,220 cases nearly 1,000 (82 per cent) were summonses for payment of money due and 200 (16 per cent) were for recovery of possession of heritable property; there were also a small number of actions for delivery of goods. The largest category of pursuers were public bodies (local authorities and public utilities) accounting for some 40 per cent of all actions raised: a further 50 per cent of actions were raised by commercial, financial and legal concerns; and less than 10 per cent of actions were raised by private individuals. The vast majority of defenders—over 80 per cent—were individuals and the remainder commercial organisations.[1] Figures from the Edinburgh Sheriff Court do not, of course, necessarily represent a nation-wide pattern, but the broad picture is sufficiently illustrative. In 1978 of 104,375 actions disposed of by decree in summary cause in Scotland as a whole, 72,885 (70 per cent) were actions for debt.[2] That actions for debt by public, commercial or financial concerns should figure largely in summary cause procedure is not surprising. The procedure is well suited to dealing with such cases relatively simply and cheaply; and, in particular, it provides a means whereby judgement can be given or settlement reached without, in the majority of cases, the need for a hearing. Of the actions disposed of by decree in summary cause in 1978, 96 per cent were granted in absence. In the other 4 per cent of cases a hearing was fixed, though not all actually proceeded to a hearing. The Scottish Courts Administration estimate that fewer than 1,000 summary cause proofs are heard in a year.[3]

11.15 The summary cause serves a useful purpose in disposing of routine cases of undisputed debt but it does not appear to encourage individuals to

[1] Scottish Office Central Research Unit: *The Social Aspects of Diligence, An Interim Report of Investigations:* Scottish Office, 1977, Volume I, pages 25–33.
[2] *Civil Judicial Statistics, 1978,* Table 11A.
[3] *Civil Judicial Statistics, 1978,* Table 11A. The estimate of the number of proofs held is based on a 10 week sample of proofs heard in Glasgow Sheriff Court in 1977.

pursue claims—either individual claims for debt or consumer and other claims. There seems to be substantial public ignorance of the summary cause procedure. In our survey of legal needs some 99 per cent of respondents had no knowledge or only inaccurate knowledge of the summary cause procedure.[1] This public ignorance is no doubt compounded by the uninformative name of the summary cause procedure. Another reason, however, appears to be the complexity of the procedure. There is, as we have said, a guide to the summary cause procedure—the only layman's guide to court procedures and much to be admired in its attempt to explain a complex system. Nevertheless, it is doubtful whether many people would be willing or competent to conduct their own cases in summary cause, even if they had heard of it or understood what it was. Indeed, the formalities make it impossible for the party litigant to conduct the whole case himself without professional assistance. A solicitor or sheriff officer must be employed to effect service and solicitors may not be willing to perform the task unless they are engaged for the whole case. It follows that where claims for small sums of money are at issue, the cost of legal representation is a significant disincentive to taking legal action. In addition, the expenses of a summary cause case which are borne by the losing party can be considerable, particularly where an action is defended. Indeed, in actions for small sums, expenses can exceed the value of the claim involved. The Scottish Courts Administration provided us with figures for a sample of 51 consecutive proofs held at Glasgow Sheriff Court culminating on 30 June 1978. In these cases, the average sum claimed was £165 and the average amount of expenses £97. In all cases of claims for sums of less than £50, the expenses exceeded the sum sought. These figures are the expenses awarded against the loser only; the total expenses of both parties will be appreciably greater. Such levels of unavoidable costs are sufficient, we believe, to deter many individuals from taking cases to court.

Dundee experiment

11.16 As we stated in paragraph 11.10, an experimental small claims procedure is at present available in Dundee Sheriff Court. This limited and voluntary small claims pilot scheme was introduced in Dundee, with effect from 1 January 1979, by the then Lord Advocate. The details were devised in consultation with consumer interests by the Scottish Courts Administration, and the experiment is being monitored. A grant from the European Economic Community has assisted towards the cost of this experiment. Parallel with the Dundee experiment, a study is being made in Aberdeen of the operation of the summary cause procedure and the scope for its simplification. Under the Dundee experimental scheme a claim against a person or business can be brought for sums up to a value of £500. Claims can be brought by individuals but not normally by a business. The sheriff clerk has been given a discretion to allow small businesses (such as a local newsagent or grocer) to bring claims under the new procedure, or to allow any business to bring a claim against an individual for non-payment of an account where the latter has refused to pay on the grounds that he is dissatisfied with the goods or services supplied. The pursuer has to complete a simple claim form and can get the help of the sheriff clerk, who sends the papers to the defender by ordinary post. The documents include a form which invites the defender to agree to have the claim disposed of under the new procedure. Agreement by the defender is essential since the scheme is

---

[1] See Appendix 4, Table 65.

not mandatory. If the defender declines, the sheriff clerk will inform the claimant and no further action under the new procedure can be taken. The claimant's only recourse then is to raise a summary cause action.

11.17 If the defender accepts the summons and the case carries on under the new procedure, the sheriff, as adjudicator, considers whether he can reach a decision without meeting the parties to the dispute. If it is necessary to have a hearing, the parties are informed that they must attend and bring their witnesses. At the hearing, the adjudicator's role is inquisitorial; he asks questions and assists both parties on any legal points. The proceedings are informal. The hearing takes place in a private room and the adjudicator does not wear a wig or gown. The adjudicator is able to accept written or oral evidence, including, for example, oral evidence by telephone, at his own discretion. Representation by a solicitor is allowed but only at the party's own expense. Representation by someone other than a solicitor is at the discretion of the adjudicator. If it proves impossible to reach an agreed solution, the adjudicator decides the case in accordance with the rules of the substantive law. Expenses may be awarded up to £25. The cost of any expert witnesses required by the adjudicator (subject to the parties agreeing to pay for the expert) may be awarded in addition. There is no appeal from the adjudicator's decision.

11.18 To date this experimental procedure has been little used. An important reason for this must be that the new procedure is not mandatory. Many potential defenders may see advantage in not agreeing to adjudication, thereby putting the claimant to the cost and trouble of taking further legal action. Few claimants have been prepared to do so.

New procedures for Scotland

11.19 We considered whether a system of hearings based on the existing court structure (as in the Dundee experiment) was preferable to a system of hearings outwith the courts such as could be provided by a special small claims tribunal. The advantages of a tribunal are informality in proceedings, the possible appointment of specialist adjudicators, and easier provision for lay representation. On the other hand, we believe that the court system ought to offer similar advantages and that it has other advantages of its own. Only a court can satisfactorily settle matters of substantive law (subject to appeal if this is allowed). The court system offers an existing widespread structure of facilities and personnel that can be augmented, if necessary, at far less cost than would be incurred in providing a wholly new tribunal system. We believe as a matter of principle that if legislation has been devised to protect the citizen (in small claims matters as well as major issues) it is the responsibility of the courts to provide efficient procedures to enforce the law. Small claims justice should not be seen as second-class justice. We wish to encourage people to look to the courts for accessible justice and not to a plethora of alternative solutions. Therefore, we prefer a procedure based on and within the existing courts.

11.20 The Dundee experiment has shown that relatively simple and informal procedures can work within the sheriff court. It is possible that the research going on in Aberdeen will show how the summary cause might be substantially simplified.

11.21 We therefore **recommend** that there should be a small claims procedure within the sheriff court which is sufficiently simple, cheap, quick and informal to encourage individual litigants to use it themselves without legal representation. In view of current activity in this field it would be wrong for us to draw up detailed recommendations about the form of the procedure; this will, no doubt, be a task for the Sheriff Court Rules Council to perform in the light of our recommendations and the results of the Dundee experiment. We do, however, **recommend** that in drawing up the rules for a new procedure, the Council should consult consumer and business, as well as legal, interests. The basic principles which we **recommend** should govern the drafting of the rules of a new procedure are:

(i) *Monetary limits*

Any civil case where the amount or value of the claim does not exceed a sum of at least £500 should be covered, regardless of whether the action is for aliment, damages, repayment of a debt or compensation. There ought to be a simple mechanism for raising the top level to maintain its value, by making provision for increases by index-linking.

(ii) *Expenses*

The risk of having to meet the other party's expenses is a major deterrent to both parties to taking part in a small claims action in court. We therefore consider that no expenses should normally be awarded to the successful party, though the sheriff should have discretion to make an exception as regards the travelling expenses of the parties and necessary witnesses.

(iii) *Convenience*

The majority of undefended cases should continue, as under summary cause procedure, to be settled by exchange of papers without any court appearance.

(iv) *Simplicity*

The simplicity of the new procedure should be seen not only in the steps of the procedure itself, but in the language and formalities of the court. The court authorities should enlist the help of consumer organisations and advice agencies in devising summonses, claim forms and so on. We have seen some good examples of simple forms and guides to procedure abroad. The summons should be issued by the sheriff clerk and served by post. This is an essential element in any 'do-it-yourself' system.

(v) *Informality*

Informality should characterise the hearing of a small claim in court just as simplicity should characterise the language and procedures used. It is, however, important to stress that informal procedures do not mean casual justice. The courts must be as firm and effective in hearing small claims as in other areas of the law.

(vi) *Pre-trial review*

During our examination of systems elsewhere—particularly in the county courts in England—we have seen the operation of pre-trial review. This is a preliminary meeting between the judge and the parties at which the judge ascertains the nature of the dispute; he may be able to act to some extent as a conciliator and he can advise the parties as to what evidence will be required and what the procedure will be at the adjudication hearing. We have no doubt that this can be an extremely useful step in procedure. However, we have heard some criticism of the English procedure, namely that the rigid division into two stages—the pre-trial review and the hearing—sometimes involves parties attending twice when, in very simple matters, an adjudication could be achieved at first hearing. We hope that any procedure introduced in Scotland will be sufficiently flexible to enable a case to be disposed of at one hearing if two hearings are not necessary.

(vii) *Scope of the procedure*

The procedure should encompass the full scope of the present summary cause, including actions concerning reparation, aliment and other matrimonial causes, or house tenancy. We rely on the pre-trial review to determine the form which proof should take in each case.

SOME DIFFICULTIES

Cost

11.22 We do not consider that the new procedure which we are recommending would involve extra public expenditure of an unacceptable order. If a 'do-it-yourself' procedure can be provided in England and Wales then no new issue of principle is involved. Equal resources should be made available in Scotland.

Staff

11.23 In England and Wales small claims cases are heard by the registrar. No such judicial officer exists in Scotland. It may be that it will be necessary to increase the complement of sheriffs in order to meet the requirements of the new procedure. Sheriff clerks may need some extra training and facilities to deal with party litigants but we are confident that they could cope without excessive expense. In evidence to us the Sheriff Clerks' Branch of the Society of Civil and Public Servants expressed the view that lay representation should be encouraged.

Debt recovery

11.24 There is a question whether the small claims procedure should supplant the summary cause and be the sole procedure available for claims of small amounts or whether two procedures for such claims should co-exist. We are in favour of the former solution, and we **recommend** its adoption. We are against proliferation of procedures which only complicate matters for the public. This does, of course, mean that the small claims procedure will, in addition to the type of case for which we wish particularly to provide, also be the 'debt collecting' procedure for the great mass of actions, where there is no dispute about liability, raised, for example, by public utilities and large companies. We believe, however, that most cases of this kind will be settled on paper without an adjudication, as they are now in the summary cause. In any event cheaper procedures mean lower debts and will be indirectly advantageous to defenders who have to pay expenses. Moreover, we do not want to exclude consumer defenders or small business defenders who at present may concede a strong case for fear of the expense of defending it.

11.25 One possible objection to the procedure we favour is that unless special provision is made, the cost of service of documents will be thrown on the public in all cases. We think, however, that this problem could readily be overcome by providing, for example, that the court will not undertake service for any party which is a body corporate. We think it important that the small claims procedure should be available even in what appears to be 'debt collecting' cases, since a small claimant's claim may take the form of a defence to a debt collecting action, rather than a claim initiated by him. We are also aware that increased use of judicial time would result from adoption of our favoured procedures but, in our view, any increased expense on this account would be a price worth paying.

RECOMMENDATIONS

			Paragraph
An improved procedure	R11.1	There should be a small claims procedure within the sheriff court which is sufficiently simple, cheap, quick and informal to encourage individual litigants to use it themselves without legal representation.	11.21
	R11.2	In drawing up the rules for a new procedure, the Sheriff Court Rules Council should consult consumer and business, as well as legal, interests.	11.21
	R11.3	The rules of the new procedure should embody the principles set out in paragraph 11.21.	11.21 (i–vii)
New procedure to supplant the summary cause	R11.4	The new small claims procedure should supplant the summary cause and be the sole procedure available for claims of small amounts.	11.24

CHAPTER 12

DEBT ENFORCEMENT AND DEBT COUNSELLING

DEBT ENFORCEMENT

12.1 Court action to recover a debt will normally only be taken after the creditor has tried by other means to recover the sum owed, for example by sending reminder letters to the debtor, getting his solicitor to threaten legal action, or using the services of a debt collection agency. Even if the creditor obtains a court decree in his favour, this does not guarantee him payment of the debt. If the debtor still refuses to pay at this stage the creditor has to take further steps, under the authority provided by the decree, to recover the debt. This procedure for enforcing the decree is known as 'diligence'.[1]

12.2 Diligence is, therefore, a vital final provision in debt enforcement procedures. Where the debtor has some resources at his disposal it is obviously important that our system of justice provides a reasonably efficient means for the creditor to gain possession of whatever proportion of them is needed to extinguish the debt. The matter is one which attracted our interest and concern.

Diligence in Scotland

12.3 If a debtor refuses or is unable to pay a sum awarded in a decree, the creditor will seek the services of a sheriff officer to enforce the decree.[2] Property belonging to the debtor held by a third party (wages due to him in the hands of the employer, for example) may be frozen by 'arrestment' and may be taken into the creditor's possession by a subsequent action of 'furthcoming' should that be necessary. Arrestment is only effective in relation to funds or property actually owed or held when the action is taken, so that to arrest four weeks' wages, four separate actions are necessary. Property held by the debtor himself may also be taken by the diligence of 'poinding'. Before poinding can take place the debtor must receive a formal demand to pay the debt (called a charge) which must be served on him by a sheriff officer. The possessions can then be sold to meet the debt at a warrant sale conducted by the sheriff officer. There are a number of other, more abstruse, forms of diligence which are rarely used.

12.4 We believe that the system of debt enforcement through these forms of diligence is capable of improvement. There are many steps in the procedure, and a fee is payable at each. Warrant sales are an inefficient and unpleasant means of meeting a debt; and there is evidence of growing public concern that the warrant sale is a degrading practice, since it is often basic domestic effects which are sold on these occasions. Fortunately, the number of warrant sales actually held is very much smaller even than the number advertised. In the very few sales that do

---

[1] Some forms of diligence may be used at an early stage in an action to force a debtor to appear in court or to compel him to find security for the sum claimed against him, pending the decision of the action. More commonly diligence is used in the execution of a judgment, and it is in this sense which we use the term here.

[2] Court of Session decrees are enforced by messengers-at-arms. For simplicity we will refer only to sheriff officers.

proceed the amount realised is usually small and the costs incurred can account for a substantial part of the sum realised.

12.5 An initial look at these problems left us in no doubt that any proposals for improving the present arrangements in Scotland could only be made following a thorough consideration of the whole field of the law relating to debt and debt enforcement. Just such a broad review is at present being undertaken by the Scottish Law Commission, who have in hand a comprehensive programme of work on diligence, including some fundamental social research into the nature and social context of debt in Scotland. It seems to us right that the problem should be treated in this thorough manner and we were concerned not to duplicate this work in any way. While we make no recommendations of our own we hope that the work of the Scottish Law Commission will come to fruition soon, as we recognise that there are problems in this area which need to be dealt with as a matter of high priority.

DEBT COUNSELLING

12.6 Debt is an inevitable feature of a society which relies on credit to the extent that ours does. It only becomes a problem when the debtor becomes unable or unwilling to pay off the debt. To the extent that he is unwilling we hope that the proposals we make on small claims in Chapter 11 will assist some creditors to obtain a court decree; and we trust that the proposals which will emerge from the Scottish Law Commission will assist the creditor in enforcing the decree. Nevertheless, we believe that many people get into debt simply because they are unable to handle their money properly. Unless they can be helped at an early stage, they can easily enter a spiral of increasing debt from which they cannot extricate themselves. Rather than wait for such people to be taken to court by their creditors, we think that there is a need in Scotland for much more effective provision than currently exists of debt counselling or, as we should prefer to call it, money management counselling. Such counselling should have three objectives: firstly, to help in the early and expeditious settlement of debts to the mutual advantage of creditors and debtors; secondly, to prevent individuals from becoming overwhelmed by mounting debts they cannot control; and, thirdly, to provide a remedy in cases of severe debt at an earlier stage than recourse to the court system allows. In this connection it is worth bearing in mind that the number of debt cases considered in sheriff courts in 1978 was over 70,000; and any measures which would help reduce this workload would thereby help to improve the efficiency of the courts.

12.7 With these ideas in mind, we were interested to study the system of debt counselling which has become an integral part of the court system in Ontario, Canada. In Ontario, court referees, as they are called, are appointed to advise the court itself of the financial situation of debtors, with a view to securing the fairest, most realistic and most constructive court orders for debt settlement. The referee interviews the debtor and reviews his whole financial position. Where necessary, creditors can be summoned and individual instalment or consolidation orders (payable either direct to creditors or through the courts) can be discussed for recommendation to the court. A somewhat similar social service office for debtors within each county court in England and Wales was recommended by the Payne Committee.[1]

[1] *Report of the Committee on the Enforcement of Judgment Debts*, (Cmnd. 3909): HMSO, 1969.

12.8 The advantages of the court referee system are to improve the quality of financial orders made by the courts and to give practical assistance to debtors in extricating themselves from financial problems. The system mainly helps those who are already floundering in very deep financial water; unhappily, it does not normally catch debtors before they get out of their depth. Whether or not it would be sensible to introduce such referees in the Scottish courts will depend in large measure on the current work of the Scottish Law Commission, because there is a very close link between diligence generally, the possibility of some kind of consolidation order for the simultaneous repayment of several debts, and the provision of counselling for debtors. Without prejudice to any development in court counselling services which might emerge from consideration of the Scottish Law Commission's work, therefore, we have confined ourselves to considering how a system of money management counselling could be made available to people who are not necessarily debtors, but who have financial problems which could land them in court unless remedied.

12.9 We are concerned that Scotland lacks virtually any accessible free service of this kind. Even those who have access to bank managers, accountants and solicitors may be reluctant to seek their advice; and there are no other generally available trained advisers on whom they can call. The nearest equivalents are social workers or advisers in Citizens Advice Bureaux, one or two of which run specialist financial advice clinics. In the course of handling many family problems, both Advice Bureaux workers and social workers must of course deal with financial problems; but this does not amount to organised, trained advice and support in budgeting and coping with debt, freely accessible to all who need it. A good example of such a service is the Birmingham Settlement Money Advice Centre.[1]

12.10 We therefore **recommend** that the Legal Services Commission which, we propose, should give high priority to developing a money management counselling service in Scotland, in consultation with the Citizens Advice Bureaux and social workers, to raise substantially the quality and accessibility of advice available to Scots in financial difficulties. This advice should be an essential component in the provision of advice services which we have recommended in Chapter 7. In so far as this advice will prevent debt cases from taking up the time of the courts, it will be immediately cost effective, to say nothing of the benefits to creditors in getting debts settled, and to debtors in terms of peace of mind and stability of family and employment. Such advice could benefit not only individual citizens but also small businesses and self-employed persons who founder into debt. Accordingly, we further **recommend** that the Scottish Association of Citizens Advice Bureaux should give higher priority to money management counselling in their training programmes; and it is similarly important that such counselling be given due priority in the training of social workers.

12.11 Once such a service has become established the courts might find advantage on occasion in seeking a counsellor's report before arriving at, for example, decisions on instalment payments. This would not detract from the authority of the court, but would provide a source of advice available to sheriffs to assist them in pronouncing judgements which were most likely to be effective, and which promoted the best interests of all parties. As we have said, we make our recom-

---

[1] The work of the Centre is described in *Simple Justice*, pages 43–44.

mendation without prejudice to the possibility of establishing a court-based system in due course, following on the recommendations of the Scottish Law Commission on diligence generally. We believe that a community-based system of money management counselling such as we have recommended could usefully work alongside a court-based system; and we see every advantage in establishing a proper service through Citizens Advice Bureaux as early as possible.

Learning to manage money

12.12 Children can and should learn how to manage money, and some of this is indeed already undertaken at secondary school. We **recommend** that as many school pupils as possible should have an opportunity, in appropriate subject departments, to learn money management.

			Paragraph
Debt counselling	R12.1	The Legal Services Commission should give high priority to developing a money management counselling service in Scotland, in consultation with Citizens Advice Bureaux and social workers.	12.10
	R12.2	The Scottish Association of Citizens Advice Bureaux should give higher priority to money management counselling in their training programmes; and such counselling should be given due priority in the training of social workers.	12.10
	R12.3	As many school pupils as possible should have an opportunity, in appropriate subject departments, to learn money management.	12.12

CHAPTER 13

ADMINISTRATION OF ESTATES

13.1 In our research into legal need we asked respondents about the nature of the business on which they had last consulted a solicitor. After conveyancing, matters concerning wills and estates were the second most common reason quoted (17 per cent of all reasons).[1] By its nature the business of dealing with wills and estates is an area which affects many people at some time. Preparing wills and administering estates is an important part of the work of Scottish solicitors: executry and trust business accounted for 19 per cent of the gross fee income of the firms who provided detailed figures in response to our survey of solicitors' remuneration.[2] While most solicitors undoubtedly conduct this business efficiently and with reasonable despatch, cases have been brought to our attention in which the settlement of a deceased person's estate has taken an unreasonable length of time. We are also aware that delay in administering an estate is the subject of a significant proportion of the complaints received by the Law Society. The delay may sometimes be occasioned by the absence of a will, or by the existence of a 'home made' will whose provisions are more confusing than helpful. It can also be caused by the executors who are appointed to administer the estate. With larger estates there can be a delay in getting determinations from the Capital Taxes Office, attributable in part no doubt to the complexity of the relevant law, and the frequency with which it is amended. In other cases, however, it appears that there is no good reason for the inordinate time taken to wind up the estate and it must be assumed that the cause has been dilatoriness, inefficiency or incompetence on the part of the solicitor concerned. We also learned that beneficiaries in an estate could find it extremely difficult to force a solicitor or an executor to proceed expeditiously with the administration, since the only procedure available was itself time consuming and costly. In order to consider in some detail the problems which arise in the administration or winding up of estates we decided to look at the matter in three distinct stages:

(i) making a will;

(ii) obtaining confirmation;

(iii) administration of the estate.

We also noted the general dearth of information available to the public about this area of the law.

MAKING A WILL

13.2 It is sometimes said that in Scotland the law of intestate succession (that is, the law controlling inheritance where there is no will) is such that it is unnecessary for many people to leave a will. Equally, it is sometimes said that making a will is one area in which the layman can do without the services of a solicitor.

[1] See Appendix 4, Table 27.
[2] See Table 3.2 and also Appendix 7, Paragraph 609.

We do not agree with either assertion. Certainly, Scots law lays down distinct principles governing succession where there is no will; and Scots law also has a long established system of legal rights for near relations who cannot be excluded by a will from all benefit in an estate. A system for the protection of the rights of all beneficiaries and creditors in the administration and division of property is clearly of importance not only to individuals but also to the community at large. However, the existence of this body of rules does not obviate the need to prepare a will setting out clear testamentary intentions. There can be no doubt that anyone who wishes to leave his or her estate in order should take the elementary precaution of consulting a solicitor about making a will. Experience shows that this is one area of the law where 'do-it-yourself' can be very unwise. From the available information, we estimate that 60 per cent of those dying in Scotland leave no will. We were concerned that many people do not consult a solicitor for fear of expense; but the preparation of a simple will should not be an expensive process. We recommend in Chapter 18 that solicitors should be required to advise their clients about the cost of such services at the outset, and our recommendations in Chapter 6 will allow solicitors to advertise fixed charges for preparing wills.

Will forms

13.3 In many stationers in Scotland will forms apparently designed for 'do-it-yourself' will-making can be found. We would wish strongly to discourage the use of these forms, many of which are wholly misleading. They are usually designed for use under English law and do not take account of the very different precepts of the Scots law of succession. Indeed, we have seen one example which specifically claims to be designed for use under Scots law but which makes reference to the English law. Home-made wills can be a major cause of delay in settlement of an estate, and can result in higher legal fees to settle the disputes arising from ambiguity than can possibly have been saved by avoiding the cost of legal advice in the first place. There is, however, one significant and important exception to our general deprecation of will forms. We are aware that the Federation of Crofters' Unions and the Crofters Commission, with the advice of the Law Society, have prepared a will form which is included in the Federation of Crofters' Handbook. We have no doubt that this particular will form is of great use to people who have special statutory rights to a particular type of property and who might not readily be able to discuss their testamentary intentions with a solicitor direct.

OBTAINING CONFIRMATION

13.4 The estate of a deceased person is administered by an executor who executes the instructions of the deceased person in the will, or in accordance with the requirements of law in the case of the estates of those who die intestate. An executor appointed by the deceased in a will is known as an executor-nominate; one appointed by the court when there is no will is known as an executor-dative. In either case, the executor's duty is to ingather the estate, to settle debts and government duties and to distribute the estate among the beneficiaries entitled to a share of it.

13.5 Before he can administer the estate, and dispose of it, the executor needs to have his appointment confirmed by the court. In order to obtain this authority the executor must apply for and obtain from the court a decree authorising him to uplift, receive, administer and dispose of the estate, and to act in the office of executor. The court to which application must be made is the sheriff court of the sheriffdom in which the deceased was domiciled; and the department that deals with these matters is the commissary office.

13.6 Before it will issue confirmation, the court requires the executor to produce an inventory or listing and valuation of the estate. In addition to personal effects such as cash and clothing, the deceased's property may include a house, its furniture, a life insurance policy, savings in banks or other financial institutions, shares in companies and the like. The first task facing an executor, therefore, is to find out exactly what property the deceased had. He must also arrange for payment of any tax on the estate and he will have to pay the court's own charges. An executor-dative appointed by the court also requires to 'find caution' (that is, provide a guarantee) that he will administer the estate properly. Normally, this is done by means of a guarantee, granted by an insurance company on the surety of the gross amount of the estate, that the estate will be properly administered. 'Caution' is not required of executors-nominate.

13.7 Solicitors are almost invariably asked to undertake the obtaining of confirmation. In their evidence to us the Law Society said "Solicitors have no monopoly over the administration or winding up of estates except in procuring confirmation in those cases which are not 'small estates'." There is no ban on other agents obtaining confirmation so long as they charge no fee, but this effectively means that solicitors enjoy a 'monopoly' in this work. Lay executors themselves are entitled to apply for confirmation at their own hand; but the apparent complexity of the procedure and the unfamiliarity of court processes and language to laymen means that in practice solicitors are generally asked to undertake the work. Since the administration of the estate follows the process of confirmation there is a tendency for most laymen also to entrust this further procedure to a solicitor who has the training and experience to carry it through. However, just because it is normally convenient to use a solicitor does not prove the need for a professional monopoly; and it is of interest that while only solicitors can charge a fee for the step of obtaining confirmation, the administration of an estate can be undertaken by other agents for reward.

13.8 We have noted that special provision is made for small estates. An estate is at present termed 'small' if, before paying off outstanding debts, it is worth less than £3,000 and if, after debts are paid, it is worth less than £1,000. These limits were set in 1961, and although the Confirmation to Small Estates (Scotland) Act 1979 increases the limit to cover estates of up to £10,000 gross, it has not yet been brought into force. We **recommend** that this statute should be brought into force without delay.

13.9 The significant feature of a 'small estate' is that, provided there is no dispute about who is executor and no doubt about the validity of the will, the sheriff clerk will assist the executor in preparing the inventory, will administer the oath of the executor, and will advise him on other procedures necessary prior to the issue of confirmation. Thus the obtaining of confirmation can generally be completed expeditiously without the services of a solicitor. With a small, simple estate including only, say, a house and its furniture, an insurance policy, a bank account and other easily accessible property, the preparation of an inventory need present no greater problem than many lay persons cope with in other aspects of their lives. The sheriff clerk is there to advise on procedure, and to check the executor's work; and he will advise the executor in appropriate circumstances, for example where complications appear, to consult with a solicitor. The size of an estate is, of course, no indication of its complexity. Some small estates are complicated and some large ones are quite straightforward. Even when the sheriff clerk and his staff are available to assist executors of estates up to £10,000 gross, most executors will still want to engage a solicitor's services. On the other hand, some straightforward estates over £10,000 in value with few beneficiaries and few or no creditors may be quite adequately dealt with by a competent layman if the documents which have to be completed are not unnecessarily complicated. We have, therefore, sought to make it possible and practical for lay executors to obtain confirmation without using a solicitor, while bearing in mind the need to safeguard the interests of the beneficiaries. The present and proposed limits of 'small estate' do not go far enough in achieving this.

England and Wales

13.10 We examined with interest the procedure in England and Wales for granting probate and letters of administration (similar to our confirmation). There is a separate, long established probate service with offices throughout the country which provide facilities for helping anyone who wants advice on obtaining probate or letters of administration (but not on administering the estate). Application may be made to the registrar of the court by way of personal application. Special personal application forms can be obtained on request, together with full instructions in laymen's language. Once the forms have been returned to the court, a probate officer will contact the applicant to arrange a personal interview. The court staff can give all the help that is necessary to complete the application forms. When they have been satisfactorily completed, the applicant has to swear an oath confirming the accuracy of the information before the grant of probate is issued. The court staff are trained to help the personal applicant; and the court charges a fee to cover the extra cost of using the personal application department. This additional fee is not charged when an application is made by a solicitor. The registrar has authority to require an application to be made through a solicitor when, for instance, cases are particularly complex, or where there is a dispute about who should be the executor.

The service in Scotland

13.11 Although we found much to admire in the probate service in England and Wales, we could not believe that the creation of an entirely new and separate service in Scotland on similar lines would be realistic or even necessary. Moreover, despite the existence of the probate service the majority of estates in England and Wales are still dealt with by solicitors. We **recommend** that in Scotland sheriff clerks should assist executors who apply in person for confirmation. They should be able to assist executors in preparing the necessary forms, much as they do in relation to small estates at present. They should be exempted by statute from any liability for the accuracy of what is contained in the application, but they should explain, for example, what sort of items should be entered in particular parts of the form. They should also issue to personal applicants a leaflet containing guidance for lay executors. In addition to explaining how to complete the application for confirmation, this leaflet should set out the legal responsibilities of executors. For such limited services it may not be necessary to make any charge over and above existing court charges. However, if the work justified it, we would see no reason in principle why a realistic charge should not be made.

13.12 We have considered whether sheriff clerks should be at liberty to provide this service regardless of the size of estate, subject only to a discretion to require a particular applicant to use the services of a solicitor. The sheriff clerk would have to take this step, for example, in any case where there was a dispute as to who was the executor. Logically this seems the right approach; but we think that in practice that would be to go too far, too fast. We think it would be better, at least initially, to restrict sheriff clerks' authority to assist personal applicants to estates which appear likely to escape liability to capital transfer tax. This approach will call for a limit to the value of estates to be set; and we **recommend** that the limit should be 80 per cent of the tax threshhold, thus allowing a 'safety margin'. At the time of writing, capital transfer tax is payable if the net value of the estate (including lifetime payments) exceeds £25,000. Accordingly, we would admit to the personal application procedure estates with a net value of up to £20,000. Sheriff clerks should at the same time, however, have a discretion to decline to assist with such estates and advise the applicant to consult a solicitor.

13.13 The training of the sheriff clerks (see Chapter 17) should ensure that they can undertake this work and advise the public efficiently. Since they already perform similar functions in their commissary court duties we do not see this as a major problem. In some courts there may be a need to provide suitable accommodation for confidential interviews between sheriff clerks and personal applicants; in other courts, more counter-space might need to be provided. We do not see these as major difficulties. One point of difficulty, however, which we have noted and which is independent of the monetary value of the estate, is the case of a will where the deceased died domiciled abroad or with no fixed or known domicile. In Scotland, only the Sheriff Court of Chancery in Edinburgh deals with these types of estates which, we are advised, create a disproportionate amount of difficulty. Sheriff clerks should normally decline to assist with such estates and advise applicants to consult a solicitor.

Scottish clearing banks

13.14 There is one common category of executor in Scotland who cannot make personal application for confirmation—the joint stock banks. All three Scottish clearing banks offer a service in the administration of estates. Solicitors, however, have a monopoly in the matter of being able to charge a fee for the process of applying for confirmation. The result is that the banks, whether as executors or acting as agents for executors, instruct solicitors to apply for confirmation. Most of the banks' business is, we understand, in estates where they are named as an executor. It strikes us as odd that the banks as corporate bodies can be entrusted to act as executors and administer estates but should be precluded from taking the essential first step of making direct application for confirmation. There is no doubt that the work of applying for confirmation could competently be done by the Scottish clearing banks, and we see no reason why in the interest of their customers they should not be able to provide this service.

13.15 We have considered whether the solicitors' present monopoly should be broken only so far as enabling the banks, if they wish, to apply for confirmation directly; or whether the public interest would be better served by the simple abolition of the monopoly, leaving it open to any person or corporate body to apply for confirmation. The original justification for the solicitors' monopoly was to ensure that unscrupulous persons had no opportunity to misappropriate executry funds. Logically, however, the public interest would have been better safeguarded if the monopoly had applied to the administration of estates rather than simply to the preliminary process of applying for confirmation. As there is no monopoly in administering estates it seems to us that there is in principle no reason to break the monopoly only in favour of the banks.

13.16 We preferred, however, a more pragmatic approach. Recognising that in practice we need only consider the banks in this context, and having regard to the fact that most of their business involves them in the role of executor rather than executor's agent, we were prepared to recommend that nominated officers of the Scottish clearing banks should be entitled to make application to the court for confirmation on behalf of the bank as executor without using a solicitor. The banks would not be restricted by the ceiling we have recommended for personal applications; but if there were anything contentious about the estate the sheriff clerk would be obliged to require the banks to act through a solicitor (who might, of course, be a solicitor in the bank's employment). The Scottish clearing banks told us, however, that they saw no need for such a change and were content with the law as it will stand following the implementation of the Confirmation to Small Estates (Scotland) Act 1979.

ADMINISTERING THE ESTATE

13.17 As we have already noted, the ingathering and distribuiton of estates, and the related accounting, are not matters in which the legal profession has any monopoly. Indeed, the Scottish clearing banks advertise a service in this area which is in direct competition with that provided by solicitors. There is no doubt, however, that the bulk of the work in the administration of estates is carried out by solicitors.

13.18 Our evidence suggests that it is in the area of administration of the estate following the grant of confirmation that dissatisfaction with the services provided by solicitors most often arises. The administration and winding up of estates by solicitors are the subject of a number of complaints each year to the Law Society—principally complaints about delay. It has been demonstrated to us by evidence from a number of individuals that some estates do take an unreasonable length of time to clear up. Sometimes the delay is not caused by the solicitor; other parties may take an excessive time to reply to his letters or to furnish necessary information. In some instances, however, delay is caused by solicitors themselves. Unlike much other legal work, there are rarely deadlines to meet in the administration of an estate. Whereas the delay of a day can be vital in a conveyancing transaction, a week here or there is not generally likely to affect the outcome of the winding up of an estate; and there is no doubt that because of pressures of other work some solicitors do not complete the administration of some estates as quickly as they should. Furthermore, beneficiaries in an estate are often reluctant to appear impatient or greedy by pressing the executor or his solicitor to complete the work of distribution. Even when beneficiaries suspect that a delay is becoming inordinate, they do not have reliable independent guidance as to what is a reasonable time for the administration of different kinds of estate. As a result, the lay executor, or the beneficiary, has no way of judging whether the solicitor is being diligent or dilatory, and has no basis for questioning the solicitor's assurance that the business in question is being attended to as expeditiously as possible. By the same token, the solicitor faced with unreasonable complaints about the time taken cannot point to any objective standard to justify the length of time being taken to resolve matters.

13.19 In Chapter 18 we recommend that the Law Society should draw up a guide to professional conduct which will put solicitors under a profesisonal duty to tell clients, at the outset of any business, how long the matter is likely to take and what it is likely to cost. As most clients will have no way of knowing what length of time is reasonable, the solicitor will also be required to indicate whether he is likely to take longer than normal owing to the pressure of other business. The client will, therefore, have the opportunity of seeking the assistance of another solicitor who may be able to deal with the matter more expeditiously. In view of what we said in the previous paragraph, we think it particularly important that these guidelines should be observed in dealing with estates; and we therefore **recommend** that, in a printed leaflet about such services made available to potential clients, an indication should be given of what kind of information the client ought to expect to receive from his solicitor at the outset of the business (see paragraph 13.26). We believe that the onus put on the solicitor by the guidelines, and the fact that the client would be aware of the information that the solicitor should be able to give, will go far to remove the source of many of the complaints which currently arise because the client has no realistic expectation of what his business is likely to cost or how long it is likely to take. Equally, if the business were to drag on longer than the solicitor had forecast, and the client received no explanation for delay, he would know that he was on much surer ground in making a complaint.

13.20 Lay executors and beneficiaries frequently feel frustrated because they do not know, and have difficulty in finding out from solicitors, what if anything is happening. Lack of communication in this area may be as big a source of unease or distress as incompetence or dilatoriness. We therefore **recommend** that the Law Society should issue rules of practice for the administration of estates which would set out a minimum frequency with which lay executors and beneficiaries would have to be informed of progress, of the steps still to be taken, and of the estimated date of completion.

13.21 Under present law and practice a dissatisfied beneficiary can have resort to the courts, for example by an action of accounting against the executor. This is a slow and cumbersome procedure and one which, in view of potential liability for expenses, a beneficiary would be advised to take only in fairly extreme cases. A lay executor also has his remedies against a dilatory solicitor. Unless the solicitor has been expressly appointed by the deceased, the executor can in theory always transfer the business to another solicitor. This, however, is not so easy in practice and may be an expensive way of dealing with the matter. The lay executor can, of course, also sue the solicitor for negligence; but, as with an action of accounting, this is to be advised only in extreme cases, and in any event is unlikely to achieve what is really wanted, namely expedition in completing the administration of the estate.

13.22 We are satisfied that the existing law provides inadequate resort to the courts in this area. We do not recommend a system, such as is operated by the Surrogate Courts of the United States, by which winding up of estates is generally under court supervision. We think that this is unnecessary. We do **recommend**, however, that there should be a procedure by which, firstly, a lay executor or a beneficiary who is concerned at delay in the winding up of an estate can, at no great trouble or financial risk, bring the matter to the attention of the court; and by which, secondly, the court can in appropriate cases, not necessarily amounting to negligence, take continuing control over the administration to ensure its expeditious completion.

13.23 We have not attempted to work out all the details, but we have in mind a procedure on the following lines:

(i) A lay executor or a beneficiary, who is aggrieved by delay or other apparent incompetence in the winding up of an estate, should be entitled to apply to the court on a simple application form setting out briefly the reasons for anxiety. Having lodged the form the applicant may, if the court thinks it essential, be required to appear before the judge in chambers either personally or through a legally qualified representative to amplify the complaint. The form of application should be such that it can be completed by the applicant himself.

(ii) The application should be accompanied by a small deposit, to prevent vexatious applications. The deposit will be returnable to the applicant if the court, after further enquiry, is satisfied that the application was reasonably justifiable. Otherwise it will be forfeited to court dues.

(iii) If the court, after hearing the applicant or his representative where this is thought necessary, considers that the complaint may be justified, it should intimate the application to the executor or to the solicitor dealing with the estate and require an explanation within a short time limit. The solicitor should be able to give his explanation in writing. If the court is not satisfied with the explanation it should require the executor or the solicitor to appear personally or through a legal representative in chambers for further explanation. The applicant or his legal representative should be entitled to be present on that occasion.

(iv) If at this stage the court is of the opinion that further action is required to ensure expeditious completion, it should have a variety of remedies available. These should include:

(a) power to require the administration to be carried on under the supervision of the court, which would involve reports of progress to the court at stated intervals;

(b) power to remove the administration from the hands of the solicitor and appoint another solicitor; and

(c) power to supersede the executors and place the administration of the estate in the hands of a factor.

(v) The court should have power to award expenses according to circumstances against the estate, against the executor personally, or against the solicitor personally.

It is our intention that this procedure should be operated not only in cases where there might be some other remedy in law, such as an action for negligence, but in any case where it appears to the court that there is a lack of reasonable expedition in completing the administration.

13.24 This procedure should be available in the sheriff court because it is a local court. We would not, however, wish to incur heavy additional cost to public funds by increasing staff or setting up complex new machinery in the sheriff courts. We therefore suggest that the Office of the Accountant of Court at the Court of Session should be expanded and adapted to provide the necessary supervision of the administration of estates where the sheriff court has ordered this. It might also be appropriate to permit the application to be to the Court of Session where a larger estate is involved. In such cases the sheriff court might also be able to remit an application to the Court of Session or, where appropriate, to another sheriff court.

13.25 We think that such a procedure would provide a greater degree of protection than exists at present for all parties involved as beneficiaries in an estate, and would represent a more direct involvement by the courts in the supervision of those whom they confirm as entitled to administer the estate on behalf of the deceased. In order to ensure that the procedure is kept as simple and straightforward as possible, we would further **recommend** that representation in chambers at the hearing should not qualify for legal aid unless at the court's discretion. In making this recommendation we have in mind the fact that most such actions will not be taken against executors or their agents until a lengthy and distressing period of delay or inadequate action has passed. At this stage, we think that most beneficiaries who might wish to take such action will wish to be sure that, as far as possible, matters are now in their own hands. We therefore believe that the court action to supersede an executor or his agent should be one which any layman can himself undertake.

PUBLIC INFORMATION

Knowing what to do: laymen's guides

13.26 Throughout our consideration of this subject we have been struck by the complexity of the problems laymen face when someone close to them dies. Some people will know that the deceased left a will, and that a particular firm of solicitors is to be entrusted with the task of arranging for the disposal of the deceased's property. If the deceased has had forethought all his papers will have been left accessible and in good order. The executor or next of kin in such circumstances has simply to contact the solicitors or bank concerned and leave it to them to act in accordance with the will. The executor or next of kin will contact a funeral director who will advise on the procedures for obtaining the death certificate and arranging the funeral. Many people, however, faced with the responsibility of winding up the affairs of a deceased person do not know what needs to be done or which way to turn for help. They do not have a solicitor, and often there is no will. Very little guidance on this subject is publicly available.

Although the booklet 'Practical Problems After a Death' published by the Scottish Association of Citizens Advice Bureaux contains much useful information, it is available for the most part only from the Bureaux. Yet we think it is important that those immediately involved should be given some guidance at the earliest possible stage about what needs to be done about the estate of a person who has died. Since the first step must be to obtain the death certificate we **recommend** that written information and guidance should be provided by the registrars when they are issuing death certificates. We have consulted the Registrar General for Scotland on this point, and he has told us that, subject to consultation with staff interests, he would see no objection to registrars issuing such guidance if they were asked to do so by central government. We think that our proposed Legal Services Commission would be the right body to produce an appropriate leaflet of guidance for laymen in simple terms.

13.27 The information contained in this leaflet would include advice on the procedure for obtaining death certificates (for those who get the leaflet before going to the registrar); what to do about insurance policies; the duties of an executor; the duties of funeral directors (with reference to their code of practice); what to do with the will, and what to do when there is no will; social security provisions regarding the death grant and widows' claims; and similar practical matters. The leaflet should also contain information about the likely cost of winding up the estate and the time it should take.

13.28 There is another kind of leaflet needed. We have noted that the administration of estates is made easier if the dead person's affairs are left in good order, so that all the relevant documents are readily found. Making a will is an important step in leaving one's affairs in good order. We **recommend** that the Legal Services Commission which we have proposed should produce a leaflet describing the steps that citizens should take to leave their affairs in order so that, when they die, others will be saved needless worry and expense. The leaflet should include a list of the documents necessary for the tidy settlement of an estate; advice about the importance of a valid will; warning against the use of pre-printed will forms; advice about choosing an executor; sources of legal advice; and so on. This is information that every citizen should have at his disposal. The leaflet should be made widely available through such outlets as solicitors' offices, advice centres, churches, community centres, social work departments, social security offices, hospitals, and libraries.

The affairs of the mentally incapacitated

13.29 There is a further matter to which we make reference here for convenience. Although we have been concerned in this Chapter mainly with the administration of the estates of the dead, we have had evidence from the Mental Welfare Commission that some particular improvements are needed in the arrangements for having a person appointed to look after the affairs of someone who is mentally ill. Firstly, when a mentally ill person has property of little value, the expense of administering it through the employment of a curator is out of all proportion to its worth. In fact such appointments are not made in these cases, so that the mentally disordered person is denied this protection. When the appointment of a curator would be uneconomic, we consider that such protection should be provided at public expense, probably by providing the services of the Accountant of Court at the Court of Session. This might be authorised, following consideration of an application, by the sheriff court. Although we have not examined this issue closely enough to be sure that there is no better solution, such an arrangement seems to us likely to be effective, and it is in keeping with what we have recommended as to the supervision of the administration of an estate by the court.

13.30 Secondly, we understand from the Mental Welfare Commission that there is a need in a few cases for an arrangement whereby the court could make a will for a person who is unable to do so. We have not considered the implications of this in detail.

13.31 Finally, it has been put to us that there is a need to revalue the limit to the worth of an estate below which a curator can be appointed by the sheriff court. The present income limit of £100 was set almost a century ago and is plainly out of date.

13.32 We **recommend** that the matters discussed in the foregoing three paragraphs should receive immediate consideration.

RECOMMENDATIONS

			Paragraph
Obtaining confirmation to an estate	R13.1	The Confirmation to Small Estates (Scotland) Act 1979 should be brought into force without delay.	13.8
	R13.2	Sheriff clerks should assist executors who apply in person for confirmation, in the ways indicated in paragraph 13.11. This assistance should, at least initially, be restricted to estates valued at up to 80 per cent of the threshold for capital transfer tax.	13.11–12
Administration of the estate	R13.3	In a printed leaflet about services in connection with estates an indication should be given of what kind of information the client ought to expect to receive from his solicitor at the outset of the business.	13.19
	R13.4	The Law Society should issue rules of practice for the administration of estates which would set out a minimum frequency with which lay executors and beneficiaries would have to be informed of progress, of the steps still to be taken, and of the estimated date of completion.	13.20
	R13.5	There should be a procedure by which, firstly, a lay executor or beneficiary can bring to the attention of the court delay in the winding up of an estate, and, secondly, the court can in appropriate cases take continuing control over the administration.	13.22
	R13.6	Legal aid should not be available for representation in chambers at a hearing under this procedure unless at the discretion of the court.	13.25
Public information	R13.7	Written information and guidance about what needs to be done about the estate of a person who has died should be provided by registrars when issuing death certificates.	13.26

			Paragraph
	R13.8	The Legal Services Commission should produce a leaflet describing the steps that citizens should take to leave their affairs in order so that, when they die, others will be saved needless worry and expense.	13.28
The property of the mentally disordered	R13.9	The measures in connection with the affairs of the mentally incapacitated suggested in paragraphs 13.29–31 should be considered immediately.	13.32

CHAPTER 14

THE COURTS

14.1 In this Chapter we look briefly at the contribution to legal services by the courts both in the procedures and in the physical facilities they provide for the resolution of disputes. Although to have made an extensive study of the court system and its facilities would have taken us outwith our remit, we considered it necessary to examine certain points where the provision of legal services to the public were most closely affected.

CIVIL COURTS AND CIVIL PROCEDURE

14.2 We have had evidence criticising civil litigation procedures as being unduly cumbersome, slow and costly. It has been suggested to us that for these and other reasons, such as excessive formality, persons wishing to assert or defend their rights are sometimes unwilling or are financially unable to resort to the civil courts in Scotland (the Court of Session and sheriff courts). We have had from a number of quarters suggestions for specific improvements.

14.3 As earlier noted, there are two particular classes of civil litigation—divorce and small claims—where, in the light of the evidence we received, we have thought it desirable and within our terms of reference to make specific recommendations. This we have done in Chapters 10 and 11 respectively. There are also a few matters, such as the winding up of estates, where we have considered it proper to propose, as ancillary to our other recommendations, certain new court procedures. This apart, we are clear that a general review of the structure and procedure of the civil courts in Scotland is outwith our terms of reference; and that, in any event, such a review, having regard to the detailed and technical knowledge required and the time involved, would need to be undertaken by another body. Nevertheless, we believe that such a general review is required, and is indeed overdue. Criminal procedure has recently been subjected to a wide-ranging review by the Thomson Committee.[1] We are not aware that civil procedure has ever been similarly treated. The last major examination in this field was that of the Grant Committee;[2] but its remit was confined to the sheriff court, and that necessarily imposed upon it a restricted approach and limited its ability to consider radical changes.

Court of Session procedures

14.4 We appreciate that civil procedures are kept under review and are subjected to frequent change, improvement and adaptation. The Court of Session itself has, under statute, wide powers of secondary legislation (Acts of Sederunt) to change and develop procedure. These powers are in regular use and numerous

[1] Reports of the Committee on Criminal Procedure in Scotland—
Criminal Appeals in Scotland (First Report), (Cmnd. 5038): HMSO, 1972.
Criminal Procedure in Scotland (Second Report), (Cmnd. 6218): HMSO, 1975.
Criminal Appeals in Scotland (Third Report), (Cmnd. 7005): HMSO, 1977.
[2] Report of the Committee on the Sheriff Court, (Cmnd 3248): HMSO, 1967.

changes have been made in recent times. We have been told that a Committee set up by the Lord President has recently made fairly radical proposals in relation to reparation actions which, if adopted and successful, might pave the way to a more general reform. However, it must be recognised that the powers of the Court are not unlimited. Some reforms which the Court may think desirable require primary legislation to remove barriers to their introduction. For this reason, and because of lack of resources, a wide-ranging review and major reform are beyond the powers of the Court itself. Accordingly, without wishing to under-estimate what has been and is being done, we do not think that reform from within the Court can be expected to be other than of a gradual and piecemeal nature.

Sheriff court procedures

14.5 The position in the sheriff courts is similar, but is rather more complex. Under the Sheriff Court (Scotland) Act 1971 there is, in effect, a division of authority in relation to the procedure and administration of the courts and the secondary legislation relating thereto. Without going into detail, it appears that the Secretary of State, the Court of Session and the Statutory Sheriff Courts Rules Council all have statutory functions and statutory restraints on their functions in this area. The structure appears on the face of it unwieldy and its suitability might well itself be a matter falling within the remit of the general review which we recommend. In any event, within the existing sheriff court structure there are also frequent reviews and reform. As with the Court of Session, however, there are limits on the scope of the secondary legislation; and, perhaps even more so than in the Court of Session, reform is necessarily piecemeal.

Cheaper alternatives to the courts?

14.6 We have had evidence, particularly from the Scottish Legal Action Group, suggesting that because of the expense, delay and formality of court procedures, there has been a 'flight' from the courts into alternative tribunals—statutory tribunals, statutory arbitrations or voluntary arbitrations. We think that there is an element of truth in this, though it can be exaggerated. It is not always the case that these alternatives are either quicker or cheaper (to the litigant or the State) than the civil courts; but cheapness, speed and informality are certainly characteristic of some of them. What we are not disposed to accept is the implication of some of the evidence that the civil courts have incurable defects and must always be looked upon as places of last resort; and accordingly that, wherever practicable, alternative tribunals should be made available. We certainly do not want to discourage arbitration or specialist tribunals for types of cases for which they are, for one reason or another, particularly suitable. We firmly believe, however, that the civil courts are, and should remain, the principal means for resolving civil disputes. We are anxious lest undue resort to remedies outwith the court may lead to the needed reform of court procedures being delayed and neglected. The aim should be to develop in the civil courts themselves those same qualities of cheapness, speed and informality in so far as these are compatible with fair and respected judical procedures. We look for a combination of improved legal aid and improvement in civil procedures to provide a system by which all manner of persons will confidently resort to the courts to assert or defend their rights in matters of substance without anxiety about expense, inconvenience or delay. We have no doubt that, at present, people are far too often deterred from asserting or defending rights, or are forced into unreasonable settlements. We believe that, in combination with the improvements in legal aid which we have recommended in Chapter 8, a major review of civil procedures might go a long way to improve the present situation.

Misuse of current procedures

14.7 We have heard it said that the present defects are due not so much to the procedures themselves as to the way they are used, or misused, by practitioners; and that if every opportunity were taken by practitioners to use available procedural devices—say be agreeing facts not seriously in dispute so as to cut down unnecessary evidence, and by agreeing not to avail themselves of the full time limits allowed for various procedural steps—cases could be disposed of more quickly and cheaply than they currently are. We are not in a position to judge to what extent delay and cost are due to the procedures themselves or to the way in which practitioners use them; but in so far as it is the latter, we doubt if further urging of practitioners to do better is any solution. There is a human tendency for even the most responsible professionals, if they are busy men, to put off work which can wait. Moreover, it frequently happens, particulary in times of high inflation, that delay and possibly increased expense are in the interests of one of the parties. No doubt there comes a point where the use of procedure as a means of delay is improper professional conduct, but the borderline between what is and what is not legitimate conduct in the interests of the client must be difficult to discern and also be incapable of precise definition. It may be that a solution to these problems is to be found in the court taking a more active role in controlling the conduct of the case than has been traditional in our brand of adversary procedure. An approach on these lines might also offer some solution to the well known but intractable problem of late settlements. We would hope that the general review which we propose would examine the practicalities of greater court involvement and consider whether, assuming the suggestion was thought useful, it could be carried out through the existing judicial structure or whether it would be desirable to introduce a new tier of judicial officers who would deal with procedural matters.

14.8 Much of the existing civil procedure involving time and expense is designed for the purpose of ensuring that each party has fair notice of his opponent's case in fact and law. We appreciate the need for this; and we would not wish to see any change which would result in litigation becoming a game in which the winner is the party who can spring the most surprises. We wonder, however, whether the present procedures in this respect are unnecessarily sophisticated and whether, again perhaps by greater intervention on the part of the court, the required result could be achieved with less delay and formality. This again is a matter which should be looked at in the proposed review.

14.9 In Chapter 11 we set out in some detail proposals for a new small claims procedure. The implementation of these proposals should not await the outcome of the review of civil procedure which we propose. It may be, however, that certain of our proposals in relation to small claims, for example the pre-trial review, might be appropriate for larger claims as well. We are not satisfied that, in the long term, it is desirable to have an entirely separate and distinct procedure for claims below an arbitrary money limit. We think it merits consideration whether the small claims procedure could be integrated with a reformed and more flexible procedure, but retaining certain particular aspects appropriate to small claims for cases below certain monetary limits. For example, the refusal of expenses of representation and the kind of informal arbitral procedure which we propose for small claims might apply to claims below one limit; the absence of a right of appeal might be appropriate below another limit; and the pre-trial review procedure might be suitable for all or at least a wider range of actions. This possibility should be considered in the proposed review.

The required remit on procedures

14.10 We have not attempted to define the precise remit of the committee which we propose should undertake the required review. Arguably, it should be wide enough to allow examination of the structures and respective jurisdiction of the civil courts both at first instance and on appeal. Certainly, it should be able to consider such fundamental questions as the extent to which it is necessary for civil litigation to be conducted in public, where no public interest is involved beyond the possible need for justice to 'be seen to be done'. In Chapter 10 we recommended that divorce and custody proceedings should in future be held in private, and we hope that this recommendation will be implemented without awaiting the outcome of a general review. In our opinion, the review should broadly cover all forms of civil litigation procedures, except perhaps such matters as diligence and bankruptcy which are already being considered by the Scottish Law Commission and which, though partly procedural, concern also the substantive law. We consider that the proposed committee should be able to look at such matters as the existing requirement for the employment of Edinburgh agents in the Court of Session and the form of documents in a court process, and also such procedures as the signetting of Court of Session summonses, the extracting of decrees, and the distinction in the Court of Session between petitions and actions to see whether there are any historical relics which cause unnecessary work and have outlived their usefulness.

14.11 We further consider that the committee, as part of its work, should pay particular attention to the simplification of all documents used in court procedures. It is important that wording should be adopted which will, as far as possible, make the documents comprehensible to laymen in order that they may understand the procedures with which they are involved and also, in appropriate circumstances, enable them to represent their own interests. We would not, however, want it to be inferred from what we have said that party litigants should be encouraged to attempt to undertake self-representation since this in most cases would certainly not be in their own interests, or in the interests of the speedy and economic administration of justice.

Composition of review committee

14.12 The subject matter of our proposed review is such that we think that the committee carrying it out would have to be composed largely of lawyers and others, such as clerks of court, experienced in civil litigation. The committee should also have lay members whose function would be to ensure that the practical interests of court users are constantly kept in mind.

Conclusion on civil procedures

14.13 We **recommend** that a committee should be appointed by the Secretary of State for Scotland after consultation with the Lord President of the Court of Session to review the structures, jurisdiction and procedures of the civil courts in Scotland.

WORKING METHODS AND FACILITIES

14.14 We also **recommend** that a separate review of the working methods of the courts should be carried out. This scrutiny should include the criminal as well as the civil courts and its primary objective should be to recommend how the courts can best adopt up-to-date working methods both in the interests of efficiency and of the courts. Apart altogether from improvements in working methods, consideration should be given to reducing the need for personal attendance of parties or agents at court.

Use of modern office machines

14.15 There seems to us scope for the use of modern office machines such as automatic typewriters and word processors which can assist in the processing of court documents. To date there has been little use of computers or data storage and retrieval systems in court administration, though we understand that a computerised fines accounting system is now being installed at Glasgow Sheriff Court, and may be extended to other courts thereafter. We also understand that other computer applications, such as the processing of statistics, are foreseen. We regard it as essential that the courts obtain the maximum benefit from such means of improving their efficiency. The use of modern business methods should result in savings of public funds in running the courts and should also reduce the cost of litigation.

Court facilities: local courts

14.16 During our review of legal services in Scotland we have visited a number of court buildings, and our Report would be incomplete without some reference to the facilities provided for the administration of justice. In the following paragraphs we consider the facilities in local courts. Our observations derive mainly from visits to and information about the sheriff courts; but in their generality we believe that our recommendations apply equally to many of the district courts.

14.17 Early in the life of the Commission, several of us paid a visit to the Glasgow Sheriff Court. It is an understatement to say that the conditions at the court—particularly for those held in custody—are very bad indeed. In fact, we were so appalled by the standard of provision for prisoners, public, witnesses and court staff that, immediately following our visit, our Chairman wrote in strong terms to the then Secretary of State for Scotland. We were, accordingly, glad when shortly afterwards we were informed that the government had decided to proceed with the building of a new sheriff court house in Glasgow, completion being expected in 1985. In the meantime, a number of short-term measures to relieve the pressure on the existing court facilities had been planned and are now being implemented.

14.18 In other courts we have visited, the deficiencies have been less pronounced, but we have noted a number of matters which concern us. A first point relating to the physical condition of the courts which we visited is the often poor standard of acoustics. It requires no subtlety of argument to observe that if the public are unable to hear the proceedings, then the court ceases to be a public hearing. In Chapter 17 we make recommendations about the training of judges and lawyers which refer to the necessity of the principal participants in court ensuring that they are heard. We would simply note here that when new courts are being designed the important question of acoustics should receive proper consideration. There is, of course, no reason why microphones should not be used in court; and we **recommend** that they should be installed in existing courts with poor acoustics.

14.19 In a number of sheriff courts which we visited, we considered that the waiting facilities for witnesses, jurors and others involved in cases were quite inadequate. Witnesses are in some instances expected to spend a very long period in the halls and corridors of court buildings, and in others they are expected to wait in the same room as the opposing party's witnesses or the witnesses for the accused person in a criminal matter. At worst, this last-mentioned arrangement could involve the danger of witnesses being intimidated before the hearing. Even when there is no question of intimidation it can be upsetting and disturbing for witnesses to have to spend what can be a very long period of time with persons accused of crimes. We feel that it is unacceptable that witnesses and parties to civil actions should have to share waiting rooms—where provided—or corridors with participants in criminal hearings. Wherever possible, the allocation of courtrooms and the arrangement of court business should seek to ensure that the participants in civil and criminal hearings are kept apart. We **recommend** that participants in civil business should not have to share facilities with participants in criminal business.

Public experience of courts

14.20 As well as making personal visits to the courts we included some questions about public experience of courts in our surveys. One hundred and eighty-five respondents from our national sample had appeared in court as a juror or as a witness since January 1971 and these respondents were asked to give their account of the facilities available to them in court. The sample was small but the responses are very similar to our own. One respondent in three described the facilities in court as inadequate in some way; the responses are summarised in Table 14.1 below:

TABLE 14.1: Reasons for dissatisfaction with court facilities*

	%
No refreshments available	28
Inadequate waiting room	26
Poor toilet facilities	15
Building cold, uncomfortable, antiquated	9
No waiting room	4
Other	3
Don't know/can't remember	15
	100
Total No. of reasons =	117

*Source: See Appendix 4, Table 70.

Facilities for witnesses, jurors and public

14.21 The results of our survey indicate that the main deficiencies which users of the local courts have found are inadequate waiting room and toilet provision, and a lack of appropriate refreshment facilities. The dissatisfactions expressed by our respondents are in the nature of basic provision, not luxury. Parties and witnesses in many of our courts have to endure lengthy waiting periods; and this means that, for many people, playing their part in the administration of justice is an uncomfortable and unpleasant experience. It is a sad commentary on the attention given to the courts of Scotland over the years that, as noted in paragraph 14.18, the city of Glasgow is having to wait until 1985 to get its first purpose-built sheriff court. Indeed, we understand that only two new purpose-built sheriff courts (at Edinburgh and Airdrie) have been constructed in Scotland during this century. We know that the court authorities are aware of the accommodation deficiencies. Part of the trouble lies in the fact that the great majority of the court buildings in Scotland date from the last century; and most are incapable of substantial extension, adaptation and modernisation without capital expenditure at a level which successive governments have felt unable to sanction. We are also aware that a number of courts have been adapted and improved and that the standard of decoration at many is reasonable. Nevertheless, much modernisation of our courts and new buildings to replace the most obsolete are required; otherwise respect for justice and the law is put at risk by imposing discomfort on those undertaking their civic responsibilities.

14.22 We consider that central and local government must give higher priority than they have done in the past to remedying the manifest physical shortcomings of many of our local courts, and we so **recommend.**

Court facilities: Parliament House

14.23 The supreme courts carry out their business, apart from criminal trials conducted on circuit, in Parliament House in Edinburgh. This building also accommodates the courts' administrative offices and a number of other organisations closely associated with the courts, notably the Crown Office and the Advocates Library with its ancillary accommodation for the Faculty of Advocates. This concentration of related organisations in one building in central Edinburgh is convenient and economical.

14.24 The accommodation within Parliament House is now substantially inadequate to meet current demands. There are insufficient court rooms and some of the court rooms are inadequate by reasonable modern standards and cannot be made adequate merely by internal alterations. The layout of the building together with the limited space available makes it impossible to secure full efficiency from the arrangement of the administrative offices and other facilities of the court. As regards accommodation for members of the public—witnesses, jurors, etc.—there have been substantial improvements in recent years, and the problem has been much reduced by the introduction of divorce procedures which make the attendance of parties and witnesses unnecessary in the great majority of cases. The position will be further slightly improved as a result of our recommendation in Chapter 10 on a divorce jurisdiction for the sheriff courts. Nevertheless, there will still be a need for improvements which require more space. Additional space would make it easier to ensure that members of the public involved with criminal procedure could be kept separate from those involved in civil litigation, though this is not as big a problem as in the sheriff courts. The facilities provided for the judges themselves we can only describe as deplorable. We were astonished to find that the judges of our supreme courts were provided with such inadequate office accommodation and secretarial facilities for carrying out their work.

14.25 We understand that in the early 1970's a proposal was developed in some detail for building an extension to Parliament House on an adjacent site; and that this planned extension together with reconstruction of part of an existing building on the site would enable all the defects above mentioned to be cured for the foreseeable future. This scheme, however, because of financial stringency has had to be put in abeyance. While we accept that the replacement of the Glasgow Sheriff Court is a matter of greater urgency than improvement to Parliament House, we **recommend** that, as soon as funds can be made available, these proposals for Parliament House should be put into effect. In the meantime, we would have thought it imperative that the site of the proposed extension be earmarked for the Parliament House scheme and should not be developed for any other purpose.

14.26 We gather that there is also a scheme under consideration for the supreme courts to use certain accommodation adjacent to, and linked with, Parliament House presently belonging to the Society of Solicitors in the Supreme Courts. Part of the building which contains this accommodation is already used for court purposes. It seems that, pending the implementation of the proposals to which we refer in the previous paragraph, this additional accommodation will be of some benefit; but, at best, it is a short term and very partial solution. It will secure little improvement to the court rooms themselves, or in the important matter of increasing the efficiency of the courts' administrative offices.

			Paragraph
Civil procedure and jurisdiction	R14.1	A committee should be appointed by the Secretary of State for Scotland, after consultation with the Lord President of the Court of Session, to review the structures, jurisdiction and procedures of the civil courts in Scotland.	14.13
Working methods of the courts	R14.2	A separate review of the working methods of both the civil and the criminal courts should be carried out.	14.14
Facilities needed at courts	R14.3	Microphones should be installed in courts with poor acoustics.	14.18
	R14.4	Participants in civil business should not have to share facilities with participants in criminal business.	14.19
	R14.5	Central and local government must give higher priority than they have done in the past to remedying the manifest physical shortcomings of local courts.	14.22
	R14.6	As soon as funds can be made available, existing proposals for improvements to Parliament House should be put into effect.	14.25

PART V

The Providers of Legal Services

CHAPTER 15

THE LEGAL PROFESSION: STRUCTURE AND ORGANISATION

15.1 In Chapter 3 we gave a brief account of the services supplied by the two branches of the legal profession in Scotland. In this Chapter we deal with the structure and organisation of the two main professional bodies, the Law Society of Scotland and the Faculty of Advocates, and then we go on to consider some aspects of the way in which solicitors and advocates conduct their business.

SOLICITORS

15.2 Although the use of the word 'solicitor' is of considerable antiquity, it has only since 1933 carried statutory recognition as the title for all members of the solicitor branch of the legal profession.[1] Prior to that time a variety of other names were also in common use—for example, advocates, law agents, procurators and writers. Many of these titles came from the old legal societies which originally represented solicitors in different parts of the country; and some (such as advocates in Aberdeen) continue to be used at the present time along with the statutory designation. Many of the older societies have continued in existence, notably the Society of Writers to the Signet which has a pre-1532 origin; the Royal Faculty of Procurators in Glasgow which dates from 1668; the Society of Advocates in Aberdeen founded in 1685; the Society of Solicitors in the Supreme Courts of Scotland formed in 1784; and the Scottish Law Agents Society dating from 1884.

The Law Society of Scotland

15.3 In 1922 a number of the existing societies formed a body called the Joint Legal Committee whose members were appointed from these societies. The activities of that Joint Committee resulted in the Solicitors (Scotland) Act 1933 which established the General Council of Solicitors in Scotland with power to deal with the admission, education and training of solicitors. The Act also set up a separate Discipline Committee to deal with disciplinary matters. In 1949 the Law Society of Scotland was established by the Solicitors (Scotland) Act of that year, and the Society were entrusted with the education, examination and admission of solicitors and with the regulation of the profession generally. In addition the objects of the Society were stated to include:

> '. . . The promotion of the interests of the profession of solicitors in Scotland and the interests of the public in relation to that profession . . .'[2]

In subsequent amending legislation the Society have been entrusted with additional powers for the protection of the public and for the regulation of the profession.

---

[1] *The Solicitors (Scotland) Act 1933.*
[2] *Solicitors (Scotland) Act 1949,* Schedule 4.

15.4 The Law Society have a governing Council consisting of forty elected members representing constituencies throughout the country and eight co-opted members representing salaried solicitors employed in public services, commerce and industry. From amongst their members the Council appoint a President and Vice-President of the Society. The business of the Society is carried out by the Council and by a large number of standing, *ad hoc*, and statutory committees and we have reproduced in Annex 1 to this Chapter a diagram provided by the Law Society which details the various committees. (Diagram 8.1 in Chapter 8 sets out the committee structure relating to the legal aid schemes for which the Law Society have responsibility.)

15.5 The day to day work of the Society is carried out by their full-time staff of 49, of whom 11 are professionally qualified; 9 solicitors and 2 chartered accountants. The office of the Society is at 26/28 Drumsheugh Gardens, Edinburgh; and it is from here that the central administration of legal aid which we discussed in Chapter 8 is also undertaken. The staff involved in the administration of legal aid throughout the country (some 183 persons) are all employed by the Society although their salaries are paid from the legal aid funds provided by central government.

15.6 All solicitors in Scotland are required by statute to be members of the Law Society; and if they carry on business by virtue of their qualification as a solicitor they are required to obtain from the Society an annual practising certificate. Solicitors who carry on business as principals are obliged by statute to comply with the Solicitors' (Scotland) Accounts Rules which specify the minimum books which they must keep in order to show their dealings with clients' monies and any other money which may be dealt with through their offices. In terms of the rules, a solicitor is required to produce annually an accountant's certificate certifying that his accounts have been kept in compliance with the rules. The Council have power to carry out at any time an inspection of the books of any solicitor or firm of solicitors in order to satisfy themselves that the accounts rules are being observed and such inspections are carried out continuously by the Society's accounting staff.

15.7 In addition to the protection given to clients by the accounts rules the private sector of the profession also maintains at its own expense a fund out of which grants are made to those who have suffered loss arising from a solicitor's dishonesty. This fund—the Scottish Solicitors' Guarantee Fund—was established under the Solicitors (Scotland) Act 1949; and the control and management of the fund are in the hands of the Council of the Society, although the routine administration is carried out by one of the Council's committees and the Society's staff.

15.8 We are satisfied that the accounts rules and the guarantee fund operate efficiently and in the interests of the public who use solicitors' services; and we see no reason for recommending any change in them. Although we received no evidence which was critical of present arrangements we have also considered whether membership of the Society should continue to be compulsory for all solicitors. We have had no hesitation in concluding that it should because it is in the interests of the public that solicitors be members of a body charged with the maintenance of high standards.

15.9 As we noted in paragraph 15.3, the Law Society are in terms obliged to be both a 'public interest watchdog' and a 'solicitors' professional association or trade union'. This dual role involves some conflict of interest and places a heavy burden on the Society to ensure that the interests of their members are not allowed to outweigh the interests of the public. In our view possible conflict of interest arises particularly in areas such as the regulation of professional standards, complaints and discipline, control of fees, the development of professional services and the administration of legal aid. Some of the recommendations that we have made throughout our Report—for example, in relation to control of fees and to professional conduct, complaints and discipline—have been specifically designed to strengthen the position of the client and the public interest.

15.10 Nevertheless, we do not want to be unfair to the Society in this matter. In our view they have in fact made creditable attempts to balance the demands of the two potentially conflicting interests which by statute they are constrained to promote. We agree with those who suggested to us in evidence that even where the Law Society are successful in discharging this statutory duty it is difficult for them always to be seen to be keeping in mind the public interest. Certainly we ourselves found members of the Council of the Society, when giving oral evidence, to have a lively awareness of their responsibilities to the public. While, therefore, we are in no doubt that the interests of solicitors and of the public can from time to time be in conflict, we consider that there is undoubted benefit to the public in having the solicitors' professional body under a wider obligation than simply to look after their own membership. Much of value we feel would be lost if the Law Society were to become simply the professional association or trade union of solicitors.

Laymen on the Council

15.11 In considering whether the Law Society could adequately look after the public interest we took account of suggestions that laymen should be appointed to the Council of the Law Society by the Secretary of State for Scotland or by the Lord President of the Court of Session. In discussion with us, members of the Council of the Law Society said that in certain of their committees there had been benefits from the contribution made by members of other professions, used as consultants, particularly in relation to the fixing of fees; they also considered that benefits accrued to the legal aid central committee and the Discipline Tribunal from the lay representation on these bodies. Nevertheless, the Society would not wish to see non-solicitors being appointed as members of the Council. Bearing in mind our view of the proper role of the Society we recognise that it would not be appropriate for their governing body to have on it lay members who were not elected by the profession and we are of the opinion that the Council should continue to be elected as at present. If the Law Society consider that any benefit is to be obtained from co-opting laymen, particularly those qualified in other disciplines, then that is a matter essentially for them. For our part, while we do not think it necessary or appropriate to make any specific recommendation on this matter, we would have thought that certain of the committees of the Society would in fact benefit from the co-option of experts such as statisticians and chartered accountants in the relevant field.

Law Society records

15.12 We feel it necessary to comment on the inadequate state of some of the records maintained by the Law Society. Our use of these records in connection with our research projects showed that all too often the records in question were not as accurate as might have been expected. The Law Society themselves accepted this; and one consequence of our requests for information is that they have asked members to advise the Society when a change occurs in a practice—for example, the assumption of a new partner or the death or retiral of an existing partner, the establishment for the first time of a practice, a change of address and telephone number, the opening of a branch office, etc.. At the present time we understand that the only relevant statutory duties on the Law Society are to maintain an alphabetical list of enrolled solicitors and to give to the Principal Clerk of Session and sheriff clerks annually, appropriate lists of solicitors holding practising certificates. We think, however, that the governing body of a profession ought to have much more information about its membership. In particular the Law Society should keep an up-to-date list of firms as well as the roll of trainee solicitors which we recommend in Chapter 16. The firm is the unit within which most solicitors practise, and we think that a list of these firms which provide the main point of access for legal services could serve a useful purpose. We also think it justifiable to require the Law Society, by statute if necessary, to keep basic factual information not only about individual solicitors and their location but also about these firms, including such details as the names and ages of partners, of qualified staff, and of apprentices; and also the number of non-legally qualified staff engaged in fee earning work. If need be, solicitors themselves should be under a statutory obligation to supply the information to the Society. Up-to-date (annual) information on the location and staffing of firms would, we believe, be of assistance both to the Law Society in appreciating developments in the profession and its organisation, and perhaps also to the Legal Services Advisory Committee which we recommend in Chapter 20. It would also make publication of the Society's directory of general services less time consuming than it is at present. We **recommend**, accordingly, that the Law Society should examine urgently the adequacy of their internal administration and records for the purposes which we see in our Report as proper; and that, if it proves necessary, the Society should be statutorily obliged to obtain the information which we have suggested.

Local faculties

15.13 As we noted earlier, there are many local bodies of solicitors in Scotland. These are entirely independent of the Law Society and the majority of them are designated as 'faculties'. Many of them undertake functions which are purely social, though a number of them actively pursue the professional interests of their members. We have shown in Annex 2 to this Chapter a list produced by the Law Society of the present local faculties or associations of solicitors. During our deliberations on various aspects of legal services we considered the possibility of these local faculties being asked to undertake a wider role. We also considered whether they should become local branches of the Law Society. On the face of it, the latter proposition had certain attractions: firstly, there would be a local point of contact with the Law Society for clients; and secondly, local branches might stimulate greater participation by solicitors in the affairs of the Society. On the other hand, we were aware from discussion with representatives of the Law Society that they were strongly opposed to the creation of local branches of the Society. They considered this would weaken the cohesive and effective role of the central organisation which itself had not been very long in existence and which now was proving to be an influential and economical body speaking for the profession as a whole. As we said in paragraph 15.11, we do not see any need to recommend any change in the way in which members of the Council of the Law Society are elected. In addition, the current system of election to represent geographical constituencies ought to mean that there is representation of solicitors throughout the country, although we are aware that elections are rarely contested and that criticism is made that the Council of the Society are at times remote from, and out of tune with, the views of the profession as a whole. We also gained the impression that some at least of the local societies or faculties might not wish to relinquish their independence; and there would undoubtedly be particular problems in achieving a simple local structure in Edinburgh and Glasgow. We finally concluded that we should make no recommendations about the existing local faculties or societies; but we consider that more effective two-way use should be made of the existing local organisations to improve communications between solicitors and the Council of the Law Society. We also concluded that this is a matter in which initiatives to meet our suggestions might appropriately be left to the Law Society.

Court advisory committees

15.14 Although we do not wish to see local faculties or societies taking on functions of the Law Society which can be dealt with centrally, there is one piece of local consultative machinery which we would wish to see established. Local solicitors generally lack, at present, any formal channel of communication with the judges in the local courts. Such a contact would be useful in ensuring the smooth running of the courts and also in improving standards of pleading (which we discuss in Chapter 16). It would facilitate consultation about any proposed alterations to the court premises or local procedures or working arrangements. It would indeed make it easier for the profession to propose such changes. We therefore **recommend** that every Sheriff Principal should establish for each court (or, where appropriate, group of courts) for which he is responsible an advisory committee comprising representatives of the local Bar, court staff, procurators fiscal, social workers and appropriate outside lay elements (to represent the users). Such an advisory committee would advise him on any matters affecting the work of the court or the convenience of its users. In making this recommendation we are aware that there are already in some courts committees operating on the lines we suggest. We **recommend** also that consideration should be given to the best form of such advisory committee or committees for the Court of Session and the High Court of Justiciary.

Edinburgh correspondents

15.15 At the present time, it is necessary for a solicitor who wishes to practise before the Court of Session to sign the Roll of Solicitors kept by the Principal Clerk of Session. Only solicitors who have a place of business in Edinburgh are entitled to do so, and the effect of this is that the services of an appropriate Edinburgh solicitor are required in any Court of Session action. The services of the Edinburgh correspondent are specifically required to sign the various papers necessary in actions before the Court; and only a solicitor who has a place of business in Edinburgh is entitled to borrow the various papers which are lodged in the Court (the process). In practice, Edinburgh correspondents consider the instructions which are sent to them by the out of town solicitor, deal with any legal aid application, and instruct counsel for all the stages of the action; generally they act as a channel of communication between the out of town solicitor, counsel and the Court.

15.16 It seems to us that this requirement inevitably involves some increase in the cost of litigation in the supreme court. We are aware that the employment of two solicitors does not mean the doubling of solicitors' fees, since the 'country' and the Edinburgh solicitors are to some extent doing different tasks both of which would have to be done by one solicitor if only one were employed. We are also advised that the Auditor of the Court of Session does not allow fees for work done by both the local and Edinburgh solicitor (known as 'double agency') and, accordingly, there is no duplication of payment for any work which appears to have been done by both solicitors. Nevertheless, we find it hard to believe that it does not involve additional expense which a client ought not to have to bear if it is not necessary. We are aware that there are technical problems connected, for example, with borrowing of productions, which might arise if the requirement were abolished. We are not entirely convinced that these problems are insoluble. A further requirement is that where an advocate is appearing before a court, the court normally requires that he be accompanied by a solicitor; and for cases in the supreme courts it is frequently much easier for the Edinburgh solicitor to be in attendance. We have not been in a position to examine the detailed implications of these requirements ourselves, but we have no doubt that they are matters which ought to be examined with a view to finding a way of abolishing or at least limiting them. We accordingly **recommend** that the committee on civil procedure which we propose in Chapter 14 should have these matters specifically included within its remit. The committee should look at the requirement that only solicitors with a place of business in Edinburgh are entitled to practise before the Court of Session and also the requirement that there should always be a solicitor present in court with an advocate, with a view to seeing whether the requirements can be relaxed.

15.17 While we have strong reservations about the requirement on the profession to use Edinburgh correspondents in connection with all supreme court business we recognise that many solicitors would no doubt choose to conduct some, if not all, such business through an Edinburgh correspondent, just as they may use solicitors in other towns as correspondents when they have to act for a client in business at a distant sheriff court. In many cases the use of an Edinburgh (or local) correspondent would be the most sensible and economical way to undertake certain business, and we see no reason why this should not continue.

Notaries Public

15.18 The office of Notary Public is an ancient one. At one time Notaries formed a distinct profession created by Royal authority, and the members were admitted after examination by the Lords of Council and Session. In 1873[1] it was provided that any enrolled solicitor could apply for admission as a Notary; and in 1896[2] it was provided that no person could be admitted as a Notary until

[1] *Law Agents (Scotland) Act 1873*, Section 18.
[2] *Law Agents (Scotland) Act Amendment Act 1896*, Section 2.

he had been admitted and enrolled as a solicitor. Now that all Notaries must be solicitors, there is no longer in Scotland, as distinct from many other countries, a separate profession of Notary.

15.19 The functions of the Notary are not now as far reaching as they once were. He has various functions in connection with conveyancing and the authentication of deeds; but his main function undoubtedly is in the administration of oaths and affidavits. The proceedings for admission as a Notary at the present time are conducted by the Clerk to the Admission of Notaries Public and are regulated by the rules of court. A petition is presented to the First Division of the Court of Session and, if this is granted, the applicant is admitted as a Notary Public and the clerk administers the declaration *de fideli administratione officii.* In evidence to us the Law Society suggested that we should consider whether all solicitors in Scotland should be allowed to exercise all the privileges and discharge all the functions at present carried out by Notaries Public. The Clerk to the Admission of Notaries Public in written evidence to us pointed out that despite the many similarities between the Scottish Notary Public and the Scottish solicitor they were fundamentally different in concept. His view was that a Notary Public was a public official while the solicitor worked within a highly confidential solicitor–client relationship; accordingly, he thought it important that the two roles should not be in any sense confused. Having considered the views expressed to us we came to the conclusion that there was no reason why all solicitors should not be Notaries Public. Although there are at present separate procedures for admission as a solicitor and as a Notary Public both procedures take the form of a petition to the Court of Session, and unnecessary expense would be saved by combining them. We **recommend**, therefore, that the status of Notary Public should be conferred on all solicitors admitted in future solely by virtue of their admission as solicitors. It should, of course, still be open to solicitors already admitted who are not Notaries Public to apply to the Court of Session to be admitted as Notaries. It may well be that the practice of international law will require the formal continuation of the office and designation of Notary Public and that persons admitted as Notaries will need to continue to take an oath. Even if this is so, we do not think that it would make our recommendations inoperative.

Incorporation of solicitors' firms

15.20 Solicitors are prevented by the terms of the Solicitors Act 1934 from practising in corporate form—that is, as limited or unlimited companies. At present, the principals of a solicitors' partnership are wholly responsible for the actions of the partnership and for its liabilities. Many solicitors today would not in fact be able to meet the whole amount of some successful claims for damages arising out of particular items of business which they undertake. The sums involved in commercial leasing or oil business, for example, run into many millions of pounds. We believe, therefore, that the protection of the client's interests is best served not by having the solicitor back his advice with his whole substance (which in modern times must be a largely formal matter), but by the provision of adequate indemnity insurance cover. At the same time, we believe that there would be considerable advantages to solicitors if they were able to practise in corporate form. Incorporation would bring with it administrative benefits in that the organisation of a firm might be better structured; financial benefits in that a company might be subject to a lesser fiscal burden than a partnership; and it might open up new possibilities for obtaining loan capital. Another point which we consider important is that increasing capitalisation of solicitors' firms ought in the longer term to benefit clients through improved efficiency. We **recommend**, therefore, that subject to suitable safeguards the restrictions on the incorporation of solicitors' partnerships should be removed. The safeguards which we have in mind include the following:

(i) solicitors practising with limited liability should be required to have a higher indemnity protection than those practising with unlimited liability or in non-corporate form; and this indemnity protection should be to a sum considered adequate by the Law Society;

(ii) the company directors as well as individual shareholders should be subject to the disciplines of the solicitor branch of the profession;

(iii) all shareholders (except perhaps nominee shareholders) and directors would require to hold practising certificates and the transfer of shares would be restricted accordingly; and

(iv) the form and content of the memorandum and articles of the company would in certain essential particulars be as prescribed by the Council of the Law Society and all alterations to them should be subject to the Council's approval.

Multi-disciplinary partnerships

15.21 Solicitors are prevented by statute from sharing fees with any other person (other than their employees or the representatives of deceased partners) who is not a solicitor.[1] In effect, this means that solicitors are unable to form mixed partnerships with any other professional group, although they can, of course, directly employ other professionals. It has been suggested to us that, particularly with the development of international legal practice and as a result of our membership of the European Economic Community, multi-disciplinary partnerships or associations might be a desirable—and perhaps inevitable—step. Against this, however, it can be argued that such partnerships would restrict client choice. A solicitor, for example, in partnership with an accountant would be unlikely to recommend his client to consult an accountant other than his partner. Even if this happened, however, it might not always be a matter for concern. Many clients who require particularly specialised advice know their requirements fairly precisely, whereas the typical problem presented by most citizens will be well within the competence of the average non-specialist practitioner. Moreover, the development of multi-disciplinary partnerships might well increase the accessibility to clients of different professional groups, and the cross-fertilisation of advice which would be available might more than make up for any restriction in choice that might result.

15.22 There are, as we recognise, areas of practical difficulty—for example, the question of which professional bodies would apply discipline to members of mixed partnerships and which rules as to indemnity insurance should be used. However, we think that these are matters which can best be resolved by dis-

[1] *Solicitors (Scotland) Act 1933*, Section 38.

cussion between the relevant professional bodies. We appreciate that there are distinctions between inter-professional partnerships and associations within the same profession i.e. the legal profession (both within the United Kingdom and elsewhere) and those between different professions i.e. solicitors and accountants. We do not consider that any significant development of multi-disciplinary partnerships is either necessary or indeed likely at the present time; but we can see no good reason for maintaining the restriction which prevents their development at all. We also envisage that there may be circumstances where a less permanent form than partnership is required and we have, therefore, also included the concept of association. The proposals will involve discussions not only between the legal professions within the United Kingdom but with those throughout the European Economic Community and elsewhere and undoubtedly substantial aspects of Private International Law and/or Community Law will apply. We therefore **recommend** that the present statutory restriction on solicitors sharing fees with others, so far as it prevents the development of multi-disciplinary partnerships and associations, should be removed so that multi-disciplinary partnerships and associations can be permitted. The professional restrictions which prevent solicitors and advocates combining in partnerships in relation to practice in Scotland should remain for the reasons which we set out at paragraph 15.37.

ADVOCATES

The Faculty of Advocates

15.23 The Faculty of Advocates are the governing body of the advocates branch of the legal profession. In origin they are an independent corporation consisting of those who have been admitted to practise as advocates before the Court of Session. The Faculty became a separate and identifiable corporate body during the late 16th or early 17th century and they were formed to administer the corporate affairs of advocates and to regulate matters of professional discipline and conduct.

15.24 Administration of the Faculty is undertaken by advocates in practice. The Faculty officers who are elected annually are, the Dean, the Vice-Dean, the Treasurer, the Clerk, and the Keeper of the Library. To assist him, the Dean nominates a Council consisting of some 20 members of the Faculty. The Council is essentially a consultative body, its main function being to advise the Dean on appropriate matters which arise for his decision or in some cases to give preliminary consideration to proposals which are to be placed before the Faculty for decision. In selecting the members of the Council it is normal for the Dean to select a reasonable cross-section of the Bar in terms of seniority and in terms of experience of different types of practice.

15.25 In the running of the Faculty the officers are assisted by a small lay staff. In 1971, in order to provide office staff and facilities for the sending out of accounts and recovering fees for work done, and for the employment of and supervision of clerks to assist practising members, the Faculty established a service company, Faculty Services Limited. The purpose of this company is to provide an efficient and economical service to practising advocates with particular reference to the relationship of such advocates with the solicitors who instruct them. The company employ four clerks who between them provide to all the practising members certain services in relation to such matters as arranging the amount of fees in particular cases and the keeping of diaries. The clerks are remunerated partly by salary, partly by a small commission on fees and partly by a per capita payment based on the number of advocates each clerk serves. Each advocate is a wholly independent practitioner and there is nothing equivalent to the chambers system in England.

15.26 While it is the Court of Session which admits individuals to the public office of advocate the Court has, since the latter part of the 17th century, left it to the Faculty to determine the conditions for admission and to determine whether these conditions have been satisfied in individual cases.

15.27 At 11 November 1979, the Faculty had 361 members; of these only 139 were in practice as advocates of whom between 30 and 40 were Queen's Counsel and the remainder were juniors. A large number of Faculty members are employed as judges in the supreme courts and in the sheriff courts; some have appointments as chairmen or members of various tribunals; others are full-time government employees in the fiscal service or elsewhere; and yet others hold full-time academic posts. Table 15.1 shows the distribution of members of the Faculty as at 11 November in the years 1962, 1967 and 1972–1979.

TABLE 15.1: Members of the Faculty of Advocates*

	1	2	3	4	5	6	7	Total
1962	74	10	17	14	96	14	56	281
1967	77	12	10	12	106	13	55	285
1972	76	13	12	11	111	16	55	294
1973	81	13	13	13	118	12	57	307
1974	87	14	13	14	115	13	60	316
1975	85	13	11	11	122	16	64	322
1976	80	12	13	9	127	16	65	322
1977	90	12	21	12	132	19	62	348
1978	91	12	23	14	134	16	60	350
1979	93	15	18	14	139	14	68	361

Key

1: Judiciary; Senators of College of Justice
Sheriffs
Temporary Sheriffs
2: Holders of full-time academic posts and not engaged in practice
3: Holders of other full-time posts and not engaged in practice
4: Holders of part-time appointments
5: Engaged in practice in this country
6: Engaged in practice or otherwise abroad
7: Not falling within any of the above classifications.

*Source: Faculty of Advocates

15.28 The practising members of the Faculty of Advocates constitute the Bar of the Court of Session and, as such, they form part of the College of Justice in Scotland. The other members of the College of Justice are the judges of the Court of Session who are designated as Senators of the College of Justice; Writers to the Signet; Clerks of Session; Keepers of the Rolls; Macers and certain other persons.

15.29 The Faculty of Advocates are not a statutory body, and their procedures are marked by a lack of formal regulation. That these arrangements work well in practice is due to the small size of the practising Bar and their concentration in Parliament House in Edinburgh. In what follows, therefore, the existence of a rule or practice cannot always be shown or proved by reference to written statements. Nevertheless, there are important rules regulating practice as an advocate which we examine below. We do not make any recommendations as to the formal constitution of the Faculty of Advocates as such.

Instruction of counsel

15.30 The general practice is that an advocate receives his instructions only from a solicitor. This practice might be thought to give rise to unnecessary expense in litigation in the supreme courts; but we do not accept that it does. The Faculty told us in evidence that advocates did not have the time or resources to trace or precognosce witnesses, or to prepare documents and lodge them with the court. If advocates were to undertake such work and to deal direct with clients, not only would their overheads rise substantially but they would cease to provide the specialised and restricted service which is the basis of the split profession. Whether or not the unification of the present separate branches of the profession—'fusion' as it is generally described—would produce on balance more advantages than disadvantages is a matter which we consider at some length later in this chapter. Meanwhile, however, we say unequivocally that so long as the profession remains split we see no advantage in principle or practice in permitting clients to instruct counsel direct in litigious matters.

15.31 In relation to opinion work it would, in our view, rarely be more efficient for clients to by-pass the solicitor. The preparation of a memorial setting forth the relevant facts and law in relation to a matter and posing certain questions for the opinion of an advocate requires a degree of skill and knowledge to ensure that the opinion is based on a proper statement of the relevant facts and that the right questions are asked. This is the main reason why memorials for the opinion of counsel are prepared by solicitors—indeed counsel is entitled to presume, when he receives a memorial from a solicitor, that all the relevant facts have been presented to him. It has, however, been represented to us that members of certain other professions should in appropriate cases be permitted to present a memorial for the opinion of counsel direct. The expertise developed by patent agents in patent matters and by chartered accountants in accountancy and tax matters does, we think, justify the members of these professions being permitted to submit memorials to counsel on behalf of clients direct in relation to matters on which they have specialised knowledge, but we think that they must accept responsibility for presenting to counsel all the relevant facts.

15.32 We reached the same conclusion in respect of representation by advocates at tribunals and inquiries. If a party involved in such proceedings prefers to entrust the handling of his case to a professional person who is not a solicitor, it seems to us undesirably restrictive to insist that the services of an advocate to present the case at the tribunal or inquiry could only be obtained through the medium of a solicitor.

15.33 On this whole issue, therefore, the rules relating to the instruction of counsel are not at present altogether clear. We think there is a need for more precision in the rules; and for this purpose we **recommend** that only solicitors should instruct counsel in court matters, but that certain other professional agents should be entitled to instruct counsel direct for an opinion or in relation to proceedings before a tribunal or inquiry although counsel may at his discretion refuse to accept such instructions.

Partnerships at the Bar

15.34 At present, all who practise at the Bar in Scotland must do so as individuals. It was suggested to us that the rule against advocates forming partnerships was harmful, particularly to new members of the profession; and that it could operate at times to the disadvantage of clients. The Scottish Legal Action Group, for example, argued that the insistence on sole practice makes it difficult for a new advocate to become established, for an advocate's work to be carried on when he is ill, and for a suitably qualified substitute to be provided if he is detained in another case. There could indeed be other advantages to be gained by advocates forming partnerships. A partnership could develop much more extensive records than any single advocate. Also a new advocate's career prospects could be considerably improved if he could join an established partnership rather than be obliged to set up business on his own from the very first.

15.35 On the other hand, the Faculty point out that at present any client can choose from among some 140 practising advocates; and that the combination of advocates into partnerships would restrict this freedom of choice, since members of a single partnership could not properly act for parties with conflicting interests. The Faculty contend that because of the small size of the Scottish Bar the consequences of restricting choice in this way could be very serious. The Faculty also take the view that a litigant instructing a partnership would have less control over who personally was to act for him at the various stages of the case; and he might in the event find his work being done by an advocate of lesser experience than he would have chosen for himself under the present system. It can, of course, be argued that it would be possible to restrict the size of partnerships so as to enable reasonable choice still to be available. It might also be expected that the delegation of appropriate work to junior advocates would result in a cheaper service; and there is no reason to think that the quality of the service would thereby diminish because the senior members of the partnerships would be likely to exercise adequate supervision and control since their reputation and future livelihood would depend on the partnership providing a fully competent service.

15.36 It was also pointed out to us by the Faculty that an advocate at present is properly accountable only to the court and to his client, and that to introduce responsibility to fellow partners might, in some cases, jeopardise the advocate's dispassionate concern to fulfil his obligations to the court as well as to his client, no matter the cost to himself. We were not persuaded that this was a strong argument for maintaining the *status quo* since solicitors, who owe a similar professional duty to clients and to the court, have long practised in partnership, and we received no evidence to suggest that this aspect of solicitors' practice produces undesirable results.

15.37 If partnerships were permitted, there would be a risk that advocates at different levels of seniority having skill and ability in particular types of work would tend to congregate into one or two partnerships, with the result that for particular types of work freedom of choice amongst advocates of adequate skill and ability might be virtually eliminated. This would not be in the public interest. In addition, younger members trying to make their way in the profession, who for one reason or another were unfortunate enough not to be able to enter any partnership having a good practice in certain fields, might be precluded for ever from the prospect of developing a good practice in those fields. This would be in the interests neither of the unfortunate person concerned nor of the public. Given the likelihood that the development of partnerships could undesirably reduce the choice of counsel available to parties, and that the Faculty themselves are firmly opposed to partnerships, we have reached the view that the existing ban on partnerships should remain.

Senior and junior counsel

15.38 As we observed early in our Report (Chapter 3), Scotland, in common with many other systems, has a two-tier Bar divided between junior and senior counsel, the latter also being known as Queen's Counsel (QCs). When an advocate takes silk (becomes a QC) he gives up the more routine work of a junior advocate such as the preparation of written pleadings and concentrates on oral advocacy and on opinion work. Advocates are at present normally appointed Queen's Counsel on the recommendation of the Lord Justice General after about 15 years' practice at the Bar. In making recommendations the Lord Justice General assesses the standing, reputation and attainments of the applicant and has regard to the required balance between seniors and juniors at the practising Bar. We do not make any recommendations as to the changing of this system.

15.39 Following the report of the Monopolies and Mergers Commission on the supply of services by senior counsel, the so called 'two counsel rule' was suspended in 1977.[1] The two counsel rule was a requirement in most civil proceedings that junior counsel had to be instructed whenever a senior was engaged; in criminal proceedings, on the other hand, it was possible for a senior counsel to be engaged on his own. Since 1977 there has no longer been any requirement to engage junior counsel when senior counsel is instructed, although the senior has a right to insist that a junior must be instructed if he considers the case warrants it. The client has the reciprocal right to decline to instruct any particular advocate who so insists; and so far as we can judge from the relatively limited period of operation of the new arrangements they appear to be operating satisfactorily.

The 'cab rank rule'

15.40 The 'cab rank rule' is a professional rule applying to advocates and it is incorporated in a rule of court which states that:

> 'No advocate, without very good cause, shall refuse to act for any person tendering a reasonable fee, under pain of deprivation of his office of advocate.'[2]

In practice, what this rule means is that an advocate cannot refuse to accept a case on the grounds that he does not like a client or his cause. The term cab rank rule is thus a misnomer, as the analogy is not with clients taking the taxi at the

---

[1] The Monopolies and Mergers Commission: *Advocates' Services; A report on the supply by Senior Counsel alone of their services:* HMSO, 1976.
[2] *Codifying Act of Sederunt of 1913,* Chapter A (VI).

head of the queue, but rather with taxis on the streets, with their 'for hire' signs illuminated, being obliged to accept as a customer anyone who hails them. There are, of course, recognised circumstances which justify an advocate declining a case, the main ones being that he is already acting for a party with a conflicting interest; ill health; or that he has already been instructed in a case which would be likely to be called in court at or about the same time. We understand that one of the main benefits of the cab rank rule so far as the public interest is concerned is that there cannot be any occasion when a litigant would find himself without representation. If the advocate of the client's choice is for a good reason unable to take the case, the cab rank rule normally ensures that another suitable advocate is available. We understand that in the last resort the Dean of Faculty would appoint a suitable advocate to take a case; but the cab rank rule, which is well understood, sees to it that intervention by the Dean is hardly ever required. We are aware of considerable complaint in relation to criminal trials, particularly in the Glasgow circuit, that an accused person may be unable to secure for his trial the services of the advocate he wants and has to make do with another advocate instructed at very short notice. This, however, is not a failure in the cab rank principle but is a result of the list system under which the circuits are operated and which makes it impossible to foretell accurately when a particular trial will start. We have been told that it would be impossible to cope with the criminal work if the list system for circuits were to be abandoned in favour of fixed diets. However, we understand that efforts are being made to ameliorate the problem by increasing the number of judges on circuit at any one time or by reducing the areas covered by the circuits, thereby in time much reducing the lengths of the lists. We further understand that progress in this direction is hampered by lack of sufficient court rooms. This is one reason why we consider that the provision of adequate court rooms and court houses is a matter which should engage the active attention of the appropriate authorities as we stated in Chapter 14.

15.41 It is, of course, essential that those who litigate in the supreme courts should be guaranteed the availability of suitable representation. The cab rank rule indeed goes further than this by guaranteeing, so far as is practicable, the services of the particular advocate preferred by the client. Because of the pressures which apply in the case of senior advocates the tendency for most is to welcome an opportunity to leave the Bar at latest by their mid 50s for a salaried post. The obligations under the cab rank rule are largely responsible for the unremitting pressures to which senior counsel are subject. We consider that if seniors over age 50 were given some dispensation from the obligations under the cab rank rule so that they could be selective in the type of work which they undertook, more senior advocates might be willing to remain at the Bar. Accordingly, we **recommend** that the cab rank rule be retained subject, however, to a change which would permit seniors over the age of 50 to be selective in the kind of work which they undertake.

Advocates' professional immunity

15.42 It is thought that advocates have a degree of immunity for liability for negligence in relation to court work. The extent of the immunity has never been laid down by a Scottish court as the matter has never been tested. The matter has, however, been considered by the House of Lords more than once in relation to English barristers and we understand that it is probable that the Scottish courts while not bound by their decisions would follow them. The principle at issue has been well stated for us by the Faculty who pointed out that any court action for negligence would necessarily involve rehearing the original case to establish whether the advocate was, or was not, negligent:

> 'The fundamental reason why the conduct of a case in court should not be scrutinised in later proceedings, has nothing to do with the particular status requirements or deserts of advocates as such or advocacy as a profession, but is an aspect of the public policy requirement that cases concluded by judicial decision should not be re-opened.'

If this is the principle underlying any immunity that advocates may have, it seems to us that it should apply equally to solicitors in their advocacy role if it does not already do so.

FUSION: A UNIFIED LEGAL PROFESSION?

15.43 In the following paragraphs we consider the issue of unification or, as it is more commonly called, fusion of the two branches of the legal profession. At present, the rules of both branches of the profession provide that no one can be a solicitor and an advocate simultaneously, although it is possible to transfer relatively easily from one branch to the other. Most transfers that take place are from the solicitor branch to the advocate branch. One of the reasons for this predominately one-way traffic, as we note in Chapter 19, may be simply that intending advocates spend a few years in the solicitor branch of the profession to enable them to save sufficient funds to tide them over the initial period at the Bar when earnings may be very low.

15.44 We received many representations on the subject of fusion both from organisations and individuals, lay and legal. The greater part of the evidence, however, was in favour of retaining the present divided profession. Within the legal profession itself there were conflicting views on fusion; but the majority of the legal groups and individual lawyers who submitted views to us favoured retention of the two separate branches of solicitor and advocate. A considerable weight of legal opinion was, however, in favour of extending the rights of audience of solicitors to enable them to appear in the supreme courts. We had the unusual experience of the Law Society, on the latter issue, submitting a divided view in their evidence to us; indeed, when they gave oral evidence to us on this topic, they included representatives who argued strongly in favour of extended rights of audience for solicitors, and others who as strongly and sincerely argued that this would be a retrograde step and not in the interests of justice. The majority view, however, was in favour of extended rights of audience for solicitors who wanted it in the Outer House of the Court of Session and also in the High Court of Justiciary. We deal with the question of rights of representation in greater detail later in this Chapter.

Arguments for and against fusion

15.45 A variety of arguments in favour of fusion were put to us. These included the suggestion that fusion would increase the speed and reduce the cost of litigation; that it would lead to more specialisation within the legal profession with a larger number of experienced and specialist lawyers becoming available; and that a larger pool of lawyers than at present would be available from which judges for the supreme courts could be chosen. The proponents of a continuing divided profession argued, on the other hand, that fusion would not lead to change, or at best only to marginal change, in the cost of litigation; that litigation would not be conducted any quicker, and indeed that specialisation in advocacy would be adversely affected; that the choice of counsel for clients and small legal firms would be restricted; that advocates are at present better placed than solicitors to undertake detailed studies and to prepare for complicated litigation; that the service which advocates provide is complementary to that which solicitors provide; that the completely independent appraisal of a case which an advocate is able to give would be lost; and that the separate Faculty of Advocates from past experience provides a suitable pool from which supreme court judges can be appointed.

15.46 We considered at some length all the views which were put to us. We have also tried to take into account, in so far as we thought they were relevant to Scotland, a great mass of arguments put forward on both sides of this question in many quarters. The arguments are so well known that we think it would be unnecessary to repeat them. In looking at the matter we have, however, concentrated on the particular needs of Scotland and have formed our conclusion on the basis of what we believe is appropriate for Scotland, rather than on any general view as to the advantages and disadvantages of a divided profession in the abstract. On the question of cost we were, of course, aware from the surveys of the income of the legal profession that because advocates are operating mainly from one centre (in Parliament House in Edinburgh) their individual overheads are much less than those of solicitors. If the profession were to be fused this overheads disparity would probably disappear with the result that fees for work presently done by advocates would have to support higher overheads. While we accept that the time taken to complete litigation is frequently lengthy, we believe that the division of the profession contributes little to this. We have in any event recommended a review of civil court procedures in Chapter 14. On questions of specialisation we are, of course, aware that many solicitors specialise in advocacy in the sheriff courts and that the volume of work at the Scottish Bar is not sufficient to enable more than a few advocates to specialise in particular areas of the law.

15.47 As we mentioned in our introductory Chapter we were able to see the evidence which the Lords of Appeal submitted to the Benson Commission. On the question of fusion they were unanimously against it, arguing that it would lead to a lowering of standards of advocacy. In support of their views many of them referred to the legal systems of the USA and Canada where fused professions exist. Some of the Lords of Appeal and English judges also referred to the Australian experience where some states have fused and others divided professions and where although the previously divided profession has been abolished by law the profession has in practice again split into two branches; their general view was that standards of advocacy were much better in the states which did not have a fused profession. We cannot but be impressed by the views which were expressed.

15.48 One argument against fusion which we found particularly persuasive was that it would result in a restriction of the choice of lawyers rather than an increase. The argument was that under fusion the better advocates would be attracted to the larger and more prestigious legal firms. As a result smaller firms would be unable to recruit their due share of the available talent and would be left disadvantaged. The smaller firms would be reluctant to instruct a lawyer in a larger firm for fear that the client would go direct to the larger firm the next time he had legal business to transact. The result might be that the small firms would attempt from within their own unsatisfactory resources to provide an advocacy service to their clients. This would be in sharp contrast to the present position in a divided profession where the small firms are not inhibited in any way from engaging the services of any one of the pool of advocates available within the Faculty of Advocates.

15.49 We are aware that at present the supreme court judges are chosen exclusively from the members of the Faculty of Advocates. It has been argued in favour of fusion that it would lead to a larger pool of appropriate talent being available from which to choose these judges since many solicitors have the intellectual capacity to serve with distinction on the supreme court bench. Such solicitors, however, because of their restricted rights of audience do not have the opportunity of practising before the supreme courts and demonstrating that they have the qualities necessary for consideration for appointment as supreme court judges. It has also been argued that some academic lawyers merit consideration for appointment as judges in the supreme courts. While there might be some force in the arguments that there would be advantage in choosing supreme court judges from a wider field than at present, we do not see this by itself as a sufficient argument to justify fusion.

Our conclusions on fusion

15.50 Our feeling after weighing the evidence is that we should be very hesitant to make any recommendation which could result in a diminution or restriction of the legal services which are available at the present time; and we are, on balance, more impressed by the arguments in favour of, than those against, the present divided profession. In particular, we see great value in having an independent advocate service which is available to all solicitors and, therefore, to all clients in Scotland. One of the strengths of the independent Faculty of Advocates based in Edinburgh is the concentration of facilities in the Advocates Library, in Parliament House, Edinburgh. This is a significant factor in keeping advocates' costs low and in making available to them adequate opportunities for research. While we appreciate that modern technological developments will in due course allow lawyers outwith Edinburgh to have equally good access to legal texts stored on electronic retrieval systems, we feel that the concentration of the Faculty in Edinburgh also allows opportunities for informal exchange of information and opinion which would not be as easy if the advocate branch of the profession were distributed up and down the country. Another benefit of the location of the separate advocates branch of the profession in Edinburgh is that it strengthens the control of discipline and the maintaining of high ethical standards and we have no doubt that for these reasons alone it is in the public interest. We **recommend**, therefore, that the legal profession in Scotland should continue to consist of two branches, namely solicitors and advocates.

Rights of audience

15.51 Our conclusion that the profession should remain divided does not, of course, of itself imply that the existing division of work between the two branches of the profession is the right one. One major distinction is that, while both solicitors and advocates are able to represent clients in cases before the sheriff and district courts and before those tribunals where legal representation is allowed, only an advocate may represent clients in the supreme courts. As we mentioned earlier, the views of the solicitor branch of the profession were divided as to whether solicitors should be granted extended rights of audience in the supreme courts. We do not feel that there is any need to consider the converse proposition (which was not raised in evidence) that there should be a restriction on advocates' rights of audience in the lower courts or before tribunals. When advocates appear in such cases, it is normally at the client's choice; and we do not consider that there would be any public interest served by restricting advocates' rights of audience in the lower courts since this would deprive clients of their present ability to choose.

15.52 In favour of the proposition that solicitors should be granted wider rights of audience, it is argued that solicitors presently represent clients in the sheriff courts in civil actions; and that such actions can, and do, at times involve more complex issues and higher sums of money than do many actions heard in the Court of Session. It is argued, therefore, that it is unjustifiable to debar solicitors from representing clients in the Court of Session. Against this it is argued that it is not the existing demarcation between rights of audience of solicitors and advocates that requires change. What needs to be reviewed is the overlapping civil jurisdiction of the Court of Session and the sheriff courts; and we have, of course, recommended such a review in Chapter 14.

15.53 In relation to criminal matters, it is suggested that many solicitors represent clients effectively and without criticism in sheriff court trials, and that there should be no objection to their being given rights of audience in the High Court of Justiciary. On the other hand, it has been suggested to us that the public interest would be jeopardised if solicitors had rights of representation in the more serious criminal cases which are reserved for the High Court, on the ground that the solicitor's close involvement with his client would make it more difficult for him always to fulfil punctiliously his obligations to the court. We do not believe that the standards of ethical integrity are in general any different in the two branches of the profession. Nevertheless, we think it may well be correct that the relative detachment of the advocate from the client which exists by reason of the nature of his function could in some types of serious criminal charges form a valuable safeguard.

15.54 Another argument against extended rights of audience for solicitors is that the standard of many solicitors' pleading in the sheriff courts falls short of the standard required in the supreme courts. Both from evidence we received and from visits to courts we are of the view that much sheriff court advocacy by solicitors is poor, and we make recommendations on this matter in Chapter 16. On the other hand, we know that advocates also do not perform uniformly well in court; and we are prepared to accept, therefore, that some solicitors are undoubtedly better oral pleaders than some advocates. On balance, however, after consideration of all the various points made to us we feel that we would not be justified in recommending extended rights of audience for solicitors in the supreme courts. We think that extending the rights of audience would involve at least some risk of substantially lowering standards in the supreme courts,

Those representatives of the Law Society who argued in favour of extended rights of audience conceded, as we understood it, that solicitors would not operate the cab rank principle. We are not surprised at this. The nature of solicitors' business might make it impractical for them to do so. We think, however, that competition in the supreme courts between the two branches of the profession, one of which could pick and choose its clients and the other of which could not, might lead to undesirable results. It could, of course, be argued that this already occurs in the sheriff courts. However, there is a difference. In the sheriff courts the advocates encroach on what is in general the domain of solicitors, but do so subject to the restraints of the cab rank rule. If the proposal to extend rights of audience were granted, the solicitor would be enabled to encroach on what is generally the domain of the advocates—and not under any restraint, but with a material advantage. Finally, on this matter, we have considered the end result of extending rights of audience. It is impossible to predict what would happen with any confidence. It may be that very little use would be made of the right, in which case an alternative to the existing system would not be justified by any substantial results. It may be, on the other hand, that the right would be very widely used. If it were, the result would inevitably be some erosion and perhaps the eventual extinction of the Faculty of Advocates. We have already decided that it is, on balance, to the advantage of Scotland that the two branches of the profession should be retained. Having reached that conclusion, it would not be sensible to support, on the basis of arguments of somewhat uncertain merits, a proposal which might have the effect of bringing about fusion by a process of slow erosion of the viability of the Faculty. Accordingly, we **recommend** that rights of audience in the supreme courts should not be extended to solicitors.

The use of computers

15.55 Any consideration of the provision of legal services now and in the future must take account of modern technology, and in particular of the actual and potential use of computers (or micro processors) by the legal profession. We received only a limited amount of evidence on the use of computers in connection with the law and legal services in Scotland—perhaps because the size of the country had not in the past lent itself to the development of the use of computers at an economic cost. We have, however, had some evidence about the use of computers in a number of other countries.

15.56 In the general evidence given to us, two major complaints about the provision of legal services were cost and delay. We have referred elsewhere to the inability of the profession to provide us with precise information of a kind which we would have thought essential to the proper management of a business. We believe that in appropriate cases, the use of computers would help to limit increases in costs and speed up some of the processes involved in the provision of legal services.

15.57 There are three main areas in which we consider that the computer can assist in the provision of legal services:

(i) in the administration and management of the solicitor's office and the advocate's practice;

(ii) in the administration of the courts and the maintenance of public registers; and

(iii) in the storage and retrieval of the law.

15.58 We are aware that the computer is generally used in commerce and industry to carry out administrative functions with a speed, accuracy and efficiency which would not be possible if undertaken by human beings. We believe that the computer can be used to make the business of a legal practice more cost effective. We therefore **recommend** that the profession should urgently examine the application of computers in, firstly, the maintenance of time and cost records, financial accounts (both for the practitioner and the client), and trust accounts; secondly, controlling and organising court work and the extensive documentation often involved in a large litigation; and, thirdly, the processing of conveyancing.

15.59 The second area in which we think the computer can help is in the administration of the courts and the maintenance of public registers. We have had evidence from North America and England of the effective use of computers for the maintenance of court lists and the processing of the various steps in a litigation. We **recommend**, therefore, that those responsible for the administration of our courts should actively examine these systems and consider implementing those which would speed up the litigation process or reduce the cost; and that any review of court procedure should be carried out against the background of the potential of the computer in this field. We are aware that the Scottish Courts Administration are already considering the introduction of computers to process fines and we would commend this initiative while hoping that they will take account of our wider recommendation.

15.60 We were impressed to learn that the Keeper of the Registers of Scotland had already developed the use of the computer in the maintenance of the Personal Registers and that, with the introduction of registration of title in 1981, he intends to keep the information for the Land Register on a computer. We also understand that, subject to suitable safeguards, it will be possible to carry out a search in these records through a terminal anywhere in Scotland. We **recommend** that this access to the records should be made available and that consideration should be given to the maintenance of other records in the same way—for example, the records kept at the Companies Registration Office in Edinburgh—and that they should be capable of being accessed (to use the computer jargon) from different parts of Scotland.

15.61 Scotland is a small country with its own laws, but the law of Scotland also encompasses statute law which is common to the United Kingdom and sometimes to the legislation of the EEC. The cost of law reports which set out the judgements of the courts is rising steeply, as is the cost of legal textbooks. The limited market in Scotland for the law reports and legal textbooks inhibits the prompt and regular publication of up-to-date reports and textbooks. These problems are probably more acute in a small jurisdiction like Scotland, but they are nonetheless real in all developed countries. There have been considerable developments in the use of computers for the retrieval of the law in North America and in the continent of Europe, but very little in the United Kingdom. We were impressed by the proposals for a computer assisted legal information retrieval system in the United Kingdom contained in a report entitled 'A

National Law Library—The Way Ahead' (prepared by the Society for Computers and Law in February 1979). We were glad to hear that the Law Society of Scotland and the Law Society in England and Wales had supported the conclusions and recommendations of the report and although we were not able to consider all these in detail, we do commend the general proposals of the report.

15.62 Associated with legal information retrieval, and to some extent a vital part of any system of retrieval, is the legislative process. During the period of our work, there were proposals for a Scottish Assembly which in the event did not come to fruition. As this Assembly would have had a substantial legislative function, the Scottish Legal Computer Research Trust decided to commission a report from Dr A G Donaldson of Edinburgh University on the role that computers could play in the drafting and enactment of legislation. The report which Dr Donaldson produced entitled 'Legislation and Computers' showed that much has been done in other countries to improve the legislative process which could be adopted in the United Kingdom.

15.63 Because we believe that a proper understanding of the use of computers is essential for the future of the legal profession, we recommend in Chapter 16 that instruction in their use should form part of the education and training of the members of the profession in the future.

15.64 It has been suggested to us that there should be set up a standing body on the use of computers in the law. We are not sure that there should be such a separate body, but if there were, it would probably need to be a United Kingdom body with adequate representation for Scotland. We do, however, **recommend** that our proposed Department of Legal Affairs and Legal Services Advisory Committee should be charged with ensuring that the development of computers with regard to the law and provision of legal services in Scotland is actively pursued.

THE ADMINISTRATIVE ORGANISATION OF THE LAW SOCIETY OF SCOTLAND*

(other than in relation to the Legal Aid Scheme)

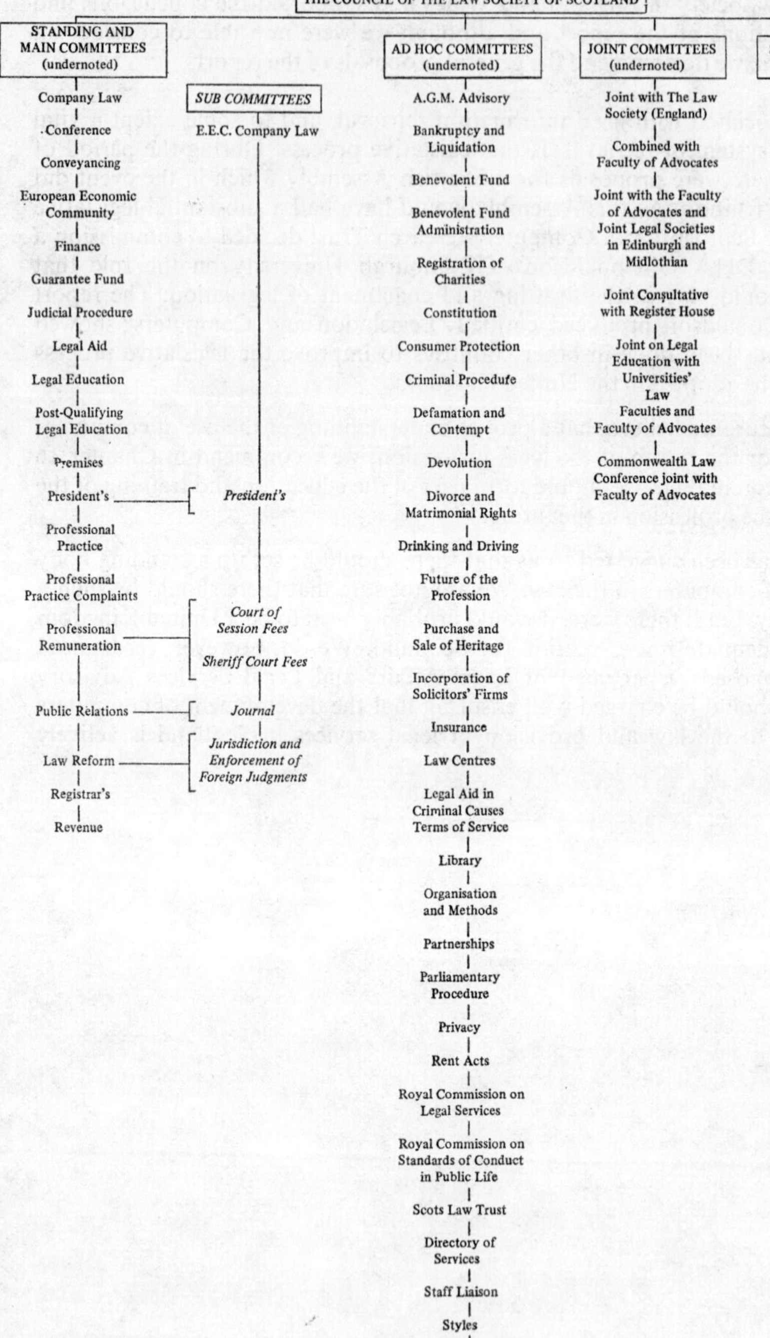
THE COUNCIL OF THE LAW SOCIETY OF SCOTLAND
STANDING AND MAIN COMMITTEES (undernoted)
Company Law
Conference
Conveyancing
European Economic Community
Finance
Guarantee Fund
Judicial Procedure
Legal Aid
Legal Education
Post-Qualifying Legal Education
Premises
President's
Professional Practice
Professional Practice Complaints
Professional Remuneration
Public Relations
Law Reform
Registrar's
Revenue
SUB COMMITTEES
E.E.C. Company Law
President's
Court of Session Fees
Sheriff Court Fees
Journal
Jurisdiction and Enforcement of Foreign Judgments
AD HOC COMMITTEES (undernoted)
A.G.M. Advisory
Bankruptcy and Liquidation
Benevolent Fund
Benevolent Fund Administration
Registration of Charities
Constitution
Consumer Protection
Criminal Procedure
Defamation and Contempt
Devolution
Divorce and Matrimonial Rights
Drinking and Driving
Future of the Profession
Purchase and Sale of Heritage
Incorporation of Solicitors' Firms
Insurance
Law Centres
Legal Aid in Criminal Causes Terms of Service
Library
Organisation and Methods
Partnerships
Parliamentary Procedure
Privacy
Rent Acts
Royal Commission on Legal Services
Royal Commission on Standards of Conduct in Public Life
Scots Law Trust
Directory of Services
Staff Liaison
Styles
Succession
JOINT COMMITTEES (undernoted)
Joint with The Law Society (England)
Combined with Faculty of Advocates
Joint with the Faculty of Advocates and Joint Legal Societies in Edinburgh and Midlothian
Joint Consultative with Register House
Joint on Legal Education with Universities' Law Faculties and Faculty of Advocates
Commonwealth Law Conference joint with Faculty of Advocates
STATUTORY COMMITTEES (undernoted)
Legal Aid Central (see Appendix II)
Legal Aid Complaints (see Appendix II)

*Source: The Law Society of Scotland: 1977

LIST OF LOCAL FACULTIES OF SOLICITORS*

The Society of Writers to Her Majesty's Signet
The Society of Solicitors in the Supreme Courts of Scotland
The Royal Faculty of Procurators in Glasgow
The Glasgow Bar Association
The Society of Advocates in Aberdeen
The Society of Solicitors in Airdrie
The Society of Procurators and Solicitors in Angus
The Faculty of Solicitors of Ayr
The Society of Solicitors of Banffshire
The Society of Solicitors in Berwickshire
The Society of Solicitors of Clackmannanshire
The Faculty of Solicitors of Dumfriesshire
The Faculty of Procurators of Dunbartonshire
The Faculty of Procurators and Solicitors in Dundee
The Society of Solicitors of Dunfermline District of Fife
The Dunoon Faculty of Procurators
The Society of Procurators and Solicitors of the Eastern District of Fife
The East Lothian Faculty of Procurators
The Society of Solicitors of the Eastern District of Stirlingshire
The Society of Solicitors of Elginshire
The Faculty of Procurators of Greenock
The Society of Solicitors of Hamilton
The Society of Solicitors of Inverness-shire
The Faculty of Solicitors of Kilmarnock
The Kirkcaldy Law Society
The Faculty of Procurators of the Stewartry of Kirkcudbright
The Society of Procurators of Midlothian
The Oban Faculty of Procurators
The Faculty of Procurators in Paisley
The Society of Procurators and Solicitors in the City and County of Perth
The Society of Solicitors in Peterhead
The Faculty of Solicitors of Ross and Cromarty
The Society of Procurators and Solicitors of Roxburghshire
The Society of Solicitors in the Shires of Selkirk and Peebles
The Society of Procurators and Solicitors of Stirling
The Faculty of Procurators of West Lothian
The Faculty of Solicitors in the Western Isles

*Source: The Law Society of Scotland: 1977

RECOMMENDATIONS

			Paragraph
Law Society records	R15.1	The Law Society should examine urgently the adequacy of its internal administration and records in the light of our Report and should, if necessary, be subject to a statutory obligation to keep the information discussed in paragraph 15.12.	15.12
Court Advisory Committees	R15.2	Every Sheriff Principal should establish for each sheriff court or group of courts, for which he is responsible, an advisory committee comprising representatives of the local Bar, court staff, procurators fiscal, social workers and appropriate outside lay elements. The advisory committee would advise The Sheriff Principal on any matters affecting the work of the court or the convenience of the users of the court.	15.14
	R15.3	Consideration should be given to the best form for a similar advisory committee or committees for the Court of Session and High Court of Justiciary.	15.14
Edinburgh correspondents	R15.4	The Committee on Civil Procedure (R14.1) should examine the requirements as to Edinburgh solicitors in Court of Session actions, and as to advocates being accompanied in court by solicitors.	15.16
Notaries Public	R15.5	The status of Notary Public should be conferred on all solicitors admitted in future solely by virtue of their admission as solicitors.	15.19
Incorporation of solicitors' firms	R15.6	The restrictions on the incorporation of solicitors' partnerships should be removed subject to suitable safeguards.	15.20

			Paragraph
Multi-disciplinary partnerships	R15.7	The present statutory restriction on solicitors sharing fees with others, so far as it prevents the development of multi-disciplinary partnerships and associations, should be removed so that they can be permitted. The professional restrictions which prevent solicitors and advocates combining in partnerships in relation to practice in Scotland should remain.	15.22
Instruction of advocates	R15.8	Only solicitors should instruct counsel in court matters; certain other professional agents should be entitled to instruct counsel direct for an opinion or in relation to proceedings before a tribunal or inquiry although counsel may at his discretion refuse to accept such instructions.	15.33
Cab Rank Rule	R15.9	The cab rank rule which applies to advocates should be retained subject to a change which would permit seniors over the age of 50 to be selective in the kind of work which they undertake.	15.41
Fusion	R15.10	The legal profession in Scotland should continue to consist of two branches, namely solicitors and advocates.	15.50
Rights of audience	R15.11	Rights of audience in the supreme courts should not be extended to solicitors.	15.54
Use of computers	R15.12	The legal profession should urgently examine the application of computers in: the maintenance of time and cost records; financial accounts, both for the practitioner and the client, and trust accounts; controlling and organising court work and the extensive documentation involved; and the processing of conveyancing.	15.58

		Paragraph
R15.13	An examination of the potential use of computers in court procedures should be undertaken by those responsible for the administration of Scottish courts.	15.59
R15.14	Subject to suitable safeguards, access to information kept on the Land Register should be available through the use of computer terminals anywhere in Scotland and consideration should be given to maintaining other public records on computer and giving access to them throughout Scotland.	15.60
R15.15	The Department of Legal Affairs and the Legal Services Advisory Committee (see R20.2) should be charged with ensuring that the development of computers with regard to the law and provision of legal services in Scotland is actively pursued.	15.64

CHAPTER 16

EDUCATION AND TRAINING I: LAWYERS

16.1 In this Chapter we consider in some detail the recruitment, education and training of lawyers. We feel it necessary to do this because we believe that the quality of the service provided by a lawyer depends in large measure on the quality of his education and training, both that which he receives before qualifying and that which he undertakes subsequently. Many areas of a lawyer's work are, for all practical purposes, the monopoly of lawyers, and there is legitimate public interest in ensuring that those who enjoy such a monopoly are adequately educated and trained to justify that privilege. What is taught, how it is taught, and the attitudes of those who teach it, will all affect the intending lawyer's perception of the role of law and of legal services in the society which he will serve. Those engaged in educating and training lawyers should aim to provide, in sufficient numbers, people qualified to provide legal services of high quality and of appropriate scope.

AN OVERVIEW OF LEGAL EDUCATION

Entry to the solicitor profession

16.2 Graduates with a Scottish LLB degree (some 95 per cent of intrants) have to complete a period of two or three years apprenticeship, the period depending on whether or not they have achieved total exemption from the Law Society examinations by virtue of the content of their degree course, or by passing any necessary examinations within the first two years of their in-office training. Graduates with degrees other than a Scottish LLB must undergo a three years apprenticeship during which they sit all the Society's examinations. The non-graduate has to serve a five years apprenticeship during which he sits the Society's examinations. (The Law Society examinations consist of two papers on the law of Scotland and papers on evidence and procedure, conveyancing, accounting, and taxation.) The apprentice is expected to gain experience in three major areas of a solicitor's work: court work, conveyancing, and either trust and executry work or public administration. A survey conducted for us showed that 87 per cent of apprentices were serving two years apprenticeships, 9 per cent three years and 3 per cent five years.[1] Ninety three per cent of apprentices work for a solicitor in private practice and most of the rest work for local authorities.

Age and educational background of apprentices

16.3 Most law students enter the course aged 17 or 18, with those taking an ordinary degree finishing three years later. Such graduates will typically complete their apprenticeship and enrol as solicitors two years after that, at the age of 22 or 23. Our survey showed that half of those undertaking two years

[1] See Appendix 6, Paragraph 142.

apprenticeships would complete them aged 23 or under. Some 95 per cent of apprentices and young solicitors have a Scottish LLB degree; 15 per cent of apprentices have a further degree (half of them a Scottish MA). Two in three apprentices are male. Thus while there are significant minorities of new solicitors who are older, more widely educated, or female, the typical intrant to the profession is a young man of 22 or 23 who has completed a three years ordinary LLB and a two years apprenticeship.

16.4 Over half of the apprentices in private practice work for the 15 per cent of firms with six or more partners; indeed firms with five or more partners have about twice as many apprentices per partner as smaller firms. Apprentices are concentrated in city firms, partly because they tend to be larger and partly no doubt because of their proximity to the university law faculties.[1] After serving his apprenticeship satisfactorily the trainee, provided he is over 21 and has gained exemption from the Law Society's examinations, or has obtained the appropriate passes, may apply for admission and enrolment as a solicitor. Most of those trainees who have completed only a two years apprenticeship must serve a further obligatory year of practical training, during which they may not practise on their own account or enter their names on the legal aid lists, although they have been admitted and enrolled as solicitors. Perhaps the most frequent exception to this arrangement is the law graduate with a good honours degree who is exempted from the obligatory third year of training. The Table below shows the number of intrants using the various methods of entry to the solicitor branch of the profession in the period 1972–79.

TABLE 16.1: Method of entry to solicitor branch*

	LLB Degree Only	*LLB Degree Plus Law Society Examinations*	*Law Society Examinations Only*	*Total*
1972	166	37	20	223
1973	189	40	12	241
1974	192	43	8	243
1975	240	39	16	295
1976	240	44	18	302
1977	217	53	14	284
1978	256	58	13	327
1979	297	58	14	369

*Source: The Law Society.

Entry to the advocate profession

16.5 Of the intrants to the Faculty of Advocates over the period 1975–78 some 95 per cent had taken an LLB degree at a Scottish university, and half of them had another degree besides.[2] Table 16.2 shows that, while half the intrants ('devils') had no previous occupation and went straight to the Bar at the start of their careers, the other half had had some work experience, with one devil in four having previously been a solicitor; when former university teaching staff are added in, the proportion rises to one in three.

[1] See Appendix 6. Comparable figures are to be found in Appendix 7.
[2] See Appendix 10.

TABLE 16.2: Previous education and employment of devils*

Previous Occupation	University Degrees		Total
	1 or less	2 or more	
None	11	10	21
Solicitor	6	5	11
Other employment	4	5	9
TOTAL	21	20	41

*Source: Appendix 10, Table 5.

The LLB degree will normally give the intrant exemption from most of the Faculty examinations, but all intrants are now required to take Faculty examinations in evidence and pleading, civil procedure and criminal procedure. Non-graduate intrants, and graduates from other disciplines than the law, may elect to qualify by taking all the necessary Faculty examinations. Intrants must spend a period as an apprentice in a solicitor's office: those with first or second class honours degrees in law have to spend 12 months, others 21 months. (These requirements may be waived by the Dean of Faculty in certain circumstances.) Following the period of apprenticeship in a solicitor's office, the intrant is attached as a 'devil' to a junior counsel who has been in practice for five years or more. The period of devilling varies between 8 and 11 months, depending on the court terms covered, though for intrants who have been solicitors for at least five years the period is reduced to a maximum of six months. The devil serves what is, in effect, an apprenticeship to his master and performs all the duties of an advocate except that he is not allowed to speak in court. At the end of the period of devilling, the intrant is admitted to membership of the Faculty of Advocates and thereafter by the Court of Session to the public office of advocate which enables him to appear before the courts.

16.6 Thus, in brief, the typical intending solicitor takes a three years Scottish LLB followed by a two years apprenticeship. Thereafter he obtains his practising certificate but must wait one further year before he can practise on his own account. Many intending advocates complete an LLB, serve one-two years with a solicitor, and then nine months or so with an advocate before being admitted. As many as half, however, will have had a previous occupation, half of them (a quarter of the total) as solicitors.

The pattern of pre-qualifying learning

16.7 While we were sitting, a number of changes in the education and training of lawyers were proposed. We discuss these below, but we should first like to comment on the existing university route which the majority of intending solicitors now follow. The present LLB ordinary degree course lasts three years; thus many undergraduates complete their university education at about age 21. They complete a two years apprenticeship and then apply for enrolment and admission as a solicitor at about age 23. The total period of university education and in-office training of five years is short in comparison with that required by lawyers in many other countries. At age 23 many young solicitors lack the maturity which clients frequently want in the advisers with whom they wish to discuss their problems. In addition, for most undergraduates the present three years LLB course is heavily orientated towards the vocational or practical subjects which will later gain exemption from the Law Society's examinations. Some improvement in the present position will be secured with the introduction in October 1980 of a compulsory postgraduate Diploma in Legal Practice. We welcome this development to which we refer in more detail below. We do not consider, however, that even four years education at university is enough for lawyers. Although for reasons of finance it may only be practicable in the longer term, we favour the introduction of a four years LLB course. We show later in this Chapter what kind of degree course we have in mind. It would mean, however, that the university education of the intending lawyer spanned five years—four years for the degree and a compulsory further postgraduate year for the Diploma in Legal Practice. With a subsequent apprenticeship of two years the solicitor would have completed a total education and training period of seven years, which is of the same order as is now required for doctors and other similar professional groups. We do not think that a truly satisfactory academic and professional training for lawyers can be accommodated within a shorter period.

THE LAW DEGREE

Admission of law students

16.8 Since the graduate entry dominates the intake to the legal profession, we felt it most important to examine the way in which applicants are selected for places in the university law faculties. (There are law faculties at Aberdeen, Dundee, Edinburgh, Glasgow and Strathclyde Universities.) These faculties receive many more applications than they have places available, and failure to enter a university law faculty will normally mean that the unsuccessful applicant will not join the profession. In selecting among the candidates who present themselves, the universities rely to a very large extent on academic attainment at school. We have reviewed this practice because there is no guarantee that those with the best school results will make either the best law students or the best lawyers. Scottish Certificate of Education Higher and Ordinary grade marks have been criticised as being measures of a student's ability to learn and regurgitate material, rather than affording a measure of intellectual potential. Further, we think that a selection procedure which depends so heavily on good school examination results is liable to produce a very homogeneous group of students, and thus limit the scope for a fruitful exchange of experience amongst them. An important unintended consequence of selecting those with the best school marks can often be the rejection of a disproportionate number of candidates from working class backgrounds and from the newer six-year secondary schools. Indeed, it has been alleged that this factor has contributed to the slowness of the profession to respond to people's need for legal assistance in the areas of personal rights, particularly those created by housing, social welfare and employment statutes in recent years.

16.9 We agree with the Ormrod Committee when they say 'the demands which the legal profession has to meet, and the roles which professional lawyers are called upon to play in society, are so varied, and require such different qualities, that the profession will always need to recruit men and women of widely differing character, temperament and intellectual attainments'.[1] We do not believe that any form of quota system for university admissions would be desirable; nor do we think that any explicit discrimination in favour of particular groups who are at present disadvantaged ('positive discrimination') would be practicable or acceptable. Nevertheless, we think that the present criteria for admission to university law faculties call for some adjustment, and we **recommend** that universities should use wider criteria than academic attainment at school when selecting law students for admission. In particular, we wish to see more account taken of the following considerations: firstly, each applicant's aptitude for, and interest in, the study of law; secondly, the need for a student population more varied in age and socio-economic background so as to create a better educational environment; and, thirdly, the need to ensure that all pupils of ability and potential, from whatever school background, have a real opportunity to study law at university if they so wish. To achieve this, the universities should continue to set a realistic minimum entry qualification based on academic attainment at school; that is, a minimum level which indicates a high probability that the student will be able to fulfil the degree requirements. The three criteria outlined above should, however, come into play when the universities are deciding which candidates to admit of those who have the necessary minimum qualifications. We wish to emphasise that the minimum qualification should not be lowered for particular candidates; rather, once the minimum has been set, the selection should not favour exclusively those who have the best school marks.

16.10 We acknowledge that there may be great difficulty in moving away from the apparently objective criteria provided by school examination results. However, we believe that there are alternatives which will be acceptable to the universities and which will be more effective in providing a genuinely objective evaluation of the potential of applicants. Glasgow University are already experimenting with Princeton Aptitude Tests to provide an objective measure of applicants' aptitude and feel for the study of the law. Such aptitude tests are used extensively in many North American universities, and in some Scottish university departments they have a place in the selection of postgraduate students. We **recommend,** therefore, that the experience gained in Glasgow University should be used as the basis for the development of a test of aptitude to study law, which would be valid and reliable for use in Scotland, so that applicants' performance in such a test could be included as one element in the process of selecting students for entry to the faculties of law.

16.11 It is essential to emphasise that the universities should select students on the basis of their aptitude to study law, not their aptitude to practise it. A better judgement of the fitness to practise law can be made after formal education has been largely completed. Some law students do not wish to enter the practising profession, and since they are not constrained by the Law Society's entrance requirements in choosing their courses, they are able to select a number of subject courses which intending lawyers seldom take. These students can make a vital contribution to the academic health of the law faculties.

The purpose of the LLB degree

16.12 We have considered what should be the purpose of a university educa-

[1] *Report of the Committee on Legal Education* (The Ormrod Committee): HMSO, 1971, p. 41.

tion in law. On our visits to Scandinavia and North America we have seen how a law degree can be used as a general education for anyone contemplating a career in business or the public service. It is not for us to recommend whether law degrees should be so regarded in Scotland; we have seen little evidence of any significant move in this direction, though our research shows that some 10 per cent of first year students do not intend to train as a solicitor on graduation, and the figure rises to about 15 per cent of students in the third and fourth years of study.[1]

16.13 If the law degree is not to be a general business education, the two main orientations left are the academic and the professional. At one extreme, law can be studied as an academic discipline without any regard to its application in professional practice, while at the other a course of study geared narrowly to the immediate needs of a practising professional would cease to be an 'education' in any proper sense of the word. The purpose of legal education was expressed to us in this way by the University of Dundee:

> 'Our aim is that students should achieve an understanding of law, regarded both as a social phenomenon and as a system of rules capable of interpretation with a measure, albeit imperfect, of rational coherence, and that that understanding should be pursued with a breadth sufficient to give it fullness and balance and with a depth appropriate to university study. At the same time it is our intention that students who intend to enter the practising legal profession should be provided with a basis on which professional competence can be built and, so far as this can be done outside the context of continuous professional practice with the main tools for acquiring that competence.'

Their evidence goes on to say that:

> 'There are aspects of legal practice for which there is no substitute for learning by day-to-day experience under the guidance of one who is already a master of the craft . . . it should not be the aim to cram everything which may conceivably be useful to the potential practitioner into the undergraduate curriculum. All that can be expected of such a student's undergraduate curriculum is that it should introduce him to the materials and techniques which when supplemented by professional training will enable him to cope with the ordinary legal problems of general practice.'

The University suggest that it is no longer adequate to try to understand the law as a rational coherent system of rules, and that:

> 'The law can now be properly understood only if there is some appreciation of the considerations which have given rise to change . . . and of the social context in which the law functions. . . . Accordingly a demand is arising for courses to be organised on the basis of interests to be protected (e.g. interests in land, interests in employment). . . . A certain tension may thus arise between conceptually-based and interests-based teaching.'

We have quoted at some length from this evidence because it seems to us to encapsulate the right approach to a university education in the law, and the proposals which we make in subsequent paragraphs are in general accord with this approach to the nature and purpose of legal education.

---

[1] See Appendix 6.

16.14 We received a number of criticisms of the existing three years LLB degree, in particular suggestions that the degree courses concentrated much too closely on subjects which would give students exemptions from the Law Society examinations. It was also said that areas such as 'welfare law' and the social context of the law were wholly or largely ignored, and that insufficient attention was paid to the new dimension in our law introduced by our membership of the European Economic Community. Some of these views were borne out by the results of a survey which we conducted into the education and training of solicitors in Scotland.[1] More than two in five of the graduate apprentices and young solicitors who responded to our survey thought that some of the courses needed to meet university requirements, or the requirements of the Law Society of Scotland, were obligatory for no very good reason. The courses most commonly mentioned in this connection were jurisprudence and Roman law. However, the proportion of university teachers who saw such courses as unnecessary was much less. Half the graduate apprentices and university teachers thought that there were courses in the law syllabus of the universities which, though not usually taken, could be useful in preparing students for work as practising solicitors. A similar proportion of apprentices and teachers thought that there were courses at their universities which, though not in the LLB syllabus, could be useful in the same way. Substantial minorities of LLB students intending to train as solicitors, and of young solicitors, shared this view. Subjects most commonly mentioned here were social security or welfare law and industrial law. Further criticisms of the three years LLB made to us were that students passing through the three years degree were insufficiently mature; that on graduation they lacked a sufficiently broad outlook; and that graduates had not learned how to think analytically and to draw conclusions, as a good lawyer must.

16.15 One way to meet some of these criticisms would be the re-introduction of the practice of taking a general degree before proceeding to a law degree. In our survey 21 per cent of heads of firms preferred this arrangement, and it certainly has attractions in combining a general education with a legal training.[2] However, we do not think that this would be the best solution. There would in any event be difficulty in justifying State finance for two full-time degrees for intending lawyers, particularly when public funds are already committed to the Diploma in Legal Practice; and, while we favour some 'clinical' experience during the law degree, when students would gain some supervised contact with clients and some practical work, we do not want to return to the regime in which law students combined apprenticeship with part-time university study for their law degree. Moreover, at least one law faculty has found that graduate entrants to law degree courses are not necessarily more broad in outlook, nor do they necessarily perform better, than their non-graduate counterparts.

16.16 Our preferred alternative way to ensure that the education of lawyers is not unduly narrow is to broaden the scope of the LLB degree. This will require a longer period of study. In the short term, more time will become available in the present degree by the transfer of some topics to the Diploma syllabus. We gather that the law faculties intend to use the space created in the LLB degree course mainly for further law teaching. This may be understandable; but we would rather see some of the space given to non-legal studies,

[1] See Appendix 6.
[2] See Appendix 6.

particularly in the social sciences, so that law students can develop a better awareness of the place of law in society, and to the study of foreign languages (but not necessarily literature). We **recommend** then, in the short term, that as the Diploma is introduced the LLB syllabus should be revised to encourage students to study a social science or a modern language.

16.17 The scope for broadening the curriculum in this way is not great. A one year course in economics, sociology or politics, for example, and a modern language, would take up most of the slack created by the transfer of some subjects to the Diploma. We also want to enable students to have an effective choice of subject while still covering the core topics reasonably required of intending lawyers. We therefore **recommend** that the Law Society, in revising their own examinations to take account of the Diploma, should reduce to the minimum the requirements they effectively place on students to study particular courses. We have rejected the more radical option of regarding any Scottish LLB as a full exemption from the Law Society's examinations, because we accept that those who intend to graduate LLB but not to practise law thereafter may wish to construct a broad curriculum suited to their own interests. There could be no guarantee that any curriculum so devised would produce a graduate with an understanding of the law appropriate to a person intending to provide legal services to clients.

16.18 The recommendations in the last two paragraphs are, however, not enough. If lawyers are to be educated in sufficient breadth and depth they will need to spend four undergraduate years at university. Only a four years LLB will provide adequate scope for studying core legal subjects; taking courses in other faculties to get a wider appreciation of the place of law in society; and acquiring deeper and more analytical knowledge of one or two chosen legal topics of interest. We therefore **recommend** that the LLB degree should require a four years course of study. While we do not think that there is any need for us to make detailed recommendations about the degree curriculum, we are concerned that too few solicitors in Scotland are sufficiently knowledgeable in the area of social law; and neither the Law Society's requirements nor the structure of the university syllabus should, in our view, inhibit the education of succeeding generations of lawyers in this field.

The honours LLB

16.19 Our recommendations for a four years ordinary degree have implications for the present four years honours degree. From our discussions with the Joint Standing Committee on Legal Education (which consists of representatives of the Scottish universities and of both branches of the profession) we are in no doubt that there would be substantial disadvantages in an honours degree requiring an extra year of study beyond the proposed four years ordinary degree course. It would be difficult to argue for funds to be made available for a five years honours LLB, when the finance already available for the Diploma will need to be supplemented for the extension of the ordinary LLB to four years. Equally, the total length of a five years honours LLB, plus a Diploma year, followed by two years as an apprentice, would be discouraging and unattractive to many intending students (although this is typical of many other countries). The alternatives are that there should be no honours degree in law (as used to be the case) or that an honours course should be of the same duration as the ordinary degree. Although there is no honours degree in medicine, which might be thought an analogous professional qualification, we think that there is a need for an honours LLB degree. Unlike medicine, a significant (although relatively small) number of law students do not intend to practise law but study the subject as an academic one. Such students should be able to obtain an honours degree. In addition, a number of students study for joint honours in law with another subject in another faculty, and we have stressed that we wish to encourage the cross-fertilisation of law and subjects from other disciplines such as the arts and social sciences. An honours degree is essential for those wishing to undertake postgraduate study, and although there is unhappily little of this in Scotland a number of students do go abroad for the purpose; and opportunities are increasing in the European context. Finally, there is some evidence that an increasing number of legal firms appreciate the advantages of recruiting honours graduates.

16.20 An honours degree should be more intellectually demanding and specialised than an ordinary degree. Although the universities have told us that devising a suitable curriculum will pose some difficulties, especially if students are to take non-law subjects after their first year, none of the difficulties that they foresee is insuperable. Indeed, the present honours LLB is a four years course; and we think that a suitable four years honours degree could be introduced without causing unacceptable difficulties. We therefore **recommend** that there should be a four years honours degree in law. From our discussions with the universities we would envisage the honours course beginning in the third year, after two years in common with the ordinary degree.

Teaching methods

16.21 Although some lecturers in at least one law faculty are making use of video tapes and closed circuit television for teaching purposes, the evidence we received is that modern teaching aids are insufficiently used in university law faculties. Teaching methods now, as in days gone by, depend too extensively on lecturing and rote learning. Insufficient use is made of tutorial techniques and there are few opportunities for students to learn from clinical experience. Indeed, no credit is given for actually going to a court to see what happens there. We asked about this in our survey of solicitors' education and training. More than two in every three university teachers who responded said that they would like to see fewer lectures and more seminars. Surprisingly perhaps, the opinions of students were more mixed, though a small majority favoured more tutorials.[1] We are unwilling to make detailed recommendations in the field of teaching practice and methods which are matters for the appropriate professionals; but we are in no doubt that the educational quality of many law courses could be enhanced by a more imaginative use of alternative teaching methods.

16.22 We **recommend** the following general principles. Firstly, there should be greatly increased participation of students in closely supervised contact with clients (or 'clinical education'), court visitation, and vacation periods spent in lawyers' offices; and for all of these activities some appropriate credit should be given. We know that in some law faculties students are already encouraged to gain practical experience through 'clinical' work under supervision. At York University, Toronto, we found that such experience could count as a full subject towards a degree.

[1] See Appendix 6.

16.23 Secondly, there should be greatly increased use of tutorials and seminars; and more lectures should be in the Socratic style (that is, involving the students in responding to questions, rather than passively noting the lecturer's arguments). Students must learn to think and react as lawyers, and not simply expect to absorb an academic view of the current state of the law.

16.24 Thirdly, although some examination papers in some universities now pose realistic problems, great emphasis is still placed on memorising statute law and leading cases. We do not think that rote learning in such a framework is of particular value; in such circumstances a 50 per cent or 70 per cent success rate is considered adequate for examination purposes, but such a performance in professional practice would be unacceptable. Although some courses in some law faculties set examinations for which students will have access to statute and standard texts, much as they would expect to have in a professional firm, there is a strong case for requiring all students to sit at least some examinations on this basis; and we so **recommend**. The pass standard should be raised accordingly. This would reduce the excessive premium on sheer memory which often exists at present and which we find inappropriate, given the rate at which statutes are introduced and amended, and their complexity of detail. For similar reasons we think that some examinations could properly be replaced by a form of continuous assessment.

Resources

16.25 Even these limited recommendations have resource implications. To upgrade the LLB degree to a four years course will require more teaching staff, lecture rooms and library facilities. Teaching methods which are not lecture-based tend to require higher staff/student ratios and smaller teaching groups than present staffing levels in the law faculties would readily allow. If, as seems likely, it will not be possible in the near future to increase the total amount spent on university education, we **recommend** that the universities, perhaps with guidance from the University Grants Committee, should ensure that law faculties are enabled to maintain student/staff ratios which are in line with those of other comparable faculties. We understand, for example, that at Glasgow University the student/staff ratio is over 13:1 in the law faculty, but 10:1 or less in other faculties. Other law faculties told us in evidence of similar disparities in their universities.

16.26 Just as important as the number of teaching staff is their quality. Lecturers' salaries do not compare well with earnings in professional practice, and while there may always be some differential it is important that it should not be so great that none of our best legal talent is prepared to contemplate an academic career. The quality of law teaching is vital to the adequacy of the subsequent provision of legal services by law graduates.

16.27 After the staff the most important teaching resource is the law textbook. Because Scotland is so small the market in legal books is too limited to sustain an adequate supply of texts, both for the student and the practitioner. In Chapter 19 we recommend the establishment of a Scottish Law Foundation which might, in addition to sponsoring socio-legal research and funding scholarships, pay for the writing of legal textbooks. In this way, the whole practising profession would contribute to the provision of adequate material for students and practitioners.

It does not follow, however, that such texts should be published in the conventional way. The Scottish Universities Law Institute, whose function is to publish Scottish legal texts, have told us that even without including a proper element of remuneration for the author the price of printed books is high, and sales are low.

16.28 In the short term, greater use should be made of alternative duplicating processes appropriate to small production runs. Indeed, the law faculties are already involved in this in the preparation of course material for the Diploma, and are co-ordinating the work to minimise cost. The possibility of selling some of this material to the practising profession should not be overlooked.

16.29 In the longer term, we think that new material on Scots law should probably be held in computer form. Computerised law libraries are already established in other countries and are currently being introduced in Britain (see Chapter 15). Such systems allow continual updating, thus overcoming a major drawback of printed texts. If the author is remunerated by the Foundation we propose that the other costs can be recovered from users, as with other viewdata systems.

The Open University

16.30 There will be those who wish to enter the profession who, though unable to attend a university course, would nevertheless prefer the graduate path of entry. Mature people who are unable to get a student grant because they already have a degree, and those with commitments to an existing job or at home, would come into this category. For such people a course provided by the Open University would be ideal. However, after consultation with the Open University authorities we had reluctantly to agree that it would not be realistic for the Open University to make such courses available for the relatively small number of potential students in Scotland.

Non-graduate entry to the profession

16.31 It is possible to qualify as a solicitor by sitting the Law Society's professional examinations independently of any university examinations or study. The number of people qualifying in this way is small and in recent years has formed a decreasing proportion of the total entry (see Table 16.1). Non-graduate intrants may find considerable difficulties in obtaining tuition for the Law Society examinations, although some will be able to employ private tutors. We believe that places in certain classes are offered to non-graduate intrants by some of the university law faculties; however, because of the pressure on limited university facilities, such places are not always available. The small number of non-graduate intrants makes it uneconomic for special classes to be mounted either by the Law Society or by further education colleges, far less to maintain a college of law.

16.32 Strictly speaking, it is possible to qualify as an advocate by passing the Faculty of Advocates' examinations without first having taken a law degree. The Faculty have told us that it is uncommon for intrants to qualify in this way, although it has been done in one recent instance. Those intrants to the Faculty who choose this particular method of entry often have some prior legal education: for example, a small number of English barristers have qualified as advocates by taking all the major papers in the Faculty of Advocates' examinations. The

Faculty, like the Law Society, are unable to organise courses for those taking their examinations. They provide reading lists and copies of previous examination papers; but it is up to the individual to acquire the necessary information by private study or tuition.

16.33 While there will probably continue to be a small number who wish to enter the legal profession as non-graduates, these for the most part will be people who have served for a number of years in a solicitor's office as an unqualified assistant and would now like to become qualified. This method of entry to the profession is likely to become even more difficult than now. However, we cannot recommend that financial and educational resources should be put into expanding this particular method of entry to the profession. We think that the universities provide the best avenue for educating lawyers and we do not want to encourage an alternative path of entry to the profession. At the same time, we do not wish to prevent people from entering the profession as non-graduates and we approve the universities' agreement to admit to the Diploma those who have taken the Law Society's examinations without obtaining an LLB degree.

THE DIPLOMA IN LEGAL PRACTICE

16.34 Following the publication of the Report of the Ormrod Committee, the Joint Standing Committee on Legal Education prepared proposals for the introduction of a Diploma in Legal Practice which would be awarded after one year of full-time study following completion of an LLB degree course. In the words of the Joint Committee the Diploma 'should be a major element in the professional training of graduates for admission to the legal profession and should concentrate on subjects particularly relevant to professional practice and on the vocational aspects and application of certain branches of law'. Plans for the implementation of the Diploma are now well advanced and the first courses will begin in October 1980.

16.35 Had we been making recommendations for the development of legal training before the proposals for the development of this Diploma had been accepted, it is not certain that we would have recommended a one year post-graduate course of this kind. There are sound educational reasons for favouring 'sandwich' training in which the practical and classroom work can be closely integrated, and assessment can take account of practical work. We have in mind teacher training as a model. However, we are aware of the practical difficulties that any recommendation on these lines would entail. Would student grants be available? Would the profession be prepared to make in-office placements available for short periods? If so, would solicitors be prepared to pay trainees anything if they only served short placements? Would teaching staff be permitted to make on-the-job assessments of trainees or even to exercise any supervision? We do not doubt, however, that the Diploma can produce real improvements by setting high standards. We accordingly supported its introduction and in the course of our work one of us had a meeting with the University Grants Committee to express that support. While we welcome the advent of the Diploma, nevertheless we **recommend** that in five years time from autumn 1980 the Joint Standing Committee on Legal Education should review, in the light of the circumstances then prevailing, whether it would be realistic and desirable to alter the Diploma curriculum to a sandwich basis.

16.36 We wish to make three recommendations about the content of the Diploma. All arise from serious inadequacies of current professional training. The first concerns oral advocacy. With notable exceptions the standard of pleading in our district and sheriff courts is bad. No one to whom we have spoken about this denies that there is substantial scope for improvement. Part of the explanation no doubt lies in the tendency for senior practitioners to withdraw from the strain of court work, so that the pool of experience in advocacy is less than in other areas of practice. Another part of the explanation may have something to do with court work remuneration (we tackle this aspect in Chapter 19). Much has undoubtedly to do with the general poverty of existing training; and we are glad that there will be a compulsory section of the Diploma devoted to oral advocacy. This will also help to limit criticism that we heard to the effect that at present some fledgling lawyers learn advocacy at the expense of their clients. In this connection we **recommend** that arrangements should be made for practice in oral advocacy with mock trials, preferably in the real court rooms after court business has ended for the day or on a day when the court is not sitting. This is done comprehensively and successfully in Norway. In addition, it seems to us desirable, as in the Norwegian course, to provide in this way an opportunity for students to play the roles not only of solicitors or advocates but also of fiscal or Advocate Depute, judge, sheriff clerk, witness and jury.

16.37 The second subject to which we want to make specific reference is ethics. We recommend elsewhere that the ethical rules of the profession should be written down. That is not enough. It should be a systematic part of the training of lawyers that they understand the high standards of conduct required by the profession of its members. We do not believe it is adequate to include ethical considerations solely as an aspect of each area of practice studied. We **recommend** that there should be a compulsory element in the Diploma on legal ethics.

16.38 Our third point is that the Diploma course should provide students with an introduction to problems of office efficiency and management. Many legal firms in Scotland seem reluctant to make use of computers and other modern business machines in running their businesses, partly no doubt because, like other people, they distrust that which they do not understand. It is vital to the efficient delivery of legal services that solicitors should be ready to adopt more efficient ways of doing things as new techniques are developed. Computers and microprocessors offer possibilities far beyond keeping the firm's accounts, and no one should be entering the profession without a basic understanding of what such machines can do. As we note in Chapter 18, a great many complaints against solicitors concern delay and lack of communication. This indicates clearly that to be a good lawyer it is not enough to know the law; knowing how to deliver a service (that is, how to manage) is just as important. We therefore **recommend** that Diploma students should have some introduction to methods of office efficiency and management.

16.39 Those who are awarded the Diploma should have an aptitude for the practice of law. Assessing aptitude is difficult, but in the same way as colleges of education reject those whose aptitude for teaching they strongly doubt, so too should the Diploma admissions officers seek to identify at the outset those who are wholly unsuited to practising law. This will require the development of an appropriate aptitude test to be taken at the time of application for admission to the Diploma, and possibly also admission interviews. Unless the time is reached when Diploma numbers have to be restricted in line with the ability of the profession to absorb intrants, the benefit of any doubt will have to be given at the admission stage. The teaching staff, however, should be ready to advise students, who by their performance demonstrate their unsuitability, to consider another career. Ultimately, suitability for practice should be an integral part of the assessment of all Diploma students. This assessment should be rigorous: the Diploma should not be awarded automatically to all students who attend the course.

A college of law

16.40 The advent of specifically professional legal training opens up the possibility of establishing a national college of law. Practically, however, the idea has too many serious defects. Apart from the cost of setting it up, a college would require all students to congregate in its area; and the college could have close links with at best only two universities. It would put the onus of practitioner involvement almost exclusively on solicitors in that area. Having rejected the idea on these grounds we were glad to learn that a central planning committee involving academic staff and practitioners had been formed to eliminate the wasteful duplication of effort between universities, and to monitor the development of professional training in all five law faculties. Such co-operation should continue so that, so far as possible, common standards prevail throughout the country. It is vital that these standards should reflect the best professional practice.

Postgraduate study

16.41 Before leaving the universities we should comment on the small number of higher degree students in law faculties and the fact that many such students are part-time, or are members of the academic staff. Although this bears only indirectly on the provision of legal services, we are in no doubt that the presence of full-time postgraduate students adds considerably to the academic vigour of a university faculty. Postgraduate study for a higher degree almost invariably involves the student in original research. Research into the law is, in one sense, what the practising profession do regularly. We believe, however, that there is scope for more fundamental work not only in pure law but in the interaction between law and society, an area which is particularly sparsely researched in Scotland. Such a development might give law students useful research experience. We have also noted the poverty of existing printed matter on Scots law; but just because the publishing market cannot justify the work does not mean it should not be done. There are several potential sources of funding for postgraduate work in law faculties. We believe that the Scottish Law Commission have already had some of their work taken forward effectively by the commissioning of papers from academics. When this is done, research staff can be used to expedite the work. There is also the Scottish Legal Education Trust to which we made reference in Chapter 6. In addition, if our recommendations are accepted, there will be the Scottish Law Foundation (see Chapter 19) and the Legal Services Commission (see Chapter 20). Although the Legal Services Commission will be concerned with the delivery of legal services and not with substantive law they might, nevertheless, find a need to commission certain work from law faculties. Indeed, they might even make possible the establishment in Scotland of an institute of socio-legal studies similar to that which exists in England, though that concept implies fairly substantial sums of money. We **recommend** that the Joint Standing Committee on Legal Education should examine these and any other possibilities for expanding the scope for postgraduate study in law.

PRE-QUALIFYING TRAINING: SOLICITORS

16.42 We referred in paragraph 16.2 to the apprenticeship which the intending solicitor has to complete before he can apply for admission and enrolment.[1] During the period of his apprenticeship he must gain experience in conveyancing, court work, and executry work or public administration although this requirement is to cease after the introduction of the Diploma. We received extensive criticisms of the apprenticeship: it was claimed that apprentices were often treated as 'cheap labour' and that little attention was paid to their real training needs. We sought to substantiate this evidence by personal visits to solicitors' offices. We found that in some offices training of a first-class standard was being given, with partners accepting full responsibility and devising thorough training programmes. However, we also met apprentices who had been given virtually no training at all. We also included questions on the apprenticeship in our survey on the education and training of solicitors in Scotland.[2] One-third of apprentices who responded to our questionnaire said that they were not given very much instruction; and a quarter said that the quality of instruction was not very satisfactory. Similar proportions of young solicitors expressed these views. More than 1 in 3 young solicitors thought that apprentices spent too much time on trivial or routine tasks; even more apprentices expressed that view.

16.43 At present the Law Society are a party to all contracts of indenture of apprenticeship, in order to satisfy themselves that the apprentice is receiving a proper training. In practice, however, they take no steps to satisfy themselves on this score unless the apprentice, or his master, complains to them. Apprentices are obviously reluctant to take such a step and prefer no doubt to sit out their time and move on quickly as soon as they qualify. At the end of the training period the trainee provides an affidavit that he has *bona fide* served his apprenticeship, the discharge of his indenture of apprenticeship, and other papers including a certificate of character and aptitude by the apprentice master. On the basis of these documents the Law Society prepare on the trainee's behalf a petition to the Court of Session for admission and enrolment as a solicitor. This whole process is in practice largely a formality. Yet although about one-third of apprentices are critical of their training period, the public has to assume that an enrolled solicitor is competent.

16.44 In future, those who have obtained the Diploma in Legal Practice will enter a two years training contract with the solicitor. The Law Society do not intend to require the trainee to gain experience in any particular areas of work, on the grounds that the Diploma curriculum will have provided the necessary minimum experience over the range of subjects fundamental to a solicitor's work. With this change the Law Society see no benefit from their continuing to

---

[1] Although the terms 'apprentice' and 'apprenticeship' are current, we understand that the Law Society intend to refer in future to 'trainees' and 'training contracts'. We use the term 'apprentice' and 'trainee' interchangeably.
[2] See Appendix 6.

be a party to each training contract. They intend to supervise training contracts through the issue of guidelines. After the trainee has completed one year, the Law Society intend that he should be entitled to be admitted as a solicitor and to hold a restricted practising certificate, so that he may appear in court during his second year.

The value of in-office training

16.45 We believe that the purpose of postgraduate training of solicitors should be to provide the trainee with experience in the practical application of the law which he has learned in theory during his university degree course. In addition, he should gain a well developed appreciation of the profession's ethics. The Diploma will, of course, go some way to giving trainees a practical view of the law; but only the direct experience provided by an apprenticeship can inculcate a genuine feeling for the work which the trainee intends to do as a solicitor. Support for this view emerges clearly from our survey: the great majority of respondents favoured the retention of an apprenticeship.[1] We believe that the Law Society are right to propose a two years training period. We could not recommend any shortening of this period in view of the inadequacies of the present provision and the importance we attach to such practical training.

Training records

16.46 We have said that the present procedures for admitting solicitors, and issuing their first practising certificates, do not provide an adequate guarantee of the intrant's competence. The Law Society should introduce a much more rigorous procedure to satisfy themselves that each trainee has had an adequate and effective training, and that he has performed well during it. As a first step to achieving this, we **recommend** that every trainee solicitor should be required to maintain a training record. This record need not be detailed or lengthy, and its precise form should be devised by the Law Society. What it should show is the approximate amount of time a trainee has spent in different areas of legal practice. Should a trainee change firms in the course of his training he will take this record with him. Upon satisfactory completion of his training period, and admission and enrolment as a solicitor, his practising certificate should be issued with his training record appended, to serve as evidence of his experience in training which he could produce when applying for his first job. We agree with the Law Society that, following the introduction of the Diploma, there is no need to stipulate particular areas of practice in which every trainee should have to gain experience during the apprenticeship. However, we believe it is necessary that all intending solicitors should have a certain breadth of view as well as depth of experience. To achieve this, we **recommend** that apprentices should be required to spend some part of their training in each of at least three areas of law (as defined by the Law Society). We do not envisage that any particular area of the law would be mandatory and there should be no requirement for the time spent in each area to be the same.

16.47 We further **recommend** that the Law Society should stipulate the minimum length of experience normally necessary to attain the required level of proficiency in each area. Thus it could be that the minimum acceptable

[1] See Appendix 6.

experience in some areas might be six months, in others four and in others eight. We recognise that our proposals for the apprenticeship might create difficulties for a trainee who has a specific goal in mind or even a post on offer, and who wishes to specialise throughout his apprenticeship in, say, company law which he foresees as being his lifetime specialism. Although specialisation in such an area of the law for such a person at the apprenticeship period might seem to be justified, we have had to bear in mind that a practising certificate entitles a solicitor to practise in all areas of the law. We do not wish to change that. In any case, we believe that for a trainee to spend six-twelve months during his training in fields peripheral to his main interest will be time well spent. We would note, incidentally, that while we speak of experience of, say, six months we do not mean that this needs to be full time for six consecutive months. A trainee who spent a quarter of his time throughout two years in a particular area should count that as equivalent to six months experience.

16.48 At present, solicitors who take apprentices have no guidance from the Law Society as to what constitutes an acceptable standard for entry into the profession. We **recommend** that training standards, linked to the prescribed minimum period for each subject, should be laid down by the Law Society. These standards should take the form of a check list of what the trainee should be able to do once he has successfully completed a particular part of his training. We do not envisage that these standards would be mandatory in any direct sense; their purpose is to provide objective and common standards for all apprentice masters to use in assessing whether or not the apprentices under their care have successfully completed a particular part of their apprenticeship. In addition, these standards will be of particular value to the apprentice master in preparing a report to the Law Society on the apprentice under his care. To ensure that a proper appraisal is made of each apprenticeship, we **recommend** that every principal who has responsibility for an apprentice should be required to report on the trainee's performance at the end of the training period and that this report should comprise a methodical consideration of the trainee's performance, using the training record in conjunction with the relevant training standards. Assessment procedures of this sort are common in companies and public bodies of any size. We also **recommend** that there should, in addition, be at least one interim report, perhaps at the end of the first year, so that no trainee is put in the position of being refused admission as a solicitor after two years without having had any advance warning. In order that the apprentice has as complete a picture of his progress as possible, we further **recommend** that these reports should be open; that is, they should be disclosed to the trainee who should be entitled to make representations on his own behalf to the Law Society where he disputes any assessment made.

16.49 No doubt most trainees will complete their apprenticeship satisfactorily in two years. There will inevitably be a few, however, who cannot be regarded as being fit to enter the profession at that stage. We **recommend** that in such cases the trainee should be required to undergo a further period of training in a different firm. We make this recommendation as we consider that it would be unacceptable to prevent anyone from entering the profession on the assessment of only one apprentice master. We would expect that most trainees who are required to undergo a second period of apprenticeship will subsequently be accepted into the profession. There will, however, be the occasional instance of a succession of reports which indicate that a trainee is not fit to be admitted as a solicitor. In such cases the Law Society should interview the apprentice and explain that on the basis of his performance he is never likely to be admitted as a solicitor and should, therefore, consider some alternative career.

16.50 We do not know of any formal training provided by the Law Society to help apprentice masters fulfil their training role. Ideally, there should be a training programme without which no apprentice master should be able to take on a trainee. However, we realise that it would be unrealistic to commit the necessary level of resources to enable such a training programme to be undertaken: it would require, for instance, teaching staff and accommodation which do not exist at present. Nonetheless, some measures must be taken in order to provide training for those apprentice masters who feel the need of it, and we **recommend** that the Law Society should include short courses for them, perhaps organised as seminars in their programme of continuing education for solicitors. In addition, there should be a set of guidelines for apprentice masters. The aim should be to bring about a common professional understanding concerning the purpose of the training period, the standards expected and the role of the apprentice master.

16.51 Provision of such a training programme, particularly one of such a limited kind, will not be sufficient to maintain an oversight of training standards. We **recommend** that the Law Society should maintain a list of firms shown by experience to be unsuitable for taking apprentices. No such firm should be allowed to employ further apprentices until they can satisfy the Law Society that the partners are fit persons to train future members of the profession. It is only fair to assume that a firm is competent to take on apprentices unless the contrary has been shown. The Law Society, however, might be alerted to potential inadequacies by such matters as convictions at disciplinary proceedings of partners or staff of a particular firm. There should be a further source of information available to the Law Society in the form of reports by trainees on the firms to whom they have been apprenticed. Such reports would have a two-fold benefit: in the first place, they would enable the Law Society to identify those firms which *consistently* got bad reports from their own apprentices; and, in the second place, they would enable the Law Society to identify and act on common criticisms of training. (We understand that medical practices are assessed for their suitability to take a trainee general practitioner.) We **recommend**, therefore, that it should be a requirement that every trainee report on the quality of his training immediately after completing his apprenticeship. We would not be satisfied simply for such reports to be optional for apprentices, because many of those who were satisfied would probably not see any need to make a report, and some at least of those who wished to make critical comment would feel inhibited from doing so in case it might adversely affect their future employment prospects. These reports should be confidential, but should be sent to the firm which provided the training as well as to the Law Society. A standard report form should be devised by the Law Society and provided for trainees to use.

Training in court work

16.52 Training in court work requires special attention for two reasons. Speaking on his feet, the solicitor in court has virtually no opportunity to reconsider his spoken remarks and prepare a 'second draft': his first choice of words must often stand. Furthermore, what is at stake may be of vital importance to the client—for example his liberty, and the outcome may well be influenced by any one act of omission or commission by the solicitor. Other work which he performs does not necessarily have this immediacy and all or nothing quality: mistakes in the office can usually be noticed and rectified. We have already referred to the unacceptably low standard of much pleading in the sheriff and district courts. The improvement which we consider is needed should begin with the advent of the Diploma but it must be consolidated by effective training in court work during the period of the apprenticeship.

16.53 At present, the Law Society intend when the Diploma is in force that the apprentice should be entitled, after serving one year of the training contract, to a restricted practising certificate which will enable him to appear in court during the second year of his training. This means that an apprentice would apply for admission as a solicitor before he had completed his apprenticeship. We are not satisfied with this proposed arrangement. The admission of the apprentice as a solicitor after the first year of his apprenticeship and the granting of a restricted practising certificate would mean a substantial change in status for the apprentice even although he still had a further year of training to undergo. He would now be an admitted solicitor with a restricted practising certificate, and allowed to act in many respects as a fully qualified solicitor, though he could not practise as a principal or enter his name on the legal aid lists. This we feel would be much too broad an approach to the narrow problem of securing a right of audience in court for trainee solicitors. It seems to us wrong in principle that a trainee should be admitted and awarded a practising certificate, even with the restrictions we have described, half way through the training period. We have already said that the full assessment of the trainee's competence ought to be made at the end of the two years period. If a practising certificate had already been awarded by that point it would be extremely difficult to take it away from the trainee, even if the quality of his overall performance were so low as to warrant such a step. We prefer, therefore, a more restricted scheme which could be seen as analogous to the process whereby a learner driver is allowed to take a car on the road so long as he is under the immediate supervision of a qualified instructor or driver. Although we do not need to work out our proposed scheme in detail, we **recommend** that the Law Society should maintain a register of trainee solicitors. A copy of this register should be sent to clerks of the courts in the same way as the list of solicitors with practising certificates is circulated. We also **recommend** that trainees who have been on the register for a year should be allowed to speak in court, but they should not be allowed to appear on their own and they should certainly not be allowed to take a case by themselves. They should always be under the immediate supervision of a solicitor in the firm to which they are apprenticed, and this solicitor should be in full charge of the case. It will be up to the responsible partner to use his discretion and judgement in assessing in what cases the apprentice may take part; and up to the solicitor taking the case to decide at what points the apprentice may safely participate. We stress again, however, that the trainee should only be allowed to speak under the immediate supervision of the solicitor in charge of the case and in his presence. It might be, for example, that it would be appropriate for the trainee to undertake routine cross-examinations designed to elicit non-contentious evidence during a criminal case, or to speak to certain procedural motions such as some adjournments. The trainee's confidence can be increased if he is allowed to do progressively more responsible work throughout the training period. We think that by this means the trainee will have adequate opportunity to gain experience on his feet without putting the interests of any client at risk. We should add that we have found no satisfactory way to designate any minor court proceedings in which the trainee could appear without supervision; and in any case it would be preferable to leave no doubt as to who is responsible to the court and the client for what is done. Training standards should be promulgated for court work as for other areas of practice.

Apprentices' pay

16.54 The Scottish Young Lawyers' Association made representations to us that the pay of apprentices should be on a par with that of other graduates, or that it should at least constitute 'a living wage'. The two views on this matter are expressed concisely in the summary to Chapter 8 of the report on our survey (Appendix 6): 'Most students, apprentices and young solicitors thought the level of salaries for apprentices too low. Heads of firms disagreed'. We think there is some merit in both sides of this argument. When a proper training is being given there is likely to be a net cost to the firm when the apprentice's immediate contribution to the firm is compared with the cost of employing him (though there may be hidden benefits to the firm from taking apprentices: many firms will find admirable members of their senior staff through having first taken them on as apprentices, for example). Equally, we do not doubt that the current remuneration of apprentices is relatively low for graduates. The 1979 edition of 'A Law Degree—Then What?' published by the Scottish Young Lawyers' Association, states that 'law apprentices in rented accommodation almost invariably qualify [for rent rebates]—usually for £3 or £4 per week'. However, it is clear to us, from the numbers wishing to enter the profession at present, that the current rates of remuneration for apprentices do not threaten the continued existence of the profession. Further, the admittedly low rate of remuneration for apprentices has to be seen against the earning profile of solicitors over their whole career. Indeed, according to the results of an exercise done for us, the internal rate of return on the costs of the education and training required for entry into the solicitor branch of the profession appears comparatively high when considered alongside that of other professions.[1] Accordingly, we do not recommend that trainees' pay should be related to the pay of any other group or to an index. We think it likely, nevertheless, that trainees who have the Diploma will, due to their increased value as assistants to the firms for whom they work, be able to negotiate a better salary than apprentices have so far achieved.

16.55 We have considered whether the costs of providing training places should be shared more equitably among solicitors. Our survey has shown that private practice provides over 90 per cent of training places, and that big city firms provide a disproportionately large number. We do not believe that those who intend to make a career as a lawyer in the public service should necessarily spend their apprenticeship there. The experience of acting for personal clients is a most valuable one. On the other hand, we think that some public sector employers are unduly restrictive in the number of trainees they will take on. Nevertheless if *all* lawyers, in the public and private sectors, are to make a fair contribution to

[1]See Chapter 19 and Appendix 12.

the cost of training, we should prefer that this be done by a levy on all practising solicitors, rather than simply by an expansion of public sector apprenticeships. Such a levy would be similar to that raised on employers by industrial training boards. It would share costs not only as between the public and private sectors, but as between private firms, many of whom contribute nothing at present by taking no apprentices. We see no objection in principle to the profession financing all or part of the apprenticeship by means of a levy, but we do not positively recommend that this should be done unless the supply of training places drops to an unacceptable level.

Restricted practising certificates

16.56 At present, as we have noted, after an apprenticeship of normally two years the apprentice is admitted as a solicitor with a restricted practising certificate (unless he is a good honours graduate in law who gets a full certificate) and he is required to practise with the restricted practising certificate for one year. After completion of this obligatory year the solicitor is free, if he wishes, to enter practice on his own account as a partner or as a sole practitioner. In England, by contrast, no solicitor may practise on his own account until his name has been on the roll of solicitors for three years. We think that the safeguarding of the interests of clients commends such an approach. A young solicitor should learn to accept more responsibility for his own work and relationships with clients before being allowed to take on the much heavier responsibility of partnership and the liability which that entails. It would be wrong to allow a solicitor who was a trainee one day to become a principal the next. A young solicitor needs time to learn about the administration of a firm's business before he assumes the responsibilities of partnership; and only a limited start on this can be made while he is a trainee.

16.57 We have already recommended that the Law Society should not issue a restricted practising certificate before the training period has been satisfactorily completed. In considering what period of restricted practice should be introduced, we differentiate between those who become partners in an existing firm and those who wish to set up practice on their own account. In the case of entry into partnership with other, experienced solicitors, the young solicitor is not wholly exposed to all the demands and needs of his clients. We think that a two years period from the end of the training contract would be sufficient before a young solicitor should be allowed to enter partnership. However, a longer period should elapse before a young solicitor can set up in business as a sole practitioner, or enter into partnership with a solicitor of no greater experience; in such cases we think that the period should be three years. We therefore **recommend** that when a solicitor is first admitted the Law Society should grant him a practising certificate which will not permit him to practise as a principal until he has had further experience for a period of (a) two years where he is to become a partner in a firm of which one partner at least has had at least three years experience as a principal and (b) three years when he is to practise on his own, or in a partnership where there is no partner with more than three years experience as a principal. A number of contingencies should be considered when the requisite rules are being drafted, such as the possibility that a solicitor of two years standing could become a partner of another solicitor who might subsequently die within the course of the first year of the partnership. In addition, the rules should be so drafted that experience of practice in, say, a London office or in another EEC country counted towards the two or three years period. Service at the Bar should also count as equivalent to post-training experience as a qualified solicitor in reckoning the two or three years period.

PRE-QUALIFYING TRAINING: ADVOCATES

16.58 Intending advocates must spend 21 months (12 if they have an honours LLB) in a solicitor's office. Thereafter, they undertake a period of devilling at the Bar. Trainee advocates are paid while they are working as apprentices in a solicitor's office but they are not paid during their period of devilling. In future, the Faculty intend that all intending advocates will be required to obtain the Diploma in Legal Practice and then to spend at least 12 months with a solicitor (regardless of their degree).

16.59 It is important to consider the balance between the periods of training with a solicitor and at the Bar, and to consider how long the total period should be. It would be possible to require all intending advocates to qualify first as solicitors. There are obvious advantages in the closer understanding between the two branches of the profession which this common training could produce. In addition, there are advantages to the intending advocate in building up a close relationship with at least one firm of solicitors during his training period: the early years at the Bar are notoriously lean ones and it will be helpful to the young advocate to have contacts in the solicitor branch of the profession. Although intending advocates might sensibly choose to qualify first as solicitors, we think that as a *minimum* it need take no longer to qualify as an advocate than it does to qualify as a solicitor; and we therefore **recommend** that the post-Diploma training of advocates should take a minimum of two years. Of this period we think that at least nine months should be spent devilling, and at least nine months should be spent in a solicitor's office. We think this gives flexibility to each trainee to adjust the balance of his training, as best suits him, between the experience of devilling and experience in a solicitor's office. We do not consider that we could justifiably go further and recommend more devilling than is at present generally required. A longer period would undoubtedly have advantages in allowing devils to obtain a wider range of experience and to participate in some limited formal training, but we do not think that a longer period should be made mandatory at this time in view of the heavy financial penalty which devilling entails.

16.60 The period an intending advocate spends in a solicitor's office should be seen as part of his training for the Bar. However, as many trainees may not decide definitely in favour of the Bar until after they have embarked on their in-office training, it is difficult to see how the Faculty could be very closely involved in any setting of standards for would-be advocates during their period in solicitors' offices. Nevertheless, we think that the Faculty should take a closer interest in the content of the work done by an intending advocate during his period in a solicitor's office. There will always be those who intend from the outset to be advocates, and even those who want to keep their options open will tend to seek training places in the relatively limited number of firms—mainly in Edinburgh—who are prepared to take on potential advocates. We believe that there is scope for the Faculty to have discussions with these firms in order to reach an understanding about what the firm, the trainee and the Faculty can each expect of the training period. The Faculty should then make this argeement available in written form to all those involved as a guide for would-be advocates training in solicitors' offices. We emphasise, however, that we are not suggesting the kind of standard setting which we recommended the Law Society should promulgate for solicitors' apprenticeships. Such supervision would be inappropriate given the lack of any formal relationship between the Faculty and individual firms of solicitors. We therefore **recommend** that the Faculty should consult with solicitors' firms who regularly employ intending advocates as apprentices, and prepare general guidelines on agreed principles for the mutual benefit of the trainee, the Faculty and the firms involved.

Devilling

16.61 At present, the content of the devil's training is a matter entirely between him and his master. In practice, the content is constrained by the range of work the master does and many trainees will inevitably find that their work is unrepresentative of the work of the Bar as a whole. On the other hand, since many newly-qualified advocates may receive some of their work through late instructions when more senior advocates have had to call off in particular cases, we have had to consider whether there should be a minimum range of experience which each devil should acquire before he can be considered qualified. It would certainly seem desirable that all devils should gain experience in both civil and criminal work. We recognise, however, that the small size of the Faculty might make it impossible for all devils to acquire such a range of experience within the necessarily short period of devilling. Without imposing an absolute requirement, therefore, we **recommend** that the Faculty should strongly encourage all devils to obtain a wide range of experience. If necessary, this could be facilitated by changing devil masters during the period of devilling. Such changes should not be seen as exceptional; and although questions of confidentiality prevent a devil from serving two masters concurrently, we can see no difficulties in principle in making flexible arrangements for changes of devil master, in order that the devil secures the widest possible range of experience during his period of training. The Faculty should, therefore, create an atmosphere, and any necessary supporting arrangements, in which devils can expect to receive every assistance in devising for themselves a training pattern which ensures a wide range of experience. In line with our recommendations for trainee solicitors, we **recommend** that devils should be required by the Faculty to keep a training record which will help them, and the officers of the Faculty, to decide whether or not the range of experience they have acquired is sufficient.

16.62 We further **recommend** that the devil master should be required to report to the Dean of Faculty on the performance of his devil at the end of his training. Where a devil has served more than one master, both should report. As with the trainee solicitor, the report should expressly recommend whether the devil is fit to be admitted to the Faculty, or whether a further period of devilling should be required of him. The devil should be given a copy of the report. The devil master should make reference not only to the devil's performance in those areas of work which he has undertaken, but also to the range and width of the experience he has acquired. The Dean of Faculty already has power to require further devilling in particular cases; and this recommendation should provide him with the necessary information to allow him to exercise this function in the best interests of the public, the Faculty and devils themselves. Although, in principle, there is no difference between trainee solicitors and advocates which should prevent the trainee advocate from submitting a report on his training to the Faculty, we do not believe that a report by the devil on training should be made mandatory in the same way as we have recommended in the case of trainee solicitors. Given the small numbers and close relationships within the Faculty we think that a formal arrangement for reporting of this kind is unnecessary and could, in some cases, be harmful to relationships within the Bar. We understand that devils who wish to draw defects in their training to the attention of the Faculty authorities can at present make an approach to the Vice-Dean. We **recommend** that this channel should be made known to all devils; and that the Vice-Dean should arrange to interview all devils on the completion of their training.

Oral advocacy

16.63 Even more than trainee solicitors, we think it important that trainee advocates should gain special experience of oral advocacy. This skill is particularly important for advocates since speaking on their feet in court comprises such a characteristic part of advocates' work. The introduction of the Diploma in Legal Practice will help in providing extra training opportunities in oral advocacy for intending advocates just as for intending solicitors. Inevitably, however, the emphasis in the Diploma courses in oral advocacy will be towards the practices of the sheriff and district courts, since intending solicitors will always be in the majority on these courses, and it will be their needs which are paramount in the minds of those planning them. We have already recommended that the courses in oral advocacy in the Diploma could include practice sessions in real courts. We think that this technique could be extended during the period of devilling to provide formal training in oral advocacy in the form of mock trials or moots. The English Bar organises such experience for its trainees and we believe this practice should be taken up by the Scottish Bar. We therefore **recommend** that the Faculty should organise mock trials at which devils would be able to plead in open court in a fictitious case; and that for this purpose the normal courts should be used after hours, or perhaps on Mondays when the Court of Session does not sit. We would expect senior members of the Faculty and judges to be prepared to co-operate in such a venture.

16.64 Although such experience will be a useful complement to the Diploma course we think it should be further extended. We have recommended that trainee solicitors should have opportunities to speak in real cases in court, and for the same reasons it is important that trainee advocates should have similar opportunities. We therefore **recommend** that devils should be able to speak in court under the immediate supervision of their devil master. They should not be able to take cases themselves. It might conceivably be possible in addition to devise a list of very restricted proceedings, such as those on the motion roll in civil cases, in which a devil nearing the end of his training could appear without any immediate supervision. If the Faculty and Lord President were satisfied that a further scheme of this kind could work without risk to the client, we should welcome its introduction.

Judges' assistants

16.65 During visits to examine aspects of legal services in Scandinavia we were impressed by the practice of providing assistants to judges from the ranks of trainee lawyers. In the Scandinavian countries this practice is, of course, designed to suit their own particular judicial structures which are radically different from our own, involving as they do a judicial career during which some time is commonly spent in the civil service. Nevertheless, we think that the practice of providing assistants to judges could be adopted experimentally in Scotland. In time, we envisage that a period—perhaps three to six months—spent as assistant to a judge might become a normal part of an advocate's training, except perhaps for those advocates who have qualified or practised as solicitors before going to the Bar. Accordingly, we **recommend** that an experiment should be carried out in the provision of a small number of posts for devils or newly-qualified advocates as assistants to supreme court judges. A small sum could be paid to each of the trainee advocates who takes up one of these posts; clearly this would not constitute a significant burden on the public purse.

Devils' remuneration

16.66 The period of unremunerated devilling is one of severe financial hardship, particularly as advocates frequently take a year to recover their fees and can thus have no effective income for about a year following their admission to the Bar. Even then, given that they are unlikely to receive a great deal of work in their first years, the total fees they receive are likely to be small. The financial barriers to entry to the advocate branch of the profession (which we discuss more fully in Chapter 19) undoubtedly affect the flow of intrants to the Bar, and it has been suggested that this leads to a bias in the class composition of the Bar in favour of those who can support themselves from private means during their period of devilling and for the first years after admission. For these reasons, and because supreme court judges and many sheriffs are recruited from the ranks of practising advocates, we think that the remuneration of devils is a matter of public interest, and we have accordingly considered the possibility of making grants available to devils from public funds. It would be difficult for student grants, for example, to be made available to devils, particularly since grants will be available at the earlier degree and Diploma stages. Nonetheless, we **recommend** that the possibility and desirability of making grants from public funds available to devils ought to be reviewed from time to time, in the light of information about the composition and flow of intrants to the Bar, by the Legal Services Advisory Committee which we recommend in Chapter 20. A further possibility would be for the Faculty to establish an arrangement with a financial institution to provide loans for devils. The Dean of Faculty already has a small loans fund at his disposal to help intrants who require assistance, but this is not sufficiently large to accommodate those who may at present be discouraged from becoming advocates by the financial difficulties that exist at the outset of a career at the Bar. We **recommend**, therefore, that the Faculty should consider the possibility of arranging a wider loan scheme for devils than is at present available, in view of the importance of maintaining a representative flow of intrants to the Bar.

CONTINUING EDUCATION AND COMPETENCE

16.67 The professional education of lawyers should not, of course, come to an end when they are admitted to the respective branches of their profession. Much new legislation is promulgated every session by Parliament. Particularly in the case of those who specialise in narrow fields, the education and training which they have had in other areas of the law becomes increasingly distant and out of date. There should, therefore, be some means by which standards of general professional competence can be maintained. The Law Society run a programme of 'post-qualifying legal education' courses to keep solicitors up-to-date with new developments and to refresh their knowledge and experience of areas of the law in which they may not be practising regularly.

Certifying competence

16.68 We have already said that the Law Society ought to take reasonable steps to satisfy themselves of the competence of those who apply for admission and for their first practising certificate; and we have made proposals to that effect. Plainly there is an argument that they should do something similar each year when re-issuing a practising certificate. We agree that the Law Society should regard the renewal of a practising certificate as re-certification of the solicitor's competence. This is clearly in the public interest. We have considered whether there should be some formal re-assessment procedure; but we have rejected this course as unnecessarily bureaucratic, and because it would lead to undesirable consequences. If obtaining a practising certificate were related, say, to attendance at specific courses in the post-qualifying legal education scheme, we think that there would be an inexorable tendency to split the profession up into sundry sub-professions, since credits for the completion of particular courses would come to be regarded as licences to practise in particular areas of the law. We do not think that this would be the right approach. In the second place, people undoubtedly learn best when they are motivated to do so by the quality of tuition and by their interest in the subject taught; and simple attendance at a course is no guarantee that the individual will make the best use of the material with which he is presented. The ability to complete a training course is not an adequate guarantee of competence on the job.

16.69 We think it fair for the Law Society to assume that an established solicitor is competent to practise and, therefore, to renew his annual practising certificate in the absence of evidence to the contrary. At the same time, however, the Law Society must be seen to be making strenuous efforts to seek out evidence of incompetence. Accordingly, we **recommend** that the Law Society should establish effective reporting arrangements with various persons and bodies who are in a position to monitor the quality of professional work done by solicitors. The kind of people and bodies we have in mind are the Keeper of the Registers, who will be able to detect deficient conveyancing work; the Accountant of Court; the Auditor of the Court; sheriff clerks; sheriffs; judges; and the indemnity insurers, as well as members of the public who have complained about their solicitor. We recognise that there may be difficulties in establishing effective reporting arrangements of the kind we have envisaged. Some of the persons and bodies we have in mind as possible sources of information may well be under statutory or other inhibitions regarding confidentiality; and in other cases professional rules or long standing practices may run counter to the suggestion that information on the competence of solicitors should be released. Nonetheless, the public interest is so strong here as to require these reporting arrangements. The arrangements should, of course, be made known to the profession.

Continuing education programmes

16.70 Programmes of continuing education are of great importance in maintaining the competence of the profession, even if participation in them is not mandatory. We were interested in a novel scheme introduced by the Institute of Chartered Accountants in Scotland whereby practitioners are required to state the amount of further education in their professional field which they have undertaken in the past year. A return detailing this information must accompany applications for a renewal of a practising certificate. A target number of hours over a period is set so that there is a strong professional encouragement for members to undertake continuing education. Nevertheless, the target number of study hours is not a minimum which members must attain in order to renew their certificate; and there are no sanctions against those who fall below what is expected of them. The fact that the minimum is recommended by a professional body which its members respect, and the fact that appropriate and attractive courses are made available to the members, secures that extensive and purposive use of the continuing education system is made. Such a scheme may not, however, be entirely appropriate in the legal profession where those doing the best work may often be researching points of law daily in the course of their work, whereas others may have very little new law to contend with. We think that the best way forward is to develop progressive continuing education courses, and to encourage the formation of permanent 'interest groups' of lawyers.

16.71 We have studied the courses made available in the Law Society's programme of continuing education and we are impressed by the range of topics covered. However, we think that the provision could be improved. At present, the courses are non-progressive—that is, courses in a particular subject are pitched at a uniform, often basic, level. We **recommend** that the Law Society should introduce a structured, progressive scheme of training in their continuing education programme so that, in particular subjects, there might be three levels of courses to be taken sequentially, perhaps one a year over a period of three years. Such programmes would be particularly useful for younger practitioners, but the final advanced course in any sequence would be attractive as a refresher course for more experienced members of the profession. In addition, many experienced members of the profession, who have specialised in particular and perhaps narrow areas of law, will find structured and progressive courses in areas of the law with which they are not familiar most useful if they wish to expand their practice.

16.72 We must also draw attention to what we believe to be the lack of adequate management courses. We have already noted that many complaints against solicitors arise, not because they are guilty of errors in the interpretation of the law, but because they fail to take effective and efficient action on behalf of their clients, to communicate adequately with their clients, or to maintain a proper control of their clients' affairs. These difficulties arise largely from poor management and poor office practice as well as a disregard for public relations. We have also noted the extremely limited use at present made by solicitors in Scotland of computers and advanced office machinery. It is of course ultimately the client who pays for inefficiencies in the organisation of legal firms and we, therefore, attach considerable importance to every means of encouraging the profession to bring its working methods up to date and to keep them under continuous review. We **recommend** that the Law Society should ensure that adequate attention is given to management techniques and modern office practice in their continuing education programmes. We also recommend in Chapter 18 that the disciplinary structure for the solicitor branch of the legal profession should be able to impose, on solicitors found guilty of minor disciplinary matters, a requirement to attend particular courses in the continuing education programme. We think that attendance at management courses will be a particularly important sanction in this area.

Court work

16.73 Throughout this Chapter our concern to improve the standard of pleading in Scottish courts will have been apparent. We have considered what should be done at the post-qualifying stage towards securing the necessary improvement. We are reluctant to be dogmatic as to what is the best approach. One possibility which we considered was the introduction of endorsements to practising certificates which would permit full practice in the courts. The endorsement would be obtained after independent assessment of a solicitor's competence in court. It would probably be necessary to make special transitional provision for solicitors already practising as principals and to concentrate on assistant solicitors wishing to obtain an endorsement. The proposal would ensure in due course that the majority of practitioners appearing in court had an endorsement and should lead to an improvement in standards; and it need not be costly to administer. On the other hand, there are drawbacks to the proposal: assessment, to be fair, could not be superficial, otherwise those doing well with a poor case would be penalised. Ultimately, the proposal might lead to a split between court practitioners and chamber practitioners in the solicitors' branch, something we want to avoid if at all possible. If no other solution produces adequate results, however, a court endorsement in some form might need to be introduced in the public interest.

16.74 An alternative proposal, which we think should be tried first, is to improve radically the advocacy course in the post-qualifying education programme. A three-stage progressive course, for example, could be coupled with a practical assessment by the tutor leading to the award of a certificate. If this proposal were to be effective the Law Society would need to give the certificate sufficient professional esteem to ensure that all those, both in private practice and in the public sector (particularly in the fiscal service), who wanted to do a significant amount of court work would feel the need to obtain it. Accordingly, we **recommend** that the Law Society should take steps through their continuing education programme to achieve a substantial improvement in court work skills, particularly of the younger members of the profession. If measures based on voluntary participation fail to achieve this aim, a court work endorsement to the practising certificate, on the lines discussed, should be considered.

16.75 There is a further way to encourage good pleading. Judges are well placed to identify weaknesses in those who appear before them. Judges should always be prepared to offer constructive criticism out of court to individual lawyers, but there is scope for a more comprehensive review of standards. We **recommend** that Sheriffs Principal should meet the local Bar of each court in the Sheriffdom from time to time to convey to the Bar as a whole, and particularly to its younger members, what the judges collectively regard as the main ways in which the presentation of cases could be improved. Such occasions could perhaps be arranged by the court advisory committees we proposed in Chapter 15, and would doubtless help to keep Bench and Bar in touch on wider matters, which would be of added advantage.

Specialisation

16.76 We considered the desirability of providing the means whereby some Scottish solicitors could obtain specialist certificates of competence in certain branches of the law. In each case initial training followed by appropriate experience would be required for such specialisation, and recertification of competence would demand continued experience in the particular field of law. We examined a number of schemes of specialisation. In particular we looked at that of the California Bar Association as a possible model, and we were told of the defects and difficulties experienced by that Association as well as the gain they hoped to obtain. In the event, we decided that it was inopportune to recommend the introduction of such specialist certification in Scotland at this time. For the foreseeable future most Scottish lawyers will practise in a number of areas of the law. Very few will be able to practise exclusively in one subject, though the number is slowly increasing. More limited specialisation, on the other hand, is highly desirable and can be encouraged by appropriate training and by the formation of interest groups of lawyers. It is this degree and kind of specialisation within a single profession that is needed in Scotland.

Interest groups of lawyers

16.77 There is substantial scope for the formation of more groups of lawyers in Scotland with special interest in particular areas of law. These achieve far more of lasting professional value than the (nevertheless desirable) local faculties embracing practitioners of all interests. We have been most impressed by what we have seen of the work of the Industrial Law Group and the Scottish Lawyers' European Group, for example; and we have no doubt that other areas of the law would benefit from the formation of similar groups. Continuing education in this kind of forum is particularly valuable for senior practitioners. We **recommend** that the Law Society, together with the Faculty of Advocates, should encourage the formation of more such groups.

Advocates

16.78 Advocates are free to take part in courses run under the Law Society's continuing education programme, and indeed the Faculty have two representatives on the Law Society Committee which runs the programme. However, we understand from the Faculty that they are disappointed at the low take-up by advocates of places on such courses. We discussed this question with representatives of the Faculty who thought that courses in company and commercial subjects in particular would be of great value to the Bar. Although the organisation of the Faculty in Parliament House gives good opportunities for contact between advocates and discussion of difficult points of law, and although advocates are of course continually engaged in researching the law when preparing cases or opinions, the Faculty find it difficult to account for the low involvement of advocates in continuing education. We think that individual advocates probably find the existing courses have a limited usefulness because many are very basic. However, our recommendations on the further development of the Law Society courses by providing progressive stages in tuition should make such courses, particularly the later stages, more attractive to advocates.

16.79 Advocates participate actively in interest groups, and could indeed give a lead in establishing more such groups. In addition, however, we **recommend** that the Faculty should organise occasional seminars for advocates conducted by judges or senior advocates, dealing with matters such as the inter-relationships of areas of the law; over-views of broader issues, such as the development of particular legal concepts, that advocates might not find time to consider during their necessarily detailed and specific research; and papers on detailed aspects of the law likely to be of interest. The Faculty of Advocates are not unlike a university faculty; and a body of this calibre ought to be pushing forward the boundaries of knowledge and understanding among its own members.

FINAL COMMENT

Women

16.80 Before concluding this Chapter, we should record that we had no evidence submitted to us regarding the opportunities for women wishing to enter the legal profession. As we have said, the Equal Opportunities Commission told us that they were unable to provide for Scotland the statistics and background that they provided for England and Wales. None of the statistics we have obtained elsewhere indicated that women, either as solicitors or advocates, are prevented from entering the legal profession or are hindered unfairly in their careers. We found women apprentices in most of the solicitors' firms we visited and one firm, taking five apprentices annually, recently took five women in one year. There is also a fair number of women partners. Inevitably, the years spent by women in child bearing affect their career prospects in this as in every profession but, on the whole, we got the impression that the legal profession, and particularly the solicitor branch, was easier to re-enter than many others. We hope that several of the proposals we have made for employment of full-time and part-time solicitors in advice services, law centres, prison clinics, etc. may provide special opportunities for women who wish to return to the legal profession without necessarily joining firms.

16.81 The lawyer reading this Chapter may think that we have made an overwhelming number of recommendations, and that many of them are unnecessary. We have, indeed, made many proposals for improving the education and training of lawyers, because we believe it is essential in the public interest that legal practices should be conducted by those who are well qualified and trained and who can organise their practices efficiently. This can only be in the best interests of the profession as well as the public.

RECOMMENDATIONS

			Paragraph
Admission of law students	R16.1	Universities should use wider criteria than academic attainment at school when selecting law students for admission.	16.9
	R16.2	A test of aptitude to study law should be developed for use in Scotland as one element in the process of selecting students for entry to the faculties of law.	16.10
The LLB degree	R16.3	As the Diploma in Legal Practice is introduced, the LLB syllabus should be revised to encourage students to study a social science or a modern language.	16.16
	R16.4	The Law Society should reduce to the minimum the requirements they effectively place on students to study particular courses.	16.17
	R16.5	The LLB degree should require a four years course of study.	16.18
The honours LLB	R16.6	There should be a four years honours degree in law.	16.20
Teaching methods	R16.7	Greater use should be made of teaching methods other than lecturing and rote learning, following the principles stated in paragraphs 16.22 and 23.	16.22–23
Examinations	R16.8	Some examinations should be conducted on the basis that students have access to statute and standard texts.	16.24
Resources	R16.9	Universities should ensure that law faculties are enabled to maintain student/staff ratios which are in line with those of other comparable faculties.	16.25

			Paragraph
The Diploma in Legal Practice	R16.10	In five years time from autumn 1980 the Joint Standing Committee on Legal Education should review, in the light of the circumstances then prevailing, whether it would be realistic and desirable to alter the Diploma curriculum to a sandwich basis.	16.35
	R16.11	Arrangements should be made for practice in oral advocacy with mock trials; there should be a compulsory element on legal ethics; and students should have some introduction to methods of office efficiency and management.	16.36–38
Postgraduate study in law	R16.12	The scope for postgraduate study in law should be examined by the Joint Standing Committee on Legal Education.	16.41
Training records	R16.13	Every trainee solicitor should be required to maintain a training record.	16.46
In-office training	R16.14	Apprentices should be required to spend some part of their training in each of at least three areas of law. The Law Society should stipulate the minimum length of experience normally necessary to attain the required level of proficiency in each area.	16.46–47
	R16.15	Training standards should be laid down by the Law Society.	16.48
	R16.16	Every principal who has responsibility for an apprentice should be required to report on the trainee's performance at the end of the training period. In addition, there should be at least one interim report. These reports should be disclosed to the trainee.	16.48

			Paragraph
	R16.17	A trainee who does not satisfactorily complete his apprenticeship in two years should be required to undergo a further period of training in a different firm.	16.49
	R16.18	The Law Society should provide training courses and guidelines for apprentice masters.	16.50
	R16.19	The Law Society should maintain a list of firms shown by experience to be unsuitable for taking apprentices. No such firm should be allowed to employ further apprentices.	16.51
	R16.20	Every trainee should be required to report to the Law Society on the quality of his training immediately after completing his apprenticeship.	16.51
Training in court work	R16.21	The Law Society should maintain a register of trainee solicitors.	16.53
	R16.22	Trainees who have been on the register for a year should be allowed to speak in court but only under the immediate supervision of the solicitor in full charge of the case.	16.53
Restricted practising certificate	R16.23	When a solicitor is first admitted the Law Society should grant him a practising certificate which will not permit him to practise as a principal until he has had further experience for a period of (a) two years where he is to become a partner in a firm of which one partner at least has had at least three years experience as a principal and (b) three years when he is to practise on his own or in a partnership where there is no partner with more than three years experience as a principal.	16.57
Professional training: advocates	R16.24	The post-Diploma training of advocates should take a minimum of two years with at least nine months spent devilling and at least another nine months working in a solicitor's office.	16.59

			Paragraph
	R16.25	The Faculty should consult with solicitors' firms who regularly employ intending advocates as apprentices and prepare general guidelines on agreed principles for the mutual benefit of the trainee, the Faculty and the firms involved.	16.60
Devilling	R16.26	The Faculty should strongly encourage all devils (trainee advocates) to obtain a wide range of experience.	16.61
	R16.27	Devils should be required by the Faculty to keep a training record.	16.61
	R16.28	The devil master should be required to report to the Dean of Faculty on the performance of his devil at the end of his training.	16.62
	R16.29	All devils should be told that they can approach the Vice-Dean in connection with their training; and the Vice-Dean should arrange to interview all devils on the completion of their training.	16.62
	R16.30	The Faculty should organise mock trials at which devils would be able to plead in open court in a fictitious case.	16.63
	R16.31	Devils should be able to speak in court under the immediate supervision of their devil master.	16.64
	R16.32	An experiment should be carried out in the provision of posts for devils or newly qualified advocates as assistants to supreme court judges.	16.65
	R16.33	The possibility and desirability of making grants from public funds available to devils ought to be reviewed from time to time.	16.66
	R16.34	The Faculty should consider the possibility of arranging a wider loan scheme for devils than is at present available.	16.66

			Paragraph
Continuing education and competence	R16.35	The Law Society should establish effective reporting arrangements with various persons and bodies who are in a position to monitor the quality of professional work done by solicitors.	16.69
	R16.36	The Law Society should introduce a structured progressive scheme of training in their continuing education programme.	16.71
	R16.37	The Law Society should ensure that adequate attention is given to management techniques and modern office practice in their continuing education programmes.	16.72
Continuing education—court work	R16.38	The Law Society should take steps through their continuing education programme to achieve a substantial improvement in court work skills, particularly of the younger members of the profession.	16.74
	R16.39	Sheriffs Principal should meet the local Bar of each court in the Sheriffdom from time to time to convey to the Bar as a whole, and particularly to its younger members, the main ways in which the presentation of cases could be improved.	16.75
Interest groups of lawyers	R16.40	The Law Society and Faculty should encourage the formation of groups of lawyers with special interest in particular areas of law.	16.77
Continuing education: advocates	R16.41	The Faculty should organise occasional seminars for advocates, conducted by judges or senior advocates.	16.79

CHAPTER 17

EDUCATION AND TRAINING II: OTHER PROVIDERS OF LEGAL SERVICES

17.1 In this Chapter we make some recommendations about the education and training of people other than solicitors and advocates in private practice who are involved in the provision of legal services to the public.

THOSE WHO WORK IN COURT

Judges

17.2 We received a limited amount of evidence about the recruitment of judges and the structure of the judiciary in Scotland. While we regarded these matters as falling within the terms of our remit, we decided that a thorough enquiry into the appointment of judges would occupy too great a part of our limited resources. Furthermore, while we have seen, for example, how a career judiciary in Scandinavia can operate effectively, we are mindful that it does so within the particular structure of the legal profession and system obtaining there. We also noted that the question of who should be the judge in the district court had been resolved by Parliament not long before we were appointed. We were glad to find that some initial training is provided for new judges, both in the district courts and in the sheriff courts.

The district court

17.3 Under the terms of the District Courts (Scotland) Act 1975 the Secretary of State for Scotland has power to make schemes for the training of lay justices, and local justices committees have responsibility for providing training courses.[1] The local provision of training is centrally monitored by the Central Advisory Committee on Justices of the Peace which is chaired by the Lord Justice Clerk. The training scheme is in two stages: inexperienced justices must complete the first stage before sitting to adjudicate, and must complete the second stage before sitting alone. The local justices committee will decide what training is required for a justice who has had previous experience. The first stage includes at least six hours attendance as an observer at the district court, during which time the justice must spend a period sitting in the body of the court. In addition to this practical experience, there is formal training in the powers and responsibilities of the justice in and out of court. The second stage of training includes much more detailed instruction on the institutional framework of the courts and the legal system; study of questions relating to legal aid in the district court; study of the principal criminal statutes and provisions at common law applicable to the district courts; the problems of punishment and treatment; and the functions of the various social and penal agencies with which the court has contact. Additionally, a newly-appointed justice must visit a prison to

---

[1] *District Courts (Scotland) Act, 1975*, Sections 14 and 16.

which his court commits offenders, and a young offenders institution, within a year of his appointment.

17.4 As well as central stipulation of the framework of training, the office of the Secretary of Commissions for Scotland issues a handbook for justices.[1] This is designed to give general guidance, and to act as a textbook to which justices can turn in case of difficulty; it includes advice and guidance on such matters as the criminal law, procedure, legal aid, sentencing and out-of-court responsibilities of the justice. It also includes a valuable section on 'principles and presumptions on which justices should proceed'; in effect, a guide to sound judicial conduct. We are impressed with the breadth of the training scheme for lay justices, and we particularly approve the very clear handbook. We **recommend,** however, that justices should in the course of their training learn something of police work and methods; and that the present requirement on them to visit penal institutions should apply before the justice tries his first case.

The sheriff court

17.5 Newly-appointed sheriffs, and temporary sheriffs, have the opportunity to attend a short course lasting about one week. The course is organised jointly by the Scottish Courts Administration, the Scottish Home and Health Department and the Sheriffs' Association, and experienced sheriffs play a prominent part in running it. These courses began in 1969 with the approval of the Lord Advocate and the Secretary of State for Scotland, and have been held approximately every other year since then. During the course the new sheriffs learn something about police methods, particularly relating to speeding offences, drunk driving and drug offences. They also learn something about police procedures for interviewing suspects, arrest and subsequent processes, and about fingerprinting and criminal records. Before or during the course, the new sheriffs have an opportunity to visit various penal establishments so that they are familiar with the institutions to which they may sentence offenders. In addition, they learn about practical aspects of sentencing and about children's hearings, adoptions and the supervision of probation and community service. The practical approach to the study of sentencing is vitally important, given the importance of the sentence to the guilty party, and the public criticism to which sentencing decisions can be subject. The necessity for all types of judges to be made familiar with the problems of sentencing, and to have the opportunity of periodic discussions on this matter, was also underlined in the recommendations of the Bridge Report.[2] We have been impressed by the informed desire for an increased measure of consistency in this area. We **recommend** that courses for new sheriffs should place greater emphasis on sentencing. Although there is very much to approve in these courses, there is perhaps an imbalance in favour of the criminal responsibilities of the sheriff courts. The sheriff courts have an important civil jurisdiction which will be amended, and increased in scope, by the implementation of our recommendations on divorce and small claims. We therefore **recommend** that more attention should be paid in these courses to developments in civil procedures.

17.6 In general terms, such courses seem to us a properly pragmatic way to approach the training needs of new judges. There is only one further area that

[1] *Handbook for Newly-Appointed Justices of the Peace in Scotland:* office of the Secretary of Commissions for Scotland, 1978.
[2] *Report of the Working Party on Judicial Studies and Information* (The Bridge Report): HMSO, 1978.

we consider this training, properly adapted as appropriate for sheriffs or lay justices, could usefully cover. New judges are already familiar with court buildings and procedures, or will be familiarised with them by their training; but the same is not true of the laymen who will be involved in the individual cases judges hear. In our survey of legal needs, we asked our respondents whether they had appeared in court as jurors or witnesses. A total of 185 respondents had so appeared since January 1971, and as many as 80 (or nearly 45 per cent) of them said that they had been apprehensive about the prospect of having to go to court. The reasons they gave for their anxiety are summarised in Table 17.1 below:

TABLE 17.1: Reasons for anxiety prior to court hearing*

	%
Didn't know what to expect	45
Worried about procedure in court	12
Nervous person	12
Prospect of cross-examination	8
Responsibility involved	6
Unpleasant case	6
Normal apprehension	6
Prospect of 'comeback', revenge	4
	100
	(N=80)

*Source: Appendix 4, Table 68.

One in four of those who had appeared in court as jurors or witnesses said that they had been anxious beforehand because they were uncertain what to expect, or unfamiliar with court procedure. Asked whether they had been nervous when actually in court, the number of positive responses is smaller, as shown in Table 17.2.

TABLE 17.2: Reasons for anxiety in court*

	%
Didn't know what to do or expect	30
Just being there/general atmosphere	24
Nervous person	16
Responsibility involved	13
Being cross-examined	8
Frightened of defender	6
Don't know	3
	100
	(N=67)

*Source: Appendix 4, Table 69.

One in five of the 185 respondents who had appeared in court as jurors or witnesses had been nervous in court because they were uncertain about what to do, or because of the 'atmosphere in the court'.

17.7 Although we have seen the clear printed guidance provided for jurors, there is clearly scope for reassuring the laymen involved in court proceedings, as witnesses or jurors, by ensuring that they know what will happen and what their job is. We have also found, from criticisms we have received and from our own experience, that laymen in court can all too frequently find the proceedings difficult to hear as well as to understand. It is clearly desirable that court proceedings should be audible and comprehensible, although we recognise that the role that judges can play in achieving this is a limited one. There is nothing the judge can do, for example, about the court room's acoustics (though we make a recommendation about the use of microphones in Chapter 14). Nor can the judge do anything about the physical layout of court furniture. Nevertheless, if the judge is alert to the need for everyone, and not simply himself, to be able to hear clearly what is being said, there are ways he can improve audibility, such as by asking the lawyer to stand further away from the witness so that he is obliged to raise his voice. Experienced judges know these techniques and it is right that newly-appointed judges should learn quickly about them. Good judges also ensure that a jury understands the procedures to be adopted, the expected time scale, and so on. It would require very little effort to cover such points in the present course for new sheriffs. Accordingly, we **recommend** that the induction training for sheriffs should devote more attention to the value of sensitive judicial handling of the court-room, informed by an awareness of how the laymen involved see what is happening; and the training should familiarise the new sheriffs with the tactics and devices within their power to help ensure that the court proceedings are both audible and comprehensible to the laymen present.

17.8 While supreme court judges may not require any extensive preliminary training on their appointment, there may well be elements of training that would be valuable and appropriate for them. We therefore **recommend** that newly-appointed senior judges should participate in induction courses, particularly on sentencing.

Continuing education for judges

17.9 In addition to this, we think that judges benefit considerably from making regular visits to the social and penal institutions with which the court has contact. Many judges recognise this and make such visits on their own account, and arrangements have been made from time to time for High Court judges to visit penal institutions in groups. We question, however, whether the existing arrangements in this area are adequate, and we **recommend** that the appropriate authorities should take steps to see that judges at all levels are familiarised with penal institutions and the practical working of criminal penalties of all kinds (including such matters as probation). All judges should, moreover, be kept fully abreast of changes and developments in this area as they occur.

Chairmen and members of tribunals

17.10 The chairman and members of tribunals need to be trained to be fully effective. We understand that there is only limited provision for this at some tribunals. In the light of our proposals for training in general, we **recommend** that the Council on Tribunals should undertake a review of the training provided for tribunal chairmen and members, with a view to establishing standards of training.

Court staff

17.11 A number of the recommendations we have made in Part IV will put extra responsibilities on to court staff in such fields as divorce, small claims and the granting of confirmation. The staff, particularly sheriff clerks, will need proper training if they are to discharge these new duties efficiently. We thought it important, therefore, to make some inquiry into the training provided for the staff in the Scottish courts. The Scottish Courts Administration run a court service training centre in Glasgow with a small full-time training staff. Individual members of staff have specific responsibilities in relation to particular courts, and the training centre provides, in addition to induction courses, both vocational and management training. The vocational courses are at two levels, basic and advanced. These courses are now a vital part of staff training, particularly since the abolition of the departmental promotion examination which, until recently, officers had to pass before they could be promoted beyond a certain grade. We were also glad to note that increasing importance is attached to management training, because it is our impression that the courts have in the past been too slow to adopt up-to-date aids to efficiency. Adequate training in these matters is all the more important because the Scottish court service is a distinct branch of the civil service, with very little movement of staff between it and the rest of the civil service. We think that these existing facilities could provide the training which will be necessary if our recommendations which affect the courts are to be implemented successfully.

Procurators fiscal

17.12 Our interest in the work of procurators fiscal was restricted to questions of professional competence, and what can be done by improved education and training to raise standards of court performance. Procurators fiscal are not exempt from the criticism we have received, or from the adverse judgments we have formed in the course of our own visits, about the general level of competence of those appearing in the lower courts. There is no doubt that the requirement to prosecute all cases in the district courts severely stretched the capacity of the fiscal service, and we have been concerned to discover just how inexperienced are most of the recruits to the service. The Crown Office have told us that in the three years 1977–79 they recruited 67 new fiscals but that only two of them, both having served more than 15 years in private practice, had sufficient experience to merit entry above the basic grade. Of the remainder, two-thirds were newly-qualified solicitors and they, together with recruits who had less than two years previous legal experience, represented 86 per cent of recruits; only 6 per cent had more than five years experience. We hope that the higher salaries payable from the start of 1980 may lead to an improvement in the standard of recruits.

17.13 In such circumstances, adequate in-service training is vitally important and we are convinced that, although some induction training for new fiscals is arranged locally, the in-service training currently provided is not sufficient. Some junior fiscals attend the Law Society's post-qualifying legal education course in advocacy; but, as we said in the previous Chapter, this is a very basic course and not at all adequate as it stands. When this advocacy course is developed in a progressive way, as we have proposed, it will doubtless be of advantage to fiscals as well as to solicitors in private practice. Some in-service training is provided by the Crown Office, including a course on forensic medicine which is of a high standard. Nevertheless, in our view, insufficient resources are devoted to the in-service training of fiscals, given the lack of experience of most of the new recruits. We **recommend** that the Crown Office should re-assess staff training needs, particularly of their less-experienced members, and should devote adequate resources to secure a satisfactory level of training.

17.14 It is important that inexperienced court lawyers should start on simpler work and move progressively to more difficult and demanding cases. While we understand that the fiscal service tries to operate in this way, we are not satisfied that adequate priority is given to the need for experienced members of staff to supervise the work in court of the more junior fiscals after the first few weeks. This, we appreciate, is a question of resources and the use of staff time; but we believe that the fiscal service needs to devote more of its senior staff time to supervising the court appearances of junior fiscals so that weaknesses can be identified and corrected and the standard of performance improved. We **recommend** that senior fiscals should devote more time to supervising the work of junior fiscals in court.

THOSE WHO WORK IN ADVICE AGENCIES AND SOLICITORS' OFFICES

17.15 In this part of the Chapter we consider two quite separate kinds of para-legal staff: those who work in advice agencies such as Citizens Advice Bureaux on the one hand; and, on the other, the non-solicitor fee-earners in solicitors' offices.

Advice centre staff

17.16 In Chapter 7 we recommended that the key to meeting the need for readier access to legal services was the provision of an expanded generalist advice service. In practice, this advice service will involve primarily the Citizens Advice Bureaux movement; but in speaking of that movement in this Chapter we intend that our remarks should apply equally to the other agencies providing advice to citizens on their rights and how to assert or protect them.

17.17 We have studied examples of the training material prepared by the Scottish Association of Citizens Advice Bureaux, and we have had a report of their training methods. Although the main responsibility for training rests with the organiser of each individual Bureau, there is a supportive national structure which provides both training materials and the specialist guidance of advisory staff. The advisory staff in turn have a direct responsibility to provide the specialised training needed by Bureaux organisers. The style of the training material impressed us and we found its presentation good and well adapted to the practicalities of Bureau work in Scotland. As the generalist advice service expands, however, we **recommend** that more responsibility for providing training should be transferred from individual Bureau organisers to national, or area, Bureaux authorities. While each Bureau will have its particular training needs, it is important that workers should get a comprehensive introduction to the work of the movement.

17.18 The Scottish Association of Citizens Advice Bureaux told us that they have not yet given much priority to advanced-level training, but we are in no doubt that they should now do so. We **recommend** that the Bureaux training schemes should be developed along progressive lines, so that individual workers may choose to specialise in one or two particular areas after they have completed their basic general training. It is into this kind of framework that training designed to meet emerging needs should be inserted. For example, there is a growing role for the Citizens Advice Bureaux to play in representation at tribunals and in money-management counselling, and specific training should be available to equip workers to meet these needs.

17.19 Hitherto, each advice agency or service has concentrated on providing its own training to its own members. We believe that this is wasteful of resources; and we **recommend** that the different advice agencies, both specialist and generalist, and including, where appropriate, trade unions, should collaborate in the provision of training to their mutual advantage. Indeed, some courses might attract participation by solicitors, just as some basic Law Society courses might accept lay advisers as course members, thereby improving lawyers' and lay advisers' appreciation of each other's capacities.

Staff in solicitors' offices

17.20 Our remuneration survey shows that legal firms in Scotland employ proportionately fewer staff who are not solicitors than firms in England and Wales. While some firms in Scotland do employ such staff on work similar to that undertaken by legal executives in England and Wales, there is no formal recognition of this by membership of a body similar to the English Institute of Legal Executives, which provides for training, examination and qualification of staff who are not solicitors but who undertake work which would otherwise be done by a solicitor. The principle can be taken even further, as we have seen in North America, to the extent that clients are met on arrival in the office by a para-legal member of staff who is trained to use standard forms and kits devised by the partners in the firm; such firms can conduct much business economically and satisfactorily. Problems which do not require the full skills of a lawyer are dealt with by a suitably trained non-lawyer, with the result that the lawyer's own time is to a much greater degree taken up with problems which require his high expertise. We think that there is a danger in Scotland that the use of solicitors to undertake certain categories of work may eventually result in costs being so great that many clients will not be able to afford the legal services they need. Throughout our Report we have stressed our concern that legal services should be provided efficiently and economically, and we think that economy and efficiency can often best be achieved by greater reliance on staff who, while suitably trained, do not have the full qualifications of a solicitor. There is scope for using these trained non-professionals in aspects of insurance work; court departments, both civil and criminal; executries/trust administration/tax; consumer problems/hire purchase/small claims; and no doubt in other fields.

17.21 We **recommend** that structured, progressive training should be provided for solicitors' staff. The Law Society have already initiated discussions with the Scottish Business Education Council (SCOTBEC) with a view to providing a specialist subject of 'elements of legal practice' in the syllabus of the basic Scottish National Certificate in Business Studies. We understand that the course will be available to those who wish to study for it part-time over two years, and also as a one year full-time course. It seems to us that this proposed course offers the prospect of a good basic general training for staff in legal firms. Furthermore, we would expect that persons who had attended the course and obtained an appropriate certificate would be able to find work in providing support services, not only for legal firms but also for solicitors in industry, commerce and the public service, in the same way that the services of legal executives are sought in these fields south of the border. The managerial skills they have acquired in their training should also prove of value to their employers.

17.22 In the longer run we believe it is desirable to provide progressive training for non-solicitors just as for solicitors. The Law Society have discussed with SCOTBEC the possibility of a higher-level Scottish Higher National Certificate course, which would provide more specialised training in particular areas of legal practice. Whether this would meet the need better than the Law Society's own continuing education programme, we cannot judge. A programme geared to a professional audience might not be as appropriate to non-solicitors as courses particularly devised with their needs in mind. On the other hand, solicitors may not be willing to allow, and their staff may not be prepared to devote, the necessary time to completing the study required for a Scottish Higher National Certificate. If, as we hope, the basic SCOTBEC course becomes established, a judgement should be made in the future as to the best way to provide more specialised, higher-level training for the non-professional staff in solicitors' offices.

			Paragraph
Judges' training	R17.1	Justices should in the course of their training learn something of police work and methods; and the present requirement on them to visit penal institutions should apply before the justice tries his first case.	17.4
	R17.2	Courses for new sheriffs should place greater emphasis on sentencing and on developments in civil procedures.	17.5
	R17.3	Sheriffs' training should devote more attention to the value of sensitive judicial handling of the court-room.	17.7
	R17.4	Newly-appointed supreme court judges should participate in induction courses, particularly on sentencing.	17.8
	R17.5	The appropriate authorities should take steps to see that judges at all levels are familiarised with penal institutions and the practical working of criminal penalties of all kinds (including such matters as probation).	17.9
Chairmen and members of tribunals	R17.6	The Council on Tribunals should undertake a review of the training provided for tribunal chairmen and members, with a view to establishing standards of training.	17.10
Procurators fiscal	R17.7	The Crown Office should re-assess staff training needs, particularly of their less-experienced members, and should devote adequate resources to secure a satisfactory level of training.	17.13
	R17.8	Senior fiscals should devote more time to supervising the work of junior fiscals in court.	17.14
Advice centre staff	R17.9	More responsibility for providing Citizens Advice Bureaux training should be transferred to national or area Bureaux authorities.	17.17

			Paragraph
	R17.10	Citizens Advice Bureaux training schemes should be developed along progressive lines, so that individual workers may choose to specialise in one or two particular areas after they have completed their basic general training.	17.18
	R17.11	The different advice agencies, both specialist and generalist, should collaborate in the provision of training to their mutual advantage.	17.19
Solicitors' staff	R17.12	Structured, progressive training should be provided for solicitors' staff.	17.21

CHAPTER 18

PROFESSIONAL CONDUCT, COMPLAINTS AND DISCIPLINE

18.1 When a person uses the services of a lawyer it is invariably about something of real importance to the individual concerned, though often it may be only a routine matter to the lawyer. However, the work of lawyers is not only of importance to their own clients; there is also a wider public interest in ensuring that legal business is conducted in accordance with high professional standards. The fact that in many areas of their business lawyers enjoy what amounts to a monopoly heightens the need for the legal profession to meet the highest possible standards of probity and professional performance. In turn, this means that there must be, and there must be seen to be, adequate machinery to maintain rigorous standards of professional care and conduct; to provide an objective system of investigation into alleged lapses of performance on the part of lawyers; and to deal with justified complaints firmly, consistently and dispassionately. Such provision is not only necessary in the public interest, it is vital to the profession itself in maintaining its high reputation. This is the subject matter of this Chapter.

18.2 In considering the machinery needed to maintain professional standards and conduct, we must consider not only what needs to be done but who should do it. This means striking a balance between the effectiveness of review of a lawyer's actions by his colleagues and the need to provide an independent expression of the public interest. In this context one might expect lawyers themselves to have the benefit of guidance through, for example, written codes of conduct or ethics as to the standards of performance expected of them. The lay members of the Commission were surprised to find how little written guidance is in fact available.

Professional conduct: solicitors

18.3 Solicitors provide their professional services subject to conditions laid down by statute, rules and regulations, and at common law. Various Acts govern them and they are also subject to practice rules made by the Law Society under powers contained in these Acts. However, the general standards of conduct and the ethical requirements which apply to solicitors are largely unwritten. There is no official code or guide to professional conduct for solicitors in Scotland. We questioned the Law Society on this matter in oral evidence; and their response was that to reduce to writing the general understanding that exists among solicitors would either produce a statement of general principles which was so general as to be of little or no use in specific circumstances, or a statement of detailed rules so restrictive as to require the continual granting of waivers in particular instances. They drew our attention to a booklet on professional ethics and practice published in 1976 by one of their former deputy secretaries.[1] In a foreword to this booklet, the then President of the Law Society said:

[1] R. M. Webster: *Professional Ethics and Practice for Scottish Solicitors:* 1976.

'This booklet has been written by Mr. R. M. Webster in response to several recent requests from members of the profession for a brief guide on professional ethics and practice.

In the field of professional practice in Scotland, it has always been regarded as preferable to work on principle rather than to attempt to prescribe detailed rules. Accordingly, the booklet sets out the main principles of professional practice and does not pretend to be an authoritative manual covering every variety of circumstances.

While the Council warmly welcomes the publication of the booklet and the contents are mainly based on decisions of the Professional Practice Committee approved by the Council over the years, the views expressed are the author's own views and are not to any extent to be taken as binding on the Council. It must be remembered that, where rules are not absolute rules, standards of behaviour depend on the social and professional climate and are always changing—for example solicitors are now allowed to use shop windows for advertising properties for sale, whereas only a few years ago this would have been frowned on.

Although the booklet has been written primarily with solicitors in private practice in mind, it is hoped that it will also be useful to those in the public service and commerce.'

The Law Society's desire to adhere to principles rather than detailed rules, accordingly, remains unchanged. What struck us as significant, however, was the explanation in the first paragraph of the foreword to the 1976 booklet that it had been written in response to requests from members of the profession for guidance on professional ethics and practice. This, we would have thought, was clear evidence of a need for authoritative standards. Moreover, a written guide to professional conduct not only provides guidance for practitioners, it also helps the client to know the standards which a solicitor is expected to maintain. It is of interest that one of the conditions governing professional practice which the Law Society listed in their evidence to us was that a solicitor must not act for persons with conflicting interests. Despite this, it is common practice for a solicitor to act for both buyer and seller in connection with the transfer of a house. This happens not only in private practice but also where employed solicitors act both for their employer and for another person, say where a local authority or new town development corporation sell a house. Conflict of interest may also arise in the case of solicitors employed by banks. In our survey of domestic conveyancing transactions which was restricted to the private sector we noted (Appendix 11, paragraph 6) that, in 18 per cent of the transactions reported on, the same solicitor or firm of solicitors acted for both parties. While this figure may be undesirably high, we think it probable that there are cases, for example in remote areas, where the economies and convenience for both parties of employing one solicitor outweigh the risks involved in the conflict of interest. However, we were concerned to note from the evidence of the Faculty of Advocates that:

'It is also pertinent to point out that in numerous problems submitted to Counsel for advice which arise out of bargains for the purchase of heritable property a common factor has been the lack of separate representation for the contracting parties.'

We think this is an example of a situation which presents difficulties, both to the solicitor and to the client, in knowing what is the proper professional practice, and in which a written statement of the appropriate rule and its application would be valuable.

18.4 Accordingly, while we accept that professional standards in Scotland have remained high in general without a written guide to conduct, we are not persuaded by the Law Society's arguments against the promulgation of authoritative rules and guidance on ethics and practice.[1] In short, we consider that the present situation cannot be regarded as entirely satisfactory. We readily accept that in drafting a guide the Law Society would have to strike a balance between the statement of principles and the prescription of detailed rules. We do not believe, however, that the practical difficulty of getting the balance right is an adequate reason for not proceeding. Law Societies and Bar Associations in other countries, including England and Wales, have produced written rules; and a comparative study of these should assist the Law Society in formulating the best approach for Scotland. We ourselves have recommended in Chapter 16 that the study of professional ethics should be a compulsory part of the curriculum for the Diploma in Legal Practice; but this by itself would not in our view be enough. Indeed, the Law Society themselves drew our attention to a new factor which we think gives added weight to the need for a fresh approach in this matter. The new factor is that solicitors (or their counterparts) from other countries in the European Economic Community are now free to choose to work in Scotland, although under obligation to work according to the rules and practice applicable to Scottish solicitors. It would clearly be of assistance to other EEC lawyers if the rules and conduct expected of them in Scotland were available in the form of a published guide. We therefore **recommend** that the Law Society should promulgate an authoritative guide to the professional conduct of solicitors in Scotland. The guide should be expressed in terms comprehensible to laymen and we think that it might be useful if the Society were to take the benefit of lay advice in preparing it.

18.5 We do not consider that there is any need for us to go into the detail of what this guide should contain, although we have already said in Chapter 6 that the present rules on advertising should be radically altered. There is, however, one other matter to which we attach considerable importance and which we feel we should mention. We believe that when a prospective client approaches a solicitor on a particular matter, the solicitor should be under a professional obligation to give his best estimate of the cost of the work, and the time which it will take to complete it; and we **recommend** that such a rule be introduced. The solicitor should also say on what basis he is giving this estimate, and should in particular say whether the work will cost more, or take longer, than would normally be the case because of his current workload, or because of some other factor peculiar to his own practice. It should also be a professional rule that the solicitor should keep his client up to date with developments, and in particular should advise the client if the original estimate as to cost or time is likely to prove significantly wrong. A proportion of the complaints made against solicitors each year could be avoided if only they took adequate steps to keep their clients informed about the progress of business.

18.6 Finally, so far as the solicitors' guide to professional conduct is concerned, we **recommend** that it should be supplied not only to the profession but

[1] After we had reached our decision on this we learned from the Law Society that they had reconsidered their view and that they now proposed to produce a guide of the kind we propose.

also to the staff of advice agencies; and it should, additionally, be available to the public.

Professional conduct: advocates

18.7 The Faculty of Advocates similarly have no written code of conduct, though advocates are subject to unwritten professional rules. The Dean of Faculty is accepted by the members of the Faculty as being the proper judge of matters of professional conduct and discipline, and in cases where he pronounces on matters of general relevance to practice his pronouncements are known as 'Rulings by the Dean' and are binding on members. It was suggested to us by the Faculty that there was much less need for written rules for advocates than for solicitors because the membership of the Faculty is so small and closely knit. These factors do indeed make it easier for the Faculty to maintain high standards on the part of their members; but it seems to us important that both solicitors and the public should know exactly the professional rules to which advocates are subject. We believe that professional rules for advocates could be stated more succinctly in the form of general principles than could rules for solicitors, who face a greater variety of individual circumstances in providing services to clients. However that may be, we **recommend** that the Faculty of Advocates should promulgate an authoritative written guide to the professional conduct expected of advocates which should, as in the case of the guide for solicitors, be supplied to advocates and made available to the public.

Misconduct and negligence

18.8 Before we turn to the present complaints and disciplinary machinery applicable to lawyers and the changes we feel are necessary, it would we think be helpful to say something about professional misconduct and negligence which are generally the reasons for complaints and disciplinary measures. The distinction that the lawyers draw between misconduct and negligence is one that is not readily apparent to many laymen; and, to make matters more complicated, some professional shortfalls in conduct or performance can involve both misconduct and negligence.

18.9 We had in evidence, or in correspondence, very few complaints about the performance or conduct of members of the Scottish Bar. We therefore limit our comments on misconduct and negligence to their application to solicitors. As we understand from discussion with the Law Society, they would endorse the English Law Society's definition of professional misconduct on the part of a solicitor as conduct which a solicitor's peers would regard as unbecoming or dishonourable. Conviction for a criminal offence such as fraud, theft or misuse of clients' monies constitutes a ready example of professional misconduct. Another example might be putting the solicitor's own interests, financial or otherwise, before those of his client. Professional negligence on the other hand is a failure to show the standard of skill and care which would be shown by a reasonably skilful and diligent solicitor in like circumstances. If it gives rise to loss, it will result in liability for damages. Negligence on the part of a solicitor need not amount to misconduct, but gross negligence or a series of incidents of negligence might. There can, moreover, be types of misconduct which are not negligence. A simple example of negligence would be where a solicitor failed to act timeously on his client's instructions to institute a claim for damages against a third party, and as a result the client's claim became 'time-barred'. In such a case, the client could sue the solicitor for negligence. Misconduct might also be deemed in a case of this kind if the negligence were particularly gross, or were one of several instances of negligence on the part of the solicitor concerned. On the other hand, an act of negligence might not have serious consequences for the client; and it might indeed be an isolated lapse on the part of the solicitor. A negligence case in this category might well not call for any disciplinary action by the Law Society, though it might result in a claim for damages.

18.10 Our reasons for trying—not without difficulty—to outline the difference between professional misconduct and negligence is that each is at present treated by the Law Society in different ways. Misconduct is treated as a disciplinary matter. Negligence, at least when it involves loss, is regarded as a matter for a civil claim for damages which must be pursued in the courts. Where the acts or omissions of the solicitor may constitute both misconduct and negligence involving a possible claim for loss in court, the Law Society normally decline to deal with the misconduct, at any rate until after any possible negligence claim is disposed of. The reason for this is that the Society consider it improper for them to take action which might prejudice the court's determination of the negligence claim. While we think that we understand the Society's attitude in this matter, we consider it unlikely that the dissatisfied client does; and we do not believe that the somewhat subtle distinctions involved are properly explained to the client, or would necessarily be understood if they were.

COMPLAINTS AND DISCIPLINE: SOLICITORS

Present arrangements

18.11 The Law Society have the principal responsibility for investigating complaints against solicitors. They see this quite properly as an important part of their statutory duty to represent the public interest. It is fair to mention here that while we received only a relatively small number of complaints against solicitors and against the Law Society's treatment of particular complaints, we nevertheless saw basic weaknesses in the procedures which we considered it important to mention and hopefully to remedy.

18.12 The Law Society's not unreasonable practice is to require complaints to be made in writing, whereupon they send a copy of the complaint to the solicitor complained against, requesting his observations. In the light of his reply, the Law Society's officials will usually attempt to resolve the matter to the satisfaction of both parties. In many cases the complaint is one of delay; and the very intervention of the Law Society is often sufficient to get the solicitor concerned to complete the work promptly. Complaints which the officials of the Law Society consider merit more detailed examination are put to the complaints sub-committee of the professional practice committee of the Law Society's Council. This committee has virtually no disciplinary powers and must, if it judges the matter serious enough, recommend that the case be taken to the Scottish Solicitors' Discipline Tribunal. Under powers provided by the Solicitors (Scotland) Act 1976 the Council of the Society can now, in respect of a complaint against a solicitor accused of undue delay in dealing with a matter, take that matter effectively out of his hands if he fails to satisfy the Council that he is responding to their exhortations or castigations. However, this is not, we have been told, a power which it is easy for the Society to operate and we ourselves do not think that it provides clients with adequate safeguards. Most complaints of unreasonable delay, accordingly, have to be reported to the Discipline Tribunal.

The Discipline Tribunal

18.13 The Scottish Solicitors' Discipline Tribunal is a successor of the Solicitors' Discipline (Scotland) Committee which existed until 1976, and which comprised five to seven solicitors recommended by the Council of the Law Society and appointed by the Lord President. Under the Solicitors (Scotland) Act 1976 the independence of this body from the Council of the Law Society was emphasised by changing its title from Committee to Tribunal, and by providing that the Tribunal should include two lay members. The cost of running the Tribunal, however, is still met by the Law Society. Normally the Law Society prosecute cases before the Tribunal, and they appoint one of their members who is not a member of the Council to conduct the case on their behalf. It is possible (though rare) for an individual client to complain direct to the Tribunal, and in these circumstances the Tribunal may refer the matter to the Council of the Society or may appoint a solicitor to represent the complainer. The solicitor complained against may conduct his own case or he can choose to be represented by a solicitor or an advocate. The Tribunal has power, when it finds a complaint of professional misconduct proved, to order that a solicitor be struck off the Roll of Solicitors, or be suspended from practice as a solicitor for such time as the Tribunal may determine. The Tribunal may also censure the solicitor, or impose a fine not exceeding £250, or do both. The Tribunal also has power to order that the solicitor's practising certificate should be issued subject to such terms and conditions as the Tribunal may direct. There is a right of appeal from the findings of the Tribunal to the Court of Session.

18.14 Another change introduced by the Solicitors' (Scotland) Act 1976 was the creation of the office of Lay Observer, whose function is:

> 'to examine any written allegation made by or on behalf of a member of the public concerning the Society's treatment of a complaint about a solicitor or an employee of a solicitor made to the Society by that member of the public, or on his behalf'.

The Lay Observer can thus only act after the complaint has been considered by the Law Society and no result which is satisfactory to the client has been achieved. In investigating a complaint the Lay Observer has power to ask the Law Society for their file, and he may submit observations to the Society on their handling of the case. The Law Society, however, are not bound to follow any suggestions made by the Lay Observer; this seems to us a fundamental weakness in the scheme of things on which we shall say more later.

Legal aid complaints

18.15 A quite different procedure applies where a complaint against a solicitor arises out of legally aided proceedings. This difference in treatment is dictated by the terms of the Legal Aid (Scotland) Scheme 1958. In such cases, the complaint must first be considered by the relevant local legal aid committee, or in appropriate cases by the supreme court committee, which determines whether or not it is 'frivolous'. Complaints not considered frivolous are referred to the Law Society's legal aid complaints committee (a committee composed of members of the Council of the Society). The legal aid complaints committee is empowered to arrange for a formal hearing of a case by three members of the committee, subject to the normal rules of procedure and evidence, cross examination and re-examination. The committee has power to recommend that a solicitor should be excluded from the legal aid list, and the Council of the Law Society must accept such a recommendation. As in non-legal aid complaints, a complainer who is not satisfied with the way the Law Society have handled the complaint can appeal to the Lay Observer. Only the solicitor, however, has a right of appeal to the Court of Session against the findings of the legal aid complaints committee, a situation which contrasts with the ability of the Law Society, or other complainer, as well as the solicitor, to appeal in the case of the findings of the Discipline Tribunal in non-legal aid cases. Moreover, unlike the Discipline Tribunal, the legal aid complaints committee has no lay membership. We do not consider that these arrangements are satisfactory and we later in this Chapter make specific recommendations for change.

Number of complaints

18.16 In 1976, in addition to 72 complaints disposed of by the professional practice complaints sub-committee, the Law Society's secretariat disposed of 791 complaints. These were all non-legal aid complaints. Of the 791, 460 were considered complaints of no substance and were rejected, and the remaining 331 were accepted as complaints of substance. The reasons given for the complaints of substance were as follows:

Delay	275
Lack of communication	104
Fees	22
Alleged negligence	57
Failure to deliver papers	43
Other reasons	61
	562*

(*this total is higher than the figure of 331 complaints referred to above because more than one reason was given in some complaints.)

Information which we received from the Law Society suggests that the number and pattern of complaints for 1979 was much the same as for 1976.

18.17 In the year 1976, the legal aid complaints committee dealt with 26 cases, 17 of which were withdrawn or dismissed as disclosing no *prima facie* case. This total excludes 41 complaints dismissed by local legal aid committees as frivolous. We think it fair to draw attention to the fact that these legal aid complaints figures have to be viewed against a total of nearly 85,000 legal aid certificates issued in 1976 in respect of civil and criminal legal aid, and legal advice and assistance. (In 1979, 53 legal aid complaints were dealt with.)

18.18 As we earlier noted (paragraph 18.10) in complaints alleging negligence by a solicitor which has given rise to pecuniary loss for the client, the Law Society inform the client that it is for him to seek his remedy in the courts, and that to assist him in this direction he should seek independent legal advice and representation. The Society refuse to investigate the complaint or (where appropriate) to take disciplinary action against the solicitor until the client has exhausted his right of redress in the courts. The Society cannot under their disciplinary procedure secure compensation for the client and their view is that it is in his own interests first to seek his remedy in the courts. If a second solicitor acting for the client considers that the first one was guilty of professional misconduct, the Society expect this to be drawn to their notice after the court action, and they will then consider the need for disciplinary measures.

Weaknesses in the present arrangement

18.19 There are, in our view, a number of shortcomings in the arrangements we have described. In the first place, we see no advantage in separate complaints machinery for legal aid and non-legal aid cases. Regardless of who is paying the solicitor, it is the nature of his service to the client which is the subject of complaint. Although the grounds for complaint may technically differ because of the statutory basis on which services are provided under legal aid, we consider it wasteful of resources to have an entirely separate procedure for the small number of legal aid complaints received each year. Moreover, our recommendations as to eligibility for legal aid will make the distinction between legally aided and non-legally aided cases even more arbitrary than it now is; and our recommendations in Chapter 8 also envisage the demise of local committees, who currently apply the 'frivolous' test to legal aid complaints.

18.20 A second shortcoming of the present arrangements is that they provide an inadequate range of response to complaints of differing severity. The Discipline Tribunal has powers where it finds a solicitor guilty of professional misconduct; but short of ordering that the solicitor be suspended from practice or struck off the roll of solicitors, the Tribunal can only censure and/or impose a fine not exceeding £250. The maximum fine of £250 seems wholly inadequate as a punishment for certain offences which scarcely merit the more extreme penalty of suspension; and we **recommend** that the maximum fine which the Tribunal should be able to impose should be at least £2,000 at present day values and should be periodically reviewed to take account of inflation.

18.21 We also regard it as far from satisfactory that the Law Society generally decline to intervene in complaints where professional negligence appears to be at issue. To their credit, they have recognised that clients in this position will be sceptical about advice to put their affairs in the hands of another member of the profession with which they are already dissatisfied; and, indeed, clients may not always easily find another solicitor who is prepared to act against one of his professional colleagues. To meet this situation, the Law Society have arranged a 'troubleshooter' scheme whereby a complainer unable to secure the services of a solicitor to act for him against his first solicitor will be supplied by the Law Society with the name of a solicitor willing to act in such cases from their 'troubleshooter' panel. Despite this, a client may conclude that his likelihood of securing adequate recovery from the solicitor in a court action for negligence hardly justifies risking further expense, even where his case seems fairly strong; and where the client finally decides not to proceed against the solicitor, the Law Society generally do not investigate whether the original complaint has disciplinary aspects which they should pursue.

18.22 As we have indicated, it seems to us fundamentally wrong that the Law Society, who are charged with representing the interests of the public in relation to the legal profession, should always leave it to the complainer in a case of alleged negligence to establish his own remedy in the courts when the Society consider that he has a remedy there. The Society should be concerned not only with misconduct but with incompetence, as we have stressed in Chapter 16. The body which issues practising certificates to solicitors cannot, in our view, disregard evidence of possible incompetence simply because the client affected may have a civil remedy in the courts. The public interest in such matters goes beyond the interest of that particular client; and we are in no doubt that a more vigorous attitude by the Law Society is needed.

18.23 We have noted that two laymen sit on the Discipline Tribunal. There is no lay involvement at all, however, in the earlier stages of the complaints and discipline process. Other professions, notably the chartered accountants in recent years, have taken steps to ensure that there is some lay involvement at all stages of their complaints procedure; and we think that this demonstrates a proper concern by a profession not to be considered to be 'looking after its own' when complaints are made against its members.

18.24 Finally, we revert to the weak position of the Lay Observer. This was stated in terms with which we wholly agree by the first Lay Observer in Scotland, the Rt. Hon. Margaret M. Herbison, in her first annual report:

> 'From my work in this first year I have reached the conclusion that the Lay Observer must have the power to take a case before the Scottish Solicitors' Discipline Tribunal. At present the Lay Observer, after investigation of a complaint, may ask the Law Society to have the complaint brought before the Discipline Tribunal. This I did on three occasions. But if the Law Society decides against this course of action as they did twice, there is nothing further the Lay Observer can do as far as the complaint is concerned. It is true that the aggrieved person has the right to take the case himself to the Discipline Tribunal but I believe for some people this would present fears and difficulties and also it might involve them in further expense. If justice is to be clearly seen to be done and if suspicion, without foundation as it may be in many instances, of what some think the closed shop of the legal profession is to be allayed, it seems to me that this can best be done by giving this additional power to the Lay Observer. Accordingly, I ask the Secretary of State to take steps to have this power introduced in legislation as soon as possible.'[1]

Our approach

18.25 We have adopted a number of principles in making our recommendations in this area. In the first place, we think that all complaints against solicitors should be made to the same focal point. Not only does this simplify matters for complainers, and those who may advise them, it also ensures that there is a single complete and authoritative source of information about complaints against solicitors.

18.26 We think that the present practice of the Law Society in refusing to deal immediately with complaints which may involve a claim for professional negligence is unnecessary, and seriously restricts the ability of the Society to

[1] *First Annual Report of the Scottish Lay Observer 1976/77:* HMSO, 1977, paragraph 26.

exercise control over the competence and diligence of their members. We therefore **recommend** that, in future, the Law Society should prosecute their disciplinary procedures in every case whether or not a claim for negligence in the courts is open to, or contemplated by, the client without waiting for the initiation or decision of court proceedings. The Discipline Tribunal also should be able to deal with such cases; and, in order to avoid risk of prejudice in the court proceedings, rules should be devised to preclude any reference being made in the court proceedings to the decision of or to any evidence given before the Discipline Tribunal. The rules should also provide that in such cases no publicity should be given to the disciplinary proceedings until after any court action has been concluded. The details of such rules could be worked out by the Lord President, the Law Society and the Discipline Tribunal. We would wish, however, to make one qualification to the above recommendation. The new professional disciplinary procedure, which we propose below, includes a power for the Discipline Tribunal to award limited amounts of compensation to clients. We do not in these circumstances consider that a client should be entitled both to such compensation and to damages for negligence. Accordingly, we **recommend** that a power to award compensation in disciplinary proceedings should only be available if the client has expressly waived any right to claim damages.

18.27 In some cases a client may have, and may wish to pursue, a substantial claim for damages while in other cases, a solicitor's incompetence or dilatoriness might have caused little or no measurable pecuniary loss. Such incompetence or dilatoriness might, nevertheless, have resulted in unjustifiable inconvenience and anxiety for the client, and also perhaps in some relatively trivial pecuniary loss. We think it desirable, therefore, that the disciplinary procedure should include a discretionary power to award the client compensation up to a limited level. It should not be an essential condition of any such award that the client should be able to show loss of a kind which would entitle him to damages in law, though this would be one matter which could be taken into account in considering whether an award should be made and, if so, the amount.

18.28 Finally, we have been concerned to secure a proper balance between the interests of a professional body in overseeing the standards and discipline of its members, and the public interest in having some independent lay participation in the assessment of complaints made against solicitors. Two differing approaches to this question are illustrated in the work of review bodies similar to ourselves in Ontario, Canada and in New South Wales, Australia.[1] We understand that in New South Wales, the Law Reform Commission found that the treatment of complaints by the Law Society there was so inadequate that they suggested in a discussion paper that the discipline of the legal profession should be put in the hands of an independent professional standards board which would have a wide range of limited disciplinary sanctions at their disposal. A further disciplinary tribunal was also proposed which would be able to deploy more severe sanctions where they found reprehensible conduct or a breach of standards indicating unfitness to practise. Although we have said that the present complaints procedure of the Law Society of Scotland and the disciplinary system of which it is part are not entirely satisfactory, the shortcomings do not

[1] The Professional Organisations Committee in Ontario, Canada; and the Law Reform Commission of New South Wales, Australia.

amount to a case for removing from the Society the initial responsibility for the discipline and standards of the profession. We believe this to be an essential duty of any professional body.

18.29 The Ontario, Canada study concluded that self-regulation of the legal profession was preferable to direct control by government because of:

> 'the high cost of error, information and enforcement and because of the need to reinforce trust relationships between practitioners and clients.'

That report argues convincingly, however, that this rationale for professional self-regulation is largely undermined if the professional body is not actively concerned to promote competence in the profession, which must imply:

> 'that the promotion of competence is a major objective of the discipline process and is actively pursued by a variety of positive strategies designed to identify and eradicate cases of incompetence.'

This is, indeed, a good expression of our own approach. To make the complaints and disciplinary process as effective as possible we think it essential that laymen be involved at all stages of that process, not only for the more objective perspective which they can bring, but to provide a visible reminder that the purpose of the whole procedure is to protect the interests of the public.

OUR PROPOSALS

18.30 Accordingly, we **recommend** the establishment of a single, reasonably simple procedure for investigating and acting on all complaints against solicitors. We want a system which will provide a wide range of lesser and greater sanctions appropriate to differing degrees of incompetence; we want to ensure a significant involvement of laymen at each stage; and we want to incorporate in the disciplinary process arrangements for relatively minor awards of compensation as an alternative to the client seeking a remedy in the courts.

New Discipline Tribunal

18.31 From this statement of general principle we make a number of detailed proposals. Firstly, we **recommend** that there should be a new Discipline Tribunal in place of the present Scottish Solicitors' Discipline Tribunal and the Law Society's legal aid complaints committee. The new Tribunal should have at its disposal a wide range of sanctions appropriate to differing degrees of misconduct or incompetence, including a power to award compensation of limited amounts to the client. An illustration of the range of sanctions we have in mind is to be found in two recommendations made in a discussion paper by the Law Reform Commission of New South Wales:

> 'Where the Board makes a finding against a practitioner, it should have power to make one or more of the following orders:
>
> (a) that the practitioner's practising certificate be restricted to the effect that he shall not practise on his own for such time, not exceeding three years, as the Board determines;
>
> (b) that the practitioner commence and complete to the satisfaction of the Board such course of legal education as the Board determines;

(c) that the practitioner make his practice available for inspection at such times and by such persons as the Board determines;

(d) that the practitioner report on his practice at such times, in such form and to such persons as the Board determines;

(e) that the practitioner take advice in relation to the management of his practice from such persons as the Board determines;

(f) that the practitioner cease to accept work or to hold himself out as competent, in such fields of practice as the Board determines;

(g) that the practitioner employ in his practice a member of such class of persons as the Board determines;

(h) that the practitioner do such work for such persons within such time and for such fee as the Board determines;

(i) that the practitioner reduce his charges for any work done by him which is the subject of the proceedings before the Board in such amount, not exceeding $1500, as the Board determines;

(j) that the practitioner pay compensation in an amount not exceeding $1500 to such persons as the Board determines;

(k) that the practitioner be fined an amount not exceeding $1500;

(l) that the practitioner be reprimanded; or

(m) that the practitioner pay such costs of and incidental to the proceedings before the Board as the Board determines.

An order should not be made under paragraph (h), (i) or (j) unless the practitioner has consented to the Board exercising the jurisdiction referred to in those paragraphs.'

The New South Wales discussion paper then deals with the more severe sanctions which their suggested Disciplinary Tribunal should have:

'Where the Tribunal makes a finding against a practitioner, it should be empowered to make any of the orders that the Board may make. But, in addition, the Tribunal should have power to order:

(*a*) that the practitioner's name be removed from any roll of practitioners on which it is entered; or

(*b*) that the practitioner be suspended from practice for a period not exceeding five years.'

Also, where the Board may make orders for terms not exceeding three years and for amounts not exceeding $1500, the Tribunal should have power to make orders for terms not exceeding five years and for amounts not exceeding $10,000. And where the Board's jurisdiction is conditional upon the consent of a practitioner, the Tribunal's jurisdiction should be subject to the same condition.

We think that the Tribunal, which we have recommended, should have a similar range of sanctions, and we discuss these in the following paragraphs.

Compensation limits

18.32 The New South Wales proposals would require the solicitor's consent to the exercise of compensation powers. We prefer that the client should decide whether the Discipline Tribunal would be the forum in which he would seek compensation (within the limits of its jurisdiction) from a solicitor in respect of alleged negligence. In fairness to the solicitor, as we have earlier noted, the client would have to renounce irrevocably his right to pursue a civil remedy for damages in the courts if he opted to seek compensation from the Tribunal. The statutory limit to the compensation powers of the Tribunal might be set (at 1980 prices) at £500 or at most £1,000. In arriving at this figure we thought it important to bear in mind that the solicitor would be obliged statutorily to defend the client's claim in this forum rather than in the courts. Compensation should not, however, be awarded in respect of any matter as to which it is thought that there would be immunity from suit on grounds of public policy (see paragraph 15.42).

18.33 We **recommend** that the Tribunal should be able to award compensation in one or more of the following forms:

(i) that the solicitor undertake for the client such further work for such fee as the Tribunal might determine, provided that all parties involved are agreeable to the arrangement;

(ii) that the solicitor pay in whole or in part for such further work for the client to be done by another solicitor;

(iii) that the solicitor reduce his fees in respect of work already done for the client by such sum as the Tribunal might determine;

(iv) that the solicitor pay compensation to the client of such sum as the Tribunal might determine up to the statutory maximum of say £500 or £1,000.

We consider that there should be no appeal from the Tribunal in respect of any award, or non-award, of compensation. In relation to disciplinary findings and sanctions, on the other hand, we **recommend** that a right of appeal to the Court of Session similar to that which exists at present should remain open to both parties.

Composition of Tribunal

18.34 We **recommend** that members of the Discipline Tribunal should be drawn from a panel of, say, five practising solicitors who are not members of the Council of the Law Society and an equal number of laymen. The solicitor members should be appointed by the Lord President of the Court of Session on the recommendation of the Council of the Law Society; and the lay members should be appointed by the Secretary of State for Scotland. The President of the Tribunal should be legally qualified and should be appointed either by the Secretary of State for Scotland or by the Lord President of the Court of Session. In all cases which reach the Tribunal we think it important that there should be equal numbers of legal and lay members along with a chairman. In most cases we would have thought a triumvirate would suffice—a chairman, one solicitor and one lay member—but in serious cases the President of the Tribunal could determine that a larger number should sit.

Complaints procedure

18.35 Complaints will come from various sources; but the main business of the Tribunal will derive from complaints by individual clients about services provided by particular solicitors. We **recommend** that all complaints should be addressed in the first instance to the Law Society for investigation. We also **recommend** that the committee of the Law Society responsible for investigating complaints should include lay members appointed by the Secretary of State for Scotland. While it should remain the duty of nominated officials of the Society to try to secure the completion of the client's work, where appropriate, they will need to be much more effective than at present in identifying and following up cases of incompetence. We have seen cases which, despite the involvement of the Law Society's complaints machinery, have been allowed to drag on for a matter of years without being resolved. This is unacceptable.

18.36 Accordingly, we **recommend** that after receiving a complaint, the Law Society should report the progress of their investigations to the complainer not later than one month after the complaint has been received. If need be, the Society at the end of a further month should provide a further progress report to the complainer. In cases not resolved by the end of the third month after receipt of the complaint the Law Society should be required to report the situation to the Lay Observer as well as to the complainer. This must be the maximum time limit permitted. In cases of urgency where further delay may be detrimental to the interests of the complainer the Law Society would be expected to observe a tighter schedule. From that point on, the Lay Observer should have the power to take over the case and, if he considers it appropriate, prosecute the complaint before the Discipline Tribunal. On the other hand, the Lay Observer may deem it preferable in particular cases to give the Law Society an extended period in which to try to bring the matter at issue to a successful conclusion. In most instances, we would expect disciplinary (and compensation) action before the Tribunal to be taken by the Law Society rather than the Lay Observer; but whichever body is involved should always keep in mind the need to inform the complainer of developments.

Lay Observer

18.37 We wish to retain the office of Lay Observer because so long as responsibility for the initial investigation of complaints rests with the Law Society, it is essential in our view to provide for an independent review in cases where the client is dissatisfied with the way his complaint has been handled by the Society. Accordingly, in addition to the role we have proposed for the Lay Observer in the previous paragraph, we **recommend** that the Lay Observer should continue to receive and investigate complaints from clients in cases where, although the Law Society have completed investigation and action on their part, the client is not satisfied. We also consider it essential, as earlier noted, that the Lay Observer himself should have authority to pursue complaints against solicitors before the Discipline Tribunal. The present situation whereby the Law Society may choose to ignore recommendations made by the Lay Observer is untenable; and we believe that the whole complaints and discipline machinery will be more effective if it is known that this independent 'legal ombudsman' has the authority to take cases at his own instance to the Tribunal.

Law Society as complainer

18.38 In the new complaints machinery that we propose, clients need not be the only complainers. The Law Society themselves will, if our recommendations in Chapter 16 are implemented, uncover a number of instances of incompetence from the reporting arrangements they establish. Some of these may not adversely affect the client at all, in the sense that the incompetence might not have cost the client anything—if, for example, what has been done wrongly, or not done at all, has been identified and put right in time. Moreover, there will be solicitors who frequently commit minor errors which taken singly would not justify any action but which, in sum, demonstrate incompetence which ought to be dealt with. The Legal Services Commission which we propose in Chapter 20 will also, in relation to legal aid work, identify cases where solicitors have acted incorrectly or improperly in relation to the provision of legal aid, though some of these may not involve any reduction in the quality of the service provided to the client. We **recommend** that all such complaints should be investigated in the first place by the Law Society who should treat the Legal Services Commission as a client for this purpose. We think that a solicitor who has consistently been rendering to the Commission accounts which claim more than he is entitled to should be subject to a penalty—not simply the abatement of particular fees to which he is entitled.

Conciliation

18.39 Finally, we attach great importance to the present function of the Law Society's officials in seeking a conciliatory solution from the start. This is particularly the case when the complaint is one of delay or failure to communicate; but it applies in other cases too. However, we should stress that satisfying the complainer is not the only purpose of the complaints machinery; even after a complainer has been satisfied, the Law Society should vigorously pursue instances of incompetence.

Funding the Discipline Tribunal

18.40 Although the Law Society have hitherto borne the costs of the Scottish Solicitors' Discipline Tribunal, we think that the funding arrangements for our proposed Discipline Tribunal should reflect its independent status. This does not mean that the Law Society should not continue to meet the cost of investigating complaints and prosecuting a case before the Tribunal; indeed in most instances the Society should be able to recover costs from the solicitor complained against where the Tribunal so orders. We **recommend**, however, that the direct cost of the Tribunal should be a charge on public funds.

18.41 The new complaints, discipline and compensation machinery which we have recommended for the solicitor branch of the profession is set out in diagrammatic form in the Annex to this Chapter.

Solicitors' lien

18.42 Solicitors in common with certain other professions and trades have by custom a right to retain property held by them but belonging to their clients until some debt or other obligation is satisfied. This right is known as 'lien', and in the case of solicitors it extends to all papers placed in their hands such as title deeds, wills and share certificates. The exercise of the lien relates only to the solicitor's professional fees and any payments made by him on behalf of his client in the normal course of business. The right permits the solicitor to retain the papers but does not enable him to dispose of them.

18.43 Although the operation of the solicitors' lien did not appear to be a contentious topic in Scotland we were aware that there could be circumstances where a client complaining about a solicitor and withholding payment of his fee might be put in difficulty if the solicitor refused to return the client's papers to him. Accordingly, we thought it desirable to consider whether we ought to make any recommendations about the lien. It seemed that there were a number of options open to us: firstly, we could recommend no change at all; secondly, we could recommend the total abolition of the lien; thirdly, we could recommend that the lien could be suspended or even abolished where the client was involved in a formal complaint against the solicitor; and, finally, we could recommend that the disciplinary body responsible for dealing with the complaint might be given a power to override the lien at its discretion while a complaint was being considered.

18.44 In essence the lien is a security right which protects the solicitor from a wilful refusal by a client to pay what is properly due to the solicitor; and since such a right is recognised in other fields of work we can see no reason why it should be abolished totally in respect of solicitors. We are at the same time concerned with the problems which can arise when a client is in dispute with his solicitor; and we consider it equally important that the rights of clients be also protected. As we suggested above, this could be done by giving the disciplinary body a power to override the lien or by suspending or abolishing the lien where a formal complaint has been made against the solicitor. Although the Law Society now have certain statutory powers[1] which enable them to uplift papers from a solicitor, the powers are not sufficiently wide to permit them to do this in all cases where a client has complained against a solicitor. We believe that the Law Society can, in most cases, successfully use their influence with a solicitor to have the papers handed over; but there will always be a residue of cases of difficulty. We do not think that we could justifiably recommend that the lien should be automatically suspended or abolished when a formal complaint has been made since that complaint may prove to be completely without substance. On balance, therefore, we are left with only two of our options—to recommend that the disciplinary body be given a discretionary power to override the lien, or to recommend that no change be made at all. In weighing the benefits to be obtained from these respective courses we have come down in favour of giving the new Discipline Tribunal which we recommend a discretion to suspend the operation of the lien where it thinks this appropriate, and we so **recommend**. We think that this will ensure that the interests of both solicitor and client will be adequately protected.

COMPLAINTS AND DISCIPLINE: ADVOCATES

18.45 The principles we have adumbrated in relation to solicitors are, in our view, equally applicable to advocates. However, we feel bound to recommend different procedures for complaints against members of the Bar. The small, cohesive and collegiate nature of the Faculty of Advocates has meant that

[1] *Solicitors (Scotland) Act 1949*, Schedule 6, paras 5 and 6: *Solicitors (Scotland) Act 1976*, Section 6.

somewhat informal disciplinary procedures have broadly sufficed to deal with the very small number of complaints that arise each year. In evidence the Faculty told us that over the period 1972–1979 an average of five complaints were received each year. About half were from members of the public, and the remainder from solicitors and judges. The Dean of Faculty is responsible for dealing with any complaints against advocates, and for any disciplinary measures which may be required as a consequence of those complaints. If a complaint requires detailed investigation the Dean may either carry it out himself, invite the Vice-Dean to do so, or appoint an *ad hoc* committee for the purpose. At any stage the Dean may consult his Council for guidance. The Faculty also told us that in recent times censure by the Dean has been the only form of discipline that has been imposed.

18.46 We think it right that complaints should continue to be investigated by the Dean, or by another office-bearer of the Faculty. Rather than recommend for advocates a standing Discipline Tribunal of the kind we have proposed for solicitors, we think that the public interest will be served if the Lord President of the Court of Session is empowered at the request of the Dean to convene an *ad hoc* Discipline Tribunal; and we so **recommend**, This Tribunal could be composed of a Court of Session judge as Chairman, an advocate and a layman. It should have similar sanctions to those proposed for the solicitors' Tribunal which we have recommended, including where appropriate the power to award limited compensation, though we think that there will be few cases where the compensation sought by a client in respect of alleged incompetence on the part of an advocate would fall below the limit of value which we have recommended. The proviso which we made in paragraph 18.32 regarding immunity from suit on grounds of public policy would also apply in the case of advocates.

18.47 We would expect most complaints against advocates to be resolved satisfactorily by the action of the Dean or an *ad hoc* committee which he might appoint. When, however, a complainer remained dissatisfied at the Faculty's handling of the complaint, we consider that the complainer should have a right of appeal to the Lay Observer. We **recommend**, therefore, that the role of the Lay Observer be extended for this purpose; and that additionally he should have power in cases where he deems the complaint to be justified to invite the Lord President to convene a Disciplinary Tribunal of the kind described in the previous paragraph. The Lay Observer should arrange for the client's case to be prosecuted before the Tribunal. Similar rules to those we have recommended in respect of solicitors should apply to the arrangements for reporting progress to the client after he has made his complaint.

18.48 Where a complaint involves both a solicitor and an advocate we **recommend** that the Faculty and the Law Society should make joint arrangements to investigate it. When necessary the Lord President could be invited to appoint an *ad hoc* Tribunal so that the complaint could be treated as a single proceeding; and on such occasions the Tribunal should comprise a supreme court judge as chairman, an advocate, a solicitor and two laymen. The Faculty and the Law Society jointly should instruct someone to conduct the prosecution.

PUBLICITY

18.49 There are two publicity aspects to be considered. Firstly, it is important that clear written guidance should be readily available so that the public may know how to complain against a lawyer, and to whom. The Law Society have recently produced a leaflet which describes how the client should complain and also the Society's role in the investigation of complaints. We consider that a single leaflet should be produced describing briefly the procedures for lodging complaints against advocates as well as solicitors; and we **recommend** that this leaflet should be made widely available—for example in Citizens Advice Bureaux, libraries, etc.. It should also be available at solicitors' offices to be given to clients who wish to complain about the handling of their business.

18.50 The second aspect is the publicity that should be given to the findings of the Discipline Tribunal. We do not consider that the proceedings of the Tribunal must be open to the public. We are content to leave the detailed procedure to be settled by the proposed Department of Legal Affairs and the professional bodies; but we **recommend** as a minimum that the findings of the Tribunal should always be released to the press as well as being adequately reported in the professional journals.

COMPLAINTS AND DISCIPLINE: OTHER PROVIDERS OF LEGAL SERVICES

The Judiciary

18.51 The statutory provisions as to the removal of members of the judiciary at different levels have been the subject of some evidence to us. We considered, however, that this was a matter which fell outwith our remit.

Advice agencies

18.52 We consider it important that any service providing first-line advice and information on which the public relies, and for which government provides funds, should establish a procedure for dealing with complaints. In time it should be possible for the proposed Legal Services Commission to make the grant of public funds to an agency conditional on its having established an adequate complaints and disciplinary procedure. Meanwhile we **recommend** that existing advice agencies should formulate and make clear to their clients their procedures for dealing with complaints.

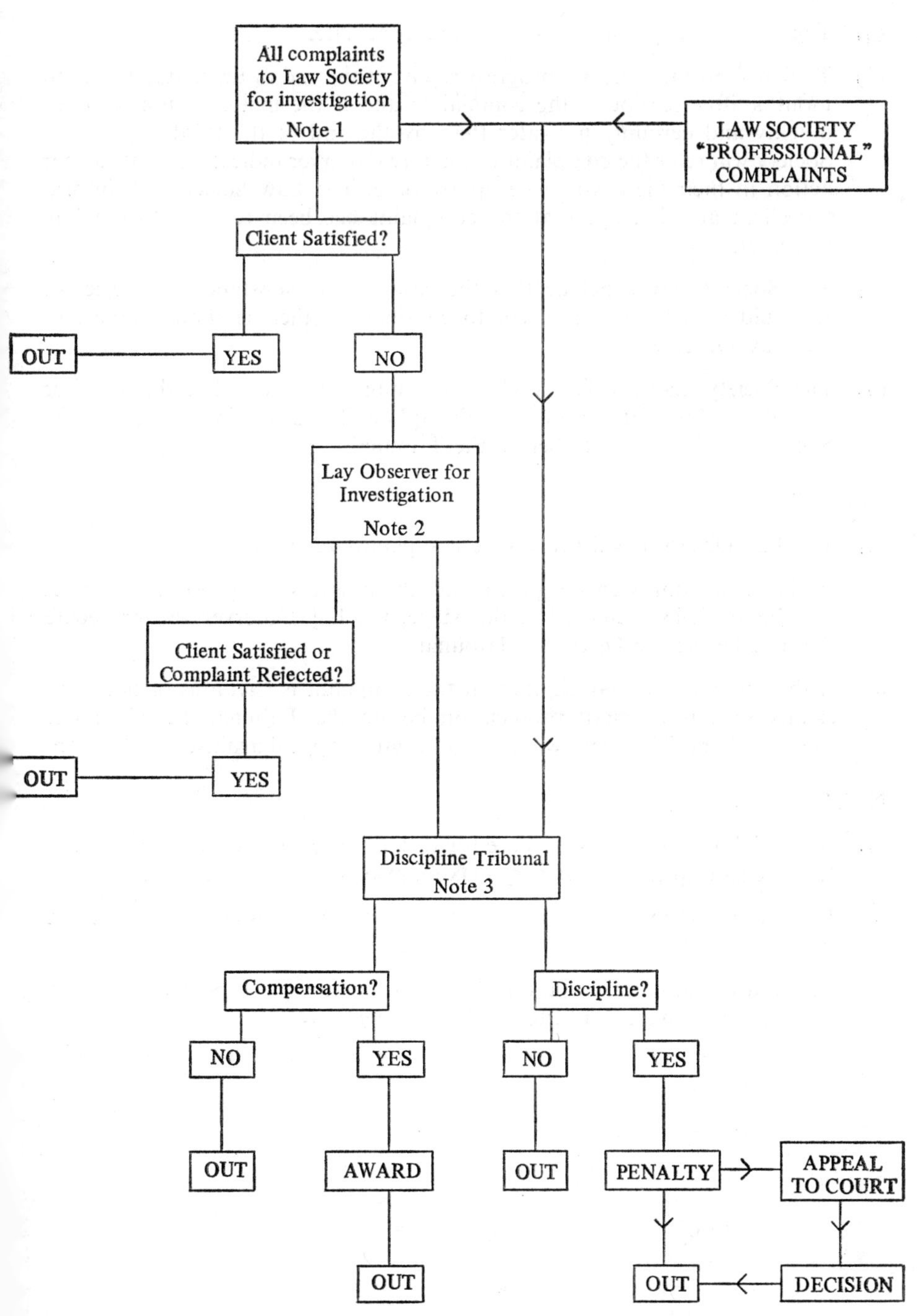
All complaints to Law Society for investigation
Note 1
LAW SOCIETY "PROFESSIONAL" COMPLAINTS
Client Satisfied?
OUT
YES
NO
Lay Observer for Investigation
Note 2
Client Satisfied or Complaint Rejected?
OUT
YES
Discipline Tribunal
Note 3
Compensation?
Discipline?
NO
YES
NO
YES
OUT
AWARD
OUT
PENALTY
APPEAL TO COURT
OUT
OUT
DECISION

NOTES ON ANNEX

NOTE 1

(*a*) The Law Society will investigate and conciliate.

(*b*) They will give the client a progress report at the end of the first and second months after receipt of the complaint; and if the matter is not resolved quickly and certainly not later than by the end of the third month, the Society will refer the complaint to the Lay Observer indicating what further action in their view would be appropriate. The Law Society will inform the client at this stage that the complaint has been referred to the Lay Observer.

(*c*) The Society may conclude that the case has no substance and reject it. It would then be for the client to consider whether he should appeal to the Lay Observer.

(*d*) The Society may satisfy the client but might conclude that the solicitor should be brought before the Discipline Tribunal: in this event the Society would prosecute before the Tribunal.

NOTE 2

(*a*) The Lay Observer will investigate complaints referred to him.

(*b*) If the complaint seems justified and there seems no prospect of client satisfaction being achieved at this stage, the Lay Observer will prosecute the case before the Discipline Tribunal.

(*c*) If the Lay Observer concludes that the complaint is frivolous or not sufficiently serious to merit prosecution before the Tribunal, he will reject the complaint. The client will have no right of appeal against this decision.

NOTE 3

(*a*) A Discipline Tribunal is proposed with the power to award compensation to the client up to the statutory maximum of say £500 or £1,000.

(*b*) It would be empowered to impose a wide range of penalties on the solicitor. (See paragraph 18.33).

(*c*) For individual hearings three members of the panel would normally suffice, a chairman, a solicitor and a lay member.

Subject	No.	Recommendation	Paragraph
Professional conduct: solicitors	R18.1	The Law Society should promulgate an authoritative guide to the professional conduct of solicitors in Scotland, which should be in terms comprehensible to laymen.	18.4
	R18.2	A solicitor should be under a professional obligation to give a prospective client his best estimate of the cost of the work to be undertaken and the time it will take to complete it.	18.5
	R18.3	The proposed guide should be supplied to the profession and to the staff of advice agencies; it should also be available to the public.	18.6
Professional conduct: advocates	R18.4	The Faculty of Advocates should promulgate an authoritative written guide to the professional conduct expected of advocates which should be supplied to advocates and be available to the public.	18.7
Discipline Tribunal: amount of fine	R18.5	The maximum fine which the Tribunal should be able to impose should be at least £2,000 at present day values and should be periodically reviewed to take account of inflation.	18.20
Disciplinary procedures: Law Society	R18.6	The Law Society should prosecute disciplinary procedures whether or not negligence is involved without waiting for the initiation or completion of civil court proceedings.	18.26
Claims for compensation	R18.7	The power which we propose for the Tribunal to award compensation (R18.10) should only be available if the client has expressly waived any right to claim damages.	18.26
New complaints procedure: solicitors	R18.8	A single, reasonably simple procedure for investigating and acting on all complaints against solicitors should be established.	18.30

			Paragraph
	R18.9	A new Discipline Tribunal should be established to replace the present Scottish Solicitors' Discipline Tribunal and the Law Society's legal aid complaints committee. The Tribunal should have a wide range of sanctions.	18.31
Compensation	R18.10	The Tribunal should be able to award compensation in the ways stated in paragraph 18.33.	18.33
	R18.11	Both the solicitor and the complainer should have a right of appeal to the Court of Session in relation to disciplinary findings and sanctions determined by the Tribunal although there should be no appeal in respect of award or non-award of compensation.	18.33
Composition of Tribunal	R18.12	The membership of the Discipline Tribunal should be drawn from a panel consisting of say five practising solicitors appointed by the Lord President and an equal number of laymen appointed by the Secretary of State. A legally qualified President should be appointed by the Secretary of State or the Lord President.	18.34
Procedure for lodging and investigating complaints	R18.13	All complaints should be addressed in the first instance to the Law Society for investigation.	18.35
	R18.14	The committee of the Law Society responsible for investigating complaints should include lay members appointed by the Secretary of State.	18.35
Progress report	R18.15	The Law Society should make regular reports to complainers on the progress of their investigations into the complaints they have received. On any complaint outstanding for three months a report should be made to the Lay Observer.	18.36

		Paragraph
Lay Observer: powers	R18.16 The Lay Observer should continue to receive and investigate complaints from clients who are not satisfied by the investigation and action taken by the Law Society. He should be empowered to take complaints to the Tribunal at his own instance.	18.37
Legal Aid: complaints	R18.17 Complaints by the Legal Services Commission against solicitors in relation to the provision of legal aid should be investigated in the first place by the Law Society.	18.38
Cost of Tribunal	R18.18 The direct cost of the new Tribunal should be a charge on public funds.	18.40
Solicitors' lien	R18.19 The Discipline Tribunal should be given a discretion to suspend the operation of solicitors' lien in cases where it thinks this appropriate.	18.44
New complaints procedure: advocates	R18.20 The Lord President of the Court of Session should be empowered at the request of the Dean of Faculty to convene an *ad hoc* Discipline Tribunal to deal with complaints against advocates. The Tribunal should be chaired by a judge and should have an advocate and a layman as members. The Tribunal should have similar sanctions to those proposed for the solicitors' Discipline Tribunal.	18.46
Lay Observer: function in relation to complaints against advocates	R18.21 The Lay Observer should be empowered to receive and investigate complaints which have not been dealt with to the satisfaction of the client by the Dean of Faculty or any committee appointed by him. The Lay Observer should have power to request the Lord President to convene an *ad hoc* Discipline Tribunal. The Lay Observer should arrange for the client's case to be prosecuted before the Tribunal.	18.47

			Paragraph
Complaints involving both solicitors and advocates	R18.22	Where a complaint involves both a solicitor and an advocate the Faculty and the Law Society should make joint arrangements to investigate it. When necessary an *ad hoc* Tribunal could be appointed by the Lord President.	18.48
Publicity	R18.23	A leaflet should be produced describing briefly the procedures for lodging complaints against solicitors and/or advocates; this leaflet should be readily available to the public.	18.49
	R18.24	The findings of the Discipline Tribunal should always be released to the press as well as being adequately reported in the professional journals.	18.50
	R18.25	Existing advice agencies should formulate and make clear to their clients their procedures for dealing with complaints.	18.52

CHAPTER 19

REMUNERATION

INTRODUCTION

19.1 Our remit required us to consider whether any, and if so what, changes might be desirable in the public interest in the arrangements for determining the remuneration of the legal profession from private sources or public funds. The reasons behind this special emphasis on remuneration, we believe, include the following:

(i) both the public and the legal profession have complained about aspects of legal charges and fees: the public because they think some fees, such as those for conveyancing and divorce, are too high; the profession because payment for some types of work, for example court work, is felt to be too low;

(ii) a significant proportion of the profession's income derives from public funds through the legal aid schemes;

(iii) some parts of a lawyer's work, as earlier explained, are covered by a form of monopoly; and, like other monopolies, it is important to know whether pricing in such areas is consistent with the public interest and also how it is monitored.

Need for special surveys

19.2 To carry out this part of our remit, we required detailed information on the income of the legal profession, its sources, its level and its distribution. Such information was necessary to enable us to make comparisons with the earnings of other professions, and others who assume comparable responsibility in their work. It was also needed to help us to form a judgement about the adequacy of incomes to attract sufficient numbers of persons of appropriate calibre into the profession. We found an almost complete dearth of information on these matters; and we decided to conduct our own surveys to attempt to remedy this deficiency.

19.3 When we reached this point, the Benson Commission had been in operation for some six months and their investigations into the income of the legal profession in England, Wales and Northern Ireland were already under way. As it seemed sensible, where possible, to obtain data for Scotland which could be compared with data for other parts of the United Kingdom, we appointed the same consultants as were already helping them. Along with representatives of the Faculty of Advocates and the Law Society of Scotland, we agreed on procedures for surveys of the structure and income of the two branches of the profession. Both bodies agreed to assist in carrying out the surveys, and the terms of appropriate questionnaires were adjusted and agreed with them.

19.4 From the survey of advocates, we hoped to learn how much they earned at different stages of their professional career, the types of work they undertook, the sources of their income, and the nature and extent of their expenses. We were aware from evidence presented to us that there were particular aspects of advocates' remuneration which gave concern: for example, scarcity of earning opportunity in early years of practice, and considerable delays between performance of work and payment for it. We hoped the survey would shed light on the severity of such problems.

19.5 While we wished to obtain similar information for solicitors, we recognised that, as solicitors largely carry on their business practising together in partnerships and provide many services to clients which advocates do not, it was important to look not only at the individual but also at the practising unit. As well as information about the income, capital and distribution both in size and geographically of legal firms, we hoped to obtain some evidence about the profitability of different classes of legal work and the extent to which some areas of activity were subsidising others.

19.6 Unfortunately, because of the limited response to some of our main surveys and the inadequate records kept by most advocates and solicitors, it was not possible for us to obtain all the information we wished. Accordingly, we tried to acquire some additional information by other methods. We put in hand two further surveys, the first to ascertain the relationship between the fees charged for domestic conveyancing and the time taken to undertake the work, and the second to get some more detailed information about the background and employment of advocates in their early years of practice. A further difficulty arose due to the lack of information on the income of other professions which might be comparable with the self-employed legal profession. We therefore commissioned a report on comparative earnings from our consultants (Appendix 9). Detailed results of the surveys are presented in Appendices to our Report. It should be noted that we do not accept in every case the interpretation of the data offered by the consultants in the various commentaries.

Response to surveys

19.7 The response to our surveys was generally disappointing; and, particularly for solicitors, was too low to justify a high degree of confidence in the results. Comparisons with other information about the attributes of the total population of lawyers and firms indicate that the respondents were generally not a truly representative sample of the profession. Nevertheless, we feel that taken as a whole, the data obtained from the surveys make a valuable addition to our knowledge on many important issues. Furthermore, detailed examination of the data encourages us to believe that we have obtained a generally reliable overall picture of the profession, its structure and earnings, at the survey dates. In the following paragraphs, we draw on this detailed analysis to develop profiles of the advocate and solicitor professions, as well as of the practice units in the solicitor branch. In this way we highlight a number of problems on which we offer comment and recommendations.

19.8 So that we might consider whether any changes in the arrangements for determining fees were desirable, we thought it necessary to examine how fees for different types of work are determined. We looked in particular at pre-fixed fees—for example, scale fees, block fees, and percentage fees, which are a characteristic of many parts of the fees charged by lawyers. We consider the criteria that ought to be used in fixing fees at paragraphs 19.85–19.93 below.

19.9 There are a few matters (notably taxation or adjudication of fees) which arose out of our consideration of the structure and remuneration of the profession on which we felt we should comment. These are considered at the end of this Chapter.

SOLICITORS' EARNINGS

19.10 In this section we discuss various aspects of the way in which solicitors in Scotland engage in their work. As we saw in Chapter 3, solicitors may be employed in a legal capacity by local authorities, central government and in commerce and industry. Others are employed by other solicitors in private practice as qualified assistants. The majority, however, are engaged in private practice as self-employed principals practising either in partnership with other solicitors in firms or as sole practitioners on their own account.

19.11 Solicitors engaged in private practice are usually the first point of client contact with the legal profession. To avoid confusion we use the term 'firm' to describe the outlets through which the private profession provides its service to clients, even though the 'firm' may on occasion be a solicitor practising alone.

19.12 We look first at the profile of a solicitor as an individual; thereafter at the structure of the firm by which legal services are provided; and finally at various problems or difficulties which we consider to be worthy of attention. **As this part of our Report is based on the results of the surveys carried out in 1977, the financial information relates to 1976/77.**

THE SOLICITOR AS AN INDIVIDUAL

19.13 We saw in Chapter 16 how the typical solicitor progressed through his university education and practical professional training. Law students generally received a student grant and in future those studying for the Diploma in Legal Practice will also do so. During his apprenticeship the intending solicitor would be paid a salary. In 1976 and 1977 the Law Society recommended for apprentices a first year salary of £1,150 and a second year salary of £1,350. The average salary paid to apprentices in the year 1976/77 was £1,678.[1]

19.14 When the period of apprenticeship ended the apprentice would apply to the Law Society of Scotland as the Registrar of Solicitors in Scotland for admission as a solicitor. The costs involved in admission totalled just under £50. Although admitted as a solicitor, he could not immediately practise on his own account but was required to undertake an obligatory year of practical training. On admission he therefore sought employment by another solicitor or firm of solicitors as a qualified assistant. About half of the qualified assistants in private practice were located in either Glasgow or Edinburgh. He would most likely remain employed as such for between two and six years during which his salary was about £4,000 per annum (although some assistants earned considerably more than this average figure). During this period, he undertook the normal range of a solicitor's work, although in many firms the young qualified assistant undertook most of the court work. Any solicitor who remained

[1] The present recommended salaries are £1900 for the first year and £2300 for the second.

a qualified assistant in private practice during the whole of his working life was unlikely to achieve high earnings.

19.15 An alternative to employment as a qualified assistant with a private firm was employment in commerce and industry; with a local authority; with a public board; or with central government, including the procurator fiscal service. In central and local government the typical solicitor received a salary greater than in the average firm (see Table 19.1).

TABLE 19.1: Comparative earnings in 1977 of solicitors aged approximately 25–29*

	Salary (£)	*Add* Superannuation and National Insurance paid (£)	Adjusted Earnings (£)	Adjusted Earnings net of tax (£)
Qualified Assistants	3,966	426	4,392	3,538
Legal Group Civil Service	4,372	1,290	5,662	4,693
Local Authority Solicitors	6,616	1,530	8,146	6,526

*Source: Appendix 9, Appendix 'F'.

19.16 After a few years as a qualified assistant in private practice our typical solicitor would seek a position as a salaried partner or as a profit sharing partner, generally in the firm in which he had been working. If he became a full-time salaried partner it was usually between the ages of 25 and 29, and he was unlikely to continue in salaried status much beyond the age of 34. As a salaried partner he earned about £5,300 while he was under 30, rising to over £6,000 in the period over 30. The top earning 10 per cent of those in the 25–29 age group earned £7,000 per annum, although those in the lowest 10 per cent earned only £3,700 per annum. The range of salaries within that age group was from between £2,000 and £3,000 up to £10,000 per annum. After age 30, the range of the salaries of full-time salaried partners was between £4,000 and £12,000.

19.17 We might note here that a salaried partnership is not a necessary step on the road to becoming a profit sharing partner. Much depends on the financial structure of the firm and the terms of the partnership agreement. Most solicitors go straight from being a qualified assistant to becoming a profit sharing partner, although the share of profits which they receive initially may be small. Our typical solicitor became a full profit sharing partner between the ages of 30 and 34 and at this stage was required to contribute to the capital of the firm. He might have done so by drawing a low share of the profits of the firm, or by providing a lump sum obtained by bank loan or from his own resources. From our surveys it appeared that less than 10 per cent of firms required payment for goodwill from their most recently appointed profit sharing partner. We think that the number of firms requiring payment for goodwill may now be dropping further.

19.18 We would also observe that the earnings of profit sharing partners are their appropriate share of the net profits of the firm (that is, the balance of the gross fee income of the firm after deduction of the expenses of running the business). These net profits are not directly comparable with the earnings of salaried persons in legal or other occupations because from these net profits the partner or partners require to make provision for capital to run the business, and for pensions. This is discussed in detail in Appendix 9. Table 19.2 below shows the earnings of profit sharing partners according to their age.

TABLE 19.2: Net profits per full-time profit sharing partner by age group: 1976 and 1977 data*

Age	1976	1977
	£	£
Under 25	Nil	5,700 (1)
25–29	8,500 (43)	7,534 (54)
30–34	9,734 (98)	9,918 (117)
35–39	13,112 (79)	11,644 (63)
40–44	12,700 (83)	13,654 (89)
45–49	13,515 (73)	13,434 (71)
50–54	13,892 (71)	13,276 (73)
55–59	11,634 (71)	14,144 (60)
60–64	11,802 (76)	11,480 (100)
65 and over	10,017 (78)	9,842 (87)

Figures in brackets show number of partners in age group.

*Source: Appendix 7, Part II, Tables 50 and 51

Although these figures do not show a smooth progression, the broad profile of earnings of profit sharing partners which is suggested is that until the age of 50–60 there is a general increase in earnings and that thereafter earnings drop away. It should be noted that a small but increasing number of solicitors become sheriffs, an appointment which is salaried and pensionable. These appointments are in the main from the ranks of profit sharing partners.

TABLE 19.3: Partners' share of net profits in 1976 and 1977*

	1976		1977	
	Number of Partners	Cumulative %	Number of Partners	Cumulative %
£				
Less than 1,000	6	0·9	1	0·1
1,001 — 2,000	1	1·0	2	0·4
2,001 — 3,000	6	1·9	8	1·5
3,001 — 4,000	14	3·9	13	3·2
4,001 — 5,000	22	7·1	23	6·4
5,001 — 6,000	41	13·0	40	11·8
6,001 — 8,000	100	27·5	96	24·7
8,001 — 10,000	123	45·2	128	42·0
10,001 — 12,000	90	58·2	126	59·1
12,001 — 14,000	70	68·4	117	74·9
14,001 — 16,000	63	77·5	60	83·0
16,001 — 18,000	62	86·4	43	88·8
18,001 — 20,000	38	91·9	29	92·7
20,001 — 25,000	42	98·0	39	98·0
More than 25,000	14	100·0	15	100·0
Total number of partners	692		740	
Total number of firms	198		246	
Mean net profit per partner	£11,739		£11,575	

*Source: Appendix 7, Part II, Tables 50 and 51.

19.19 The wide range of profit sharing partners' earnings is reflected in the Table 19.3.

19.20 We next consider net profits by size of legal firm.

TABLE 19.4: Mean net profit per partner by size of firm*

	1 Principal	2–4 Partners	5–9 Partners	10 or more partners
1976	34 firms 34 partners £8,870	115 firms 315 partners £10,977	44 firms 263 partners £12,108	5 firms 80 partners £14,747
1977	62 firms 62 partners £9,431	143 firms 387 partners £11,355	37 firms 230 partners £12,141	4 firms 61 partners £13,012

*Source: Appendix 7, Part II, Tables 50 and 51.

The above Table shows net profits per partner increasing with the size of firm. However, these average figures do not reveal the range of earnings. More detailed information shows that for both the 1976 and 1977 figures the majority of profit sharing partners who earned more than £25,000 were in partnerships of between 2 to 4 partners. A total of 29 partners earned more than £25,000 per annum (2 per cent of the sample): of these, 2 were sole practitioners; 20 were in partnerships of between 2 and 4; 5 were in partnerships of between 5 and 9; and 2 were in partnerships of 10 or more.

19.21 Profit sharing partners, being self-employed persons, have no fixed retirement age. Just over 11 per cent of full-time profit sharing partners in our survey were aged 65 or more.[1] Some solicitors in private practice instead of retiring completely from the firm become consultants to the firm often at a relatively low salary. The mean salary of consultants was just under £3,400 although the range was from under £1,000 up to £14,000.

THE SOLICITOR IN THE FIRM

19.22 Table 19.5 shows the distribution of firms throughout the country at the time of our survey in 1977. The largest number of firms was in the practice size of 2–4 partners (48 per cent); sole practitioner units came next (32 per cent); units with 5–9 partners (16 per cent); and 3 per cent of units had 10 or more partners. One-third of practice units were run by sole practitioners.

Size and structure of firms

19.23 The typical Scottish legal firm practised from one office located in the business centre of a city or town. (In Chapter 15 we discussed the location of offices.) It had three profit sharing partners, one qualified assistant, one apprentice, one unqualified assistant and nine other staff.

19.24 About one firm in four had at least one branch office in addition to its headquarters. We have, incidentally, noted in the course of our work an increas-

[1] In 1976 of 4,877 solicitors on the Roll of Solicitors, 1,179 (24 per cent) were over 60, and of these 849 (17·4 per cent) were aged over 60 and under 70, 272 (5·6 per cent) were over 70 and under 80, and 58 (1·2 per cent) were aged over 80. Not all of them, however, would be working solicitors.

as at November, 1977

Region	Number of firms							No. of Practitioners		Proportion of single-principal firms in region	Number of Solicitors' offices per 10,000 population
	Total	Number of Partners									
		1	2	3	4	5/9	10 or More				
Lothians:											
(a) Edinburgh	153	54	17	19	13	36	14	631		35%	3.9
(b) Other Places	18	7	6	3	1	1	–	39	670	39%	1.8
Strathclyde:											
(a) Glasgow	215	72	39	28	28	38	10	742		33%	2.9
(b) Other Places	180	71	40	24	21	24	–	475	1,217	39%	1.6
Tayside	81	24	21	14	9	13	–		235	30%	2.4
Central	31	6	10	6	3	5	1		104	19%	1.6
Fife	35	10	9	5	9	2	–		93	29%	1.6
Borders	22	4	9	4	2	3	–		63	18%	2.5
Dumfries and Galloway	36	4	17	9	5	1	–		92	11%	3.0
Grampian	96	24	23	15	13	19	2		326	25%	2.5
Highland	34	11	11	5	3	4	–		88	32%	2.2
Western Isles	1	–	1	–	–	–	–		2	(0%)	0.7
Shetland	3	3	–	–	–	–	–		3	(100%)	1.6
Orkney	3	2	1	–	–	–	–		4	(67%)	2.2
Totals	908	292	204	132	107	146	27		2,897	32%	2.3

* Source: Law Society of Scotland (except for final column which required a separate exercise based on 1979 data)

ing number of branch offices being opened in poor outer urban areas. We commend this initiative and would like to see the trend continue. A small branch office makes the lawyer's services more readily accessible to many citizens; and the branch office's access to the resources of the firm's headquarters makes a much wider range of services effectively available than would otherwise be possible. In Chapter 7 we made recommendations for public funds to be available to meet the initial expenses of establishing such offices in areas of unmet legal need.

19.25 Although the size of firms varies over a wide range, we have observed a growing number of larger firms, some of them the result of amalgamations. We expect this trend to continue, so that firms can reap the benefit in improved efficiency of relatively expensive office equipment such as computers, time-recording systems, law retrieval systems and word processors. Larger firms are better able to generate the capital required to instal such equipment (and our recommendation on the incorporation of partnerships should help to make loan finance more readily available). We appreciate that leasing may develop as an alternative to borrowing for capital expenditure; but it will still be the larger firms which are generally able to get the best return from such expenditure by using it more intensively. Another factor pointing to a probable increase in the number of larger firms in future is the likely development of increased specialisation which may require small general practices to enter into liaisons with larger city firms for a variety of particular requirements.

19.26 Although our typical firm had one qualified assistant, 42 per cent of firms had none; their only legally qualified personnel were the partners. The larger the firm, the more likely it was to have qualified assistants.

19.27 The average amount of capital invested in a firm was £41,000, an average per partner of £12,000. Up to about age 40, partners earned substantially more each year than they had invested in the firm, though their capital contribution increased markedly over that period.

TABLE 19.6: Sources of income 1976-77*

	All firms		*Sole Practitioner*		*2–4 Partners*		*5 or more Partners*	
	£	%	£	%	£	%	£	%
Domestic Conveyancing	29,154	34·0	8,303	34·4	22,551	34·9	71,078	33·1
Executry and Trust	18,180	21·2	5,183	21·5	15,244	23·7	41,059	19·1
Court	13,544	15·8	4,734	19·6	9,768	15·1	33,982	15·8
Company (incl. Commercial Conveyancing)	10,025	11·6	1,382	5·7	5,055	7·8	33,569	15·7
Commission on sale of heritable property	5,150	6·0	1,810	7·5	5,045	7·8	9,235	4·3
Other (including all other commissions)	9,789	11·4	2,720	11·3	6,941	10·7	25,688	12·0
	£85,842	100·0	£24,132	100·0	£64,604	100·0	£214,611	100·0
Number of firms	431		100		243		88	
Income per fee earner	£12,624		£10,969		£12,667		£12,125	

*Source: Appendix 7, Part I, Paragraph 605.

Sources of fees

19.28 Table 19.6 shows the sources of solicitors' fee income. The principal sources of income were domestic conveyancing (34 per cent), trust and executry work (21 per cent), court work (16 per cent) and company work (11 per cent). About 60–70 per cent of the average firm's fee income was likely to have come from work done for individual private clients.

19.29 Table 19.7 shows the proportion of their income which firms derived from legal aid. This Table is based on responses from fewer firms than Table 19.5 and in consequence the totals in the two Tables differ. Moreover, 3 out of 4 firms could only give an estimate of the amount of their income which came from legal aid, so the figures must be regarded merely as indicators rather than precise measurements. Perhaps 8–9 per cent of the typical firm's fee income was in respect of work carried out under the legal aid schemes. It is notable that the figure for single-principal firms was roughly double the average.

TABLE 19.7: Legal aid fees earned per firm*

	All Firms £	*Sole Practitioner* £	*2–4 Partners* £	*5 or more Partners* £
Legal Aid Fees for court work	7,185	4,301	5,011	15,324
Other Legal Aid Fees	780	570	763	991
	7,965	4,871	5,774	16,315
Total fee income	91,671	27,496	67,238	208,712
Legal Aid fees as a percentage of firm fee income	8·7%	17·7%	8·6%	7·8%
Number of firms	345	62	206	77

*Source: Appendix 7, Part I, Paragraph 614.

19.30 Some limited information was obtained on the profitability of court practices which were defined as practices thought by their partners to devote more than 40 per cent of their time to court work. This definition is one previously used by the Law Society; but we feel, in retrospect, that it may be too restrictive. Court practices so defined were found to have a higher net income per partner than others as Table 19.8 shows.

TABLE 19.8: Net profit per partner for court and non-court practices*

	1975(£)	1976(£)	1977(£)
Court practices	10,175	11,485	13,039
Non-court practices	9,868	10,883	11,163
All firms	£9,900	£10,956	£11,418

*Source: Appendix 7, Part I, Paragraph 610.

A firm's expenses

19.31 Salaries represent the principal part of a legal firm's expenses: in 1976 gross salaries were 61 per cent of the average firm's expenditure (excluding tax); and this proportion varied little with the size of the firm. The remaining expenditure of firms went on the usual office overheads such as rent, rates, heating, lighting and interest charges; and on stationery, etc..

Profitability

19.32 Table 19.9 shows for 1976 the profitability of firms of different sizes.

TABLE 19.9: Profitability by size of firm 1976*

	All firms £	Sole Practitioner £	2–4 Partners £	5 or more Partners £
Total income	83,251	22,035	63,405	199,900
Total expenditure	47,567	14,097	34,335	117,835
Net profit (before tax, and before charging interest on partners' capital and current accounts)	35,684	7,938	29,070	82,065
Net profit margin	43%	36%	46%	41%
Number of firms responding	432	93	248	91

*Source: Appendix 7, Part I, Paragraph 410.

Although the comparative data we obtained in our survey appeared to show a downward trend in profitability, this may be cyclical rather than a long-term trend. Table 19.9 constrasts vividly with Table 19.13 below: whereas expenses accounted for well over half of solicitors' fee income, they represented only a quarter of advocates' income.

Pensions

19.33 Some solicitors becoming profit sharing partners are required to make goodwill payments. We understand that in some cases goodwill payments by incoming partners have been used by outgoing partners as a method of funding their retiral. We do not think that this is appropriate: there are much more suitable and effective methods of providing for retiral.

19.34 We were able to obtain information about the limited provision made by firms on behalf of their staff. Less than half of firms made any provision for their staff and even those that did, appeared to make inadequate provision. From the information obtained we inferred that most firms had not contracted out of the State earnings-related pension scheme. We **recommend** that firms should make adequate pension provision for their staff. Many firms required to make provision for payment of pensions to retired partners and/or their dependants. The average annual amount of these payments was about £1,500 and if this is the retired person's only source of income other than the flat-rate State pension then we must assume that the provision is inadequate. We **recommend** that firms should make adequate pension provision for partners.

19.35 The foregoing profiles provide a cross-section of the profession and its structure which is useful in considering two questions which seem to us important: the adequacy of solicitors' remuneration, and the relative profitability of different classes of work.

19.36 Firstly, there is the general question whether the remuneration of the profession is adequate in the sense that it supports a sufficient number of solicitors to satisfy the public interest in the supply of legal services. A related question is whether the rate of recruitment to the profession and the retention of recruits are adequate to satisfy likely future needs. Simple means of answering these questions are not readily available; but we have been able to draw on a number of pieces of evidence which, when added together, suggest reasonably firm conclusions.

19.37 At a superficial level, we have found no substantial evidence of a shortage of solicitors, though we are aware of difficulties arising in outlying urban areas and in small, isolated communities about which we make proposals elsewhere. We have also observed that the profession has been expanding fairly rapidly in recent years; and that there is no lack of applicants to study for law degrees, or of graduate lawyers for apprenticeship places. Indeed, the competition for entry to law faculties and for apprenticeship places is extremely strong. Even this evidence, of course, does not necessarily provide a guarantee that future demands for legal services will be satisfactorily met, for we have no means at present of predicting the long term course of demand for solicitors' services. We comment in Chapter 20 on the desirability of a more systematic approach to the forecasting of future needs, at least in broad terms. On the available evidence, however, there is no obvious sign of deficiencies in the general supply of solicitors now, or in the foreseeable future.

19.38 We recognise that one very important factor in determining the rate of new entry to any profession, especially one in which there is a lengthy period of training, is the relationship between remuneration in that profession and in others which might compete with it for new recruits. This introduces the problems of earnings comparisons. Table 19.10 is the comparison made by our consultants and explained fully in their report which appears at Appendix 9. From the Table showing earnings adjusted for capital requirements, pensions and other benefits, we conclude that the Scottish solicitor principal (to which status most of the profession may reasonably aspire) fares reasonably well relative to broadly comparable groups in society. We note, however, that he is marginally less well remunerated than his English counterpart, and our consultants' report suggests that this relationship holds good not only in the middle but also in the upper earnings ranges of the profession. We do not think, however, that this small difference has any great significance; nor do we think it poses any problem for the provision of legal services in Scotland. Assistant and salaried solicitors obviously have much lower rates of remuneration, but since these are for the most part stages on the way to principal status, we think that these rates reflect a reasonable progression.

19.39 One further piece of evidence remains to be introduced. Solicitors, like other professional workers, have lengthy training periods during which their earnings are low or non-existent, and the costs of education and training are incurred. On entry to professional employment, the solicitor may reasonably expect that his earnings will rise as he acquires experience; and that over his working life he will earn at least enough to compensate him for the early lack of earnings and the costs of training. Indeed, the decision to acquire professional training is a form of investment decision which may be expected to yield a reasonable rate of return, just like other types of investment decision. Economists have developed techniques to evaluate this rate of return on education and training investments, and estimates of the return in different occupations have been made. We commissioned a similar exercise using data from the survey of firms; and this further exercise revealed a rate of return for solicitors which is quite high relative to other professions at recent dates.[1] The result suggests that, as matters now stand, the solicitor profession offers attractive net lifetime income prospects; and that some further expansion of the profession would be unlikely to reduce the rate of return to such an extent that it would be unattractive to young people choosing among alternative professional careers.

TABLE 19.10: Median adjusted earnings in 1977*

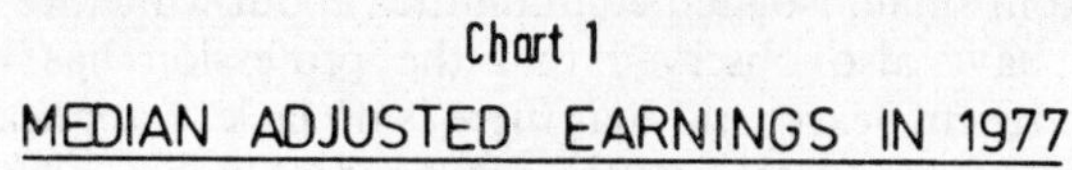

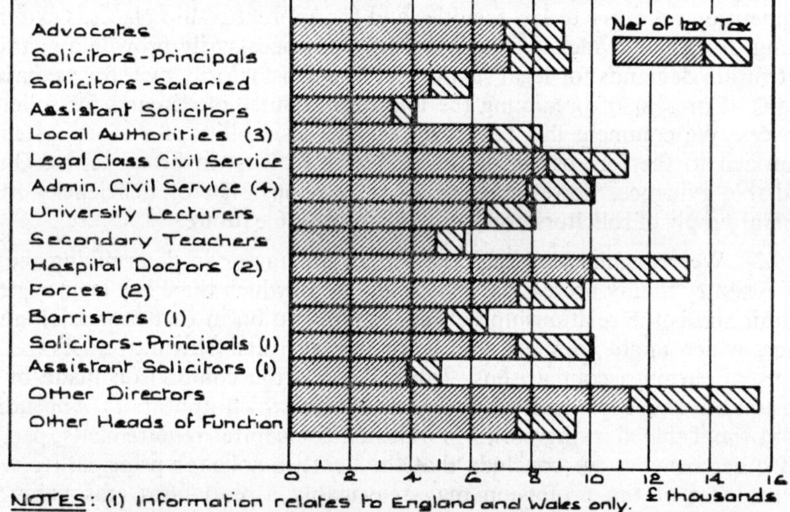

NOTES: (1) Information relates to England and Wales only.
(2) Information relates to the United Kingdom.
(3) Solicitors employed by Local Authorities.
(4) Assumed career pattern after entry as an administration trainee.

*Source: Appendix 9, paragraph 509.

19.40 Accordingly, taking all these points together, we conclude that the remuneration available to the Scottish solicitor is adequate to maintain and, if necessary, increase the size of the profession. In drawing this conclusion, we are not unmindful that some of the changes we propose elsewhere in this Report will have implications for remuneration, and that changes will occur in the need for solicitors' services and in the pattern of their remuneration.

[1] Charles Mulvey: *The Internal Rate of Return to Solicitors and Advocates in Scotland.* Appendix 12.

RELATIVE PROFITABILITY OF DIFFERENT TYPES OF WORK

19.41 As stated in paragraph 19.5 we also hoped to obtain from our surveys reliable information about the extent to which different types of work contribute to the remuneration of solicitors and the profitability of their practices. Although we have seen what proportion of their income solicitors derive from different categories of work, and from legal aid, we have not been able to obtain satisfactory evidence on the relationship between the costs of, and the income obtainable from, different kinds of work. In short, we have to say that we found it impossible to obtain sound information on the relative profitability of different classes of legal activity. This was regrettable, for we had representations from outside the profession alleging that large profits are made from domestic conveyancing, while within the profession many members regarded court work as being inadequately rewarded. We made a number of attempts in discussion with the Law Society to discover a method by which information of the kind we wanted could be obtained; but our proposals were regarded as impracticable or (as in one case) proved to be unacceptable to the profession. The sole area where we were able to make some limited progress was in a survey of domestic conveyancing transactions, a report on which is at Appendix 11. We also comment briefly on this survey later in this Chapter.

19.42 From the lack of evidence available to us, and the obvious difficulties of acquiring information of the kind necessary for our purpose, we can only draw one conclusion—that the vast majority of Scottish legal firms have no soundly-based knowledge of the relative profitability of the different types of work which they undertake. This means that they have no capacity to direct the resources of the firm to types of work in which they had a comparative advantage, which would, in principle, lead to some increase in specialisation and greater efficiency. We hope that our later recommendations with regard to the fixing of fees and taxation, and the use of modern business equipment, will make a contribution to more efficient organisation of firms.

19.43 Until better evidence on these matters is available than we were able to obtain, we can say little about the relative profitability of activities such as conveyancing and court work. We can, however, report on a few strands of information which are indicative rather than conclusive. We have seen that court practices had a higher net income per partner than others. This would suggest that even with the structure of court fees then current, a degree of specialisation enabled above-average net profits to be obtained. Inquiries indicated that solicitors adopted various methods to cope with court work that would otherwise have been unprofitable: for example, it appears common for the correspondent system[1] to be used, whereby one practice instructs another specialist or more conveniently located practice to appear in court, with an agreed sharing of fees between the practices. We see no objection to this, *provided that the client's interests are adequately safeguarded throughout;* and the division of labour involved appears to us to be a sensible adaptation of practice methods leading to increased efficiency.

19.44 A survey of conveyancing alone could not be expected to yield conclusions about relative profitability in the sense of comparing profits from con-

[1] This should be distinguished from the Edinburgh correspondent arrangement which though sharing a common principle has a restrictive element on which we comment in Chapter 15.

veyancing with profits from other types of business. We hoped that the survey would provide factual information on the extent to which scale fees as recommended by the Law Society were adhered to; on the reasons why scale fees were modified in particular cases; and particularly on the hours of work associated with conveyancing transactions over a range of property prices. At the very least, reasonable success in such an exercise would show that it was possible to obtain cost information which could be used to provide a sounder basis for scale fees, if their use is to be continued in future. Additionally, the results might shed some light on the relative profitability of different types of conveyancing transactions, including the extent to which cross-subsidisation between high and low price conveyancing occurs.

19.45 Despite a lower than desirable response rate, we were satisfied that for our purpose we obtained a reasonable cross-section of firms and transactions. The possibility of using a similar method to yield improved cost information seems assured; and there seems no reason why the method should not be extended to other types of business. We **recommend** that any body that may be involved in fee-fixing should consider the adoption and development of this approach, since we believe that if pre-fixed fees are to be used they must be based on sound cost information (see paragraphs 19.98 and 19.99).

19.46 Although the results of the conveyancing survey are set out in Appendix 11, some brief comment on the results is relevant here. Firstly, it emerged clearly that the total costs to a client engaging in the purchase or sale of a property are substantial. The average bill for a sale was £544, and for a purchase £478: these figures relate to an average property price of £17,200 for sales, and £16,800 for purchases. Simultaneous sale and purchase of houses (which is common) would thus result in a solicitor's bill of over £1,000 on average properties. But of this total, only about 45 per cent is due to the transfer, completion of missives and mortgage work, the remainder being accounted for by VAT, unavoidable outlays including stamp duty and (in sales) commission.

19.47 Secondly, the survey indicated clearly that there was a close relationship between the Law Society's recommended scale fees and the fees actually levied by solicitors for transfer of property, by far the most important element in the solicitor's conveyancing fee. Both for sales and for purchases the average charge for transfer work was slightly below the recommended scale fee. This would suggest that on average solicitors tend to modify charges down from the scale, though exceptions in the other direction exist. The most common instances of downward modification were where the client was buying and selling simultaneously or where the solicitor was acting for buyer and seller. The scale fee, then, appears to be the dominant influence on solicitors' conveyancing charges.

19.48 That being so, it is vitally important that the scale fee should be fair both to solicitor and client. The scale fee for transfers of property has a minimum charge of £100 for properties under £5,000: thereafter the fee rises by £10 for every £1,000 of property price. We might expect that as the price of property rises there would be a gradual rise in the time devoted by the solicitor to the transaction. This would conform to the progression of the scale fee, though one might also expect higher price transactions to reflect an element of greater responsibility. Such an element, however, should probably be small, for the essence of the solicitor's function is assurance of a good title which is as important to the client buying a £5,000 house as to one buying a £25,000 house. In practice, our evidence shows no clear correlation between hours of work on the transaction and property price (see Appendix 11, Table 11). From this point of view, the basis of the scale is unsound.

19.49 Furthermore, when the transfer charges (which we know are based primarily on the scale fees) are converted to an hourly basis (Appendix 11, Table 12), we find that the average charge per hour for properties over £25,000 is almost 70 per cent higher than that for properties under £25,000. This, together with other evidence (see for example, Appendix 11, Figure 4), would seem to indicate clear cross-subsidisation from high price to low price property transactions. In other words, the profit margin on higher priced transactions, based on fee-earners' hours as a measure of cost, is much higher than that on lower priced transactions. For reasons given later in this Chapter we think that cross-subsidisation is undersirable; and to the extent that this cross-subsidisation derives directly from the Law Society's recommended scales, we can only conclude that, as presently constructed, it does not operate in the public interest. The present evidence is based on a small sample and to that extent our conclusions must be qualified. We would welcome further inquiries of this kind to provide better information. We should also point out that although the evidence points to cross-subsidisation *within* conveyancing, it does not allow us to say anything about the extent of cross-subsidisation from conveyancing to other types of transaction. It is still possible that clients engaging in lower price conveyancing transactions, though benefiting from a subsidy deriving from high price transactions, may be in turn subsidising clients with other types of business.

19.50 In the light of our inability to obtain satisfactory information about relative profitability, we considered it worthwhile to mount a small statistical exercise based on the data from the remuneration survey of firms. This involved the use of multiple regression analysis, the purpose of which in this case was to seek to explain variations in relative profitability (net profit before tax and interest) per profit sharing partner, in terms of a number of characteristics of the firms. A number of alternative formulations were agreed with the Law Society's statistical consultants, who undertook the necessary calculations and reported the results to us. The results were not altogether satisfactory in statistical terms, since only about half the variation in profitability was accounted for. However, we were able to draw the following *tentative* conclusions:

(1) that capital invested per partner was a powerful influence on profitability;

(2) that, less firmly, conveyancing, commercial work and court work were a positive influence on profitability;

(3) that trust and executry work, and legal aid, tended to have a depressing effect on profits;

(4) that larger firms (those with more partners) had some tendency to show greater profitability; and

(5) that after allowing for other variations of circumstance (size, capital, composition of business), Edinburgh and Glasgow firms showed no greater profitability, and possibly even less, than other firms: in other words, their access to concentrations of population and commercial work is apparently offset by higher expenses.

We must stress that these conclusions are by no means firm; and, indeed, we report them here only because of the dearth of other information. Nevertheless, the results are on the whole compatible with common assumptions regarding profitability, and they are broadly consistent with our earlier findings on court work and conveyancing.

19.51 The fact remains, however, that this evidence falls far short of what we needed to reach conclusions on the relative profitability of different types of legal work, and the effects of specialisation. To say the least, we find it surprising that a profession which prides itself on being a general adviser to the public in matters of business should have such a poorly developed system of cost and income analysis; and we would wish to see immediate steps taken to improve this situation. Nor is this a matter which is of interest to the profession alone. We believe that a better understanding of costs, fee income and profits would lead to improved organisation in solicitors' firms, which would in the long run be to the public advantage. It would also provide essential information on these matters to those concerned with the setting of various types of legal fees, advising on fee structure, or otherwise regulating legal charges in the public interest: this is of particular importance in those areas where the solicitor has a legal monopoly for certain types of transaction and where fees are paid from public funds. We make recommendations on these lines later in this Chapter.

ADVOCATES' REMUNERATION

Profile of the advocate

19.52 The profile which we give in this part of this Chapter is based on information we obtained from two sources. Firstly, we had a survey carried out on our behalf in 1977 in which a questionnaire was sent to all practising advocates; and, secondly, we undertook a survey of advocates admitted to the Faculty of Advocates in the period 1975–78.[1] **The financial data in the main survey related to the fiscal year ended on 5 April 1976 and the remuneration figures which we mentioned are, therefore, for that period.**

19.53 There are no age limits on entry to the Bar in Scotland; and, from our surveys, the typical (median) newly admitted advocate was age 27. The ages of those called ranged from 24 to more than 31 (in some years very much more) so that the average (mean) age on entry was 28. This is shown in Table 19.11.

TABLE 19.11: Advocates admitted in 1975–78*

Age on Admission	Number	%
23–24	8	20
25–26	11	27
27–28	13	32
29–30	3	7
31+	6	15
	41	100

*Source: Appendix 10, Table 2.

[1] Appendix 8.

19.54 Before deciding to come to the Bar the prospective advocate would have to assess the financial implications. He would have to find funds to meet:

		1976	1979
(a)	the cost of providing himself with court dress, say	£130	£380
(b)	the entry fees to the Faculty of Advocates, although these could be paid over a number of years	£356	£365
(c)[1]	living expenses for a period of at least 9 months while he was devilling	£260	£370
(d)[1]	living expenses for possibly two years after he was called, because there would inevitably be some period before he could show his paces and be properly employed; and even when he became employed, there might be a period of up to a year before he was paid for the work he had done	£900	£1300
(e)	his annual fee to the Faculty of Advocates, which depended on the seniority of the advocate. In the first year of practice this was	£30	£40
(f)	dues to Faculty Services Limited which were a percentage of the fees paid to him through Faculty Services Limited	*	*
(g)	professional indemnity insurance premiums for at least the compulsory insured figure of £25,000	£25	£30
(h)	a contribution to the Advocates Widows' Fund, on average	£4.77	£9.19

The total of these expenses largely depended on the style in which the advocate lived; but, taking as a minimum figure the supplementary benefit figures for subsistence, an advocate who was admitted to the Faculty in April 1976 required to have available a sum of approximately £1,700 (in April 1979, the sum would be approximately £2,500). In the calculation we have ignored any fees he may have received and any percentage payment due to Faculty Services Limited. There were no grants available to the prospective advocate while he was devilling and the Faculty had only £1,000 per year available to make loans. He had, therefore, to finance the foregoing expenses either from savings, private resources, other earnings or loans. He may decide to qualify and work as a solicitor and save to enable him to cover the expenses and the initial period of low earning.

19.55 Gross fees for our typical advocate during the first three years at the Bar averaged £3,144 per annum. He would probably try to supplement this fee income by seeking out additional sources of income, such as law reporting or tutoring. His average annual expenses were £1,072 or about one-third of his gross fees. The position is clearly shown in Tables 19.12 and 19.13.

[1] The estimates for living expenses relate to a period of 2 years and 9 months from July 1973 to April 1976 and July 1976 to April 1979. The estimates are based on the appropriate rate of supplementary benefit for a single person and are purely for illustrative purposes.

* The percentage payable is revised annually—at the present time it is 7%. A further 4½% is collected by Faculty Services Limited for the running expenses of the Faculty.

TABLE 19.12: Advocates' average expenses 1975–76*

	Faculty Services Limited £	Faculty Rates £	Telephones etc. £	Travel £	Premium for Professional Indemnity £	Other £	Total £
QCs	1,370	237	353	493	59	1,106	3,618
Juniors							
9–15 years	1,239	170	423	504	28	1,347	3,711
4–8 years	678	107	285	387	6	592	2,055
3 or less years	244	31	120	340	5	332	1,072
Overall	£1,049	£163	£341	£456	£29	£989	£3,027

*Source: Appendix 8, paragraph 38.

TABLE 19.13: Advocates' expenses as a percentage of gross fees 1975–76*

	Average Gross Fees £	Faculty Services Limited %	Faculty Rates %	Telephone %	Travel %	Premium for Professional Indemnity %	Other %	Total %
QCs	16,038	9	1	2	3	0·4	7	22·4
Juniors								
9–15 years	13,086	10	1	3	4	0·2	10	28·2
4–8 years	6,481	11	2	4	6	0·1	9	32·1
3 or less years	3,144	7	1	4	11	0·2	10	33·2
Overall	£11,395	9%	1%	3%	4%	0·3%	9%	26·3%

*Source: Appendix 8, paragraph 40.

19.56 The net annual incomes (gross fees less expenses) of young advocates in their first three years ranged widely. The top 25 per cent earned more than £3,830, the typical (median) advocate £2,132, while the bottom 25 per cent earned £425 or less. The average (mean) was £2,024.

19.57 In his first three working years the young advocate probably devoted over 60 per cent of his time to divorce work; about 16 per cent to reparation work; and the remainder to a variety of different matters. During the first few years of practice he would undertake four or five speculative actions a year.

19.58 After the advocate had been called for about three years, he would be receiving a reasonable flow of fees but continuing to suffer from the lag between carrying out work and being paid for it. Although this was a particular problem in the early and low earning years, it remains a problem throughout the working lifetime of the advocate. It affects the tax position of senior advocates who take up salaried appointments but continue to receive payments of fees from their previous practice. The problem arises partly because an advocate does not normally submit his fee note until after he has completed the work, and partly because there is a delay of about a year in payment of his fees whether from private sources or the legal aid fund. The position is shown in Table 19.14.

19.59 After about 12 years at the Bar as a junior our typical advocate would consider whether he should apply for silk (that is, become a senior or QC). If he did, as we noted in Chapter 15, he gave up dealing with most of the preliminary work in a case, such as the drafting of the papers setting out his client's case, and appearances in court at the procedural stages. He would be much more dependent on his abilities to deal with a case in court, examining witnesses or arguing the merits of the case. He had, of course, to assess the risks involved in giving up one form of practice to take up another. If a junior of some years seniority did not wish to become a QC either because of his limited prospects, or for reasons of personal preference, he would leave the practising Bar, probably by applying to be appointed as a sheriff or by seeking some other similar appointment.

TABLE 19.14: Average period of delay between work and collection of fees*

Type of work	Period
Criminal Legal Aid	10 months
Civil Legal Aid	14 months
Civil Non-Legal Aid	9 months
Overall	12 months

*Source: Appendix 8, paragraph 71.

19.60 The average (mean) net annual income for a QC in 1975/76 was £11,713 with the top 25 per cent earning £13,147 or more, the median £10,502, and the bottom 25 per cent £8,514 or less.

19.61 We hope that the profile that we have given of our typical advocate derived from our remuneration and other surveys will be helpful, in particular to lay readers of our Report. One conclusion clearly emerged. The pressures of maintaining an active practice at the senior Bar impose a strain on the advocate which probably makes it difficult to continue even to age 60. There are hardly any practising advocates over the age of 55. By that age nearly all have taken up full-time salaried appointments, mainly as judges of the supreme and sheriff courts, chairmen of tribunals or academics, and a few may have left the profession of law entirely. The salaries payable in the main judicial full-time appointments are noted in Table 19.15.

TABLE 19.15: Salaries payable in judicial full-time appointments open to advocates*

	April 1976 £	April 1979 £	April 1980 £
Lord President	20,425	29,849	34,000
Lord Justice Clerk	19,300	27,730	31,000
Other Supreme Court Judges	16,675	24,786	28,500
Sheriff Principal of Glasgow and Strathkelvin	14,500	19,590	21,000
Sheriff Principal (elsewhere)	13,500	19,040	21,000
Chairman, Scottish Land Court	13,500	19,040	21,000
Sheriff A	13,000	18,015	19,500
Sheriff B	11,210	16,656	18,750
Sheriff C	10,000	14,215	15,600

*Source: Scottish Courts Administration.

Pensions for judges and sheriffs are favourable, non-contributory and, like those of others in the public service, index-linked to take account of inflation. There is a compulsory retiring age of 75 years for supreme court judges; but they can retire voluntarily at age 70 or after having completed 15 years service, and are then eligible for a lump sum payment equal to twice the annual amount of pension. Sheriffs Principal and sheriffs are obliged to retire at age 72 but may retire voluntarily at age 65. They are eligible for the same lump sum payments. Members of the judiciary may retire before the stipulated ages, with appropriate proportionate benefits being payable at the age at which the pension would normally have become payable.

Sources of fee income

19.62 We have been largely unable to ascertain the contribution made by different types of work to advocates' total income. Advocates' records do not permit any such analysis, and our consultants found that 82 per cent of advocates who responded to our survey had to estimate the breakdown shown in Table 19.16. The fees received through Faculty Services Limited are analysed in more detail in Table 19.17, which shows the heavy dependence of the junior Bar on civil legal aid work (mainly divorce).

TABLE 19.16: Sources of fees 1975–76*

	1975/76 Total Gross Fees of those responding £	*QCs Total Gross* £	%	*Juniors Total Gross* £	%
Criminal Legal Aid	53,762	9,408	3	44,354	10
Criminal Non-Legal Aid	16,670	4,194	1	12,476	3
Civil Legal Aid	151,371	20,518	6	130,853	29
Civil Non-Legal Aid	446,235	230,739	65	215,496	47
Miscellaneous fees	11,107	9,108	3	1,999	1
Total through Faculty Services Limited	679,145	273,967	78	405,178	90
Advocates depute or part-time procurators fiscal	41,408	22,038	6	19,370	4
Other fees	86,712	56,827	16	29,885	6
	128,120	78,865	22	49,255	10
	£807,265	£352,832	100	£454,433	100

*Source: Appendix 8, paragraph 30.

Pensions

19.63 Of advocates who responded to our survey, 60 per cent were making no pension provision; among QC's the proportion was 40 per cent. Even fewer advocates took out sickness insurance. The failure to make pension provision may be partly explained by advocates' good prospects of entering salaried employment before reaching retirement age. The time lag in receiving fees may mean that advocates use outstanding fees as a form of insurance.

TABLE 19.17: Fees received through Faculty Services Ltd in 1975/76*

	Legal Aid				Non-Legal Aid		Total Received
	Criminal £	*Civil* £	*Total* £	%	£	%	£
QCs	9,408	20,518	29,926	10·9	244,041	89·1	273,967
Juniors							
9–15 years	25,599	81,251	106,850	40·4	157,765	59·6	264,615
4–8 years	18,119	43,338	61,457	47·5	68,024	52·5	129,481
3 or less years	636	6,264	6,900	62·3	4,182	37·7	11,082
	44,354	130,853	175,207	43·2	229,971	56·8	405,178
	£53,762	£151,371	£205,133	30·2	£474,012	69·8	£679,145

*Source: Appendix 8, paragraph 33.

Adequacy of advocates' remuneration

19.64 From the information which we have obtained, and which is reflected in the profile we have given of an advocate's career, it appears that in the early years of his career an advocate has to bear certain costs, reflected partly by a lack of income, which are much greater than those of his counterpart in the solicitors' branch and in other professions. We have already commented, in relation to solicitors, on the significance of these costs in comparing earnings in different occupations—a comparison which no doubt plays some part in the choice made by young people to enter one profession or another. Just as we were able to obtain an estimate of the rate of return to the investment in training to be a solicitor, so we used data from the advocates' survey to obtain a rate of return for advocates.[1] This turned out to be significantly lower than that for solicitors, but still a little higher than for engineers and scientists, for example. The result tended to confirm our concern about the possible effects of this financial disincentive to enter the advocate branch of the legal profession. In practice, however, the low initial income, and the relatively low rate of return on training, do not appear to be discouraging entry, or reducing the size of the profession. Indeed, the numbers in full-time practice at the Bar have increased in recent years as we have seen; and the rate of entry of new advocates has also been rising.

19.65 We were aware, and were concerned, that in recommending the transfer of divorce jurisdiction to the sheriff court we would add to the financial difficulties facing new advocates, since much of their limited income derives from divorce work. However, we understand that this process is already under way, in that since the introduction of the affidavit procedure for undefended divorces some divorce work is already going to more experienced juniors rather than recently admitted advocates. To some extent the loss of this work may be alleviated by our proposals to extend the availability of legal aid. This might generate extra work in the Court of Session in other types of litigation, a proportion of which might be expected to fall to junior advocates. It may also be that new areas of work will develop at the Bar or that demand for greater specialist knowledge will result in greater recourse to advocates.

[1] See Appendix 12.

19.66 If, on the other hand, there is no expansion in the work which advocates do, many junior advocates are going to have an even more difficult time than those whose income was reflected in our profile. Increased competition at the lower end of the Bar may not simply mean that only the strongest and best advocates remain in the profession; it could be that only those with sufficient financial resources of their own would be able to last the course. We doubt whether the latter eventuality would be in the long-term interests of the profession; but another possible outcome might be that the age of entry would rise further with new members usually having had a number of years experience as solicitors. This we think could well be an advantage.

19.67 We are in no doubt, however, that monitoring of entry to the Bar in the next few years will be important, particularly as advocates have access to the most senior judicial appointments. We therefore **recommend** that the Legal Services Advisory Committee, which we propose in Chapter 20, should keep the position under continuing review.

Payment of counsel's fees

19.68 Another matter which concerned us was the time lag after work has been undertaken before payment is received by the advocate. This problem persists throughout the career of advocates and in a period of inflation inevitably has an adverse effect on the income of advocates. This is particulary serious in legal aid matters when no payment is made until the legal aid authority is satisfied about the accounts rendered by the solicitor as well as the advocate. This is a matter which has been exercising the Faculty of Advocates for a number of years, but a satisfactory solution has not yet been found. While we accept that there are sometimes difficulties in establishing what exactly is owed to counsel by way of fees, we can see no reason why payment in full, or some payment to account, should not be made before the solicitor's account is received and approved. We therefore **recommend** that this should be done. Indeed, when our revised proposals for legal aid are implemented, solicitors themselves will normally accept responsibility for the need to instruct counsel and, if need be, to justify such action to the legal aid authority paying the account. If, after the event, the legal aid authority considers the payment to counsel unreasonable it can dispute the payment to counsel.

Advocates' outlays

19.69 An advocate normally meets his travelling and accommodation expenses in a case from his fees. The Faculty have not proposed any change in this as they say that it allows the advocate to decide himself the level of the expenses which he should incur. We believe, however, that it would help to establish a more realistic approach to the determination of fees, particularly for the more junior Bar, if expenses were a separate charge on the client. We are sure that a guide as to what constituted a reasonable level of expenses could be prepared by the Faculty to cover normal circumstances. We therefore **recommend** that advocates' outlays should be charged separately from fees.

FEES

19.70 The basic principle on which all fees are based is understood, at least in theory, to be that they should be fair and reasonable. One of our major difficulties, however, has been to ascertain the methods used in practice to calculate fees.

19.71 In the legal profession there are two main types of fees—those for litigation work known as judicial fees, and those for advice and the preparation of documents, termed non-judicial fees. For solicitors, the difference is that court fees are fixed in Tables laid down under statute whereas non-judicial fees are not prescribed, although some guidance may be given by the Law Society or from the practice of auditors of court. Ultimately, however, the fee to be charged for any particular piece of work can be determined by the court as, in any action to recover a fee, the court will have to be satisfied before granting a decree that the fee charged is fair and reasonable.

19.72 The fees payable to advocates are not subject to any statutory tables, and there are no scales of fees except an informal one for certain classes of legal aid work which is used as a guide by the legal aid taxation staff (see paragraph 19.76 below). We understand that this informal scale is sometimes used as a guide for charges for non-legal aid business. An advocate's fee for any piece of work is agreed between him (or by his clerk on his behalf) and the solicitor instructing him or the legal aid fund, but it is always subject to possible audit by the auditor of court.

19.73 The fees chargeable by solicitors for work in civil courts are laid down in Acts of Sederunt (subordinate legislation made by the judges in the Court of Session). There are two sets of Acts of Sederunt, one relating to the Court of Session and the other to the sheriff courts. The Lord President of the Court of Session, as the senior judge, has on behalf of the other judges the main responsibility in regulating fees; and to assist him he has recently set up an advisory committee which is chaired by one of the judges. Acts of Sederunt for sheriff courts require to be laid before Parliament and are subject to its negative resolution procedure, while those relating to the Court of Session come into operation with the authority of the Court itself. We understand that the effect of this court fee regulating procedure is that an element of indirect governmental control exists over the fees that can be charged.

19.74 One particular feature of civil court procedure is that the award of expenses against the loser normally follows success; that is, the successful party is entitled to have his opponent pay the legal fees and outlays necessarily incurred by him in connection with the action. This means that the fees payable in this way by the losing party are usually subject to the process known as taxation, or audit, and this check is normally done by the auditor of the court in which the case was heard, subject to right of appeal to the court itself.

19.75 For general work in the criminal courts there is no table of fees prescribing the charges to be made by solicitors. For work carried out under criminal legal aid, however, fees have been prescribed and are laid down in various Acts of Adjournal (the equivalent in criminal matters of Acts of Sederunt) made by the judges in the High Court of Justiciary. These lay down the fees payable to those participating in the duty solicitor schemes and the range of fees for other criminal work paid under legal aid.

Checking legal aid fees

19.76 In all legal aid matters the fees claimed are submitted to the legal aid taxation staff who assess what fee is to be paid taking account of any fees laid down in the court tables. If any adjustment that they propose is not acceptable to the solicitor or advocate, and if negotiation fails to reach an agreed fee, then the fee will be referred to the appropriate auditor of court for determination. We understand, however, that not many cases require to be decided by an auditor and that usually the figure proposed by the legal aid staff is accepted—though not always with equanimity.

Law Society's table of fees

19.77 Fees for advice and general business undertaken by solicitors are normally charged in accordance with a table of fees approved by the Law Society. This 'Table of Fees for Conveyancing and General Business' sets out the recommended charges for professional services provided by solicitors in Scotland, and it is applicable to all legal work except in so far as fees are otherwise prescribed by statute. The range of work covered by the Table encompasses the drafting of deeds of all kinds, advice, conveyancing, trust and executry work, partnerships and incorporation of companies, the sale, purchase or lease of property and the handling of cash for clients.

19.78 Notwithstanding the recommended charges, the Law Society's Table of Fees provides that a solicitor may enter into a special charging agreement with his client which may take the form of a total fee or a rate per hour. Solicitors are obliged, however, to quote only the fee recommended in the Law Society's Table to any prospective client who is not an established client of the firm. We have reason to believe this is not always observed, and in any case we recommend in Chapter 6 that this restriction should be abolished.

19.79 Where there is a dispute, the fee payable is normally determined by the auditor of court. The auditors in the sheriff courts are normally sheriff clerks or members of the court staff, while in the Court of Session there is a separate office of auditor which has its own staff. We discuss who should adjudicate on fees at paragraphs 19.118–19.122 below.

19.80 From the above very brief summary it is clear that a number of persons and bodies are presently involved in fixing different fees. It has, however, proved a difficult task to find out the basis on which prescribed and recommended fees are calculated. In many cases the bases on which these fees had originally been fixed are unclear. There have been various updating exercises, but in some cases these simply involved a percentage addition to take account of changes in the law or procedure and the passage of time, particularly in recent years of high inflation.

Pre-fixed fees

19.81 So far as we can ascertain, the original basis for many fees in court tables and Law Society Tables was laid down many years ago. In times of low inflation only occasional minor amendments had to be made. The phenomenon of high inflation, and the adjustments that have been made to reflect this, have brought into question the whole basis on which fees have been historically fixed. In some areas of work, however, such as conveyancing and trust and executry work, the solicitor may to some extent be protected from the effects of such inflation since the value of the property on which his fee is based will have risen (see paragraph 9.67). In the middle 1970s the Law Society had to satisfy the Price Commission before certain changes could be made in the

Table of Fees. This required them to obtain certain information from the profession. Sufficient information was obtained for the purposes of the Price Commission but this was of limited value in determining whether particular fees for specified work were appropriate. The basic problem seemed to be that the Society did not have, and could not obtain from the profession, proper information about the time taken to complete different types of business and hence about the costs of such business. This was largely because the profession, with very few exceptions, did not keep records of time spent on different transactions. Such recording takes time and can be expensive to maintain manually, and the very existence of Tables prescribing fees often made time and costing records seem unnecessary. We expressed our concern to the Law Society at their inability to provide us with evidence to justify the figures in their Table of Fees. They informed us that they have been trying to obtain more information about the cost of carrying out different types of work but so far without success.

19.82 The Lord President's advisory committee on court fees told us that they tried to take account of various factors when recommending adjustments in the court tables of fees. They do not, however, have the resources to undertake the investigations which we think necessary to arrive at a proper table of fees for court work.

19.83 The Auditor of the Court of Session is not involved in the determination of any pre-fixed fees. He informed us that in adjudicating on particular fees he tries to take into account the market forces prevailing in salaries and overheads, but again we feel that although he has a long practical experience he does not have the resources needed for a systematic review of these matters.

19.84 We are in no doubt that if pre-determined fees for lawyers' business are to be maintained, any person or body who fixes such fees, whether judicial or non-judicial, mandatory or recommended, should know and be able to demonstrate what it costs to do the work, so that the fees can be seen to be charged on a proper basis. We are encouraged by our limited conveyancing exercise, discussed earlier (19.44–19.49), to believe that substantial progress on this matter can be made.

Factors which determine fees

19.85 In the Law Society's Table of Fees there are types of work where no specific fee is recommended and the fee is to be 'according to circumstances'. In such a situation a number of factors have to be taken into account in determining the appropriate fee. These factors are similar to those taken into account by the Auditor of the Court of Session, by the Faculty of Advocates, by the Taxing Masters in England and, subject to some variations, by the appropriate authorities in many other countries. We have no doubt that the factors in question are relevant in ascertaining what is to be a proper fee. There does not, however, appear to be any criterion to determine the emphasis which should be placed on each factor in any particular case. The factors as stated by the Law Society are:

(a) The importance of the matter to the client.

(b) The amount or value of any money or property involved.

(c) The complexity of the matter or the difficulty or novelty of the question raised.

(d) The skill, labour, specialised knowledge and responsibility involved on the part of the solicitor or assistant.

(e) The time expended.

(f) The length, number and importance of any documents or other papers prepared or perused.

(g) The place where, and the circumstances in which, the services or any part thereof are rendered, including the degree of expedition required.

19.86 We are agreed that time is an important factor and that in all cases it should be used as the base factor. We are, however, aware that there are cases where the time factor may be very minor and where other factors might be particularly important. The weight to be given to the various factors is to our minds a question of judgment.

19.87 Fees should be related to the cost of carrying on an advocate's or solicitor's practice and overall should be such as to provide an adequate supply of advocates and solicitors, remunerated in a way which properly reflects the skill, training, work, risk and responsibility involved. A system taking into account all the elements involved in providing a service would be the fairest way of remunerating the profession and of charging the client. The elements should include the overheads involved in providing the services and the qualifications and experience of the person undertaking the work subject to these being appropriate and necessary.

19.88 How can this be done in practice? We take the view that in assessing the fees of a solicitor or of an advocate there should be two main factors. Firstly, 'time' which should be embodied in an hourly cost rate reflecting the cost of undertaking a particular type of work in a particular case with reasonable efficiency; and, secondly, a sum reflecting 'skill and knowledge, responsibility and special attention'. The first of these we may call the base factor, and the second the supplementary factor.

The base factor

19.89 The hourly cost rate should be set to a rate to cover the cost of a reasonable 'salary' for a solicitor or employee of the grade necessary to undertake the work, plus a share of the direct and indirect overheads attributable to that person; and it should include an element of profit to reflect a return on the capital necessarily involved in running the practice. Such cost rates might vary for different types of work, and from district to district depending on local factors; and we see no objection to this.

The supplementary factor

19.90 The supplementary factor should vary according to the professional skill and responsibility of the person carrying out the work and would have regard to the elements 'skill and knowledge, responsibility and special attention'. Where the work is carried out with particular skill and knowledge or responsibility, or most expeditiously, then the supplementary factor should be higher; where these elements are limited, or absent, the factor should be less or nil.

19.91 It would also be important to ensure that the person undertaking the job is not too highly skilled for the work being undertaken: the hourly rate and the supplementary factor should always be based on a person of the appropriate grade undertaking the work.

Effect of new system

19.92 This system, if properly developed, would be very competitive. The effect of proper pricing would be to encourage firms to adopt good practices which would enable them to compete and to organise their business efficiently; and there should be consequential reductions in fees. It may be argued that such a method of fixing fees could lead to fees for work at the lower end of the market, such as low-price conveyancing transactions and other small matters of business, becoming so high as to make such work too expensive for the client. This might arise because the skill and training of the solicitors made it uneconomic for their degree of expertise to be employed below a certain figure. We do not think that this is a serious risk since such cases would involve little time on the part of high cost fee earners, or they might be catered for by firms adjusting their staffing to deal with this kind of business. We accept, however, that this is a matter which ought to be kept under review by the Legal Services Advisory Committee which we recommend in Chapter 20. It would be for this body to consider whether a service so affected might be more economically provided in some of the other ways suggested in Chapter 7.

19.93 Our proposals mean that solicitors and advocates must keep better records than they do at the present time. The proven use of modern business equipment in this field, including computers and time recording systems, makes the keeping of such records not only possible but simple. So far as we are aware, there are in Scotland at the present time no advocates and very few solicitors' firms who have any form of time recording which is related to cost rates and which would be adequate to enable fees to be calculated on the basis we have described. This compares unfavourably with the situation in England where much more extensive use of such systems is made. We recognise that computers and other equipment will have costs, but machines are becoming cheaper, economies in expensive staff time may be made, and above all they should enable greater efficiency and better forms of financial control to be achieved. This can only lead to the long term advantage of the lawyer's client.

The case for pre-fixed fees

19.94 If all fees were to be calculated as we would prefer, there would be no need for any pre-fixed fees. Nevertheless, it may be some time before our cost rate approach to charging could be implemented in every firm; and, indeed, there might be other advantages in retaining some of the present pre-fixed fees. We have, therefore, examined the arguments for and against such fees to see whether any could usefully be retained and, if so, in what form.

19.95 Pre-fixed fees may take one of four forms:

(i) one fee prescribed for an individual item of work, such as 'serving summons on defender';

(ii) a block fee for whatever work is involved to complete a stage in an action, such as 'a series of steps in a court action';

(iii) a scale fee, such as that for conveyancing; and

(iv) percentage fees, such as those for executry work.

19.96 The main assertions made in favour of pre-fixed fees are these:

(a) potential clients know what fees will be charged;

(b) the advocate or solicitor can more readily quote what the fee for a piece of work will be;

(c) in court cases, a litigant will have some idea of his possible liability for fees to be paid to the other side if he loses;

(d) in professional areas of business, maintenance of standards requires that competition should be on quality of service and not on the fee charged for that service; and

(e) the small client is protected by a pre-fixed fee from being exploited.

Against pre-fixed fees it is argued that:

(a) cross-subsidisation between different areas of work (eg conveyancing and court), or between different categories of work within the same area (eg lower-priced and higher-priced houses), may be built in, with the effect that some clients are paying more than they should in order to reduce prices for others;

(b) only rarely will a pre-fixed fee applied to a particular matter be fair to both the lawyer and the client, whether the pre-fixed fee is a maximum, a minimum or a norm;

(c) they tend not to be susceptible to change in line with changed circumstances, particularly in times of high inflation;

(d) the appropriate fee for each piece of work is always a matter of judgement in the light of the circumstances and fixed fees do not recognise this;

(e) a national scale is unlikely to be fair or correct everywhere; and

(f) a pre-fixed fee does not easily reflect the experience or ability of the persons doing the work.

These points are not invariably argued in the direction we have indicated. For example, there are those who think it a merit of pre-fixed fees that they permit in-built cross-subsidisation.

19.97 We are quite clear that cross-subsidisation should be avoided, not only as between categories of work but within a single category. Pre-fixed fees should not be adopted with this end in view.

19.98 Our principal objection to pre-fixed fees, no matter how accurately established, is that they are only fair and reasonable charges in the exceptional case. While this does not matter to the solicitor, who will be correctly remunerated over a total of 100 cases, for example, it does matter to each of the 100 clients who pay only once. Those with comparatively simple cases will pay too much, subsidising those with more difficult cases. Our second objection to pre-fixed fees is that, as presently constituted, there is no evidence that they are based on sound information as to the proper costs of the business they cover.

19.99 If these objections could be overcome, we think there would be advantage, at least for the next few years, in maintaining pre-fixed fees in appropriate areas of business. Such a policy would provide guidance for solicitors and clients alike while the development of time recording and other business methods is taking place; and, indeed, we think this approach would help to get a cost rate based system of fee-charging off the ground. To get round our objections, two criteria would need to be satisfied. Firstly, any pre-fixed fees should be set as maxima and should be promulgated by a statutory independent legal fees body with membership representative of the profession, court auditors, and laymen (possibly including an accountant, a statistician and an economist). This body should be appointed by the Secretary of State and should take over from the Lord President responsibility for court fees, though it should promulgate not mandatory but maximum fees. Any Table of Fees which the Law Society recommended to their members would not be operative unless it had been approved by this body. We so **recommend**. Secondly, it would be necessary for any such fees to be based on proper information on the necessary costs of business covered by the fee structures. This will require an investigative or research facility which will, over time, build up and up-date the relevant information on current practice and costs, and to this end we **recommend** that the statutory fees body should have adequate staff and resources for this purpose. The statutory body should further investigate and report on any other fees at the request of the Legal Services Advisory Committee which we recommend in Chapter 20. This Advisory Committee should have the power to require any body involved in fixing fees, whether mandatory or recommended, to make available the basis on which it has arrived at its conclusions.

Block fees

19.100 Block fees were, we understand, introduced to cut down the amount of detailed information that had to be submitted by solicitors when an account for certain court work was submitted for taxation. While this object is desirable, and we deal with the problem of long detailed accounts in paragraph 19.101, we consider that, if block fees are to continue to be used, two things must be corrected. Firstly, it is quite wrong that solicitors should be able to charge for part of an action using block fees, and for another part of the same action according to detailed accounts. No solicitor should get the 'best of both worlds', because inevitably the client would get the 'worst'. Secondly, the blocks must be small enough to ensure that cases which involve least work are not grossly overpaid.

19.101 We were very concerned at the way in which fee notes submitted for adjustment with the legal aid fund, or for taxation by an auditor of court, had very often to be set out item by item in chronological order at great length—some could run to more than 20 pages. The obvious cost of preparing these long documents alarmed us and we wondered whether they were really necessary. Part of the reason for the length of these documents in court cases is the detailed way in which the court tables set out the fee for each item. Court fees should not, we believe, require to be set out in such great detail. We believe that ultimately all fees including court fees should be charged on the basis which we set out in paragraphs 19.89–19.91. If this discretionary fee basis were adopted fee notes would need to state only the number of hours worked by, and the hourly cost rate for, each class of fee earner and a short statement of the nature of the business, where it had been performed, and the main elements to be taken into account in respect of the supplementary factor. Fee notes in this form should be used by both advocates and solicitors. Both the advocate and solicitor would, if required, have to be able to justify the number of hours for which they are charging and their hourly cost rates and the elements which they consider appropriate for the supplementary factor. We believe that if any form of tables of fees for court work are thought to be desirable in particular cases, they must be in a form which will minimise the work involved in preparing fee notes and having them checked or taxed.

19.102 We **recommend** in the long term that fees should be calculated by use of an hourly cost rate for each fee-earner, based on adequate time-records, a proper apportioning of the overheads and a fair return on capital.

The bases of taxation (adjudication of fees)

19.103 Where an action is raised for payment of any fees (court or non-court) the court insist that the account should be taxed by the auditor of the court. Where the expenses of a party in a court action are to be paid by the other party to the action, it is usual for these expenses to be taxed by the auditor of court. It is also open to a solicitor or his client to ask an auditor of court to fix what should be an appropriate fee for the services rendered. In carrying out his function of fixing or checking fees the auditor is not bound by, for example, the Law Society's Table of Fees, although in evidence we have heard from the Auditor of the Court of Session that he will take account of what that Table recommends. Sheriff court auditors, on the other hand, would appear to give a greater weight to what is contained in the Law Society's Table of Fees. In cases where the fees are prescribed by Act of Sederunt or Act of Adjournal, the responsible auditor is bound by what is laid down.

19.104 There are four bases of taxation of judicial fees, that is to say fees which an unsuccessful party to a litigation will have to meet:

(a) agent and client—client paying;
(b) agent and client—fund paying;
(c) agent and client—third party paying; and
(d) party and party.

Agent and client—client paying

On this basis, the party paying is liable for all expenses reasonably incurred by the solicitor for the protection of his client's interest, including any expenses which the solicitor's client has specially authorised.

Agent and client—fund paying

This is a special basis where the legal aid fund is paying the fees. According to the Auditor of the Court of Session what this covers has never been precisely defined but in practice it is slightly less generous than agent and client—client paying, but more generous than agent and client—third party paying.

Agent and client—third party paying

This basis is not so generous to the successful party as that in agent and client—client paying. It is, however, more favourable than party and party.

Party and party

On this basis, according to the rules applicable to the Court of Session, 'only

such expenses will be allowed as are reasonable for conducting the case in a proper manner'. In the sheriff court, the rule is that 'only such expenses shall be allowed as are necessary for conducting the case in a proper manner with due regard to economy'. In consistorial cases between husband and wife there are certain variations of these rules.
The way in which these bases are operated is in the discretion of the auditor of court who examines the account.

19.105 In non-judicial matters the auditor of court will fix a fee which in all the circumstances of the particular case provides reasonable remuneration to the solicitor or advocate for his work and responsibility.

19.106 We **recommend** that the expenses payable by the losing side should be those necessary for the successful party to have his case conducted in a proper manner. We further **recommend** that the statutory bases for taxation be clarified and simplified and would suggest that this might be undertaken by the appropriate Rules Councils of the Court of Session and Sheriff Courts.

19.107 We see advantages in allowing the present freedom for a client and his advocate or solicitor to agree what the fee for a specific job should be. There are some dangers in that the client may not have separate advice when making the contract, and it might become a method of contracting out of the taxation system. We **recommend** that such special charging agreements should be permitted, provided that such agreements are in writing and include a statement that one effect of the contract will be that the fee will not be subject to taxation. We would also **recommend** that it should be a practice rule that an advocate or solicitor who took an unfair advantage of a client in such an agreement by charging a grossly excessive fee could be subject to professional discipline.

Court auditors

19.108 There is a need at present to co-ordinate the taxation or adjudication of legal fees throughout Scotland so as to ensure uniformity of approach in the way in which fees are fixed and charged. Our proposals to rationalise the fee fixing process make this even more desirable. Moreover, we feel that a solicitor should have an obligation to give his client, when taking instructions, an estimate of the fee that will be charged, or to tell him the basis on which the fee will be charged; and that the fee can be subject to adjudication. This means that there should be a simple fee adjudication system readily available, easily accessible, reasonably cheap and having the authority and status to make it acceptable both to the public and the profession. We think that such a coordinated or integrated system should be introduced in Scotland for the adjudication of all legal fees. We did consider a system of Remuneration Certificates as in England which would be issued by the Law Society on the request of a client who asked the Law Society to certify whether a fee charged was reasonable; but we do not recommend this, partly because the Law Society were not in favour of it, and partly because we did not feel such a system would be seen to be impartial and independent.

19.109 The integrated system for the adjudication of all legal fees should be organised on the basis of a Department of the Auditor of Court which would be a department of court and not a government department and we so **recommend**.

19.110 The Department of the Auditor of Court would deal with the adjudication of all fees whether court or non-court which were submitted to it. It would not be compulsory for all fees to be submitted for approval; but if a client asked his solicitor for an adjudication of his account it would have to be submitted to the appropriate office of the department (unless it had been the subject of a special charging agreement) and only fees approved by the department would be enforceable through the courts.

19.111 The chief officer of the department would be 'The Auditor of Court' with such deputes as he might require. Taxing or adjudication officers should be sheriff clerks but answerable in relation to audit work to the Auditor of Court. In time a staff of specialist auditors might be needed with no other court duties.

19.112 Any account for court work which required to be examined would normally be submitted, as appropriate, to the supreme court taxing office or the local taxing office for sheriff court or district court cases. Where a client in a non-court matter required a solicitor to have his account vetted, the account should be submitted to the taxing office in the area in which the solicitor practised. The Auditor of Court should have the power to require particular accounts or classes of accounts to be remitted to himself.

19.113 Appeals from local taxations should be to a deputy auditor or the Auditor. Appeals from a deputy auditor or the Auditor should be to a judge of the High Court or Court of Session, as appropriate. In order to develop consistency it would be preferable not to have appeals taken to the sheriff. An appeal to the court would only be permitted where the Auditor or deputy auditor who had dealt with the matter certified that a principle of general importance was raised which should be put before the court, although it would be open to the court to review the decision of the Auditor (or deputy) and allow an appeal to be heard.

19.114 Where the rules of court require adjudication (on whatever basis) the cost of the process would be payable as the expenses of the action. Where a solicitor was required by statute to have his account 'taxed' or a client asked a solicitor for an adjudication of his account, it would be for the auditor to decide who should meet the cost of the adjudication. The rule that presently applies in some adjudications whereby the cost is borne by the client unless more than 20 per cent is 'taxed off' appears rather arbitrary; and we consider that it would be preferable for the auditor (or the Auditor of Court or judge on appeal) to decide who should meet the expense of adjudication and how. It would be important to ensure that the expenses of the department would be met from the adjudication fee income; but the level of fee charged should be kept as low as possible—perhaps of the order of 2 or 3 per cent of the fee fixed.

19.115 As the proper adjudication of accounts involves judgment from experience as to what is (and is not) involved in different types of cases or transactions, it would be desirable for the Auditor to have at least 15 years experience of private practice as a solicitor and for any deputy auditors also to be solicitors with considerable experience in private practice. In addition, the officials in the Department of the Auditor of Court should be all salaried and all fees accruing from taxation would go to the Treasury. Indeed we see no reason why this department, like the Department of the Registers, should not be broadly self-financing on the basis of the fees which it charges. At present, the fees charged for non-judicial accounts are paid to, and retained by, auditors personally. This practice does not seem to us to be in the public interest and we therefore **recommend** that, whether or not our other proposals for amending the system for taxing fees are accepted, all auditors of court should be salaried and that all the fees charged should be payable to the Treasury.

19.116 In addition to the present powers of adjudication which an auditor has, we consider that auditors should clearly have the power to consider the necessity or relevance of work which has been done and the extent to which there has been unreasonable delay in completing it. If it is considered that the work has not been carried out expeditiously or that the work, or part of it, was unnecessary, there should be a power to adjust the fee to take account of these circumstances. It might even be that in particular circumstances the auditor would disallow a fee completely. Accordingly, we **recommend** that court auditors should have power to adjust fees for the reasons we have described in this paragraph.

19.117 To sum up, the new Department of the Auditor of Court should in our view be responsible for:

(a) ensuring consistency throughout the system;

(b) training and supervising taxing officers;

(c) issuing notes of guidance to taxing officers (which would also be available to the public and the profession);

(d) an annual report to the Department of Legal Affairs about their work which should be published;

(e) advice in the making up of any tables of fees laid down by statute or the courts; and

(f) carrying out regular research into advocates' and solicitors' costs.

Adjudication of legal aid fees

19.118 In all legal aid matters, as we noted in paragraph 19.76, the fees claimed both by solicitors and advocates are submitted to the legal aid central committee. The fees are then subjected to a form of 'taxation' by the staff of the committee's audit department who seek to agree with the advocate or solicitor the amount of the fee which is to be paid. In undertaking this work the staff take account of any fees which have been prescribed by the courts; but if agreement cannot be reached with the advocate or solicitor it is necessary to submit the account to the auditor of court for a formal adjudication. We gave considerable thought to whether the function presently undertaken by the legal aid central committee's audit department should be assumed by our proposed Legal Services Commission which would have as one of its main functions the administration of legal aid; or whether the proposed new Department of the Auditor of Court should have the responsibility of assessing legal aid fees which would, after examination and, if necessary, adjudication, be passed to the Legal Services Commission for payment.

19.119 One of our number was unable to be present during the discussion of these matters and, with the other Commissioners being equally divided, he felt the best course for him would be to abstain. We were thus equally divided in our views on this question.

19.120 Some of us considered that there would be advantage in requiring all legal aid accounts to be dealt with by the new Department of the Auditor of Court. This could be done either by establishing a legal aid section of the department in Edinburgh which would absorb most of the existing staff of the audit department of the central committee and make use of their expertise; or, alternatively, by having legal aid fees dealt with in local taxing offices. The second option might increase costs, although any such increased costs might be offset to some extent by the additional income brought in by the other adjudications which the legal aid staff could also do. In either case once the fees had been adjudicated, either centrally or locally, they would all be sent to the Legal Services Commission for payment. At that stage the Commission might require to check that the fees which had been fixed were in fact payable in terms of the legal aid certificate which had been granted, although it might be possible to arrange for this check to be carried out as part of the adjudication process in legal aid cases. An advantage of having the legal aid accounts dealt with in this way would be that there would be a consistency throughout the fee fixing system—fees for legal aid cases would be dealt with in the same way as fees for private legal business. Under our earlier proposals, legal advice paid from public funds will be much more available. This will mean that there will be a new dimension in the adjudication of fees paid from legal aid funds which will mean that a new expertise will require to be developed by those presently involved. The proposed Department of the Auditor of Court will be an independent department of the Court and well able to ensure that the fees payable from public funds are properly charged. The Auditor of the Court of Session, in his evidence to us, felt that it would be much more appropriate foı all legal aid accounts to be subject to taxation by the Auditor of Court rather than assessed by the legal aid authority. Legal aid accounts in England are almost entirely dealt with by the Taxing Masters or Taxing Officers (court officials similar to auditors of court in Scotland). It is not suggested that the present right of appeal to the court of the advocate or solicitor or the legal aid authoıity should be removed and there does, therefore, seem to be considerable advantage in having all legal aid accounts dealt with initially in the Department of the Auditor of Court (with its inbuilt appeal system). It should also, we believe, be more economical. The examination and adjudication of legal aid accounts by the new department would certainly improve its viability. Without this substantial infusion of legal aid work the new department would start with a small staff, some of whom might be part-time; and only if the demand for the adjudication service in respect of non-legal aid accounts increased, would additional staff need to be recruited. The view of this group of Commissioners is that all legal aid fees should be taxed or adjudicated by the Department of the Auditor of Court, and not by the Legal Services Commission or whoever may be responsible for the administration of legal aid.

19.121 The other group of Commissioners, however, were opposed to the function of examining and determining fees in legal aid matters being taken away from the proposed Legal Services Commission. This group considered that that Commission, as the body paying for the services which were being provided, should be in the same position as clients paying for services privately.

In other words the Commission, like a private client, should be able to question an account submitted by an advocate or a solicitor and, if possible, reach agreement on the fee to be paid. We think it wrong that the Legal Services Commission should be deprived of an opportunity which a private client would have. If the Commission and the lawyer could not agree about the amount of the fee to be paid then either party could go to the new Department of the Auditor of Court and would be bound to accept its adjudication, subject of course to the proposed final right of appeal to the courts. The right of appeal to the department would be an important protection for solicitors and advocates dissatisfied with the fee proposed by the Commission. On this basis, therefore, the Commission would have full responsibility for the proper and efficient working of the legal aid scheme. They would also be responsible for checking for abuses, but it would make this task much more economical and manageable if they had the related task of examining legal aid accounts. The first group of Commissioners considered that under their preferred option it would only be necessary for the Commission to undertake spot checks but it seemed to the second group that if the new department were given the task of examination and adjudication of legal aid accounts, even the limited task of spot checks by the Commission would entail some duplication of staff and staff effort. A consideration which weighed very heavily with the second group was that a Legal Services Commission having responsibility for spending as much as £9 million from the public purse (the 1978/79 level of legal aid expenditure) should, like other public bodies, have full responsibility for ensuring that those public funds are properly expended.

19.122 In these circumstances we are unable to make a recommendation one way or the other. Nevertheless, the matter is important and a decision must be taken at the appropriate juncture.

Money held by solicitors

19.123 We were aware that solicitors handle considerable sums of money on behalf of their clients. To protect the clients where money is being handled the Law Society have, in terms of their statutory powers, made rules which regulate the opening and keeping by solicitors of bank accounts for clients' money. The 1977 survey of firms, described in Appendix 7, disclosed that a total of £89 million of money was held on behalf of their clients by the 447 firms which responded to this part of the survey. On the basis of this evidence, we estimate that as at 1977 the legal firms in Scotland probably held some £165 million for their clients. The sum we have estimated is not an amount which they would hold throughout the year; much of the money is held only for short periods of a few days or a week or two in connection with conveyancing and trust and executry matters.

19.124 The rules made by the Law Society provide that, where the solicitor is likely to hold money in excess of £500 for a client for a period of more than two months, he should arrange matters so that interest can be obtained and be paid to the client. In some cases, funds are held for clients in separate accounts for which the client's name is specified, and any interest then payable on the account must be paid to the client. In other cases, where interest has been earned on a general account for unspecified clients, there is no requirement to account to any individual client for the interest obtained and the solicitor may retain it himself. We have no information to show how much of the £165 million that we estimate is retained by solicitors is held in specified clients' accounts. We assume, however, that a considerable part of this sum must be. On the basis of the limited data which we obtained from the 1977 survey of firms we estimate that all legal firms in Scotland probably earned about £3·5 million from interest on money held by them. There will, we think, be substantial parts of the total sums held on which no interest at all will be earned, because we understand that many solicitors run their clients' accounts, or part of their clients' accounts, on bank current accounts.

19.125 It has been suggested to us in evidence that where interest on funds held by a solicitor is not paid to a client, there is a case for paying the interest not to the individual solicitor but into a new fund to be used for a variety of public purposes in the legal services field. Legislation for such purposes has recently been passed in both Canada and Australia, and there are supporters for the introduction of such a scheme here.

19.126 We have considered the views put to us and we are agreed that, if at all possible, clients should be given the benefit of any interest which ought to have been obtained for them. We recognise, however, that there are circumstances in which this will not always be possible and that there will, therefore, be a benefit which at the present time accrues to solicitors. We think it more appropriate that, where it is not possible for the client to be given the benefit, then that benefit, after deduction of any related expense that the solicitor may have incurred, should be used for public purposes in the field of legal services. We accordingly make the following **recommendations** to deal with interest which is obtained on money belonging to clients but retained by solicitors in Scotland:

(1) Clients *should* wherever possible be given the benefit of any interest on funds of theirs held by a solicitor, and the rules of the Law Society regulating this matter should make this clear.

(2) An investigation should be undertaken into the interest which can be and is actually obtained, with a view to introducing legislation so that where it is not possible for the interest to be paid to individual clients it should be used for public purposes in the field of legal services by establishing a Scottish Law Foundation. The Foundation should have trustees appointed from the profession, from the universities and other appropriate interests, and should have among its functions financial involvement in the preparation of text books, the establishment of a computerised law retrieval system, the provision of scholarships and the support of socio-legal research.

(3) In the interim period until such legislation can be introduced, there should be a general levy on all solicitors who are principals in private practice and who might, therefore, be likely to benefit from interest on money held on behalf of clients.

(4) The levy should be collected by the Law Society and used to set up and sustain the Foundation which we have recommended.

Subject to the further investigations which we have recommended, we would suggest that the initial levy should be fixed at £30 but that this should be adjusted annually to take account of inflation and other financial considerations arising from the interest available.

			Paragraph
Pensions	R19.1	Solicitors' firms should make adequate pension provision for their staff.	19.34
	R19.2	Solicitors' firms should make adequate pension provision for partners.	19.34
Surveys to assist in fixing fees	R19.3	Any body that may be involved in fee fixing should undertake surveys of different types of work undertaken by solicitors to ensure that if pre-fixed fees are used they are based on sound cost information.	19.45
Entry to the Bar	R19.4	The Legal Services Advisory Committee should keep under continuing review entry to the Faculty of Advocates to ensure a sufficient supply of advocates.	19.67
Payment of counsel's fees	R19.5	Where appropriate, payment in full or to account of counsel's fees should be made by solicitors and in the case of legal aid fees by the legal aid authority before the solicitor's account is received and approved.	19.68
Travelling, etc. expenses	R19.6	Advocates' outlays should be charged separately from their fees.	19.69
Pre-fixed fees	R19.7	The Secretary of State for Scotland should appoint a statutory independent legal fees body with appropriate membership to promulgate any pre-fixed fees which should be set as maxima. The body should take over from the Lord President responsibility for court fees. It should have adequate staff and resources to enable it to undertake investigation and research. Any table of fees proposed by the Law Society should not be operative unless approved by the body.	19.99
Fee fixing	R19.8	Fees should be calculated by use of an hourly cost rate for each fee earner, based on adequate time records, a proper apportioning of the overheads and a fair return on capital.	19.102

			Paragraph
Bases of court fees	R19.9	Expenses payable by the losing side in a court action should be those necessary for the successful party to have his case conducted in a proper manner. The statutory bases for taxation should be clarified and simplified by the appropriate Rules Councils of the Court of Session and Sheriff Courts.	19.106
Special charging agreements	R19.10	Special charging agreements between lawyers and their clients should be permitted provided they are in writing and include a statement that one effect of the contract is that it excludes taxation of the fee.	19.107
	R19.11	It should be a practice rule that an advocate or solicitor who took an unfair advantage of a client in such an agreement by charging a grossly excessive fee should be subject to professional discipline.	19.107
Fee adjudication services	R19.12	An integrated taxation system should be organised on the basis of a Department of the Auditor of Court.	19.109
	R19.13	All auditors of court should be salaried and all fees charged for adjudication of fees should be payable to the Treasury.	19.115
	R19.14	Auditors of court should have the power to adjust fees to take account of whether work has been necessary or there has been any delay in completing it.	19.116
Legal aid fees	R19.15	We make no recommendation as to the way in which legal aid fees should be taxed or adjudicated.	19.118–19.122
Interest on money held by solicitors	R19.16	Interest on money held for clients should wherever possible be paid to clients. A Scottish Law Foundation should be established for public purposes in the field of legal services funded in the ways stated in paragraph 19.126.	19.126

PART VI

THE MACHINERY OF GOVERNMENT

CHAPTER 20

CENTRAL OVERSIGHT OF LEGAL SERVICES

20.1 Scotland is, we think, probably unique in being a country with its own wholly distinct legal system but without a distinct Ministry of Justice or similar department of government. The functions which one would expect to be carried out by such a department are presently split between the office of the Secretary of State for Scotland and the office of the Lord Advocate. The division of responsibilities between these two offices (apart from matters relating to the Lord Advocate's Law Officer function and to the prosecution of crime) is based upon no readily discernible principles.

A Department of Legal Affairs

20.2 It is not surprising that we received evidence criticising this division of functions in responsibility for legal affairs in Scotland. The Lord Advocate is responsible for the prosecution of crime, in which he is assisted by the Solicitor General, the Crown Agent, Advocates Depute and the procurator fiscal service. The Lord Advocate is also one of the government's Law Officers and as such is their chief legal adviser on Scottish matters. To assist him in this work he has a small staff in the Lord Advocate's Department in London. The main function of the staff in the Lord Advocate's Department, however, is drafting Scottish legislation and any parts of United Kingdom legislation that apply to Scotland. In 1972, the then Prime Minister made a Parliamentary announcement about a reallocation of functions between the Secretary of State and the Lord Advocate.[1] An Order to give effect to these changed responsibilities was laid at the same time.[2] This resulted in our view in the Lord Advocate having a rather curious assortment of functions in relation to the jurisdiction and procedure of civil courts, the enforcement of judgements, procedure in inquiries in certain tribunals, approval of the programme of the Scottish Law Commission, prescription and limitation of actions, and certain other matters.

20.3 The Secretary of State for Scotland, on the other hand, is responsible for criminal justice policy, and civil law excluding those matters for which the Lord Advocate is responsible. The subjects with which the Secretary of State is concerned include, among many others, divorce, conveyancing reform, and legal aid—and these particular subjects we have dealt with in our Report. He discharges his legal functions through the Scottish Home and Health Department. The Secretary of State is responsible for the administration of the courts. He is also responsible for recommending to H.M. the Queen appointments to the supreme court and shrieval benches, except that in the former case the Prime Minister is responsible for recommendations relating to the appointment of the two most senior judges—the Lord President of the Court of Session and the Lord Justice Clerk.

---

[1] *House of Commons, Official Report 21 December 1972:* Written Answers Cols. 455–457.
[2] *The Transfer of Functions (Secretary of State and Lord Advocate) Order 1972 (S.I. 1972/2002).*

20.4 The Scottish Courts Administration which had already been carrying out on behalf of the Secretary of State certain of his legal functions, including in particular functions relating to the courts, also assumed responsibility for discharging some of the Lord Advocate's functions. On behalf of the Secretary of State they see to such administrative matters as the accommodation and staffing of the courts, the pay and conditions of service of the clerks of court and the other officers who assist the judges in the running of the courts. Among the matters which Scottish Courts Administration discharge on the Lord Advocate's behalf are the law relating to:

—the jurisdiction and procedure of Scottish courts in civil (but not criminal) proceedings;
—the enforcement of the judgements of Scottish courts in civil matters and the recognition and enforcement of judgements of foreign courts;
—evidence;
—prescription and limitation of actions; and
—arbitration.

20.5 The Secretary of State for Trade is primarily responsible for central government support to the Citizens Advice Bureaux; and he is also responsible for policy in the realm of commerce and contracts where, although policy is determined for the United Kingdom as a whole, the provisions of Scots law are particularly distinctive. A similar position also arises in respect of other United Kingdom departments where their Ministers have functions which may produce legislative effects on a variety of legal relationships under the law of Scotland.

20.6 The Lord President of the Court of Session also exercises certain executive functions in the field of legal affairs. For example, he is responsible for determining the fees for solicitors for litigation work.

20.7 We believe that the Scottish legal system will never be adequately serviced by central government unless Scotland is given a Department of Legal Affairs of standing, authority and independence from other Scottish departments. The United Kingdom is no doubt one economic and legislative unit, but as regards legal systems it comprises two quite separate countries. It follows, in our view, that as regards its legal system, Scotland ought to have a central government department in this area of a kind which is appropriate to a separate country. We believe it to be an essential characteristic of such a department, if it is to have the required standing and authority, that it should be separate from, and not merely a part of, some other Scottish department; and, in particular, that it should have as its head a Senior Minister who would have no other departmental functions. In this connection, our views on this matter are broadly in accord with those expressed by the Scottish Law Commission in their Memorandum No. 32 commenting on the White Paper relating to the proposals for devolution. While the Memorandum was written in the context of devolution proposals, it is clear that the views expressed in the Annex to the Memorandum reflected the Scottish Law Commission's views as to what was needed whether there was devolution or not.

20.8 Our view is that there is a clear need for a single Scottish Legal Affairs Department, as the only way to ensure that policies and practices are reviewed sensibly in relation to each other. To achieve the coherent central government responsibility we favour, there would appear to be three options: a department of the Scottish Office with a Senior Minister; a department under the Lord Advocate; or a totally new department under a new and wholly independent Minister. We have considered the various options at some length but the one that appealed to the majority of our number was the first. On this basis, the department would have the Secretary of State to speak for it in Cabinet. We therefore **recommend** that all Scottish legal affairs, except for the Lord Advocate's functions of providing legal advice to the government and of prosecuting crime, should be the responsibility of a new Department of Legal Affairs under a Senior Minister who should have no other departmental responsibilities.

Advice to government

20.9 In the course of our work we have been impressed by evidence of the valuable work done by the Lord Chancellor's Advisory Committee on Legal Aid in England and Wales. There is no counterpart to this Committee in Scotland. We believe it is vital that in securing the provision of legal services our recommended Minister of Legal Affairs should have access to an advisory body of high standing; and that the members of such a body should be intimately acquainted with the delivery of legal services including not only the practical aspects of running a solicitor's business or a practice at the Bar, but also the day to day work of lay advice agencies, courts and tribunals. We have not tried to formulate the precise remit of this advisory body. We have in mind that its area of continuing survey would be roughly co-extensive with the area which we have examined as a Commission so that it would keep under continuous review the interests of the citizen in relation to the legal system. We think that the cost of such an advisory body could be largely offset by the contribution it would be able to make to improving the efficiency with which public funds are expended on the provision of legal services. We therefore **recommend** that there should be a Legal Services Advisory Committee to which the Minister for Legal Affairs could look for guidance on the delivery of legal services in Scotland. The membership of the Advisory Committee should consist of equal numbers of legal and lay persons appointed by the Secretary of State for Scotland; and the chairman should in our view be a person of standing (and not necessarily a lawyer) who would also be appointed by the Secretary of State.

An executive Commission

20.10 We have made recommendations in earlier Chapters that a Legal Services Commission which we would be proposing in this Chapter should be responsible for:

—the provision of public information as to legal rights and services in Scotland (Recommendation R6.7);

—developing lay advice and representation at tribunals and training for lay representatives (R7.3);

—studying and experimenting with the best use of Law Centres in Scotland (R7.4);

—grants to advice centres and Law Centres, the conduct of research, experimenting with ways to provide services, and the setting of standards (R7.7);

—providing financial assistance to firms of solicitors to establish themselves in under-provided areas (R7.10);

—administering legal aid (R8.27);

—developing money management counselling in Scotland (R12.1);

—publishing advice on how to leave one's affairs in good order (R13.8);

In exercising all of the foregoing responsibilities, we consider that the fundamental principle guiding the Legal Services Commission should be to secure in the provision of legal services the best possible value for money consistent with justice.

20.11 In Chapters 6 and 7 we explained why we thought an executive Commission was the most suitable type of body to carry out functions connected respectively with the dissemination of public information about legal services and the disbursing of public funds to advice agencies. As regards the administration of legal aid, with which we dealt in Chapter 8, some of us considered that if there were cogent arguments for taking this responsibility away from the Law Society, it should be given instead to the proposed Department of Legal Affairs. An associated issue was that under our proposed legal aid scheme solicitors would be responsible for the granting of legal aid, although they could refer to an independent central committee, composed mainly of solicitors, cases of particular difficulty. Given the establishment of this independent central committee, there would seem to be no compelling reason why the Department of Legal Affairs should not take charge of and run the legal aid administration directly. The majority of us, however, preferred that a Legal Services Commission should administer legal aid because of the advantages attaching to a single body, one stage removed from central government, being responsible for the various ways of providing subsidised legal services as a supplement to statutory legal aid. As we noted in Chapter 7, comparisons as to the relative cost-effectiveness of different modes of provision ought to be made centrally through a properly co-ordinated approach. We want, however, to avoid having competing interests regularly pressing their own case for extra finance on the responsible Minister. It is much better in our view that the responsible body should be free of day to day political pressures and that it should be able to weigh the respective merits of different options additional to the statutory provision of legal aid.

20.12 Under no circumstances have we contemplated the possibility that legal aid might at some time become a cash-limited service. We are strongly of the view that the Commission should not itself set the conditions of eligibility for legal aid; this we consider is a matter to be determined by Parliament although no doubt in doing so it will take account of the views of the Commission, and of the Advisory Committee which we recommended in paragraph 20.9. These views should be published. The task of the Commission would be to administer as efficiently as possible what must remain an 'open-ended' scheme in financial terms. The grant-aiding of advice services, on the other hand, is in our view more susceptible to cash limits.

20.13 As noted in paragraph 20.10 above, we had suggested in Chapters 12 and 13 certain other responsibilities which we thought an executive Commission could appropriately carry out. Though the range of responsibilities may seem wide, the Commission which we are envisaging and recommending should not be a large body. In view of the major changes we have proposed to the legal aid schemes fewer staff in total should be required for the administration of legal aid than at present. Those who are required should if possible be transferred from the present legal aid administration to the Commission. It should not require a large staff to disburse funds to advice agencies, nor to disseminate information if the publicity material is commissioned from outside experts rather than composed by the Commission's own staff.

20.14 We therefore **recommend** that there should be a Legal Services Commission in Scotland whose main executive responsibilities would be to administer legal aid in accordance with rules laid down by Parliament, to allocate public funds to advice agencies, and to inform the public about the law and advice services.

20.15 We considered whether the distinctive roles of the Legal Services Advisory Committee which we recommended in paragraph 20.9 and of the Legal Services Commission could be combined in a single body. Certainly, we want to limit so far as possible the number of new public bodies that we recommend should be established. We took the view, however, that the Minister of Legal Affairs should be able to look for expert and objective advice to a body of high standing which has no executive interests of its own to defend against criticism. Some of the particular matters remitted to the Advisory Committee might first have been raised with the Minister by the Legal Services Commission. It seems to us that the Minister will have more confidence in the advice of his Committee if it has no executive responsibilities.

Manpower forecasting

20.16 At present very little manpower forecasting is undertaken in the sphere of the legal profession and the provision of legal services. The Law Society recently commissioned a report for their legal education committee particularly related to the number of persons entering the profession; and they helpfully made it available to us. We were interested to note that the solicitor branch of the profession is expanding at a significant rate—some 4½ per cent per year—and this is causing some anxiety about longer term over-supply as well as practical difficulties in the shorter term in meeting the demand for training places. We noted also in Chapter 15 that the number of practising advocates is increasing.[1] The paper prepared for the Law Society did not make a forecast of any change in the level or pattern of demand for legal services which might affect the number of solicitors required and we accept that it might not be simple to do this; such information would, however, be useful to the profession. It is not only the professional bodies, of course, who would stand to benefit from some attempt to forecast future manpower requirements. The universities, particularly as providers of tuition for the Diploma in Legal Practice, should be able to avoid wasteful allocation of training resources if they have some early warning of likely downward changes in demand. We do not believe that forecasts should attempt too much detail, as experience has shown that it is extremely difficult to make accurate predictions about manpower requirements in particular spheres. Nevertheless, we believe that manpower forecasting which attempts to recognise in advance the probability of any major

[1] Table 15.1.

over-supply or under-supply of lawyers, is both necessary and possible. We consider that this could be done most economically by the appointment of appropriate consultants and we **recommend** that the Department of Legal Affairs should convene a meeting perhaps once a year with representatives of the Law Society, the Faculty of Advocates, the Legal Services Commission and the University Grants Committee, and other interested parties, to consider reports prepared by the consultants. These reports should cover a forecasting period of perhaps five years, rolling forward each year. It may well be that manpower forecasting techniques might prove of additional benefit in assessing the likely impact of policies under consideration.

Information and research

20.17 The need for manpower forecasting is just one aspect of the dearth of information about legal services in Scotland. We have already recommended that the Law Society should review the records they keep. We have remarked on the absence of adequate information about the cost of providing particular legal services, and about the relative profitability of different categories of work. Within central government's sphere, it is not at present possible to distinguish between sheriff summary courts and district courts in the annual publication of criminal statistics; and the legal aid statistics are based on the financial year to 31 March whereas criminal statistics and civil judicial statistics are based on the calendar year. Not only does this lend weight to the need for a single department to have responsibility for such matters, it demonstrates also that to date no-one has been concerned to make the kind of comparisons and analyses which are essential to a proper understanding of the operation of legal services in Scotland. We **recommend** that there should be a review of the information on legal services collected and published by government.

20.18 Apart from the regular collection and dissemination of statistical information, we have no doubt that in future more research into the provision, operation and utilisation of legal services in Scotland would be in the public interest. We ourselves have made no more than a start through the studies we felt it necessary to commission against a background of almost no relevant and up-to-date research. The Scottish Law Commission told us that they found it indispensable to a proper review of the law on debt enforcement to instruct original research into the social context of debt, so that their recommendations could be based on a proper appreciation of the circumstances in which debt arose. We believe that there is a similar need for research in many other areas of legal services. The Legal Services Commission should be able to conduct experiments into new ways of delivering legal services. It is equally important that the Department of Legal Affairs should also have a research budget both for its own internal research and for the commissioning of research by outside bodies such as the universities. In particular, part of this budget should be earmarked to provide the Advisory Committee, which will have a key role to play in determining research needs and priorities, with the capacity to set in motion such research as it thinks necessary to fulfil its remit. We **recommend** that a research budget adequate for these various purposes should be available to the Department of Legal Affairs.

			Paragraph
Department of Legal Affairs	R20.1	All Scottish legal affairs, except for the Lord Advocate's functions of providing legal advice to the government and of prosecuting crime, should be the responsibility of a new Department of Legal Affairs under a Senior Minister who should have no other departmental responsibilities.	20.8
Legal Services Advisory Committee	R20.2	There should be a Legal Services Advisory Committee to which the Minister for Legal Affairs could look for guidance on the delivery of legal services in Scotland.	20.9
Legal Services Commission	R20.3	A Legal Services Commission should be established with a range of executive functions for publicly funded legal services as outlined in paragraph 20.10.	20.14
Manpower forecasting	R20.4	The Department of Legal Affairs should convene regular meetings with appropriate interests to consider forecasts of legal manpower requirements.	20.16
Information and research	R20.5	There should be a review of the information on legal services collected and published by government.	20.17
	R20.6	An adequate research budget should be available to the Department of Legal Affairs to cater both for its own research and for research which it commissions from outside bodies.	20.18

PART VII

RECOMMENDATIONS

RECOMMENDATIONS

CHAPTER 6: INFORMING THE PUBLIC

			Paragraph
Legal education in schools	R6.1	All pupils should be taught for one period per week in the third year of their secondary school curriculum about the law, the legal system and legal services.	6.6
	R6.2	The Department of Legal Affairs (see R20.1) should be associated with the Scottish Education Department in ensuring that appropriate school courses are made available.	6.8
	R6.3	The Department of Legal Affairs and the Scottish Education Department, in conjunction with the Law Society, should consider what part solicitors might play in the provision of legal education in schools.	6.8
Public information	R6.4	It should be the responsibility of government to ensure that important changes in the law are widely advertised in the press and by radio and television as they are implemented.	6.15
	R6.5	The financial and explanatory memorandum introducing each government Bill should include a statement of the amount proposed to be spent on initial publicity for the measures the Bill contains.	6.15
	R6.6	Community education should be recognised as an important part of the work of Citizens Advice Bureaux and Law Centres.	6.17
	R6.7	The Legal Services Commission (see R20.3) should carry initial responsibility for securing the adequate provision of public information on legal rights and legal services in Scotland.	6.18

			Paragraph
Advertising by solicitors	R6.8	As proposed by the Monopolies and Mergers Commission, the Law Society should replace their present rules on advertising with practice rules drawn up after consultation with the Office of Fair Trading, breach of which should be treated as professional misconduct. These practice rules should embody the principles set out by the Monopolies and Mergers Commission and reproduced in paragraph 6.34.	6.36

CHAPTER 7: ACCESSIBILITY OF ADVICE

			Paragraph
Generalist advice services	R7.1	Improved access to legal services should be promoted by the development of generalist advice centres.	7.5
Lay help at tribunals	R7.2	Encouragement should be given to developing the provision of lay advice and representation before those tribunals in which lay participation is appropriate, and adequate training should be provided for lay representatives.	7.12
	R7.3	Responsibility for developing the system of lay advice and representation before tribunals, and for ensuring that adequate financial resources are made available, should be given to the Legal Services Commission.	7.12
Law Centres	R7.4	The Legal Services Commission should study and experiment with the best use of Law Centres in Scotland, bearing in mind the principles stated in paragraph 7.15.	7.15
	R7.5	A code of practice regarding the circumstances in which clients should be required to pay for Law Centre services should be drawn up by the Legal Services Commission after consultation with the Law Society and lay users.	7.17
Administration	R7.6	In special cases Citizens Advice Bureaux management committees should be able to authorise their solicitor to proceed under legal aid, if applicable, or to charge fees.	7.20
	R7.7	The Legal Services Commission should, with funds allotted to it by central government, give grants to advice centres and Law Centres, conduct research, experiment with ways to provide services and set standards for advice services.	7.28

			Paragraph
	R7.8	Each centre should be run by an independent local management committee.	7.28
	R7.9	Area advice services committees should be established.	7.29
Assistance to legal firms	R7.10	The Legal Services Commission should have power to provide financial assistance to firms of solicitors to establish offices in under-provided areas of the country.	7.32
	R7.11	District councils should be ready to give planning permission for solicitors' offices in shopping centres and residential areas, and to let residential property to solicitors for use as offices where this will make legal services more readily accessible.	7.32

CHAPTER 8: PAYING FOR LEGAL SERVICES

			Paragraph
The scope of civil legal aid	R8.1	Legal aid for advice and assistance and for representation in civil matters should only be available to help citizens to assert or protect their rights, and not to assist them in arranging their affairs for the benefit of themselves or others.	8.17
	R8.2	Legal aid should be available for representation at a tribunal, but only if the client would otherwise be unable to follow the proceedings and if there is no lay representation available locally which is recognised by the tribunal as suitable.	8.21
	R8.3	A tribunal should have power to grant legal aid where it considers that the matter before it gives rise, or is likely to give rise, to a substantial point of law.	8.21
	R8.4	All tribunals at which a substantial point of law is likely to arise should include a legally qualified member.	8.21
	R8.5	Legal aid should be available to pursue or defend an action of defamation.	8.22
	R8.6	The civil legal aid scheme should have no upper eligibility limit of disposable income, and should have a scale of contributions which rises sharply with income and is reviewed annually.	8.26
	R8.7	No account should be taken of capital in assessing eligibility for civil legal aid, or in computing the contribution payable.	8.27
	R8.8	Civil legal aid should not be available to businessmen or traders for litigations relating to a business or trade, even if the business or trade is owned by an individual, this exclusion to be in addition to the exclusion of bodies corporate or unincorporate.	8.28

LS—N

			Paragraph
Liability for expenses	R8.9	The expenses of the successful opponent of a legally-aided party should be recovered from the unused balance of the legally-aided party's contribution; to the extent that they exceed any such balance, they should be met by the legal aid fund.	8.29
	R8.10	The right of recovery from the legal aid fund should extend to individuals and one-man businesses, but not to litigants who are bodies corporate or unincorporate unless such a body can satisfy the court that inability to recover from the legal aid fund would result in severe hardship to individuals.	8.29
An integrated scheme	R8.11	Civil legal aid and legal advice and assistance should be integrated into a single scheme, which should simply be a legal aid scheme.	8.31
	R8.12	The assessment of an applicant's eligibility for civil legal aid and the setting of a maximum contribution should be done by the solicitor to whom the client applies.	8.32
Collecting contributions	R8.13	Where contributions are to be paid by instalments to the central administration every effort should be made to introduce alternative and convenient methods of payment, such as by post office giro.	8.36
	R8.14	It should always be possible for the solicitor and client by mutual agreement to make their own arrangements for payment of the contribution direct to the solicitor.	8.37
Assessing the merits of proposed litigation	R8.15	(i) Where the solicitor has assured himself that the 'probabilis causa' and reasonableness tests are satisfied, he should be able to grant legal aid himself;	8.40

			Paragraph
		(ii) Where the solicitor is in doubt he should refer the application to a statutory independent committee to be set up by the body responsible for administering legal aid;	
		(iii) Where the solicitor thinks the tests are not satisfied he should have no power to refuse legal aid, but should have to refer the application to the committee, unless the client is satisfied, on the solicitor's advice, that such a referral would be hopeless.	
Recovery of expenses	R8.16	The present rule, whereby the legal aid fund undertakes the recovery of all the expenses awarded to successful assisted persons, should be changed.	8.45
Sums recovered	R8.17	While the legal aid fund should still look to sums recovered to defray its expenses when recovery of expenses from the other side is difficult, the assisted person should have first claim on a part of any sum recovered.	8.47
The statutory deduction from civil legal aid fees	R8.18	The ten per cent deduction from civil legal aid fees should be abolished.	8.49
Legal aid for accused persons	R8.19	Legal aid should be provided to enable all accused persons to receive initial advice on how to plead and, where appropriate, to be given help in the preparation of a plea in mitigation.	8.51
	R8.20	The criteria for granting criminal legal aid to defend a summary prosecution should be laid down in statute. Legislation should specify the offences where there is no risk of imprisonment or where the risk is so small as not to justify a grant of criminal legal aid.	8.52–8.54
	R8.21	Authority to grant, but not refuse, criminal legal aid should be delegated to sheriff clerks in suitable cases, provided that the clerks receive adequate training for the purpose.	8.57

			Paragraph
	R8.22	Where a decision on an application for criminal legal aid has to be taken by a judge, it should be done in chambers.	8.57
	R8.23	Accused persons who receive criminal legal aid, and are tried and found guilty, should be liable to contribute to the cost of their defence.	8.59
Duty solicitor	R8.24	All accused persons in custody should be entitled to see a duty solicitor and before they do so they should have full details of any crime alleged against them.	8.62
	R8.25	Court advisory committees (see R15.2) should prepare duty plans to ensure the attendance of solicitors to provide legal services for accused persons.	8.63
Legal advice in prison	R8.26	Public funds should pay for regular legal clinics in prisons.	8.64
Administration of legal aid	R8.27	Legal aid should be administered by an independent authority in the form of the Legal Services Commission which we propose in Chapter 20.	8.73–8.74
Choice of defence agent	R8.28	An accused person should be entitled to choose his own defence agent, using legal aid if he is eligible.	8.79
Public defender	R8.29	There should be an experiment to assess whether or not a public defender system could with advantage be introduced in Scotland to run in parallel with the service provided by solicitors in private practice supported by legal aid. The points detailed in paragraph 8.82 should be borne in mind in the design of the experiment.	8.81–8.82
Public interest litigation	R8.30	The Department of Legal Affairs should consider the use of legal aid to facilitate appeals where an important legal point is at issue.	8.91

CHAPTER 9: CONVEYANCING

			Paragraph
Registration of Title	R9.1	Any extra cost incurred on first registration in the Land Register of properties over what might be charged for recording under the present system should be borne by the State.	9.12
	R9.2	The land certificate should disclose as many as possible of the overriding interests affecting a property.	9.13
	R9.3	There should be set up a Standing Committee appointed by, and reporting to, the Secretary of State for Scotland which should have responsibility for overseeing the new Land Register, recommending such improvements and simplification as seem desirable, and considering the longer term operation of the system. The membership should comprise representatives of the Land Register staff, the legal profession and any other related profession, and the general public.	9.15
	R9.4	The Standing Committee should advise when registration of title should become universally compulsory. When this happens without any change of ownership the full costs of such a registration should be borne by the State.	9.15
Simplification of procedures and documents	R9.5	The Standing Committee should examine the feasibility of introducing a simpler system of transferring property which might be provided by the State at a much reduced cost to the public.	9.16
	R9.6	The legislature and the profession should ensure that the documents used for conveyancing are written so far as possible in simple language.	9.18

			Paragraph
	R9.7	A specialist committee with lay representation should be appointed to review the scope for simplification and standardisation of legal documents used in conveyancing.	9.20
The conveyancing monopoly	R9.8	The present monopoly should not be extended to bring within it the missives stage of the purchase and sale of heritable property.	9.31
	R9.9	Domestic conveyancing should no longer be restricted exclusively to the legal profession; members of other professional bodies who satisfy prescribed standards as detailed in paragraph 9.45 should be entitled to undertake conveyancing work for a fee.	9.45
Building society valuations	R9.10	Building societies should adopt standard specifications for valuations, appoint a common panel of valuers and instruct all valuations through a common agency.	9.53
	R9.11	An expert committee should consider the difficulties involved in making building society valuation reports available to potential borrowers.	9.57
	R9.12	The same expert committee should examine whether the difficulties in requiring sellers to provide a survey report can be overcome.	9.59
	R9.13	The same expert committee should consider whether sellers should be obliged by statute to provide certain information to purchasers.	9.61
	R9.14	The same expert committee should consider whether a person who instructs a survey but does not buy the house should pay the surveyor for his time only.	9.62

			Paragraph
Instalment purchase	R9.15	A detailed study should be made of instalment purchase contracts with a view to effecting changes in the substantive law which will offer the purchaser in an instalment sale better protection than the law at present affords.	9.75
Oppressive conditions in missives	R9.16	The question of oppressive conditions in missives should be referred to the Office of Fair Trading.	9.76

CHAPTER 10: DIVORCE

			Paragraph
Jurisdiction to sheriff courts	R10.1	Sheriff courts should be granted jurisdiction in actions for divorce.	10.17
	R10.2	In divorce actions the sheriff court should have exclusive jurisdiction as a court of first instance.	10.18
Power to remit cases to Court of Session	R10.3	A sheriff on cause shown by the parties, or of his own accord, should have power to remit divorce actions to the Outer House of the Court of Session.	10.19
Designation of particular divorce courts	R10.4	Sheriffs Principal, when they think it appropriate, should designate particular courts within their sheriffdom to deal with divorce cases.	10.20
Right of pursuer to select court	R10.5	The pursuer in a divorce action should be able to choose between raising the action in his or her local sheriff court or in the defender's local sheriff court if this were different.	10.21
Sheriff's right to remit action to another sheriff court	R10.6	A sheriff of his own accord should have power to remit any divorce action to any other sheriff court where, for instance, he has grounds for believing that this would be in the the best interests of any children affected by the action.	10.21
One category of divorce based on separation	R10.7	Parliament should consider whether there should be only one category of divorce based on separation; whether this category of divorce should not require consent; and whether the period of separation which would establish evidence of irretrievable breakdown should not be longer than two years.	10.23
Special reports on custody of children	R10.8	Special reports on custody arrangements should be obtained in all divorce actions involving children.	10.25

			Paragraph
	R10.9	In every divorce action (defended as well as undefended) where children under the age of 16 are involved the case should be referred by the court to the appropriate reporter to the children's panel for special reports on custody arrangements.	10.31
Review of custody or access orders	R10.10	In any case where a court has made an order for custody or access, the reporter to the children's panel should be under a duty to review the working of the order after a period of, say, 6 months and to report to the court if he considers that any change is required.	10.34
	R10.11	Any child over the age of 10 to whom a custody or access order relates should be entitled as a matter of right to contact the reporter directly and seek a review. In such cases the reporter would have a duty to review and report to the court if he considered a change were required.	10.34
Review of supervision or committal orders	R10.12	Any local authority subject to an order which has placed children of divorced parents under its supervision or care should be required after, say, one year after the making of the order to report to the court as to whether or not the order should remain in force.	10.35
Grants to authorities for services of reporters	R10.13	The Department of Legal Affairs in discussion with the local authorities concerned should make *ad hoc* grants to cover the extra costs incurred by the courts' use of reporters' services.	10.36
Privacy for divorce actions	R10.14	Defended divorce actions in the sheriff court should be heard in private, subject to the right of the press to attend and report the minimum that is considered essential in the public interest.	10.40

			Paragraph
Restrictions on press reporting in custody of children cases	R10.15	Privacy of proceedings with restrictions on press reporting should apply in all cases concerning custody of children, whether they are divorce actions or not.	10.40
Law reports	R10.16	Divorce actions held in private should still be subject to reports in law journals but using the 'A v B' technique to preserve privacy.	10.41
Evidence and corroboration	R10.17	In undefended divorce actions the court in place of affidavit evidence should be able to proceed on written forms completed by pursuers with a signed declaration that what is stated is the truth, and without need for corroborative evidence.	10.45
Need for simple forms in divorce actions	R10.18	Simple forms should be introduced which would enable a litigant to apply personally for a divorce, if he or she so wishes.	10.46
Cessation of full legal aid for undefended divorce actions	R10.19	Only initial legal advice and assistance under the proposed integrated legal aid scheme should be available to parties seeking divorce where there are no matters in dispute.	10.47
Entitlement to expenses	R10.20	Consideration should be given to the proposition that no expenses should be awarded against the defender in undefended divorce actions.	10.48

CHAPTER 11: SMALL CLAIMS

			Paragraph
An improved procedure	R11.1	There should be a small claims procedure within the sheriff court which is sufficiently simple, cheap, quick and informal to encourage individual litigants to use it themselves without legal representation.	11.21
	R11.2	In drawing up the rules for a new procedure, the Sheriff Court Rules Council should consult consumer and business, as well as legal, interests.	11.21
	R11.3	The rules of the new procedure should embody the principles set out in paragraph 11.21.	11.21 (i–vii)
New procedure to supplant the summary cause	R11.4	The new small claims procedure should supplant the summary cause and be the sole procedure available for claims of small amounts.	11.24

CHAPTER 12: DEBT ENFORCEMENT AND DEBT COUNSELLING

			Paragraph
Debt counselling	R12.1	The Legal Services Commission should give high priority to developing a money management counselling service in Scotland, in consultation with Citizens Advice Bureaux and social workers.	12.10
	R12.2	The Scottish Association of Citizens Advice Bureaux should give higher priority to money management counselling in their training programmes; and such counselling should be given due priority in the training of social workers.	12.10
	R12.3	As many school pupils as possible should have an opportunity, in appropriate subject departments, to learn money management.	12.12

CHAPTER 13: ADMINISTRATION OF ESTATES

			Paragraph
Obtaining confirmation to an estate	R13.1	The Confirmation to Small Estates (Scotland) Act 1979 should be brought into force without delay.	13.8
	R13.2	Sheriff clerks should assist executors who apply in person for confirmation, in the ways indicated in paragraph 13.11. This assistance should, at least initially, be restricted to estates valued at up to 80 per cent of the threshold for capital transfer tax.	13.11–12
Administration of the estate	R13.3	In a printed leaflet about services in connection with estates an indication should be given of what kind of information the client ought to expect to receive from his solicitor at the outset of the business.	13.19
	R13.4	The Law Society should issue rules of practice for the administration of estates which would set out a minimum frequency with which lay executors and beneficiaries would have to be informed of progress, of the steps still to be taken, and of the estimated date of completion.	13.20
	R13.5	There should be a procedure by which, firstly, a lay executor or beneficiary can bring to the attention of the court delay in the winding up of an estate, and, secondly, the court can in appropriate cases take continuing control over the administration.	13.22
	R13.6	Legal aid should not be available for representation in chambers at a hearing under this procedure unless at the discretion of the court.	13.25
Public information	R13.7	Written information and guidance about what needs to be done about the estate of a person who has died should be provided by registrars when issuing death certificates.	13.26

			Paragraph
	R13.8	The Legal Services Commission should produce a leaflet describing the steps that citizens should take to leave their affairs in order so that, when they die, others will be saved needless worry and expense.	13.28
The property of the mentally disordered	R13.9	The measures in connection with the affairs of the mentally incapacitated suggested in paragraphs 13.29–31 should be considered immediately.	13.32

CHAPTER 14: THE COURTS

			Paragraph
Civil procedure and jurisdiction	R14.1	A committee should be appointed by the Secretary of State for Scotland, after consultation with the Lord President of the Court of Session, to review the structures, jurisdiction and procedures of the civil courts in Scotland.	14.13
Working methods of the courts	R14.2	A separate review of the working methods of both the civil and the criminal courts should be carried out.	14.14
Facilities needed at courts	R14.3	Microphones should be installed in courts with poor acoustics.	14.18
	R14.4	Participants in civil business should not have to share facilities with participants in criminal business.	14.19
	R14.5	Central and local government must give higher priority than they have done in the past to remedying the manifest physical shortcomings of local courts.	14.22
	R14.6	As soon as funds can be made available, existing proposals for improvements to Parliament House should be put into effect.	14.25

CHAPTER 15: THE LEGAL PROFESSION: STRUCTURE AND ORGANISATION

			Paragraph
Law Society records	R15.1	The Law Society should examine urgently the adequacy of its internal administration and records in the light of our Report and should, if necessary, be subject to a statutory obligation to keep the information discussed in paragraph 15.12.	15.12
Court Advisory Committees	R15.2	Every Sheriff Principal should establish for each sheriff court or group of courts, for which he is responsible, an advisory committee comprising representatives of the local Bar, court staff, procurators fiscal, social workers and appropriate outside lay elements. The advisory committee would advise the Sheriff Principal on any matters affecting the work of the court or the convenience of the users of the court.	15.14
	R15.3	Consideration should be given to the best form for a similar advisory committee or committees for the Court of Session and High Court of Justiciary.	15.14
Edinburgh correspondents	R15.4	The Committee on Civil Procedure (R14.1) should examine the requirements as to Edinburgh solicitors in Court of Session actions, and as to advocates being accompanied in court by solicitors.	15.16
Notaries Public	R15.5	The status of Notary Public should be conferred on all solicitors admitted in future solely by virtue of their admission as solicitors.	15.19
Incorporation of solicitors' firms	R15.6	The restrictions on the incorporation of solicitors' partnerships should be removed subject to suitable safeguards.	15.20

			Paragraph
Multi-disciplinary partnerships	R15.7	The present statutory restriction on solicitors sharing fees with others, so far as it prevents the development of multi-disciplinary partnerships and associations, should be removed so that they can be permitted. The professional restrictions which prevent solicitors and advocates combining in partnerships in relation to practice in Scotland should remain.	15.22
Instruction of advocates	R15.8	Only solicitors should instruct counsel in court matters; certain other professional agents should be entitled to instruct counsel direct for an opinion or in relation to proceedings before a tribunal or inquiry although counsel may at his discretion refuse to accept such instructions.	15.33
Cab Rank Rule	R15.9	The cab rank rule which applies to advocates should be retained subject to a change which would permit seniors over the age of 50 to be selective in the kind of work which they undertake.	15.41
Fusion	R15.10	The legal profession in Scotland should continue to consist of two branches, namely solicitors and advocates.	15.50
Rights of audience	R15.11	Rights of audience in the supreme courts should not be extended to solicitors.	15.54
Use of computers	R15.12	The legal profession should urgently examine the application of computers in: the maintenance of time and cost records; financial accounts, both for the practitioner and the client, and trust accounts; controlling and organising court work and the extensive documentation involved; and the processing of conveyancing.	15.58

		Paragraph
R15.13	An examination of the potential use of computers in court procedures should be undertaken by those responsible for the administration of Scottish courts.	15.59
R15.14	Subject to suitable safeguards, access to information kept on the Land Register should be available through the use of computer terminals anywhere in Scotland and consideration should be given to maintaining other public records on computer and giving access to them throughout Scotland.	15.60
R15.15	The Department of Legal Affairs and the Legal Services Advisory Committee (see R20.2) should be charged with ensuring that the development of computers with regard to the law and provision of legal services in Scotland is actively pursued.	15.64

CHAPTER 16: EDUCATION AND TRAINING I: LAWYERS

			Paragraph
Admission of law students	R16.1	Universities should use wider criteria than academic attainment at school when selecting law students for admission.	16.9
	R16.2	A test of aptitude to study law should be developed for use in Scotland as one element in the process of selecting students for entry to the faculties of law.	16.10
The LLB degree	R16.3	As the Diploma in Legal Practice is introduced, the LLB syllabus should be revised to encourage students to study a social science or a modern language.	16.16
	R16.4	The Law Society should reduce to the minimum the requirements they effectively place on students to study particular courses.	16.17
	R16.5	The LLB degree should require a four years course of study.	16.18
The honours LLB	R16.6	There should be a four years honours degree in law.	16.20
Teaching methods	R16.7	Greater use should be made of teaching methods other than lecturing and rote learning, following the principles stated in paragraphs 16.22 and 23.	16.22–23
Examinations	R16.8	Some examinations should be conducted on the basis that students have access to statute and standard texts.	16.24
Resources	R16.9	Universities should ensure that law faculties are enabled to maintain student/staff ratios which are in line with those of other comparable faculties.	16.25

			Paragraph
The Diploma in Legal Practice	R16.10	In five years time from autumn 1980 the Joint Standing Committee on Legal Education should review, in the light of the circumstances then prevailing, whether it would be realistic and desirable to alter the Diploma curriculum to a sandwich basis.	16.35
	R16.11	Arrangements should be made for practice in oral advocacy with mock trials; there should be a compulsory element on legal ethics; and students should have some introduction to methods of office efficiency and management.	16.36–38
Postgraduate study in law	R16.12	The scope for postgraduate study in law should be examined by the Joint Standing Committee on Legal Education.	16.41
Training records	R16.13	Every trainee solicitor should be required to maintain a training record.	16.46
In-office training	R16.14	Apprentices should be required to spend some part of their training in each of at least three areas of law. The Law Society should stipulate the minimum length of experience normally necessary to attain the required level of proficiency in each area.	16.46–47
	R16.15	Training standards should be laid down by the Law Society.	16.48
	R16.16	Every principal who has responsibility for an apprentice should be required to report on the trainee's performance at the end of the training period. In addition, there should be at least one interim report. These reports should be disclosed to the trainee.	16.48

			Paragraph
	R16.17	A trainee who does not satisfactorily complete his apprenticeship in two years should be required to undergo a further period of training in a different firm.	16.49
	R16.18	The Law Society should provide training courses and guidelines for apprentice masters.	16.50
	R16.19	The Law Society should maintain a list of firms shown by experience to be unsuitable for taking apprentices. No such firm should be allowed to employ further apprentices.	16.51
	R16.20	Every trainee should be required to report to the Law Society on the quality of his training immediately after completing his apprenticeship.	16.51
Training in court work	R16.21	The Law Society should maintain a register of trainee solicitors.	16.53
	R16.22	Trainees who have been on the register for a year should be allowed to speak in court but only under the immediate supervision of the solicitor in full charge of the case.	16.53
Restricted practising certificate	R16.23	When a solicitor is first admitted the Law Society should grant him a practising certificate which will not permit him to practise as a principal until he has had further experience for a period of (a) two years where he is to become a partner in a firm of which one partner at least has had at least three years experience as a principal and (b) three years when he is to practise on his own or in a partnership where there is no partner with more than three years experience as a principal.	16.57
Professional training: advocates	R16.24	The post-Diploma training of advocates should take a minimum of two years with at least nine months spent devilling and at least another nine months working in a solicitor's office.	16.59

			Paragraph
	R16.25	The Faculty should consult with solicitors' firms who regularly employ intending advocates as apprentices and prepare general guidelines on agreed principles for the mutual benefit of the trainee, the Faculty and the firms involved.	16.60
Devilling	R16.26	The Faculty should strongly encourage all devils (trainee advocates) to obtain a wide range of experience.	16.61
	R16.27	Devils should be required by the Faculty to keep a training record.	16.61
	R16.28	The devil master should be required to report to the Dean of Faculty on the performance of his devil at the end of his training.	16.62
	R16.29	All devils should be told that they can approach the Vice-Dean in connection with their training; and the Vice-Dean should arrange to interview all devils on the completion of their training.	16.62
	R16.30	The Faculty should organise mock trials at which devils would be able to plead in open court in a fictitious case.	16.63
	R16.31	Devils should be able to speak in court under the immediate supervision of their devil master.	16.64
	R16.32	An experiment should be carried out in the provision of posts for devils or newly qualified advocates as assistants to supreme court judges.	16.65
	R16.33	The possibility and desirability of making grants from public funds available to devils ought to be reviewed from time to time.	16.66
	R16.34	The Faculty should consider the possibility of arranging a wider loan scheme for devils than is at present available.	16.66

			Paragraph
Continuing education and competence	R16.35	The Law Society should establish effective reporting arrangements with various persons and bodies who are in a position to monitor the quality of professional work done by solicitors.	16.69
	R16.36	The Law Society should introduce a structured progressive scheme of training in their continuing education programme.	16.71
	R16.37	The Law Society should ensure that adequate attention is given to management techniques and modern office practice in their continuing education programmes.	16.72
Continuing education—court work	R16.38	The Law Society should take steps through their continuing education programme to achieve a substantial improvement in court work skills, particularly of the younger members of the profession.	16.74
	R16.39	Sheriffs Principal should meet the local Bar of each court in the Sheriffdom from time to time to convey to the Bar as a whole, and particularly to its younger members, the main ways in which the presentation of cases could be improved.	16.75
Interest groups of lawyers	R16.40	The Law Society and Faculty should encourage the formation of groups of lawyers with special interest in particular areas of law.	16.77
Continuing education: advocates	R16.41	The Faculty should organise occasional seminars for advocates, conducted by judges or senior advocates.	16.79

CHAPTER 17: EDUCATION AND TRAINING II: OTHER PROVIDERS OF LEGAL SERVICES

			Paragraph
Judges' training	R17.1	Justices should in the course of their training learn something of police work and methods and the present requirement on them to visit penal institutions should apply before the justice tries his first case.	17.4
	R17.2	Courses for new sheriffs should place greater emphasis on sentencing and on developments in civil procedures.	17.5
	R17.3	Sheriffs' training should devote more attention to the value of sensitive judicial handling of the court-room.	17.7
	R17.4	Newly-appointed supreme court judges should participate in induction courses, particularly on sentencing.	17.8
	R17.5	The appropriate authorities should take steps to see that judges at all levels are familiarised with penal institutions and the practical working of criminal penalties of all kinds (including such matters as probation).	17.9
Chairmen and members of tribunals	R17.6	The Council on Tribunals should undertake a review of the training provided for tribunal chairmen and members, with a view to establishing standards of training.	17.10
Procurators fiscal	R17.7	The Crown Office should re-assess staff training needs, particularly of their less-experienced members, and should devote adequate resources to secure a satisfactory level of training.	17.13
	R17.8	Senior fiscals should devote more time to supervising the work of junior fiscals in court.	17.14
Advice centre staff	R17.9	More responsibility for providing Citizens Advice Bureaux training should be transferred to national or area Bureaux authorities.	17.17

			Paragraph
	R17.10	Citizens Advice Bureaux training schemes should be developed along progressive lines, so that individual workers may choose to specialise in one or two particular areas after they have completed their basic general training.	17.18
	R17.11	The different advice agencies, both specialist and generalist, should collaborate in the provision of training to their mutual advantage.	17.19
Solicitors' staff	R17.12	Structured, progressive training should be provided for solicitors' staff.	17.21

CHAPTER 18: PROFESSIONAL CONDUCT, COMPLAINTS AND DISCIPLINE

			Paragraph
Professional conduct: solicitors	R18.1	The Law Society should promulgate an authoritative guide to the professional conduct of solicitors in Scotland, which should be in terms comprehensible to laymen.	18.4
	R18.2	A solicitor should be under a professional obligation to give a prospective client his best estimate of the cost of the work to be undertaken and the time it will take to complete it.	18.5
	R18.3	The proposed guide should be supplied to the profession and to the staff of advice agencies; it should also be available to the public.	18.6
Professional conduct: advocates	R18.4	The Faculty of Advocates should promulgate an authoritative written guide to the professional conduct expected of advocates which should be supplied to advocates and be available to the public.	18.7
Discipline Tribunal: amount of fine	R18.5	The maximum fine which the Tribunal should be able to impose should be at least £2,000 at present day values and should be periodically reviewed to take account of inflation.	18.20
Disciplinary procedures: Law Society	R18.6	The Law Society should prosecute disciplinary procedures whether or not negligence is involved without waiting for the initiation or completion of civil court proceedings.	18.26
Claims for compensation	R18.7	The power which we propose for the Tribunal to award compensation (R18.10) should only be available if the client has expressly waived any right to claim damages.	18.26
New complaints procedure: solicitors	R18.8	A single, reasonably simple procedure for investigating and acting on all complaints against solicitors should be established.	18.30

			Paragraph
	R18.9	A new Discipline Tribunal should be established to replace the present Scottish Solicitors' Discipline Tribunal and the Law Society's legal aid complaints committee. The Tribunal should have a wide range of sanctions.	18.31
Compensation	R18.10	The Tribunal should be able to award compensation in the ways stated in paragraph 18.33.	18.33
	R18.11	Both the solicitor and the complainer should have a right of appeal to the Court of Session in relation to disciplinary findings and sanctions determined by the Tribunal although there should be no appeal in respect of award or non-award of compensation.	18.33
Composition of Tribunal	R18.12	The membership of the Discipline Tribunal should be drawn from a panel consisting of say five practising solicitors appointed by the Lord President and an equal number of laymen appointed by the Secretary of State. A legally qualified President should be appointed by the Secretary of State or the Lord President.	18.34
Procedure for lodging and investigating complaints	R18.13	All complaints should be addressed in the first instance to the Law Society for investigation.	18.35
	R18.14	The committee of the Law Society responsible for investigating complaints should include lay members appointed by the Secretary of State.	18.35
Progress report	R18.15	The Law Society should make regular reports to complainers on the progress of their investigations into the complaints they have received. On any complaint outstanding for three months a report should be made to the Lay Observer.	18.36

			Paragraph
Lay Observer: powers	R18.16	The Lay Observer should continue to receive and investigate complaints from clients who are not satisfied by the investigation and action taken by the Law Society. He should be empowered to take complaints to the Tribunal at his own instance.	18.37
Legal Aid: complaints	R18.17	Complaints by the Legal Services Commission against solicitors in relation to the provision of legal aid should be investigated in the first place by the Law Society.	18.38
Cost of Tribunal	R18.18	The direct cost of the new Tribunal should be a charge on public funds.	18.40
Solicitors' lien	R18.19	The Discipline Tribunal should be given a discretion to suspend the operation of solicitors' lien in cases where it thinks this appropriate.	18.44
New complaints procedure: advocates	R18.20	The Lord President of the Court of Session should be empowered at the request of the Dean of Faculty to convene an *ad hoc* Discipline Tribunal to deal with complaints against advocates. The Tribunal should be chaired by a judge and should have an advocate and a layman as members. The Tribunal should have similar sanctions to those proposed for the solicitors' Discipline Tribunal.	18.46
Lay Observer: function in relation to complaints against advocates	R18.21	The Lay Observer should be empowered to receive and investigate complaints which have not been dealt with to the satisfaction of the client by the Dean of Faculty or any committee appointed by him. The Lay Observer should have power to request the Lord President to convene an *ad hoc* Discipline Tribunal. The Lay Observer should arrange for the client's case to be prosecuted before the Tribunal.	18.47

			Paragraph
Complaints involving both solicitors and advocates	R18.22	Where a complaint involves both a solicitor and an advocate the Faculty and the Law Society should make joint arrangements to investigate it. When necessary, an *ad hoc* Tribunal could be appointed by the Lord President.	18.48
Publicity	R18.23	A leaflet should be produced describing briefly the procedures for lodging complaints against solicitors and/or advocates; this leaflet should be readily available to the public.	18.49
	R18.24	The findings of the Discipline Tribunal should always be released to the press as well as being adequately reported in the professional journals.	18.50
	R18.25	Existing advice agencies should formulate and make clear to their clients their procedures for dealing with complaints.	18.52

CHAPTER 19: REMUNERATION

			Paragraph
Pensions	R19.1	Solicitors' firms should make adequate pension provision for their staff.	19.34
	R19.2	Solicitors' firms should make adequate pension provision for partners.	19.34
Surveys to assist in fixing fees	R19.3	Any body that may be involved in fee fixing should undertake surveys of different types of work undertaken by solicitors to ensure that if pre-fixed fees are used they are based on sound cost information.	19.45
Entry to the Bar	R19.4	The Legal Services Advisory Committee should keep under continuing review entry to the Faculty of Advocates to ensure a sufficient supply of advocates.	19.67
Payment of counsel's fees	R19.5	Where appropriate, payment in full or to account of counsel's fees should be made by solicitors and in the case of legal aid fees by the legal aid authority before the solicitor's account is received and approved.	19.68
Travelling, etc. expenses	R19.6	Advocates' outlays should be charged separately from their fees.	19.69
Pre-fixed fees	R19.7	The Secretary of State for Scotland should appoint a statutory independent legal fees body with appropriate membership to promulgate any pre-fixed fees which should be set as maxima. The body should take over from the Lord President responsibility for court fees. It should have adequate staff and resources to enable it to undertake investigation and research. Any table of fees proposed by the Law Society should not be operative unless approved by the body.	19.99

			Paragraph
Fee fixing	R19.8	Fees should be calculated by use of an hourly cost rate for each fee earner, based on adequate time records, a proper apportioning of the overheads and a fair return on capital.	19.102
Bases of court fees	R19.9	Expenses payable by the losing side in a court action should be those necessary for the successful party to have his case conducted in a proper manner. The statutory bases for taxation should be clarified and simplified by the appropriate Rules Councils of the Court of Session and Sheriff Courts.	19.106
Special charging agreements	R19.10	Special charging agreements between lawyers and their clients should be permitted provided they are in writing and include a statement that one effect of the contract is that it excludes taxation of the fee.	19.107
	R19.11	It should be a practice rule that an advocate or solicitor who took an unfair advantage of a client in such an agreement by charging a grossly excessive fee should be subject to professional discipline.	19.107
Fee adjudication services	R19.12	An integrated taxation system should be organised on the basis of a Department of the Auditor of Court.	19.109
	R19.13	All auditors of court should be salaried and all fees charged for adjudication of fees should be payable to the Treasury.	19.115
	R19.14	Auditors of court should have the power to adjust fees to take account of whether work has been necessary or there has been any delay in completing it.	19.116

			Paragraph
Legal aid fees	R19.15	We make no recommendation as to the way in which legal aid fees should be taxed or adjudicated.	19.118–19.122
Interest on money held by solicitors	R19.16	Interest on money held for clients should wherever possible be paid to clients. A Scottish Law Foundation should be established for public purposes in the field of legal services funded in the ways stated in paragraph 19.126.	19.126

CHAPTER 20: CENTRAL OVERSIGHT OF LEGAL SERVICES

			Paragraph
Department of Legal Affairs	R20.1	All Scottish legal affairs, except for the Lord Advocate's functions of providing legal advice to the government and of prosecuting crime, should be the responsibility of a new Department of Legal Affairs under a Senior Minister who should have no other departmental responsibilities.	20.8
Legal Services Advisory Committee	R20.2	There should be a Legal Services Advisory Committee to which the Minister for Legal Affairs could look for guidance on the delivery of legal services in Scotland.	20.9
Legal Services Commission	R20.3	A Legal Services Commission should be established with a range of executive functions for publicly funded legal services as outlined in paragraph 20.10.	20.14
Manpower forecasting	R20.4	The Department of Legal Affairs should convene regular meetings with appropriate interests to consider forecasts of legal manpower requirements.	20.16
Information and research	R20.5	There should be a review of the information on legal services collected and published by government.	20.17
	R20.6	An adequate research budget should be available to the Department of Legal Affairs to cater both for its own research and for research which it commissions from outside bodies.	20.18

ALL OF WHICH WE HUMBLY SUBMIT FOR YOUR MAJESTY'S GRACIOUS CONSIDERATION

Hughes (Chairman)
William Brown
J. R. Clark
Ethel Houston
Laurence C. Hunter
Donald Macgregor
Joan Macintosh
Peter Maxwell
Donald B. Robertson
George Sharp
A. S. Weatherhead

G. M. Fair (Secretary)
Kenneth F. Barclay (Legal Secretary)
P. M. Russell (Assistant Secretary)

29 February 1980

Some of our number have dissented on certain of the matters in the Report and their Notes of Dissent are set out in Part VIII.

PART VIII

NOTES OF DISSENT

NOTES OF DISSENT

CONTENTS

The Notes of Dissent in this Part of the Report are concerned with the subjects shown below. The order conforms with the sequence of the Chapters in the Report.

NOTE OF DISSENT BY MISS E. M. HOUSTON

ND1.1 I am against the recommendation which (without more detailed conditions) adopts the Monopolies Commission recommendations on advertising by Solicitors. There is evidence that many of the professions still oppose advertising, both for themselves and by the Legal Profession. The Medical and Dental Defence Union of Scotland in their evidence to us stated 'the MDDUS would be averse to any form of advertising by members of the Legal Profession from an ethical standpoint as they see the Legal Profession in the same position of ethical standards as the Medical Profession'. The Consultative Committee of Accountancy Bodies expressed the view 'we are not aware of any advantage to be obtained by the public from advertising by professional people. That is our view on the profession of accountancy (and it has been expressed in detail in evidence to the Monopolies and Mergers Commission on behalf of The Institute of Chartered Accountants for Scotland, The Institute of Chartered Accountants in England and Wales and the Association of Certified Accountants) and we see no reason to regard the Legal Profession in any different light. The increased costs, which must ultimately be borne by the client, in a labour intensive profession; the danger of misleading claims whether made wilfully or innocently; and any drop in standards consequent on a price war initiated by advertising, far outweigh the advantage of removing of what appears to be a purely theoretical difficulty a prospective client may have in obtaining professional advice'.

ND1.2 There was evidence from individuals and other users of legal services that they did not like individual advertising by Solicitors. 'We should not like to see legal firms advertising for business or competing with one another so far as fees are concerned. Competition should be on service alone and not by price.' (Viewpoint Housing Association). This concern, specifically from not only the legal profession but other professions, is reflected throughout the community and cannot readily be discounted.

ND1.3 It is difficult to distinguish between price advertising by Solicitors to compete on fees for 'standardised products' (see BATES case THE UNITED STATES LAW WEEKLY 45 LW pp. 4895/4910 for discussion on 'standardised products') and self-promotional advertising. The Monopolies and Mergers Commission in the Report (p. 16) already referred to stated "the Advertising Association told us that there was little distinction between 'informative' and 'persuasive' advertising and that it was 'virtually impossible to give information without some overtones which create persuasive impressions' ". I would maintain that legal services in Scotland taken in the framework of our legal system, e.g. 'a simple Will', 'a simple Divorce', cannot be accurately priced as 'standardised products' and that in any event it is not possible to advertise without giving the impression of superiority of 'product' or service.

ND1.4 The Monopolies and Mergers Commission in their Report on the services of Advocates (subject to recommendations on minor matters), did not consider that the present restrictions against advertising for Advocates operated against the public interest. They considered that the public were not denied adequate information as, in the main, Advocates are instructed by Solicitors who know the market. (This argument was based to some extent on the existing practice of the Edinburgh 'Correspondents' system.) The Monopolies Commission considered the efficiency of an Advocate's work must be thought of in terms of personal ability rather than in terms of office organisation, methods and machinery. (In our Report we have, however, made reference to the advisability of the Faculty of Advocates using modern technology.)

ND1.5 The Solicitor in Scotland has a substantial advocacy role in the Sheriff Court—a court of unlimited monetary jurisdiction with possibly increased jurisdiction with regard to divorce actions and a court dealing with much of the criminal prosecution work. In arguments, for or against advertising, I see no reason why the advocacy role of the Solicitor should be treated differently from that of the Advocate. Both have immunity from suit in their advocacy role and both have an equal duty to the Court as to their client. I consider it is against the public interest for a lawyer to advertise legal services performed in his role as a pleader in the Court whether he is an Advocate or a Solicitor because of his duty to the Court. Also, intrinsically, a pleader in all courts must be judged in terms of personal ability and efficiency.

ND1.6 Not enough emphasis has been given by the Monopolies Commission to the mixed roles of the Scottish Solicitor—court pleader/estate agent/general practitioner/specialist in commercial work and taxation/employed solicitor in Banks and other institutions and public companies. If advertising were to be effective in price competition (assuming price competition of legal services to be possible) it would require a fragmentation and identity of professional roles which I do not consider possible or desirable in Scotland. In private practice there has developed in Scotland greater emphasis on the partnership of Solicitors and to provide a wide range of legal services to the client could be considered in the public interest. It would be virtually impossible to make rules distinguishing which legal services can be advertised.

ND1.7 In the main, many individual Solicitors in Scotland (whether in partnership or otherwise) are likely to operate as general practitioners. It would not be at all unusual for a Court practitioner to make Wills. What is the rationale for allowing him to advertise the price of a 'simple Will' if he may not advertise his services for litigation? Advertising his services for making a Will could bring him other work, specifically litigation, for which advertising might not be in the public interest.

ND1.8 I consider that the best way to approach advertising by Solicitors is to place a Statutory obligation on the Law Society to ensure:

(a) that the public are fully informed of the range of legal services and the qualifications and experience of those offering legal services (including specialist knowledge if adequately certifiable) and

(b) that the public are fully informed of ascertainable legal charges.

I take the view that the Law Society subject to this obligation should be free to decide its own policy on advertising after consultations with the Lord President as head of the Judiciary; after canvassing throughout the Membership from time to time; after a programme of independent Surveys of public attitudes and specific groups of major users of legal services in consultation with bodies representing the public interest; and after consulation with other professional bodies, specifically the legal professions within the EEC.

NOTE OF DISSENT BY MR. D. B. ROBERTSON

ND2.1 I cannot agree with the recommendation that solicitors should advertise prices for specific work and services other than for an initial interview or consultation.

ND2.2 I think there is considerable force in the Law Society's views on price competition. While I have strong reservations about the reality and scale of the so called unmet need for legal services in Scotland, it would appear from our own assessment of the problem that it is fear of the unknown and an initial ignorance which may deter some persons from approaching a lawyer for help. It seems plain from the evidence we had that once over the first jump to an interview and the getting of advice there is no barrier to future use (paragraphs 5.16 to 5.21).

ND2.3 If that is so then the nub of the problem is convincing the public that using a lawyer need not be excessively costly and having a price tag for consultation which the potential client can decide is reasonable and affordable gets him into the position where he can obtain a fairer and franker estimate for the cost of resolving his problem by further action.

ND2.4 As is recognised by us (paragraph 6.30) the nature of legal work makes price advertising difficult as every case is different, and in my view in many cases to advertise prices for specific jobs would be downright misleading; the client who enters the office relying on an advertisement that a particular service is priced at £X only to be told that in his or her case because of the circumstances the price will be £X plus may well, with some justification, feel that he has been deceived.

ND2.5 It seems to me that the pricing of initial consultation for advice will solve the problem.

NOTE OF DISSENT BY LORD MAXWELL, MR. D. B. ROBERTSON AND MR. A. S. WEATHERHEAD

ND3.1 We do not agree with the recommendation that the Legal Aid Scheme (for litigation) and the Legal Advice and Assistance Scheme (for legal advice) should be integrated in one scheme.

ND3.2 We accept that there is a superficial logic in combining the two schemes as advice and representation are, in many cases, complementary to each other. There may also be some advantage in having one name for the two different types of aid.

ND3.3 We are, however, persuaded that the integration of the two schemes is impracticable. We are also concerned that the integration of the scheme may seriously affect the extent to which solicitors will be able to give quick advice within certain limits to clients who are eligible for aid.

NOTE OF DISSENT BY MISS E. M. HOUSTON

ND4.1 I concur with the Note of Dissent on the integrated legal aid scheme by Lord Maxwell, Mr. Robertson and Mr. Weatherhead.

ND4.2 While I fully agree with the highly desirable object of extending Legal Aid more widely throughout the community, I have grave reservations as to the practicality of the proposals that the proposed criteria for granting Legal Aid should be altered (paragraph 8.17); that Solicitors should themselves assess contributions (paragraph 8.32); that they should collect the contributions (paragraph 8.37); and that Solicitors should have primary responsibility for assessing *probabilis causa* and for the operation of the reasonableness test (paragraph 8.40).

NOTE OF DISSENT BY MISS E. M. HOUSTON, LORD MAXWELL, MR. D. B. ROBERTSON AND MR. A. S. WEATHERHEAD

ND5.1 We do not agree with the recommendation that a Legal Services Commission should administer legal aid within the framework described by Parliament (Chapters 8 and 20).

ND5.2 Some of us have reservations about the validity of the arguments for removing the administration from the Law Society as most of the objections to leaving it with the Society could be overcome and in any event, the ultimate control of the administration is with Parliament and the Government as legal aid is a creature of statute. It may, however, be that there is an unacceptable inconsistency in having the administration of the public funds for legal aid administered by the members of the profession who are paid from these funds for services provided and we do not therefore dissent from the recommendation that legal aid should be administered by some other authority (paragraph 8.73).

ND5.3 We do, however, dissent from the recommendation that the appropriate independent authority should be the proposed Legal Services Commission. While some of us have reservations about the need for a Legal Services Commission, we do see the need to have some body separate from Government to co-ordinate the setting up and funding of a variety of types of advice centres and law centres and the funding of other types of publicly funded legal services and it is probably not inappropriate for this body to provide public information about legal services.

ND5.4 It appears to us that there is a radical difference in kind between the administration of legal aid and the functions proposed for the Legal Services Commission. Legal aid is now and if the Royal Commission's proposals are accepted, will continue to be available to persons entitled thereto as a matter of right. There are now and will be no cash limits. Any changes in the rights of individuals to obtain the support of public funds, for example by altering the contribution levels, will require legislation and any change in detail in the methods of operating the scheme which do not require legislation can be and we consider should be made by the appropriate Government Department. We do not think that a body set up with the function of making policy decisions on the expenditure of funds within cash limits is an appropriate type of body to control the detailed administration of the financial rights of the individual.

ND5.5 We note with some concern the proposed function of the Legal Services Commission in relation to legal aid set out in paragraph 8.74. It appears from items (1) and (3) of this paragraph, that the Legal Services Commission is to keep under continuous critical review, the relative merits of the legal aid scheme and other methods of providing publicly funded legal services, the creation and disbursing of funds for these other methods being matters for its own policy decisions and one of the principal reasons for its existence. We have no doubt that there should be review and advice to the Government and through the Government to Parliament as to whether the amounts available as a matter of right to individuals should be increased or diminished, whether any savings should be used to increase the cash limits available for other methods of providing legal services, but we think it wrong that the functions of critical review and pressing for amending legislation should rest with a body having both an administrative responsibility in relation to the rights and a policy making responsibility in relation to the creation and extension of other methods. We think that the review should be the function of a body that has no executive function in relation to either rights under legal aid or the alternative methods of delivering publicly funded legal services and which would therefore be seen to be disinterested and impartial.

ND5.6 The Royal Commission has recognised the need to have such a body in its unanimous recommendation that there should be a strong Legal Services Advisory Committee which will be the principal vehicle for making recommendations to the Government with regard to the provision of legal services of all kinds. We therefore think that the review function proposed for the Legal Services Commission is properly the function of the proposed Legal Services Advisory Committee.

ND5.7 If and in so far as a law centre and other establishments falling under the executive functions of the Legal Services Commission were self financing in the sense that clients paid for the services with, in appropriate cases, financial legal aid, the recommendation from which we dissent would mean that the Legal Services Commission would be in charge of the administration of legal aid, part of which would go to the financial support of institutions which were its own creations, or in any event, for which it had financial and executive responsibility. We think that this is undesirable in principle.

ND5.8 If the Law Society is not to continue to administer legal aid subject to some improvements in the arrangements, then we would recommend that the administration of legal aid should be the function of the Department of Legal Affairs which is also unanimously recommended by the Royal Commission, or by a body quite independent and separate from the proposed Legal Services Commission.

NOTE OF DISSENT BY MR. D. B. ROBERTSON AND MR. A. S. WEATHERHEAD

ND6.1 We dissent from the view of the Commission that a public defender employed by the State is an acceptable way to provide advice and representation for persons accused of crime whether use be compulsory or not (paragraph 8.81).

ND6.2 This view is a radical change from the well tried arrangements for providing advice and representation for accused persons in Scotland by the private profession to provision by a State agency. It is not merely a change in the way such advice and representation is funded.

ND6.3 We recognise that considerations of economy are important in any State funded scheme but a change of this nature and in this field should never be considered on grounds of administrative convenience or financial savings the reality and extent of which are at best highly doubtful. There are a number of ways in which the cost of Criminal Legal Aid might be reduced some of which are presently under review.

ND6.4 The prosecution of crime is organised and administered by the State as accuser in the public interest. A defence agent while owing duties to the court and to his profession and operating under certain restraints, is representing an interest which is in sharp conflict with the State. It is fundamental that justice should be done and be seen to be done and the first imperative is that accused persons should have advice and representation that are and are seen to be absolutely independent, impartial and fearless and not in any way subject to or influenced or inhibited by State considerations of any kind including expense, inconvenience or even public opinion.

ND6.5 It is worth bearing in mind that the present system of Criminal Legal Aid delivered by the private profession has operated now for some years following a careful inquiry by the Guthrie Committee in 1950. That Committee considered and rejected proposals for a 'public defensor'. It considered that in certain circumstances in the Burgh and Justice of the Peace Courts the *Law Society* might appoint a salaried solicitor to act for persons before these courts but, in response to a suggestion of a salaried 'defensor', again employed by the *Law Society*, in the busier sheriff courts for even limited services up to the plea stage it was 'strongly inclined' to the view that a rota of independent private practitioners was preferable.

ND6.6 A view was strongly expressed to the Commission that to be viable at all, such a system would require to be compulsory. We agree with this and we also agree with the Commission that there must be a choice and therefore there can be no compulsory system.

ND6.7 Apart from the fundamental objections we think that the proposed experiment is impracticable if not impossible mainly because the very criteria proposed by the Commission make it so. Even in the case of a non-compulsory system there is a real danger that once such a bureaucratic organisation is set up and funded for some years there would be a disinclination to disband it and the temptations to encourage use and diminish choice or to make it compulsory might be irresistible.

ND6.8 A State agency, as the public defender system envisaged by the Commission is, cannot ultimately guarantee independence in reality or appearance. That is the fundamental objection.

NOTE OF DISSENT BY MISS E. M. HOUSTON

ND7.1 The Commission decided not to make recommendations supporting the *status quo* i.e. they agreed there should be no change over the existing prohibition of contingency fees but did not make any specific recommendation. I wish to support consideration of contingency fees and other methods of funding legal services, other than by the provision of state financed Legal Aid. The Law Society in their evidence to us canvassed the arguments for and against a contingency fee basis and decided that on the whole, a contingency fee system (largely based on the experience in the United States), would be against the public interest. It is certainly true that public reaction to an uncontrolled contingency fee basis is one of dismay, particularly (and rightly in my view) from the medical profession but also from a wide section of the public. However, I consider that the matter has not been widely canvassed in Scotland in recent times. The common law prohibition in Scotland, based on the Roman Law that *pactum de quota litis* was illegal has been reinforced most by decisions in the 19th century, largely on the basis that a lawyer under a contingency fee arrangement could take advantage of the ignorance or inexperience of the client. It is also considered to be against the public interest that the lawyer should be in a position where it can be alleged that he can make a profit out of encouraging litigation and putting forward excessive claims.

ND7.2 In England contingency fees were considered in some detail by the Appeal Court in *Wallersteiner v. Moir* (no. 2) 1975 1 A.E.R. 849. Lord Denning (his two colleagues dissented) took the view that in the special circumstances under consideration, i.e. a derivative action involving litigation on behalf of minority shareholders, a contingency fee arrangement might be equitable subject to strict safeguards, e.g. (1) Counsel's Opinion of reasonable chance of success; (2) notification of the contingency fee arrangements to the other side and (3) approval of the Court and/or the Law Society.

ND7.3 The Law Commission of England and Wales and Northern Ireland in their Report number 7, paragraph 19, (Proposals for Reform of the Law Relating to Maintenance and Champerty) although recommending that the criminal aspects of Champerty and Maintenance be abolished, commented that the question of allowing contingency fees in litigation was one on which the professional bodies, as well as the public, must have further time for reflection before any solutions could or should be formulated. I think it could be argued that apart from some or all of the safeguards mentioned by Lord Denning, a contingency fee basis might also be restricted to certain clearly defined types of action, specifically to exclude the worst aspects of what both the legal profession and the public here consider these to be in the United States. It could also form the basis for the funding of certain class actions for which there is inadequate provision at the moment.

ND7.4 Although these are quite separate issues from the consideration of contingency fees, I am in favour of the proposals to the Benson Commission by the Bar Council (of England and Wales) of a Suitors Fund and of proposals by JUSTICE for a Contingency Legal Aid Fund being given serious consideration in Scotland.

NOTE OF DISSENT BY MISS E. M. HOUSTON, LORD MAXWELL, MR. D. B. ROBERTSON AND MR. A. S. WEATHERHEAD

ND8.1 We cannot accept the decision of the Commission that the preparation of Missives for the sale and purchase of residential property on behalf of purchasers or sellers for a fee should not be restricted to solicitors or those who may be entitled to undertake conveyancing on behalf of other persons. The Missive constitutes the binding contract between the parties and is therefore of vital importance to them—in some ways more important than any documents which may follow thereon. Almost all the evidence to us on this matter was to the effect that there should be some restriction on those who are entitled to prepare Missives on behalf of others including the evidence from those who wished to widen the conveyancing monopoly to other than solicitors.

ND8.2 Historically, Missives were among the documents excluded from the statutory monopoly of solicitors with regard to the preparation of deeds generally. We do not know why this should have been so, but they are included along with other documents *in re mercatoria* and at the time, it would have been rare for anyone other than a solicitor to have prepared Missives for the purchase and sale of heritable property. We believe that the importance of Missives to purchasers and sellers—and particularly probably purchasers—is such that those who prepare these documents for the signature of a client or for signature on his behalf should be restricted to those who have the necessary legal skill and knowledge and who are subject to appropriate rules of conduct, such as on the issue of conflict of interest. We would so recommend.

NOTE OF DISSENT BY MISS E. M. HOUSTON

ND9.1 I do not agree with Recommendation 9.9 that domestic conveyancing should no longer be restricted exclusively to the legal profession.

ND9.2 In my view, it is not possible in the present Scottish Legal System to isolate the professional services involved in the preparation of the documents transferring and mortgaging heritable property, from the professional services involving legal advice in the whole area of Scots law. The new registration of title procedures will simplify conveyancing in Scotland and it is important that the implementation of these Reforms be given the greatest priority, not only in terms of public funding, but professional support. Despite the simplification of conveyancing, which will result from these Reforms, a legal knowledge of the Scottish Feudal System and of the formalities which are a protection to the public at large, as well as the ability to interpret the rights and burdens which continue or may continue with the lands, will still be essential requirements. In their evidence to us the Building Societies Association and the Scottish Building Societies Association stated:

> 'it might be contended that the Solicitors' monopoly in preparing instruments relating to heritable or real property is unjustified because such preparation can be carried out by a person with specialised knowledge of land law and conveyancing who does not possess all the wide ranging legal knowledge which a person requires to qualify as a Solicitor. The Associations think however that this is a rather superficial contention'.

ND9.3 In their evidence, they did not rule out the possibility that there could be a 'new breed of conveyancers' to compete with the legal profession, but they stressed the importance from their side as representing investors that such a new profession would virtually have to duplicate the education and training, licensing and discipline procedures which have a strong similarity to those already existing within the legal profession.

ND9.4 The recommendation that the services involved in providing conveyancing should be restricted to 'domestic conveyancing' is totally unworkable. The views of the Building Societies Association are relevant here.

> 'Building Society advances are very largely confined to domestic property, so commercial conveyancing is not a matter with which Societies are normally concerned. However, in the Associations' view a distinction between commercial and domestic conveyancing is impracticable and undesirable, quite apart from the fact that in Scotland conveyancing relates to the land and the nature of the buildings on the land is incidental, so that any distinction between domestic and commercial conveyancing is illogical'.

ND9.5 Institutional users of legal services in the field of conveyancing might be expected to support the *status quo* but it is difficult to assess fully public reaction since the methodology and basis of our Research and Surveys in the field of domestic conveyancing related to the present position. There was no evidence from Surveys or Research as to public attitudes to a change in the delivery of these services.

ND9.6 Looking to the future, the introduction of the practical application of computers and machine intelligence methods in the field of conveyancing (and in many other fields) can revolutionise documentation. The duties involving land transfer, though still reflecting many aspects of the law may not be carried out by individuals on the basis of traditional drafting skills. To protect the public against computer fraud and false titles, those likely to be essential personnel will more than ever be required to exhibit qualities of integrity and public accountability. In my view the legal profession is the best candidate for this role.

ND9.7 The proposals for the assessment of legal fees by reference to a body independent of the legal profession and having appropriate membership representing the legal profession, the public and specialists, should remove the basis of discontent that the fees are self regulated by the profession. That these fees are maxima, will provide greater competition from within the profession than is perceived at the moment. To extend the monopoly to other bodies not subject to the same independent fee assessing body would require the setting up of further independent machinery or the 'non legal conveyancer' being subject to the same controls as to discipline and fees as the solicitors. There could be an enlarged body of conveyancers, (legally qualified and otherwise) still operating a monopoly and still criticised for not producing effective competition and reduction in costs.

ND9.8 While I have put forward arguments, which I consider to be valid, for the retention of the monopoly by the profession it is clear to me that the profession must be seen to discharge its duty of public accountability not only on the matter of legal fees, but in the process of Law Reform to 'demystify' the law. This is particularly relevant in Scotland. The Scots as a whole have a profound sense of history and legal traditions are and have been influential but changes in the Scottish Land Tenure system involve social, political and commercial considerations and the future pattern of land tenure is not just a matter of conveyancing. The issue continues to be whether the system of conveyancing requires to adapt itself to matters of land tenure or whether the system of land tenure should adapt itself to the increasing demand for house ownership and thus to a greatly simplified system of conveyancing. The evidence we have had indicates that a large section of the public do want to be able to buy property with simplicity, safety and at a cost which reasonably reflects the time and skill involved. More information, too, must be given to the public to reflect the element in legal charges attributable to the solicitor's efforts as an Estate Agent—a role particularly bound up in the Scottish System of Sale and Purchase. The conveyancing monopoly—along with the other monopoly aspects of legal services (e.g. advocacy and a 'knowledge monopoly' of legal skills) must be seen to be in the public interest. The privilege of self-government, or independence involves public accountability. So far, public accountability has been a matter entirely for the profession to discharge, largely within its internal organisation. There is evidence that the public wish to be involved at levels of decision and policy making. The experience of the legal professions, particularly in most of the Provinces of Canada and the legal professions in Australia, indicates that public involvement can assist the profession in discharging public accountability without detracting from the independence of the profession.

NOTE OF DISSENT BY MR. A. S. WEATHERHEAD

(This Note of Dissent is supported by Miss E. M. Houston and Lord Maxwell)

ND10.1 I cannot accept the recommendation of the Commission (paragraph 9.53) that building societies should establish a common agency through which all requests for house valuations from individual societies should be channelled so that there would be only one valuation of a house used by the building societies. I doubt very much whether this is practicable and I do not think that the full implications for the seller of such an arrangement have been fully appreciated. This is a matter which I think should have been treated like similar matters and remitted to an expert body to examine.

NOTE OF DISSENT BY MISS E. M. HOUSTON

ND11.1 I am in disagreement with the recommendation expressed (paragraph 10.18) and the arguments put forward to support the view that the Sheriff Court should have exclusive jurisdiction as a Court of first instance in divorce matters. I fully agree with the object of achieving a Family Court System in Scotland and I agree that for divorces involving custody and welfare of children, the Sheriff Court as envisaged in our Report is the more suitable forum. But of 8,782 divorces granted in 1978 (Civil Judicial Statistics Cmnd 7762 Tables 4 (a) and (b)) 3,836 divorces did not involve children. I consider there should be concurrent jurisdiction with the Court of Session in divorces not involving children.

ND11.2 My reasons for supporting this are:

1. *Cost and Competition*

   There will be cases, whether legally aided or otherwise, where it is possible to predict, by the specific choice of forum, a reduction in cost. Competition could also lead to greater efficiency and speed.

2. *Client Choice*

   Client choice should be available provided:

   (a) The pursuer's solicitor has specifically advised as to possible relative costs and payment is being made by the pursuer or,

   (b) where the defender is found liable, he has the right to challenge the expenses awarded against him on the grounds that the choice of a forum against his agreement has resulted in greater costs to him.

NOTE OF DISSENT BY MR. D. B. ROBERTSON

ND12.1 I dissent from the recommendation that the Sheriff Court have exclusive jurisdiction in divorce. I consider that all defended divorce actions ought to be heard at first instance by the Court of Session, and, having regard to the efficiency and elimination of inconvenience now achieved by the affidavit procedure in undefended causes, the recognised fact that mere transfer to a lower court will not materially reduce cost, and to the burden it would place upon an overburdened Sheriff Court, I see little point in transferring undefended causes as at present processed.

ND12.2 Undefended divorces with no dispute or difficulty as to children or finance may become even simpler, particularly if some of the Commission's recommendations are implemented and legal aid is not available (paragraph 10.47). Be that as it may, defended causes are often fought vigorously, can involve difficult and delicate questions, and matters which are of importance to the parties and to society.

ND12.3 Contrary to what is so often tritely claimed, a transfer of jurisdiction will not of itself reduce cost significantly (paragraph 10.13). This is particularly so in defended causes and if legal aid be abolished for undefended causes a large amount of the public expense will go. I have seen no compelling evidence that the cost of a defended cause in the Sheriff Court would be significantly less than in the higher court; such statistics as we have are not helpful to a firm or sound conclusion on this point. I doubt if the present affidavit undefended causes would be significantly cheaper merely by transfer without alteration in procedure.

ND12.4 Like the alleged saving in cost, the inconvenience to parties of having causes heard in the Court of Session has in my view been exaggerated. In undefended causes this argument has disappeared but would remain for defended ones. The main centres of population are within reasonable distance of Edinburgh and, without wishing to seem dismissive of this point, I do find it difficult to believe that even the not numerous consistorial litigants from really far flung outposts in the far north or the Isles seriously regard the trip to Edinburgh as a matter of great concern, or out of proportion, if they are locked in combat probably and hopefully for the only time in their lives over issues which must be of major importance to them.

ND12.5 I fear I do not really understand the view that the division of labour, between the solicitor, the Edinburgh correspondent and the advocate is wasteful of resources, inefficient and bound to result in cases taking longer than they need. It is recognised that these three agents are not duplicating or triplicating work and that the client pays only once for any particular item of business (paragraph 10.13). It follows logically that the only difference if the work was being done locally would be that the fees would be paid to perhaps one person if he performed all these functions. There might be a saving in postage charges. I cannot see how cases are bound to take longer because papers are transmitted by post. The time taken to process a case is prescribed by court procedure and the availability of court time. If I am correct as I indicate later that many Sheriff Courts are overloaded the litigants may have to wait much longer to get a hearing or decision than they would in the Court of Session.

ND12.6 If some of the issues in defended divorces are to be regarded as special and of importance not only to the parties but as a matter of public concern (and no-one would surely dispute that at least the treatment and disposal of the offspring are special and important) I agree that ideally there should be family courts along the lines recommended by the Finer Committee. I honestly cannot see the busy Sheriff Courts in Scotland with their wide and varied criminal and civil jurisdiction and in most cases inadequate accommodation ever playing a proper and adequate role as family courts. If defended divorces involving children, finances and ancillary matters, which are often protracted and sometimes fragmented, were to be dealt with in the Sheriff Court it would likely result in further delay and a risk that less time and consideration could be given to the difficult and delicate issues that often arise. Many Sheriff Courts are already overloaded and recent legislation such as the Criminal Justice Bill, which gives very time-consuming new roles to the Sheriff is not likely to diminish their workload; on present staffing many Sheriff Courts could not cope. At present there are 'specialised courts' within the Court of Session some staffed by particular judges who operate under special procedures and it would be more practical and much easier to have a centralised family court within the Court of Session. Such a specialised unit might not necessarily require to be restricted geographically for hearings just as the Land Court operates from time to time. A smaller group of judges dealing with consistorial matters is better able to build up an expertise and develop the law in a rational and coherent basis of principle.

ND12.7 While I have some reservations about the total role of reporters and children's panels as envisaged in the Report, I cannot see any real difficulty in their role being played within the context of the Supreme Court as the Court rather than the Sheriff Courts. I do not agree that access to the 'machinery' envisaged would be materially more complex from the Court of Session.

ND12.8 I agree that the jurisdictional divisions (or lack of them formally) between the Court of Session and the Sheriff Court in civil business has become anomalous and is overdue for review with a view to rationalisation (Chapter 14). One can see the sensible division of jurisdiction to some extent in our criminal courts. Matters more important to the State and to the public, more serious charges with more serious consequences and of more importance to the accused citizens are all reserved to the Supreme Court. Up until about the middle of this century one could see the same division operating broadly as a matter of practice in civil matters as between the Court of Session and the Sheriff Court but in recent years it has become blurred and requires refocussing by legislation, not further blurring as the proposal on divorce will do.

ND12.9 I agree that it would be wrong to retain divorce work in Edinburgh merely for the benefit of the Junior Bar and at the cost of the divorcing public regardless of the latter's best interests (paragraph 10.16). The mere transfer of undefended and defended divorces under the present procedures would not of itself materially reduce expense and might well cause delays. I am of opinion for the reasons stated that it is in the best interests of the litigants and in the public's best interests in this field, which does often involve matters of private and public importance, for the Supreme Court to remain the ordinary forum.

NOTE OF DISSENT BY MR. D. B. ROBERTSON

ND13.1 I am against the disciplinary bodies proposed for solicitors and advocates having any powers to award money compensation.

ND13.2 So far as the advocates are concerned the new set up proposed seems over elaborate and smacks of taking a cannon to kill a fly having regard to the nature and tiny number of complaints, but as regards money compensation this is apparently to be awarded not on the basis of negligence but upon some concept of 'solatium' for inconvenience trouble or worry and presumably of a minor nature looking to the restriction of the level of award. I really do not understand this proposal. The present disciplinary tribunal for solicitors seems to me both potent and severe as any one who has attended a hearing can testify. It may be reasonable for them to have powers to require reduction of fees (although that can be done otherwise) and that in a sense is an indirect way of awarding money compensation, but to give power to award damages on grounds which are doubtfully competent in law seems to me going too far.

ND13.3 The lawyer's customer is already in a somewhat special position compared with his situation dealing with most other purveyors of Goods and Services. If there is a real case for reparation the client should sue in the ordinary courts. For the minor kind of claim envisaged it would probably be a 'small claim' and I would think few claims would be contested if pressed.

ND13.4 This is another type of proposal which it seems to me is likely to be detrimental to the whole atmosphere and professional relationship between lawyer and client; it is not in anyone's interests to encourage clients with minor disappointments only to claim damages.

ND13.5 So far as the advocate is concerned in particular, since this provision for money compensation could not presumably be considered in respect of actual advocacy in court or the preparation therefore, the field is very restricted; having regard to the advocate's position in respect of suing for his fees and choosing a client the position would be peculiarly anomalous.

NOTE OF DISSENT BY MR. D. B. ROBERTSON

(This Note of Dissent is supported by Lord Maxwell)

ND14.1 The proposal that advocates' outlays should be charged separately from fees is likely in my opinion to add to cost and lead to delay with no corresponding benefit to the client that I can see. I am therefore against it.

ND14.2 This proposal must be read along with the other that fees should be calculated by hourly rates. That proposal will add to administrative cost and will as I read it mean a departure from the traditional approach of counsel being paid by the day at least for court appearance and may involve a new head of charges for preparation, akin to brief fees in England. This outlay proposal I cannot see as a benefit to anyone and certainly not to the paying client.

ND14.3 At present one of the advantages of the average fee note from counsel is its simplicity. If outlays such as travelling, accommodation, subsistence and stationery and the like are to be calculated and detailed in the account it will certainly put up the cost of producing the account; I am advised that it would almost inevitably entail extra staff for Faculty Services.

ND14.4 At present I would guess that in many cases the advocate loses out to some extent with outlays being inclusive. Separate outlays would, I think, end up with increased cost to the client overall and it would also be a fertile field for dispute on detail with consequent delay in payment which we are trying to minimise. There is adequate provision for challenge and taxation of counsel's account and if the element of expenses is inflated this can be and is revealed for discussion before the auditor.

ND14.5 This proposal is counterproductive in terms of cost time and benefit to the client.

NOTE OF DISSENT BY LORD MAXWELL

(This Note of Dissent is supported by Miss E. M. Houston and Mr. D. B. Robertson).

ND15.1 I agree with the proposal that there should be set up a new Department of Legal Affairs (or Ministry of Justice) for Scotland, that this should be a distinct department of authority and standing and that, to this end, it should have as its head a senior Minister having no responsibility to or for any other department.

ND15.2 I disagree however with what I understand to be the view of the majority of the Commission that the Ministerial head of this department need not be a lawyer. I accept that, in some areas of the proposed department's functions, including some of the areas which this Commission has considered in the course of its work, a non-lawyer could give at least as good and, arguably, better service to the public than a lawyer. Nevertheless I am convinced that, looking at the whole range of the proposed department's functions in the Scottish and United Kingdom context, the Ministerial head of the department could not adequately carry out his duties unless he was a lawyer of standing and experience.

ND15.3 It is evident that the number of Scottish Parliamentary constituencies is insufficient to ensure that every Prime Minister would be able to find from among the Members of Parliament supporting the Government a lawyer of suitable qualifications for the post and some other arrangement would therefore be required to give effect to what I consider essential. I have given some thought to what this arrangement should be, but have come to the conclusion that I am insufficiently informed to offer an opinion upon this matter.

ND15.4 The Scottish Law Commission in the appendix to the Memorandum referred to in Chapter 20 propose that the Lord Advocate should be the Ministerial head of the Department. This may well be the best solution. It does, as observed by the Scottish Law Commission, involve consideration of the extent to which the Lord Advocate might have to be relieved of his othei functions, notably those concerned with legal advice to Government and the public prosecution of crime.

ND15.5 It may be that there are better solutions than that proposed by the Scottish Law Commission, including, possibly, the creation of some wholly new office.

ND15.6 Consideration would also require to be given to the question of how the Ministerial head of the Department, if he was not a Member of Parliament, could have a 'voice' in Parliament. The Scottish Law Commission refer to the possibility of conferring upon him a life peerage, but again there may be other and better solutions.

ND15.7 My position therefore is as follows:

(1) I endorse the Royal Commission's recommendation on the setting up of a Department of Legal Affairs with its own Ministerial head.

(2) I consider, however, that it is essential that the Minister should be a lawyer of standing.

(3) I hope that the best method of achieving (1) and (2) can be made the subject of immediate study by those better qualified than I, as I think that the Royal Commission's proposal is important and valuable and that its implementation ought not to be delayed.

INDEX

References are to chapter and paragraph number

Printed in Scotland for Her Majesty's Stationery Office
by McCorquodale (Scotland) Ltd. Dd 630139, K20, 4/80